Just and Unjust Peace

STUDIES IN STRATEGIC PEACEBUILDING

Series Editors
R. Scott Appleby, John Paul Lederach, and Daniel Philpott
The Joan B. Kroc Institute for International Peace Studies
University of Notre Dame

STRATEGIES OF PEACE
Transforming Conflict in a Violent World
Edited by Daniel Philpott and Gerard F. Powers

UNIONISTS, LOYALISTS, AND CONFLICT TRANSFORMATION IN
NORTHERN IRELAND
Lee A. Smithey

JUST AND UNJUST PEACE
An Ethic of Political Reconciliation
Daniel Philpott

Just and Unjust Peace

Peace

An Ethic of Political Reconciliation

———◦◦———

DANIEL PHILPOTT

OXFORD
UNIVERSITY PRESS

OXFORD
UNIVERSITY PRESS

Oxford University Press, Inc., publishes works that further
Oxford University's objective of excellence
in research, scholarship, and education.

Oxford   New York
Auckland   Cape Town   Dar es Salaam   Hong Kong   Karachi
Kuala Lumpur   Madrid   Melbourne   Mexico City   Nairobi
New Delhi   Shanghai   Taipei   Toronto

With offices in
Argentina   Austria   Brazil   Chile   Czech Republic   France   Greece
Guatemala   Hungary   Italy   Japan   Poland   Portugal   Singapore
South Korea   Switzerland   Thailand   Turkey   Ukraine   Vietnam

Published by Oxford University Press, Inc.
198 Madison Avenue, New York, New York 10016
www.oup.com

Library of Congress Cataloging-in-Publication Data

Philpott, Daniel, 1967-
Just and unjust peace : an ethic of political reconciliation / Daniel Philpott.
p. cm.
ISBN 978-0-19-982756-5
1. Reconciliation—Religious aspects.   2. Restorative justice—Religious aspects.
3. Abrahamic religions.   I. Title.
BL65.P4P57 2012
201'.7273—dc23
2011037890

1 3 5 7 9 8 6 4 2
Printed in the United States of America
on acid-free paper

To Brian Cox

Contents

PART THREE: *Practicing Political Reconciliation*

Acknowledgments

I WOULD BE remiss to write a book on reconciliation without acknowledging the many relationships that made it possible. At the height of helpfulness were those who read and commented on most or all of the manuscript: Asma Afsaruddin, Paolo Carozza, Michael Griffin, Charles Mathewes, Colleen Murphy, Monika Nalepa, Robert Schreiter, Alex Tuckness, and Paul Weithman. At a high altitude were also those who commented helpfully on some portion of the manuscript: Gary Anderson, Thomas Brudholm, John Carlson, Phil Clark, Paige Digeser, Steven Harsono, Robert Johansen, Jason Klocek, Jay Landry, John Paul Lederach, James Lee, Jennifer Llewellyn, Louise Mallinder, Atalia Omer, Stephen Pope, Rasoul Rasoulipour, Andrew Reiter, Jack Snyder, Jason Springs, Ernesto Verdeja, Charles Villa-Vicencio, Leslie Vinjamuri, and Stewart Wood.

On several occasions, I profited greatly from having the manuscript read in a group setting. While a visiting fellow at the Edmond J. Safra Foundation Center for Ethics at Harvard University in 2005 and 2006, I benefited from sharing a paper-length draft with colleagues: Jeffrey Abramson, Arthur Applbaum, Elizabeth Ashford, Thos Cochrane, Elizabetta Galleoti, Renee Jones, Maria Merritt, and Dennis Thompson. In fall 2009, I was privileged to have my nearly completed manuscript read by a working group on love and justice at the Institute for Advanced Studies in Culture at the University of Virginia, whose members included Geoffrey Clausen, Jennifer Geddes, Karen Guth, Regina Schwartz, Gregory Thompson, Nicholas Wolterstorff, and Joshua Yates. Immensely helpful, too, was a workshop on the manuscript sponsored by the Kroc Institute for International Peace Studies at the University of Notre Dame, whose participants included Asma Afsaruddin, Scott Appleby, Michael Griffin, Daniel Groody, Charles Mathewes, James McAdams, Colleen Murphy, Monika Nalepa, Gerard Powers, Robert Schreiter, Ernesto

Verdeja, and Paul Weithman. Most of them also read the manuscript in its entirety. Finally, the students in my graduate seminar "The Politics of Reconciliation" in spring 2008 and spring 2011 read and commented on portions of the manuscript.

Crucial as well was institutional support. The Kroc Institute for International Peace Studies has been a wonderful setting for my scholarship, with its emphasis on religion; its active work in peacebuilding around the world; its scholarly focus on strategic peacebuilding, a concept that converges strongly with reconciliation; and, finally, its collaborative community. I thank in particular Kroc's director, Scott Appleby, for supporting this project from the beginning, for generously enabling me with the indispensable resources to complete it, and for his friendship. I am also grateful to the research committee at the Kroc Institute, which awarded me a grant to fund my manuscript workshop of May 2010. Vital to the writing of the book were three academic leaves. The first was supported by the fellowship at Harvard mentioned above, which I held from September 2005 to May 2006. The second was as a research fellow of the Alexander von Humboldt Foundation from August 2006 to August 2007, during which I was a scholar in residence at the Hertie School of Governance and the Social Science Research Center (Wissenschaftszentrum) in Berlin, Germany. I thank my sponsor, Ulrich Preuss, for his kind assistance during that year. The third was as a visiting fellow at the Institute for Advanced Studies in Culture at the University of Virginia from August 2009 to December 2009.

I have presented portions of the manuscript at the University of Oklahoma, where I delivered the True Family Lecture; at the University of California, Riverside, where I delivered the Forrest S. Mosten Conflict Resolution and Peace Studies Lecture; and at the University of California, Berkeley; Arizona State University; the Social Science Research Center, Berlin; the University of Bern, Switzerland; Humboldt University, Berlin; the International Symposium on Religions and World Peace, Osnabrück, Germany; Wheaton College; Calvin College; Gordon College; the University of Nijmegen, Netherlands; the University of Notre Dame Law School; Taylor University; the University of Virginia; Trinity School; St. Andrews University, Scotland; the Kroc Institute; the Institute for Theology and Peace, Hamburg, Germany; and the New Hampshire Institute of Politics.

I thank several research assistants for background research on several parts of the book, including Peter Campbell, Tito Contreras, Erin

Kelly, and Deborah Kwak. I also thank Kirstin Hasler for a conscientious job of checking the manuscript. The cheerfulness and reliability of Vonda Polega at the Kellogg/Kroc Information Center saved me countless hours of research time. I am deeply grateful, too, to my editor at Oxford University Press, Theo Calderara, for his thorough and virtuoso editing and his constant support on numerous fronts, as well as to Oxford's copy editors for their conscientious work.

The book finds its origins in the kindness and vision of a close friend, Brian Cox, whom I first encountered in July 1996 soon after I alighted in Santa Barbara, California to take up my first academic position as an assistant professor at the University of California. An Anglican priest who would later become the founding senior vice president for dispute resolution training of the International Center for Religion and Diplomacy, Brian trotted the globe building reconciliation in divided and warring countries. Although at this point I had not thought much about reconciliation, I found myself unable to resist Brian's invitation to accompany him to Sarajevo, which we visited in fall 1996. There, amid makeshift graveyards and bombed-out buildings, the impulse to reconciliation seized me, as it still does. Over subsequent years, Brian imparted to me his formidable vision of faith-based reconciliation and mentored me in the active work of faith-based reconciliation, most importantly over seven years in Kashmir. Today, as I continue this work in central Africa under the auspices of the Catholic Peacebuilding Network, I bring with me all that Brian has taught me. I dedicate the book to him, whose vision is stamped on every page.

Finally, I offer thanks, surely inadequate, to the person who supported writing this book more than any other, indeed with a constancy and commitment that often exceeded my own: my dear wife, Diana.

—Notre Dame, Indiana
April 15, 2011

Just and Unjust Peace

Introduction

OVER THE PAST generation, all over the world, societies have sought to confront histories denominated in commas and zeroes. Rwandans face a genocide that killed some 1,000,000, Cambodians one that left 2,000,000 dead. Bosnians look back on a death toll of 100,000. South Africa's truth commission documented some 38,000 human rights violations; Guatemala's, 55,000. Even where death tolls are lower—Northern Ireland, the Arab-Israeli conflict—other injustices abound and conflict is all-consuming. Were they stood upright, the collected files that recorded East Germany's surveillance of its citizens would stretch 121 miles. In the Jewish scriptures, the prophet Ezekiel describes a society overcome by evil as a valley of dry bones. Still today, chroniclers of enormities often select geographic images—rivers and lakes clogged with bodies in Rwanda, killing fields in Cambodia.[1]

The desolate aftermath of evil makes it difficult to talk about justice. The overthrown *caudillos* or communist *apparatchiks* may threaten to retake power. A peace settlement may relapse into civil war. Studies show that up to 43 percent of negotiated settlements revert to war within five years.[2] It is urgent, then, to achieve at least the minimal peace that Thomas Hobbes envisioned during the English Civil War of the seventeenth century, one where a sovereign government, a leviathan, holds a monopoly on force. Monitor the cease-fire; quell rampant crime; establish a civilian police force; resettle refugees, whose camps can be breeding grounds for counterattacking militias. Disarm, demobilize, and reintegrate armed factions. If there is time, bury the dead.

Yet talk about justice does take place, even where violence has been monumental. Some of these sundered societies manage to pursue a liberal, democratic peace in the spirit of Hobbes's seventeenth-century successor, John Locke. They hold and monitor elections, create constitutions that guarantee human rights and establish independent courts, reform military and police sectors, create the structures for free markets, and place human rights violators on trial. These goals dominate what is now called the liberal peace, the preferred approach of the United Nations, the World Bank, and powerful Western governments.[3]

In virtually all of these societies, though, people demand even more: a wider set of measures to "deal with the past," to borrow a phrase prevalent in Northern Ireland. They ask that we examine the stories that the commas and zeroes obscure. "Years of terror and death have displaced and reduced the majority of Guatemalans to fear and silence. *Truth* is the primary word, the serious and mature action that makes it possible for us to break this cycle of death and violence and to open ourselves to a future of hope and light for all," proclaimed Bishop Juan Gerardi upon presenting the report of the Recovery of Historical Memory Project, just two days before government soldiers assassinated him.[4] "[Some people] say that offering amnesty helps the truth come out. But I don't believe that knowing alone makes you happy. Once you know who did it, you want the next thing—you want justice!" protested Mhleli Mxenge, the brother of Griffiths Mxenge, a human rights lawyer who was brutally assassinated by the counterinsurgency unit of the South African apartheid government.[5] East German political activist Bärbel Bohley held that opening the files of the Stasi, or East German secret police, was "critical." How else, she argued, "can we get the lies...out of our public life? Unsparing accountability is the point of departure for responsible political action."[6] To these logics Archbishop Desmond Tutu of South Africa adds: "There is no future without forgiveness."

Inquiries into past injustices have a long history. As early as the fifth century BCE, Thucydides described a debate in the assembly at Athens over the place of justice in treating the captured inhabitants of the city of Mytilene during the Peloponnesian War. The current generation has produced innovations. Two international war crimes tribunals, the first since the Nuremberg Trials of 1945, were established in Rwanda and Yugoslavia in the 1990s and then made permanent through the International Criminal Court in 1998, while countries such as Timor-Leste and Sierra Leone have developed hybrid courts combining domestic and international authority. Even more innovative are truth commissions, roughly forty of which have appeared since 1974. Reparations are also becoming more common as are public apologies, of which political scientist Barry O'Neill identified 121 instances from 1980 to 1995.[7] Apology's twin practice, forgiveness, is far less common in public contexts but also far less obscure than it was in the past, evident as of late in the political proceedings of South Africa, El Salvador, Northern Ireland, Guatemala, Timor-Leste, and Chile, among other places. Efforts to deal with the past have become intense, global, and replete with moral quandaries.

Should war criminals be granted amnesty if their assent is needed for a peace settlement? What sort of punishment do human rights violators merit? Do truth commissions have a restorative effect? May leaders apologize on behalf of entire nations? Are reparations owed to representatives of past generations? Can states practice forgiveness? Arising from this generation's innovations but resounding perennial issues of justice, questions such as these have been posed around the world in stump speeches, parliamentary debates, newspapers, sermons, seminars, negotiations, street conversations, and the books and journal articles of legal scholars, political scientists, historians, sociologists, philosophers, anthropologists, and psychologists. Each reflects the central question of this book: What does justice consist of in the wake of its massive despoliation?

Thoughtful and useful answers to these questions have arisen from the speeches and the debates, the books and the articles. Yet answers to any one alone—or two or three—cannot account for justice. Sometimes the answers are complementary: An answer to one may be incomplete or distorted without reference to another. Sometimes the answers are contradictory: A solution to one dilemma may give rise to a new dilemma. A given solution may also beget demurrals and rebuttals, which in turn beget new syntheses. Some victims of forced labor during the Holocaust criticized proposed reparations from the German government in the 1990s as being nothing but "blood money" if not accompanied by apologies and public acknowledgment of the victims' suffering. Some South Africans blamed their Truth and Reconciliation Commission for stressing truth telling and the forgiveness of perpetrators while doing nothing to alter the economic injustices that apartheid had wrought. Injustices and all of their accompanying wounds demolish partitions between categories of justice and wash out conceptual retaining walls. What is needed is a framework for justice that considers the past as a whole, integrating all of the important facets of justice while attending to the particularities of each.

This book aspires to such a framework. Its orienting concept is one that has emerged in recent years but also has ancient roots: *reconciliation.* The term is eponymous for truth commissions in Chile, South Africa, Timor-Leste, Sierra Leone, and Peru. It has shown up in the texts of one-third of all peace settlements since 1989, and it has arisen in discussions around the world about dealing with the past.[8] Constructing an ethic of reconciliation, discovering its justifications, strengthening its synergies, ironing out its contradictions, and explaining its relevance for political orders is this book's mission.

Holism is a central theme. The argument begins by charting the distressingly diverse ways that war and dictatorship wound their victims and diminish all who are involved in them. Such wounds are not only intrinsically injurious, but also, by spawning emotions of hatred, vengeance, and fear, they lead to further injustices and hinder the creation of just political orders. The response that I propose is similarly holistic. Justice involves practices that redress, insofar as is possible, the many forms of these diminishments and increase the flourishing of those who have suffered them. These practices are not only intrinsically just but they also create vital capital for political orders in the form of legitimacy, trust, and identification with the nation.

There are six of these practices. They are the struts and gears that put the ethic into political practice and include:

- building socially just institutions and relations between states
- acknowledgment
- reparations
- punishment
- apology
- forgiveness

Each of these practices addresses unique wounds in unique ways. What justifications for them best describe their moral logic, are consistent with one another, and reflect a common ideal of reconciliation? What concrete, practicable guidelines do they generate for political societies and relationships between political societies that have suffered war and dictatorship?

In politics, of course, peace is always less than just—sometimes it is thoroughly unjust—nor does reconciliation always find favor. Its detractors complain that it forgoes retribution, masks inequalities of power, interferes in matters of the soul, and is too religious and too utopian. My argument engages these criticisms and, through this engagement, takes on complexity and qualification. It acknowledges political evil, holding that evil cannot be reversed, understood, left behind, philosophically "solved," or in any way construed as occurring for a greater good.

Reconciliation is not so much a solution to evil as it is a response to evil, a response that in the political realm will always be partially achieved, compromised by power, challenged by its sheer complexity, and often delayed in its enactment. West Germany undertook an intense wave of Holocaust remembrance four decades after the events took place. Spanish activists began to dig up mass graves from the civil war of the 1930s only in the early 2000s. To think of peace holistically is not to argue that it will be achieved completely but only that its components are interdependent and require integration.

This book does not account for the forces that shape how countries deal with the past—that is, whether trials, amnesties, truth commissions, and reparations are the product of power, ideology, or culture. It aims rather to provide a set of standards by which the justice of peacebuilding can be evaluated. But neither is the ethic one of mere ideals. Each of the six practices, alone or in combination with others, has been attempted numerous times, and among these attempts can be found a mixture of breakdown and breakthrough, of failures as well as moments when, in the words of poet Seamus Heaney, "hope and history rhyme." The predicament that emerges is one in which restorative practices occur but are suffused with blemish. It is such a predicament that calls for an ethic. If the practices were ineffectual, the ethic would be futile; if they did not involve partiality, compromise, and intractable dilemmas, the ethic would be pointless.

Restoring a Restorative Ethic

Reconciliation is a concept of justice, that is to say, a set of propositions that tells us who ought to do what to whom, for whom, and on behalf of whom and the reasons why. The central meaning of reconciliation is the restoration of right relationship. The idea will seem strange to modern Westerners, for whom justice means individual rights, a just distribution of wealth, just punishment, and other matters of desert, entitlement, and rights. But there are other traditions and schools of thought—Judaism, Christianity, Islam, and the contemporary restorative justice movement— for which justice means something much like right relationship.

The ethic of reconciliation defended here concerns right relationship in a particular realm—the political realm—where the goal is respected citizenship defined by human rights, the rule of law within political communities, and respect for international law between political communities. The ethic, then, is not concerned with reconciliation in all of life—in families, personal friendships, civil society organizations, or religious organizations. It is an ethic of political reconciliation. But political reconciliation is not limited to human rights and the rule of law. It involves a broad portfolio of practices that redress the multiform wounds that massive political injustices inflict. Redressing this range of wounds is also part of political reconciliation.

The core argument of the book overlaps strongly with what has come to be known as restorative justice. The concept surfaced in the 1970s as a proposal for reforming criminal justice in the United States, Canada, Australia, the United Kingdom, and New Zealand. In the 1990s, it was employed to rehabilitate national political orders, most famously by Archbishop Desmond Tutu of South Africa. Political reconciliation carries on this project, developing restorative justice into an ethic for dealing with past injustices on a national or international scale.

Restoration animates each of the ethic's six practices—even punishment. In country after country, punishment is pitted against reconciliation, just as justice is posed against mercy and retributive justice is positioned against restorative justice. With political reconciliation, however, punishment is restorative—of the political community, of law, of victims, and potentially of perpetrators—and therefore an essential part of reconciliation. The most dramatically restorative practice is forgiveness, which involves not merely a victim releasing her perpetrator of claims but also her constructive invitation to a better future. When forgiveness and punishment are each justified restoratively, they become complementary. The other practices—acknowledgment, reparations, apology, and building socially just institutions—are restorative as well, alone and in conjunction.

To call each of these practices restorative is to reject any distinction between "backward-looking" activities that focus on the past and "forward-looking" activities that construct the future. All of the practices are Janus faced, peering in both directions. Reparations, punishment, and public apologies address past injustices, to be sure, but they do so in an effort to create a better political future. Constructing strong democratic constitutions not only builds a better future but also seeks to repair a past condition where violence and oppression prevailed.

The cardinal virtue running through the practices is mercy. This, too, may sound strange to citizens of the modern West, where mercy most often means forgoing punishment and is understood to be in tension with justice. Yet mercy, as articulated by the religious traditions considered here, is something far broader: a will to relieve the misery, grief, sorrow, or distress of another. This sense, a restorative sense, is the one that the present ethic of political reconciliation adopts and proffers. Mercy is quite similar to restorative justice and characterizes each of the six practices, even punishment.

What is true of mercy is also true more broadly of reconciliation and restorative justice: These are odd visitors, discordant entrants, in modern Western thought, law, and politics as well as in global institutions. Reconciliation has played little role in Western law since it emerged in the Middle Ages and is not a major theme in the Greek and Roman sources of Western law and thought or in the natural law tradition of ethics. Only shards of reconciliation can be found in the major philosophers of the modern liberal tradition: John Locke, Immanuel Kant, John Stuart Mill, and John Rawls. Georg Wilhelm Friedrich Hegel, who gave more extended treatment to reconciliation in *The Philosophy of Right*, is exceptional among these, though he meant something different from what is argued for here and stood at a critical distance from the liberal tradition. Reconciliation has little status in international law. Among international organizations, Western governments, international lawyers, and human rights activists, the liberal peace is far more dominant.

How, then, did reconciliation find its way into global political discourse? It is largely religious leaders and communities who have sponsored it, though not exclusively. Tribal traditions in New Zealand, the United States, Canada, and sub-Saharan Africa have helped to inspire restorative justice, while secular voices have defended reconciliation eloquently. Even religious traditions have applied reconciliation to politics only recently, having for centuries confined it to families, friendships, civil society, or the confessional.[9] Still, in recent years religious leaders have done the most to escort reconciliation into politics. Tutu and Pope John Paul II articulated it most famously. Religious leaders have been some of the strongest advocates of reconciliation in South Africa, Sierra Leone, Northern Ireland, Chile, Brazil, El Salvador, Guatemala, Germany, Rwanda, Timor-Leste, Iraq, and elsewhere. Among reconciliation's theorizers, theologians and religious ethicists are disproportionately represented.

What religious voices bring to troubled political proceedings are the texts and traditions in which reconciliation finds its oldest and most thorough expression. In the scriptures of Judaism, Christianity, and Islam, reconciliation characterizes God's purposes and actions, which human relationships in all spheres of life are then meant to reflect. Justice, in each of these schools, is not only a comprehensive state of righteousness that reflects God's original intention for his relationship to humanity but also a process of restoring this righteousness that reflects God's response to evil. Closely related and complementary are these scriptures' concepts of peace and mercy. In the stories, revealed laws, injunctions, and grand narratives of these texts can be found all of the major themes of political reconciliation—restorative justice, mercy, holistic peace, restorative punishment, forgiveness—and groundings for all of the six practices. It is a core claim of this book that reconciliation, as embedded in these religious traditions, holds great promise for restoring political orders with calamitous pasts.

The claim comes at a time when religion seems to be as much a source of conflict as of reconciliation. Radical Islam battles the West, other Muslims, and non-Islamic cultures in Iraq, Afghanistan, Europe, the United States, the Middle East, South Asia, East Asia, and Africa. Armed conflicts inspired at least in part by religion have raged over the past several decades in Yugoslavia, Sudan, Kashmir, Israel and Palestine, Sri Lanka, Lebanon, and Northern Ireland. Hindu nationalist parties have pursued religious claims antagonistically and often violently in India, while Buddhist nationalists have done the same in Sri Lanka. In Latin America and even more so in the United States and Canada, religion pervades debates over abortion, marriage, sexuality, stem cell research, education, and the role of religion in public life. In Europe, cultural clashes escalate between Islamic communities and an incompletely secularized surrounding Christian civilization. Can religion really be an irenic force?

There are good reasons for religion to have a role in an ethic of political reconciliation. Most of all, religious traditions are "carriers" of an ethic that has much to offer political orders addressing legacies of injustice, whether their citizens are religious or secular. The ethic's religious character, though, also will make it attractive to religious believers themselves. Defying the erstwhile dominance of the secularization thesis among Western intellectuals, religion not only has failed to decline over the past generation but has grown in political influence among all of the major religions and regions of the globe, even in western Europe, long thought to be the ground zero of secularization.[10] An ethic that claims global relevance ignores religion only to its detriment. In sites of past injustices that involve large religious populations or where religious leaders play a pivotal role, religious justifications may be critical for building a consensus around the practices of reconciliation. I also take issue with arguments for religion's exclusion from political reconciliation, particularly the claims of some Western philosophers that political arguments must always be expressed in a secular, "public" language. To be clear, this book is not primarily about peace among religions, interreligious dialogue, or the work that religious people and organizations do to achieve peacebuilding and reconciliation. It proposes, rather, that religious traditions have a great deal to contribute to the question of what constitutes justice in dealing with past injustices.

I also offer secular justifications for political reconciliation. There are good reasons for this, too. In settings of past injustice that feature a religious divide or a split between religious and secular perspectives, secular language can facilitate a critically needed consensus on principles of reconciliation. Integral to the ethic, in defining both the senses in which relationships need restoration and the kind of regime to which political reconciliation aspires, are human rights and other norms of international law, which are typically articulated in a secular, legal language. Political reconciliation might also be carried out or supported by organizations that operate in secular language—governments in many parts of the world, the United Nations, the World Bank, and many nongovernmental organizations (NGOs). Compelling secular rationales for the practices are available and compatible with religious justifications. Contemporary arguments for restorative justice, one of reconciliation's justifying rationales, are often expressed in secular terms.

The ethic of political reconciliation also merges in part with the liberal peace, incorporating its core commitments to human rights, democracy, and the rule of law. Human rights have strong foundations in religion and can achieve a wide consensus involving holders of secular perspectives. In some respects, the ethic also comes into tension with the liberal peace and its commitments. Both convergences and divergences emerge through a dialogue with the liberal tradition.

What I propose, then, is a grafting in which religious justifications are offered fully and publicly but are accompanied by secular justifications and in which concepts from ancient scripture merge with ideas drawn from the modern liberal tradition. Just this sort of grafting can be found in religiously inspired political reform movements of the last two centuries that have sought to promote liberal democratic politics, including nineteenth-century campaigns to abolish the slave trade and then slavery itself, the early feminist movement, Mahatma Gandhi's campaign for Indian independence, the American civil rights movement, and more recent prodemocracy movements in Poland, Turkey, the Philippines, Brazil, Chile, Mexico, Indonesia, Malawi, Kenya, South Africa, East Germany, Ukraine, and Lithuania. It is through this grafting that ancient sources of reconciliation can be marshaled for the restoration of modern political orders.

Settings for Reconciliation

So an ancient idea has entered global politics. But why now? A resurgent public religion may well have revived the idea, while lightning-fast global communication then rocketed the idea from Chile to South Africa and on to Timor-Leste, Peru, Sierra Leone, Northern Ireland, and many other locales. The occasion for the idea, though, is the historically novel wave of societies that have come to address massive injustices. Social scientists Ellen Lutz and Kathryn Sikkink have charted a "justice cascade" of truth commissions and trials in the 1980s and 1990s.[11] These efforts to face the past, along with the many other activities through which societies aim to replace violence and lawlessness with stability and the rule of law, may be thought of collectively as peacebuilding. The global breadth and intensity of these efforts over several decades make our time an age of peacebuilding. An ethic of political reconciliation is a moral standard for the interrelated activities that peacebuilding comprises.

In what contexts has peacebuilding taken place? One is a global wave of democratization that began in 1974, came to include some ninety transitions to democracy by 2008, and has recently resurged in what is called the Arab Spring of 2011.[12] Addressing injustices committed under the previous authoritarian regime—communist, right-wing military, and apartheid—has been a common task in building constitutional orders based on the rule of law, human rights, and democratic governance.

Another common context is civil wars—in Sudan, Cambodia, Sierra Leone, Northern Ireland, the former Yugoslavia, Timor-Leste, Uganda, and many other countries—more of which ended through negotiation between 1989 and 2004 than in the previous two centuries.[13] Often these settlements involve international organizations. The United Nations (U.N.) revolution of 1987 to 1994 involved a multiplication in the number, scope, size, and budget of U.N. efforts to build peace after civil conflicts. Far beyond securing cease-fires, these efforts involve monitoring elections, demobilizing combatants, reforming security sectors, resettling refugees, and a range of efforts to address past injustices. These operations have had mixed success, but they persist.[14] To improve their effectiveness, the U.N. Security Council formed the Peacebuilding Commission in 2005.

Reconciliation is rarer today between states. Civil wars, after all, have dwarfed international conflicts since World War II.[15] Yet peacebuilding still occurs in international contexts. Issues of justice in the settlements of both World War I and World War II—with their very different results—are staple topics in international relations textbooks. In some cases, states engage in practices of reconciliation with other states long after war has ended. Contrast Germany, which over six decades following the crimes of the Nazi period has carried out to some degree all of the six practices except for forgiveness (which was not its place to bestow), with Japan, which has done far less. Today, Germany enjoys a deep and stable peace with its neighbors France and Poland, while Japan experiences ongoing tensions with China and South Korea.

Still another occasion for practices of peacebuilding is the aftermath of intervention. Since the end of the cold war, the United States has encountered its most difficult foreign policy dilemmas in trying to build peace overseas—in Somalia, Afghanistan, and Iraq—as has the European Union in Kosovo and Congo and Germany in Afghanistan. Building peace has proved far more difficult than military victory. It is not surprising then that in late 2005 the Department of Defense raised postconflict reconstruction operations to a "core mission" or that the Department of State and the Agency for International Development have made similar moves.

The work of peacebuilding and several of the six practices of reconciliation also have been carried out by civil society organizations, which do not speak for entire political orders, though they may contribute to their restoration. These include religious communities, local and tribal organizations, and nongovernmental organizations. Though civil society organizations lack the official imprimatur to carry out practices such as punishment, reparations, or building just institutions, they are often better equipped than states for practices that involve the transformation of emotions and attitudes.

All of these contexts—democratization, the settlement of civil wars, international conflict, the aftermath of intervention, and civil society— are ones in which peacebuilding takes place and thus where the ethic of political reconciliation finds its setting. What, then, is the case for viewing reconciliation as a concept of justice? What does this justice consist of? And what payoff does it yield for contemporary political societies facing devastating pasts? Answering these questions is the task of the chapters that follow in Part One.

Reconciliation as a Concept of Justice

I

Whose Justice?

WHAT IS JUSTICE in the wake of large-scale injustice? That is the central question of this book. During the age of peacebuilding, debates over this question have been framed by the nature and scale of the massive injustice (was it genocide? a large civil war? a dictatorship?), the character of transitions (was it a violent overthrow? a negotiated settlement?), and configurations of power. But that is not all. These debates have also been shaped by competing philosophical, religious, and cultural world-views. South Africa's Truth and Reconciliation Commission of 1996 to 1998, the most globally recognized and mimicked of any recent attempt to deal with the past, was pervaded by religious language and ritual despite the fact that it was an official, legally mandated proceeding. Within South Africa, disputes took place over the appropriateness of this religious influence. Even more spirited, as sociologist Jonathan VanAntwerpen argues, were debates about the South African experience that took place in North America and Europe, whose societies are much more secular and where religion's role in public life is far more controversial.[1]

The secular-religious divide shaped debates over the justice of dealing with the past in many other countries too. In Uganda, for instance, the Acholi Religious Leaders Peace Initiative, a coalition of Christian and Muslim clerics, advocates amnesty, forgiveness, and traditional tribal reintegration rituals for soldiers who have left the Lord's Resistance Army (LRA). The coalition is at odds with human rights activists and international lawyers who advocate the indictment of LRA leaders by the International Criminal Court. In other settings, it is the presence of two or more religions rather than the religious-secular divide that must be accommodated. In Sierra Leone, for instance, a truth commission was established and national trials were held in a country that is 60 percent Muslim, 30 percent Christian, and 10 percent indigenous African religions.

Given the existing wide range of philosophical and religious convictions, is a universal standard of justice even possible? Formulating such a standard may not seem problematic if the only task of this book were to persuade people to think of justice in a certain way. In that case, some would agree with the standard, others would not, others would agree partially, and so it goes, just as it does with any argument about ethics. The aspiration of developing an ethic such as this one, however, is to guide concrete practices and institutions—truth commissions, trials, the conduct of forgiveness—in the rough-and-tumble here and now of political settings around the globe. To be strong and effective, these practices and institutions require the assent of the people who participate in and live under them. They require legitimacy. Yet the people involved often belong to diverse philosophical and religious traditions, a diversity that may well inhibit the broad consensus on which practices of political reconciliation depend. So the problem returns: Whose justice? Which standards? Before the argument for political reconciliation can get under way, then, it must confront the problem of pluralism.

Two Tasks

My defense of an ethic of political reconciliation centers on two broad tasks. The first task is straightforward in its aim (if not in its execution), and one that philosophers of justice have long pursued: to describe, develop, and defend a concept of justice; to offer arguments for it; and to explain what features make it more attractive than the alternatives. The concept of justice that I defend here is political reconciliation. Its core content is the restoration of right relationship within or between political communities. Integral to the ethic is also the idea of human rights, which define political injustice and right relationship.

The reasons and arguments that best make the case for the ethic find particularly strong expression within three religious traditions: Judaism, Christianity, and Islam. Political reconciliation, though not necessarily human rights, also resonates with certain tribal traditions around the world as well as with the restorative justice school of thought. I will aim to show how four of these frameworks can ground the ethic on their own, independently of the others. I will also show how reconciliation converges with and diverges from other concepts of justice—chiefly, the liberal peace.

The approach of rooting the ethic in multiple traditions and schools is also designed to perform the second task: achieving consensus among diverse traditions. Let us call this task surmounting the problem of pluralism. The problem of pluralism is a practical one. It arises from the hope that a political ethic might guide concrete action. The institutions and practices of reconciliation are strengthened vastly if those who participate in and live under them believe that they are just, right, and beneficial. Perhaps such convictions are not strictly necessary. A war crimes tribunal might be imposed on a country by international lawyers or by victorious rebels in a civil war. Even institutions begotten in this way, though, suffer when a country's citizens view them askance. Far more often, legitimacy matters from start to finish. Truth commissions, trials, vetting schemes, and reparations are often created by parliaments through democratic deliberation. Their conduct involves the participation of officials, judges, lawyers, victims, perpetrators, outside NGOs, sometimes the United Nations, as well as onlookers, perhaps thousands or millions of them. They involve agreed-upon standards of what political injustices are and how they are to be redressed. They are usually created with the hope that they will contribute to national stability and cohesion in the wake of war or dictatorship. In all of these respects, the people's assent to institutions for dealing with the past is crucial. Not only crucial but often urgent: In many cases, truth commissions and trials, reparations and apologies are demanded here and now, propelled by the clamorous momentum of a transition, a ticking clock that leaves little time to work out cultural, philosophical, and religious differences.

Could the ethic of political reconciliation developed here elicit assent in Sierra Leone, a country divided among Christian, Muslim, and tribal peoples? Could it garner legitimacy in Iraq, Afghanistan, India, Israel, and Nepal, whose cultures differ from one another as well as from the West? What about within the United Nations or an NGO such as the International Center for Transitional Justice that typically operates in secular language? Does the world's diversity stand in the way of the ethic of political reconciliation being practiced widely, across continents?

The first task is designed to anchor the ethic in solid reasons, while the second task aims to give the ethic reach. The first task strives for depth of justification, the second task breadth of justification. The tasks may also be thought of as advancing two different forms of legitimacy. The first one aims at what may be called substantive legitimacy, the kind obtained when a norm or practice is shown to be truly just. The second aims at what can be termed empirical legitimacy, the sort that comes about when institutions are seen as just by the people who live under them.

More on the Second Task: Strategies for Consensus

Through what strategy can the second task be achieved? Is it even think-able that Christians, Muslims, Jews, Hindus, Buddhists, and secularists of different philosophical stripes could all endorse the ethic of political reconciliation developed here? What sort of strategy might elicit such a consensus?

One strategy holds that members of diverse traditions can best achieve consensus by placing boundaries and limitations on the kind of reasons, arguments, and language that they use. Interlocutors might agree, for instance, to argue only in secular language. This approach, however, does not turn out to be promising. As I will argue in chapter 6, it fails to offer strong principled grounds for why some kinds of reasons are acceptable in political discourse and others are not.

This book pursues consensus through a different strategy, one that invites participants in a dialogue to voice the full range and depth of their beliefs. This approach may be called rooted reason. To this table of dia-logue, interlocutors may tote the complete set of their convictions. They also carry convictions about justice that they have derived from these beliefs—the fruit of the first task. They come, too, with a motivation to find common ground with other traditions in order that such justice might be realized more widely in the world—the hope of the second task. Through comparing, conversing, listening, seeking to understand, and sometimes revising their own views in light of the conversation, they may arrive at common ground on principles of justice.

They reason in this way, of course, from the standpoint of their dif-ferent religious and philosophical convictions. Yet if they disagree on some important matters, they might also agree on others. Subsequent chapters will aim to demonstrate that Judaism, Christianity, Islam, and restorative justice can converge substantially on an ethic of dealing with the past. Such convergence can be called an *overlapping consensus*, philosopher John Rawls's term for agreement on principles of political justice among representatives of diverse religious and philosophical con-ceptions. Unlike Rawls's overlapping consensus, however, the one here is not sought through any sort of restrictions on reasoning but rather through a dialogue in which participants draw from the depths of their own convictions.[2]

Among the religious faiths, why are these three, in particular, chosen for a demonstration of overlapping consensus? Because of their wide reach. The followers of two of them comprise a healthy portion of the world's population—Christianity, about one-third, Islam, more than one-fifth. All three are central to global political controversies, Judaism's importance far exceeding its comparatively tiny proportion of followers among the world's population. Of the states that have undertaken transitional justice over the past three decades or so, the preponderance of them harbor largely Christian populations, while some, such as Sierra Leone and Bosnia, have mixed Christian-Muslim populations, and a few, such as Morocco, are almost totally Muslim. All three faiths inhabit Israel and Palestine, a region that sorely demands practices of reconciliation. The purpose here, though, is not to show how these faiths can get along with one another—say, by plumbing Islam's views of Jesus or Christianity's complex relationship with Judaism—as important as this task may be for interreligious reconciliation and dialogue. Rather, it is to show that the conceptual groundwork for an ethic of political reconciliation lies in these traditions.

In many places where a popular consensus is needed for reconciliation, these three faiths will be sparsely represented. The potential of other traditions to support the ethic, then, ought be considered as well. For a justification of the ethic in secular language, I look to Western writings on restorative justice. First Nations peoples in North America, the Maoris of New Zealand, the Ubuntu tradition of sub-Saharan Africa, and many other cultures exhibit strong practices of restorative justice too. Certain strands of feminism, particularly what is called care feminism, also contain notions amenable to reconciliation.[3] Other major religious traditions, and doubtless other philosophical and cultural traditions that I have failed to note here, are also worth exploring. The scope of this book, though, permits only three religious traditions along with secular arguments for restorative justice to be plumbed.

Whatever the traditions and schools involved, the use of rooted reason respects participants by not requiring them to shed their cherished and considered convictions before entering dialogue. Rather, it allows that beliefs about justice that emanate from traditions' separate sources might upon examination bear resonances and resemblances. Because rooted reason welcomes deep religious and philosophical convictions, it carries hope for assembling a consensus across cultures.

The concept of an overlapping consensus through rooted reason is illustrated through a Venn diagram in Figure 1.1. The area of overlap in the center represents the set of propositions that members of respective traditions have found in common. What the diagram shows is how several philosophical and religious perspectives can converge in endorsing the propositions of an ethic of political reconciliation. The traditions and schools justify these propositions on the basis of warrants that they draw from their own texts and teachings. Still, their conclusions about justice—at least some of them—converge.

Agreement derived from rooted reason will always be partial. The area of overlap represents only a portion of each tradition or school's beliefs. Particularly in the case of the religious traditions, beliefs about justice are only one component of each tradition's vast array of teachings, claims, beliefs, rituals, and practices; but it is a portion that is shared with other traditions.

The ethic of political reconciliation defended here will hardly command agreement among all religious and philosophical traditions and

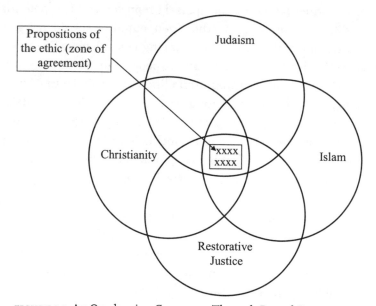

FIGURE 1.1 An Overlapping Consensus Through Rooted Reason.

schools. Here, the range of agreement among Judaism, Christianity, Islam, and restorative justice is explored. If other perspectives were involved in the dialogue over political reconciliation, the zone of shared agreement would range from all of the ethic's propositions to some of them to none of them. Prior to a dialogue between traditions, it is difficult to say how much agreement will be possible. It depends on which traditions are involved.

Partiality of agreement applies within traditions and schools as well. An ethic of political reconciliation, as we shall see, is not plainly stated in the texts or basic beliefs of Judaism, Christianity, or Islam. It has evolved through their traditions and requires still further development. Nor will the ethic be accepted by all within each tradition or school; sometimes it will meet with sharp internal opposition. It is worth recalling philosopher Alasdair MacIntyre's definition of a tradition as an "extended argument."[4] Within traditions, dialogue, argument, and interpretation must take place if a consensus is to be widened.

When members of different traditions or of different strands of the same tradition arrive at an agreement on principles of justice, they often will not understand these principles in the same way or endorse them for the same reasons. The dialogue that takes place in rooted reason is not best described as translation, which implies a process of beginning with a set of ideas from one tradition and aiming to re-express them in another. Describing rooted reason better is mutual resonance, involving a reciprocal back-and-forth process of comparison and efforts at mutual understanding, something more like a five-way intersection than a one-way street.

The consensuses that arise from rooted reason will be ad hoc, unpredictable, and shifting, reflecting the pragmatic character of the second task—achieving the consensus required for the practical operation of the ethic. What is sought is legitimacy for and reflective cooperation in truth commissions, trials, and reparations, not a grand global ethic of justice that reflects the putative true common meaning of sundry philosophies and religions. Reasoning similarly, philosopher Jacques Maritain reflected on the compromise between cultures that was necessary for the negotiation of the Universal Declaration of Human Rights in 1948, which he took part in drafting:

> How is an agreement conceivable among men assembled for the purpose of jointly accomplishing a task dealing with the future of the mind,

who come from the four corners of the earth and who belong not only to different cultures and civilizations, but to different spiritual families and antagonistic schools of thought? Since the aim of UNESCO [United Nations Educational, Scientific and Cultural Organization] is a practical aim, agreement among its members can be spontaneously achieved, not on common speculative notions, but on common practical notions, not on the affirmation of the same concept of the world, man, and knowledge, but on the affirmation of the same set of convictions concerning action. This is doubtless very little, it is the last refuge of intellectual agreement among men. It is, however, enough to undertake a great work; and it would mean a great deal to become aware of this body of common practical convictions.[5]

"We agree about the rights, but on condition no one asks us why," Maritain also quipped. In the same way, members of "different spiritual families and antagonistic schools of thought" might also come to an agreement on truth commissions, trials, reparations, and apologies, even if they only partially agree on why these institutions ought to exist. They are far more likely to arrive at this agreement if they can endorse it on the basis of their most deeply rooted convictions rather than reasons to which they have been confined.

2

The Basic Standards of Justice

RECONCILIATION REQUIRES STANDARDS. Whenever and wherever the practices of reconciliation have occurred in global politics, they have operated according to standards of justice, usually ones adopted from international law. What is the truth that the vast majority of truth commissions investigate? The truth about human rights violations and war crimes. What are the offenses of concern to the International Criminal Court and to the international criminal tribunals for Rwanda and Yugoslavia? War crimes, genocide, and crimes against humanity. What are the misdeeds to which national trials, vetting policies, reparations schemes, and even official apologies almost always respond? Those that international conventions define.

It should not be surprising that truth commissions, trials, and reparations presuppose these standards. If standards were absent or continually disputed, such practices could hardly be initiated. A truth commission cannot operate without a notion of truth nor can trials take place without a definition of crime. This is not to deny that controversies over human rights and the laws of war occur in the aftermath of massive injustices. What is usually disputed, though, is not the basic justice of torture or the massacre of innocents but rather matters such as whether such acts occurred, who committed them, whether the commands of a superior made them excusable, and whether a national state of emergency made them necessary. In any event, it remains the case that the heads of state, international officials, parliaments, courts, lawyers, or parties to a negotiated settlement who give trials, truth commissions, reparations, and other practices their legal authority typically establish certain criteria of justice in advance. If some standard were not authoritative, then already contentious practices would be further laden, perhaps unmanageably so, with the added and formidable task of coming to an agreement on principles of justice.

The ethic of political reconciliation that I defend here also rests on standards of justice drawn from international law. These standards are basic and foundational to the ethic, defining those political injustices with which reconciliation is concerned as well as the essential features of justice in a restored political community. While it is an essential argument of this book that justice involves far more than human rights and the laws of war, it still encompasses these standards. Because of the foundational status of these standards, a closer look at them is a good place to begin the defense of the ethic.

Standards of Political Injustice

Political injustices are unjust deeds that people commit or unjust regimes, laws, or constitutions that people build or sustain, in both cases in the name of a political organization, program, or ideal. Political injustices violate the terms of right relationship in or between political communities, the behavior that citizens have the right to expect from one another, from the state, and from other states. By political community I mean a group of people organized under a unified set of laws whose aim is to coordinate its members' pursuit of the common good.[1] The primary form of political community today is the territorial state. Another, the European Union, coexists with and does not supplant the state.[2] International relations are relations among political communities, involving war, diplomacy, commerce, and much else. Political injustices may occur in any of these realms and involve diverse perpetrators. Agents of the state—soldiers, policemen, intelligence officers—commit political injustices when they create and enforce unjust laws, start wars of aggression, or commit crimes in the course of wars, smaller military actions, or any operation in which they seek to maintain order and security, national unity, or simply the survival of their regime. Opposition forces—guerrillas, insurgents, conspirators, terrorists, secessionist rebels—perform injustices in pursuit of a new regime, a more just regime, or national independence. Perpetrated in the name of a political organization, program, or ideal, political injustices differ from other crimes, even serious ones such as rape and murder that have no political purpose. Political injustices have been the subject matter of practices of political reconciliation wherever and whenever these practices have occurred.

Which deeds exactly are unjust? International law is again our source. Over the past century, more and more standards of justice—such as human rights, norms defining war crimes, and genocide law—have come to be embedded in conventions, protocols, declarations, charters, and conventions. Dorothy V. Jones documents this expansion in her book *Code of Peace*, finding that by 1989 the world's states had created seventy-nine legal instruments that define standards of justice in nine separate issue areas.[3] Since then, international law has only continued to expand.

Human rights and laws governing the just use of force are the standards to which the past generation's practitioners of truth commissions, trials, and reparations have returned again and again, as if to an oracle, in defining injustices to be redressed. Presidents, prime ministers, commissioners, parliamentarians, judges, lawyers, military commanders, deposed high officials, guerrilla leaders, dissidents, and ordinary victims and perpetrators from all of the world's major religions and a wide assortment of its ethnicities and nationalities have invoked these principles.

The most serious crimes are those with which the Nuremberg tribunal charged Nazi war criminals: crimes against peace, or military aggression; war crimes, especially the deliberate killing of civilians; and crimes against humanity, involving the violent persecution of a body of people. The crime of aggression between states also became the bedrock norm of the United Nations Charter in 1945. Shortly thereafter, the United Nations added genocide —acts designed to destroy particular peoples, defined on a national, ethnic, racial, or religious basis—to these crimes when it adopted the Genocide Convention in December 1948. In 1987 the United Nations Convention Against Torture added the prohibition of another common and serious form of political cruelty to international law. Other standards are more recently codified—prohibitions of rape and other sexual crimes, for instance. All of these standards were empowered in the 1990s through the establishment of international tribunals for Yugoslavia and Rwanda and then through the creation of a permanent tribunal that encompassed all signatory states, the International Criminal Court.

Not all political injustices involve mass atrocity. Surveillance, the imprisonment of dissidents, and the obstruction of oppositional journalism, public speech, gatherings, and religious activity, backed by the threat of force and smoothed by a measure of popular acquiescence, enables some regimes to achieve through pervasive fear what others gain through crude bloodshed. Eastern European communist regimes largely fit this description, at least apart from their founding brutalities in the late 1940s and their episodic armed crackdowns. Addressing this sort of political injustice is the broader portfolio of human rights.

Over the past half century, civil wars have been the most common form of violence and are now frequently the subject of trials and truth commissions. Between 1945 and 1976, a total of 85 percent of all wars occurred mainly on the territory of a single state and concerned mainly that state's affairs, in contrast to the period 1900 to 1945, when 80 percent of all wars were fought between states.[4] Sudan, Cambodia, Angola, Nigeria, Bangladesh, Indonesia, and Sierra Leone have hosted some of the worst internal conflicts. Is it justifiable to overthrow a government? International law, founded on a charter designed with the first half of the century in mind, is largely silent about the initiation of civil war, though it has much more to say about conduct once a civil war has broken out. In chapter 10, I argue that the use of force can be justified against egregiously unjust regimes and that an ethic that would absolutely prohibit it risks being one of cheap reconciliation. Still, the civilian death toll and the morally dubious outcome of the bulk of civil wars over the past few decades demand that the criteria of last resort, proportionality, and the clear prospect of a more just replacement regime be strongly applied.

The picture of restored justice that these standards imply includes not only the guarantee of human rights and the laws of war in the constitutions of states and in international law but also recognition of the legitimacy of these standards by those who live under them—a recognition that contributes immeasurably to their strength. All of this amounts to the core meaning of *right relationship* within and among political orders. Within a political community, right relationship involves a much wider set of obligations, loyalties, and pursuits than those prescribed by human rights and the rights of people and states under the laws of war.[5] These latter rights, though, are substantial enough to be meaningful yet minimal enough to be demanded of all humankind.

The Justification of Human Rights

It is not enough for an ethic to identify, assert, or adopt rights; it must also justify them. What grounds human rights? Which, if any, are universally valid? Are there exceptions to rights such as those protecting

against torture or barring the killing of noncombatants? The growing number of international legal agreements testifies to the fact that
answers to these questions can achieve an overlapping consensus, albeit
a consensus whose constituent traditions contain dissenters who remain
outside the sphere of overlap. To follow the method set forth in the last
chapter, however, a demonstration that agreement is possible is only
the second task of the ethic. Are the propositions found in the sphere
of overlapping traditions and schools valid ones? Reaching beyond consensus for justification—the first task of the ethic—requires doing what
Jacques Maritain warned against after he helped negotiate the Universal
Declaration of Human Rights: asking why. We will see in later chapters how human rights can be the subject of an overlapping consensus,
though one that is partial and accompanied by disagreement between
and within the traditions and schools.

Add to these disagreements a further one: whether religion and human
rights are compatible. Views range widely. Religion strongly supports
human rights, one perspective holds, and is even necessary for human
rights in some versions of this perspective.[6]

An opposite view contends that religion is inimical to human rights.
Some holders of this view profess religion and reject human rights as
a by-product of an individualism, legalism, and acquisitiveness that allegedly originated either in Latin Christendom or the Enlightenment.[7] Other
holders of this view take the opposite tack, celebrating human rights and
rejecting religion, which they believe shackled human rights until the
Enlightenment freed human rights from sacral claims.

From still another standpoint, human rights are not necessarily at odds
with religion but can be defended adequately in secular terms. Included
here are the arguments of religious people who see human rights as
grounded in a dignity conferred by God but also intelligible and defen-
sible apart from revelation.[8] Others scholars argue for human rights on
wholly secular terms.[9]

Still others are skeptical altogether, doubting the claims of religion as
well as the validity of any attempt to place human rights on a foundation
of reason. Some such skeptics still favor human rights as a useful detriment to political injustice but view them as rooted no deeper than the laws
that legislatures pass or that courts mandate: no laws, no rights. Others
are simply skeptical through and through.[10]

My own view, for which I will argue in more detail in later chapters, is
that religion—at least Judaism, Christianity, and Islam—supports human

rights and the laws of war and their incorporation into an ethic of political reconciliation. Consistent with the last chapter's caveats, some of these faiths and some theological strands within these faiths are more favorable toward human rights than others. Doubtless, unfavorable strands have contributed to episodes of religious leaders violating human rights. In all of these faiths, support for human rights has grown stronger and wider over the course of history. Still, I will argue that faiths that profess a God who creates human beings in the divine image, confers love on them, and gives them universal commands in regard to their treatment of one another are distinctly well equipped to explain essential features of human rights: the human dignity and worth that rights protect, the universality of rights and their applicability to every person, and the sense in which no set of goods or states of affairs, no matter how valuable or attractive, can justify certain kinds of acts or omissions toward vulnerable people like torturing them, killing them if they are not engaged in combat, or denying them subsistence or nourishment.

A fourth perspective, restorative justice, which offers a secular justification of political reconciliation, contains no original argument for human rights. It is mainly an approach to criminal justice. There is no reason, though, why an expansion of restorative justice to the scale of the nation-state cannot incorporate human rights. Other scholars and public leaders, not least South Africa's Archbishop Desmond Tutu, have already pointed in this direction.[11] A secular justification for an ethic of political reconciliation, though, requires secular arguments for human rights—secular at least in the sense that they do not directly invoke God. The best of these arguments, in my view, are ones of common morality, the most prominent of these falling in the natural law tradition of Thomas Aquinas and the Kantian tradition of ethics.[12] Certain ethical precepts are rationally knowable and universally applicable, common morality maintains. These precepts include prohibitions of murder, lying, stealing, and adultery and an injunction to practice universal benevolence. Entailed in these precepts are both duties and corresponding rights. The prohibited actions should not be undertaken as an end or as a means or justified by some greater good; common morality arguments often render the prohibitions exceptionless. A stress on the inviolable dignity of the person—as an end in itself, as a legislator of the moral law, or as a rational being who is fulfilled through basic human ends such as life, health, knowledge, friendship, and play—is behind these precepts. Such bases for dignity exist independently of the person's social utility, abilities, race, gender, ethnicity, religion, or location. All of these features of common morality undergird essential corresponding features of human rights—their universality, their basis in human dignity, and their moral precedence over competing goods.

A thorough defense of human rights that meets all the objections of cultural relativists, postmodernists, premodernists, political realists, utilitarians, communitarians, legal positivists, feminist skeptics, and theological skeptics is more than I can offer in this book. What I aim to show in later chapters, rather, is that religious traditions contain such arguments and that these rights can garner an overlapping consensus among these traditions and secular schools. The argument for a political ethic of reconciliation, pursued according to the method outlined in the last chapter, then, can incorporate human rights as foundational standards.

Conclusion

The standards of justice that define political injustices as well as the essential features of justice—or right relationship—in a restored community consist of human rights and the norms governing war that are set forth in major international law documents. Yet these standards only begin to describe the fracture that political reconciliation seeks to mend and the justice that repairing this fracture involves. Like the web of cracks that spread from the hole a bullet makes in a wall, the wounds of political injustice extend far wider than political injustices themselves. The restoration of the sufferers of these wounds, then, also involves far more than filling the hole—that is, an end to laws and acts of political injustice. The first dimension of this holism—the multitude and variety of wounds of political injustice—is explored in the next chapter.

3

The Wounds of Political Injustice

WHILE RIDING THROUGH the forested hills of Bosnia in September 1996, less than a year after the Dayton Accords had brought an end to more than four years of civil war in Yugoslavia, I had occasion to observe the checkerboard imprint of ethnic cleansing. Passing through towns, I saw neighborhoods where homes stood intact—with lamplight shining through the windows, trimmed rows of bushes, and people walking in and out—next to homes reduced to crumbling, burnt concrete walls that framed hollowed-out windows and were wrapped in twisted branches of rebar. The burnt homes were the ones where Muslims lived on the day that Serb armies swarmed through town, where Serbs lived when the Croats showed up, where a Serb was married to a Muslim, or simply where the wrong person lived at the wrong time.

Behind this macabre pattern was the array of deeds, motivations, and culpability that characterized the war. Of the three major communities involved, Serb nationalists best qualified as aggressors, though they would claim that they were only protecting their endangered countrymen. Assuredly, Croat leaders such as Franjo Tudjman whipped up his share of deadly nationalist sentiment while Bosnian Muslims adopted assertive designs too. Some Serb, Croat, and Muslim soldiers joined their side's armies out of fervent nationalist inspiration. Others fought in defense of their towns and families. Some fought out of fear or social pressure. Others were simple thugs. The Serbs' massacre of Muslims at Srebrenica in July 1995 was the war's most notorious atrocity, but soldiers on all sides committed war crimes. Others did not, killing in a defensive manner that did not strictly involve political injustices.

Not all conflicts are symmetric in this way. Even Yugoslavia's symmetry is only a rough one. The paradigmatic asymmetric conflict is the

Holocaust. Even this evil, though, included architects, zealots, "ordinary men" who conformed to social pressure, fearful followers, and thugs.[1] Philosopher Karl Jaspers, who wrote his classic *The Question of German Guilt* shortly after these events came to an end, sought to distinguish criminal guilt, whose bearers were legally responsible, from the political guilt of those who voted, attended meetings, voiced verbal approval, or remained passively indifferent.

That guilt is hotly disputed underscores a crucial characteristic of political injustices: their complexity. Another major feature of political injustices, at least those that I consider in this book, is that they are systemic, affecting a wide spectrum of the inhabitants of societies. "Everything's broken," as Bob Dylan's political song puts it.

If political injustices are complex and systemic, so are the wounds they inflict. One of the core claims of the book is that the justice of reconciliation is a justice that aims to bring repair to persons and relationships that political injustices have wounded. An effort to depict and categorize these wounds and the ways in which they diminish human flourishing, then, is essential to the argument at hand.

What Are Wounds of Political Injustice?

A wound of political injustice can be defined as some respect in which a political injustice ruptures right relationship within or between political communities and diminishes the human flourishing of those who are involved in that injustice. Any political injustice involves four parties. First, there are victims whose human rights have been violated.[2] Second come perpetrators or wrongdoers who violate the human rights of others. Third are members of the community at large, citizens of the state who are neither victims nor perpetrators. Finally, there are the governing institutions of the state, which may at different times, in their very different modes, represent any of these parties, coordinate among them, enforce the rule of law, promote practices of reconciliation, or sanction or commit political injustices. Each party is what the great sociologist Max Weber called an ideal type—a simplified category that captures an important part of social reality. In later chapters, I will admit greater complexity, acknowledging, for instance, that parties can play gradations of each role and sometimes more than one role. Here, though, I keep the roles simple so as to describe the multiple ways in which wounds sever right relationship.

What makes political injustices distinctive from, for example, natural disasters or even "ordinary" crimes in stable communities are the intentions of the wrongdoers. Perpetrators of such acts directly disregard or purposely seek to violate their victim's human rights and dignity in the name of a political regime or ideology. Sometimes, the subordination of human rights and dignity constitutes the very rationale of a regime. Philosopher Jean Améry thought this was true of Germany's National Socialist regime.[3] The question of intent is essential to how the parties involved, especially victims, understand the loss of loved ones, bodily injury, and trauma that these injustices produce—namely, as losses that are compounded by their political, communal dimension. Of course, not every injustice committed in the context of war, genocide, or dictatorship is political. Wars often involve acts of rape and plunder that have little instrumental value for a military or political end. Political processes for determining amnesty often make just such a distinction between political crimes, which have intelligible strategic ends, and other crimes, which do not.

Types of Wounds

In what ways, then, do political injustices wound those who are involved in them? I identify six. Each wound involves a unique configuration in which the four parties afflict and are afflicted by suffering. All of the wounds can in turn take two different forms. Primary wounds are unprompted by prior wounds of injustice and the memories that they leave. Secondary wounds, by contrast, are caused by primary wounds through a chain of events involving memories, emotions, and judgments, culminating in further acts of injustice. Secondary wounds are identical to the six primary wounds in the ways that they diminish human flourishing. They differ only in that they are caused by primary wounds themselves. The point of this distinction is not that wounds can be rigidly and clearly separated into those that are caused by prior wounds and those that are not. Almost every primary wound is inflicted by an act of political injustice that is motivated by a grievance or responds to some previous injustice. Scholars will debate the degree and manner in which memories of previous injustices served to bring about any particular war, massacre, genocide, or authoritarian regime. The point in distinguishing the two types is rather to convey the dynamic by which wounds beget more wounds and to identify emotions, memories, and judgments as part of the rupture in right relationship to which restorative practices must attend.

Primary Wounds of Political Injustice

1. *The Violation of the Victim's Human Rights*

The first wound of political injustice is the violation of the victim's human rights. This may seem confusing. Is not the violation of a victim's human rights the definition of a political injustice in the first place? And do not wounds result from political injustices, meaning that they must be something other than these injustices themselves? Would it not make more sense to say, for instance, that the violation of the right to life is an injustice while the loss of life itself is the wound?

It is my claim that the violation of a victim's human rights is not only the definition of a political injustice but is also a form of wound, one that is suffered in addition to the many other ways that human rights violations damage human flourishing. The reason is that rights are a form of respect. To heed a person's human rights is to respect that person by recognizing and refraining from violating her dignity and worth. This respect is broadened when rights are enshrined, recognized, guaranteed, and enforced in public law. What obtains, then, is a form of right relationship involving a complex set of claims, obligations, and entitlements among citizens, between citizens and government institutions, or between states and citizens of other states. The state's message is reinforced when citizens also view public rights as legitimate. Such respect, where rights are not only esteemed and practiced among people but are robustly recognized and guaranteed by the state, is itself an aspect of human flourishing, one that complements the good that rights protect. When perpetrators violate human rights, they not only injure or extinguish a victim's life, bodily integrity, property, or whatever good it is that rights protect, but they also disrespect the status and recognition that the victim rightly enjoys under the law. Perpetrators make their own cause superior to the goods, rights, and prerogatives that they owe to others because these others are citizens—or even combatants, prisoners of war, or simply human beings—and treat them instead as people whose membership, allegiances, or race merit them no status at all. Likewise, when political institutions that guarantee and recognize human rights are restored, so too a dimension of human flourishing is also restored even if victims experience no restoration of the health, possessions, or other things of value that they lost when their rights were violated. That dimension is respect.

2. Harms to the Victim's Person

If the violation of human rights amounts to more than damage to human well-being, though, it certainly does involve such damage. Most raw and perceptible among the wounds of political injustice are the many forms of harm to the victim's person, in body and soul, in the most basic aspects of his flourishing. These forms of harm damage the good that rights protect. Their effects are recorded by victims through their disfigurations and testimonies. They involve death, the loss of loved ones, permanent injury from torture or assault; grief; humiliation; trauma; sexual violation; loss of wealth, property, and livelihood; the conquest and subordination of the victim's community; the taking of the victim's land; the defilement of the victim's race, ethnicity, religion, nationality, or gender; and many other diminishments of human flourishing. Admittedly diverse, these harms are grouped here because they are all direct harms to the flourishing of victims.

For survivors of political injustice, harms persist in radically altered lives. "Whoever was tortured, stays tortured," writes Améry, who was tortured by the Nazis. "Torture is ineradicably burned into him, even when no clinically objective traces can be detected."[4] Often, of course, "objective traces" are detectible. South African writer Antjie Krog quotes Anglican priest Michael Lapsley's description of losing his hands in a mail bomb: "When I made my political choice, I often thought of death. What I never thought of was being maimed. After the explosion, I felt that it would have been better if I were dead."[5]

In the mind and the soul, the persistent scars of political injustices take the form of what psychologists call trauma. Derived from the Greek word for "wound," trauma involves, in psychologist Judith Herman's words, a "diminished life, tormented by memory and bounded by helplessness and fear."[6] Traumatized patients, she describes, are "hyperaroused" to the point where memories of wounds effortlessly permeate the consciousness and stimulate anxious episodes of recall. In response, patients often detach themselves from the world through "constriction." Anger, depression, and broken relationships among family and friends are common symptoms. Many patients report a sense of having been forsaken by God. Trauma is long term, its symptoms often continuing to show up decades after the wounding event.[7]

When wounds are inflicted on body and soul, their political dimensions move from the motive of the perpetrator into the understanding of the victim. David Becker, a psychologist who observed survivors of political injustices in General Augusto Pinochet's Chile, takes to task his field's official concept of trauma, post-traumatic stress disorder, for its neglect of the political dimension. If politics is the source of wounds, politics must be included in their diagnosis: "[W]e would differentiate between a person who has experienced torture in Chile, a Bosnian refugee or a Vietnam veteran much more than between depressive, hysteric, or obsessive symptoms."[8] Becker describes a Chilean family that he treated in the 1980s whose children experienced psychological disorders resulting from their dissident father's kidnapping and torture at the hands of the police during the previous decade. Remarkably, even though their father was no longer politically active, their symptoms worsened and abated in tandem with the fortunes of the Pinochet regime.[9]

Once the political dimension of a wound has encamped in the victim's understanding, it will compound his experience of the wound. "The first blow brings home to the prisoner that he is helpless," Améry says of torture.[10] Overwhelmed by the force of the regime, the very regime whose moral duty it is to uphold justice (or by an opposition movement, which claims a right to exercise such a duty), the victim is left without recourse. With helplessness comes intensified fear. Yet there is something more insidious about political injustice that emerges especially vividly in writings about torture. It involves the attempt by the perpetrator not just to stupefy the victim but to erase his beliefs, commitments, and even identity and replace them with the message of the regime or the opposition force. This particular intention is what makes this sort of killing and harm different from nonpolitical harm. In her acclaimed book, *The Body in Pain*, literary theorist Elaine Scarry depicts the language-destroying, world-destroying act of torture, through which a regime makes pain into the victim's lived reality and then stamps its own insignia onto that pain.[11] When torture is used in this way, its goal is not so much to extract valuable information or even to inflict as much pain as possible but rather to gain the victim's assent. A crucial step toward the torturer's victory is the victim's betrayal of his own beliefs and morality. Even more strongly, regimes will sometimes succeed in making their opponents feel guilty for their resistance or even for the death of their loved ones, as the Guatemalan army did in its suppression of Mayans in the early 1980s.[12] The annihilation of victims' core beliefs in the face of such a brutal elicitation of assent helps to account for why high numbers of them commit suicide.

3. Victims' Ignorance of the Source and Circumstances of Political Injustices

Compounding this annihilation, truth commission reports from eastern Europe, Latin America, and South Africa testify, is a third dimension of woundedness: ignorance of the source and circumstances of the injustice. Professing this ignorance most commonly are relatives of the missing and the dead. "If they can just show us the bones of my child, where did they leave the bones of my child?" asks the mother of one missing South African political activist.[13] Friends of the victims not only want others to know of brutalities borne but want to learn who committed them, how, and why. André du Toit, a South African political philosopher, heard many such entreaties at his country's Truth and Reconciliation Commission hearings:

> Over and over again people pleaded to know what happened to a father, a mother, a sister, a brother, a son, or a daughter. They wanted to know where he or she was buried. They wanted to know why they were killed and under what circumstances. This was a common refrain at every public hearing. Almost exactly the same set of words has been used by witnesses whether they lived in South America, Northern Ireland, or South Africa.[14]

This is the trauma of uncertainty. In Argentina, Brazil, and Ireland, stories have surfaced of relatives maintaining the bedrooms and offices of the missing in the hope that they will return.[15] "I do not image hell as beds with shackles where the condemned must lie," writes Argentinian author Matilde Mellibovsky, "but rather as a couple of easy chairs in which one can sit comfortably and wait for the postman to bring news— which will never come."[16] It is females—widows and mothers—who are most vocal about such ignorance, Brandon Hamber and Richard Wilson argue.[17] Far from a by-product of brutality, the trauma of uncertainty flows from regimes' strategies of silence, strategies that they maintain long after they commit their injustices. Splicing all of these themes into renowned protest are the Argentinian mothers of disappeared human rights activists who, every Thursday from 1977 to 2006, marched silently in Buenos Aires' Plaza de Mayo to demand knowledge of their sons' fate, first from the military junta that carried out the country's Dirty Wars, then from a democratic government that pledged continually to foster reconciliation and the restoration of victims. Knowledge of these circumstances, these stories imply, is a step toward greater flourishing.

4. Lack of Acknowledgment of the Suffering of Victims

Exacerbating victims' ignorance of their wounds is a lack of acknowledgment, through ignorance or indifference, of the suffering of victims on the part of members of the community and the state.[18] This deficiency amounts to a fourth dimension of woundedness. "The effective refusal to acknowledge [atrocities and violations] in public amounts to a basic demonstration of political power," writes du Toit. "For the victims, this actually is a redoubling of the basic violation: the literal violation consists of the actual pain, suffering and trauma visited on them; the political violation consists in the refusal (publicly) to acknowledge it."[19] In its failure of acknowledgment, what the government and community withhold is a value quite similar to what public rights confer: recognition of the dignity of persons. Yet there is an added dimension of recognition that the restoration of robust rights alone does not perform: an acknowledgment not only that a victim has rights but also that his rights were violated and that he suffered because of this violation. The wound involved when such acknowledgment is missing can be understood as the political analogue of the plight of one who suffers alone in the hospital from a disease or from the wounds of a crime yet receives no attention, encouragement, or help from loved ones. His isolation itself is a wound. The victim of political injustices is isolated, too, though in his case it is from the members of the political order in whose name the injustice was committed. The political character of the injustice gives special importance to the role of governments and fellow citizens in acknowledging this violation. Just as agents and members of the political order confer the recognition on which public rights depend, so, too, they owe recognition to those victims whose rights have been egregiously violated in the name of the political order to which they and other citizens belong. This recognition is also a feature of right relationship in political orders. Thus, a communication is demanded. When it does not take place, as du Toit avers, the victim's wound is compounded.

The community's withheld regard indeed perpetuates the "strategy of invisibility," in the words of theologian William Cavanaugh, that authoritarian regimes deploy.[20] In order to achieve dominance, the regime must not only suppress the victim's communication but also prevent other citizens from communicating with the victim or speaking out on behalf of the victim. Torturers in such regimes even take great care to avoid killing their victims so they do not become martyrs, figures who historically have strengthened political resistance. The anonymity of the victim's suffering is the regime's dogged legacy.

5. The Standing Victory of the Wrongdoer's Political Injustice

The fifth and sixth dimensions of woundedness focus on the perpetrator. The fifth dimension is the standing victory of the wrongdoer's political injustice. When the perpetrator commits a political injustice, he breaks right relationship with the victim as a bearer of rights and with the community whose role it is to recognize and uphold these rights. In committing this deed, he asserts the superiority of a political order or a program, one whose instrument he may well have allowed himself to become, as had Adolf Eichmann when he came to accept Adolf Hitler's words as the absolute and binding law of his land.[21] In the wake of a perpetrator's injustice, what then remains is not only the harm to the victim, perhaps compounded by lack of knowledge or recognition, but the ongoing triumph of the perpetrator's evil deed, which persists victorious and unchallenged. As is true with lack of acknowledgment, the victory of the injustice persists even if just political institutions are restored. The injustice continues to "stand over" the victim and to stand against the norms of a just community—at least until it has been defeated decisively by a forceful, countervailing message of justice.[22]

The idea of a standing injustice may seem abstract, but it is real to the people involved. Wrongful words and deeds create realities to which other people must respond, just as a person creates a reality when she places a boulder on her neighbor's front walk, forcing her neighbor to choose between stopping and looking at it, walking around it, or calling for its removal—but leaving her unable to ignore it. In the same way, if Bill insults Susan, he has created a new "moral fact" in their relationship, one that cannot be ignored. Susan must then decide whether to return Bill's insult, refuse to talk to Bill, forgive him, or ignore the insult—in itself a response. Of course, for his part, Bill may apologize, explain that he was joking and misunderstood, or plead that he snapped under pressure, responses that all presuppose the moral fact that his insult has created. "I suggest," writes philosopher Pamela Hieronymi, "that a past wrong against you, standing in your history without apology, atonement, retribution, punishment, restitution, condemnation, or anything else that might recognize it as a *wrong*, makes a claim. It says, in effect, that you can be treated in this way, and that such treatment is acceptable."[23] The injustice that the perpetrator has committed stands and must now be dealt with in some way by victims, the government, members of the community, and the perpetrator. Even doing nothing is a real response, one that may well incur outrage.

Something much like the standing victory of a perpetrator's injustice is what human rights activists have in mind when they decry a "culture of impunity." A Rwandan whose entire family was killed in the genocide of 1994 expressed the idea to researchers Timothy Longman and Théonèste Rutagengwa:

The problem is that they ask us for reconciliation. It is true that it is necessary, because we can't continue with cyclical massacres. But you feel bad when you see those who killed your family strolling around with impunity. I say this because it is the case for me. I lost all my family in the genocide. My home was destroyed, and I live badly. But I feel bad when I know that the author of all this lives in Kigali. I know that [when he visits] he arrives at night and leaves early the next day [to avoid] arrest. How can I be reconciled with him when he doesn't come to ask my forgiveness or at least to reimburse my goods that he destroyed?[24]

The victim holds open the possibility of reconciliation, but only upon witnessing the "punity" that is lacking in "impunity" or at least receiving a reimbursement of goods, actions that would, in their different ways, bring down the standing victory implied by "strolling around" and evading arrest. The same sort of standing victory is also a good way of thinking about what Chilean human rights activists wanted when they sought to prosecute Pinochet for torture, murder, and other human rights violations years after he was no longer Chile's president and even after he had become infirm. What they sought was not the further suffering of an ill and elderly man but rather the defeat of the honor that Pinochet continued to enjoy in the eyes of many of his fellow citizens—a defeat that could occur through the countervailing public communication of a judge's verdict.

6. Harm to the Person of the Wrongdoer

Like a discharging cannon, a political injustice not only wounds its victim but also recoils, wounding the wrongdoer as well. How is this so? In

Judaism, Christianity, Islam, and the arguments of many philosophers can be found the idea that the one who respects and promotes the good of others also strengthens his own soul and character. He deepens his integrity in the sense of integrating his actions with rightness, his deeds with virtue, and the good that he understands and pursues with the true good. This is no less true of political actions. Evil, by contrast, is disintegrative. It separates the wrongdoer's actions and commitments from his true moral self and is thereby destructive. In Plato's *Gorgias*, Socrates avers that to do evil is to damage one's soul, which is in turn the worst evil that one can suffer. This, too, occurs in the political realm.[25] "Like sin, crime that is a gross violation of human rights almost always hides its true nature from its own self," writes South African psychologist Pumla Gobodo-Madikizela. "It is by its very nature delusional: perpetrators of human rights violations redefine morality and start believing that they can commit systematic murder and other atrocities 'for the greater good.' "[26]

The sixth wound involves the harm that a political injustice brings to the wrongdoer. It captures the idea that in doing evil wrongdoers diminish themselves. It implies, too, that evil disintegrates, even if this erosion is invisible or unacknowledged. Many, if not most, of the Latin American generals who ordered or committed crimes on behalf of military dictatorships in the 1970s and 1980s remained stalwart even after their regimes gave way to democracies: Subversion had to be defeated, civilization had to be defended. "I did my job," explained former Argentinian naval captain Alfredo Astiz.[27] Only a minority of apartheid officials evinced remorse or turmoil after their regime had fallen. "Repentance is for little children," Hannah Arendt quotes Adolf Eichmann as saying.[28] If doubt, shame, guilt, or trauma roils within such characters, it is not apparent to others. Their woundedness is objective and undeniable, though, if their true self flourishes through right action.

The wounds of other wrongdoers are more apparent. In a remarkable series of prison interviews, Gobodo-Madikizela discovers them readily in Eugene de Kock, the former commander of the Vlakplaas, the unit of the apartheid government charged with suppressing the armed resistance of the African National Congress. Known popularly as Prime Evil, de Kock had become the most reviled white person in South Africa, especially after the Truth and Reconciliation Commission revealed story after story of his direct orchestration of the most gruesome acts of torture and murder. When Gobodo-Madikizela spoke with him, he was serving a 212-year term at Pretoria's Central Prison.[29]

At the outset, she nearly abandoned her project, first out of fear for her safety, then out of a worry that her relationship with de Kock involved an "intimate complicity" in his evil. Still, she continued and came to see that de Kock's evil had poisoned him. In his cell, his surfacing conscience increasingly brought accusations, leading to what psychologists call splitting, an unconscious strategy whereby a wrongdoer projects his evil deeds and motives onto a second self, whom he then separates from his true self. Yet splitting fails. The tenancy of the second self cannot be revoked, and it remains behind as an in-house enemy of the conscience. De Kock related to Gobodo-Madikizela an incident evocative of Shakespeare's Lady Macbeth in which, after one murder, he took a shower in order to remove "the smell of death" from his clothes but found that the smell would not go away. This sense of evil as separation without severance is also found in Judaism and Christianity, where sin means the condition of being separated from other people and even more so from God. Here, too, separation is a wound. "The distance between evil and sickness is not that great," Gobodo-Madikizela writes. "The evil component of crimes against humanity is the moral failing. The sickness aspect is the defect in perspective, the distortion in mental processing that both precedes the evil and is intensified by it."[30]

Ample evidence that political injustices wound those who commit them comes from other psychologists as well. Writer Frederica Mathewes-Green reports psychologist Rachel McNair's finding that members of the Einsatzgruppen, the most elite killing specialists in the SS division of the Nazi military, experienced nightmares about their victims, some of them becoming insane or committing suicide, most of them ending up dependent on alcohol. It was when SS chief Heinrich Himmler witnessed the work of firing squads that he came to favor the more sterile and bloodless gas chambers.[31] Even he worried about what killing does to killers. Unless reversed, the disintegration of the self leads to death. Wounded perpetrators testify to this fact. "[Images of death] are there in the day, they are there in the morning. They are there at night when the sun sets. You can forget about forgetting—it's like a daily calling card," de Kock told Gobodo-Madikizela.[32]

Secondary Wounds

Primary wounds are not the end of political injustices' despoiling work. They may then redound, multiply, spread, and further destroy a just peace through secondary wounds—wounds that are identical to the six wounds previously described in the ways that they diminish persons, relationships, and political orders but that differ in that primary wounds are one of their chief causes. It is through a chain of memories, emotions, judgments, and, finally, actions that primary wounds lead to secondary wounds. When this sequence occurs among a group, the memories, emotions, judgments, and actions take on a collective form that can result in further civil wars, international wars, rebellions, and massacres or can give birth to political orders that suffer from shaky legitimacy and to relations between states that are frosty and fraught. The acts that create secondary wounds may also take place years after the primary wounds, sometimes through memories and emotions that are passed down over generations. To say that primary wounds can lead to secondary wounds is to say that the Germans' support for the Nazis and their aggression resulted in part from World War I and its outcome; that Hutus in Rwanda carried out genocide in 1994 in part because of their domination at the hands of Tutsis prior to the late 1950s; that Croats and Serbs fought one another in the early 1990s in part because they fought during World War II; that Korea and China continue to experience tensions with Japan today because of Japan's colonization and conquest during the first half of the twentieth century; and that stability in Iraq today is threatened in part by Saddam Hussein's massacres of Shiites and Kurds and his exclusion of them from political rule. Secondary wounds can be inflicted by either the victims or the perpetrators of primary wounds or by parties that fought each other on an equal footing at some prior time.[33]

Memory

The path from primary to secondary wounds begins with memory, the vehicle that transports the wounds of political injustice forward in time. Here *memory* means the present ideas that people hold about a past episode—what happened, who did it, who intended what, who suffered what, and what it was like. Memories are not just brute facts; they involve meaning and interpretation. Citizens do not remember simply that people were killed at this battlefield on that day but rather that one country's army killed another country's soldiers for a particular reason. Kashmiri Muslims remember that the Indian government took their land by making a deal with the Hindu maharaja and sending troops to Kashmir in 1947. Rwandan Hutus remember being subordinated at the hands of

Tutsis under Belgian colonial rule. Germans in the 1920s remembered the aggrandizement of the Allied powers at the Versailles settlement of 1919 and the complicity of their socialist and communist countrymen.

The forces that shape these meanings are in good part collective ones. Through the interpretations of others—via conversation, literature, songs, stories, newspapers, textbooks, teachers, film, mass media, museums, monuments, public commemorations, political speeches, regional cultures, the literature and discourse of political parties, civil society organizations, and religious organizations—people remember battles and negotiations and structures of oppression that they were not present to witness and that may have occurred decades or centuries earlier, while those who were present come to remember them in new ways. Memories are shaped both organically, at the popular level, as well as by the social, cultural, and political elites who persuade their citizens. Collective memory is memory shared among people and formed through social processes. It is not the same as a national mind or a group psyche. "We tend to vest our nations with conscience, identities, and memories as if they were individuals," Michael Ignatieff comments. "It is problematic enough to vest an individual with a single identity: our inner lives are like battlegrounds over which uneasy truces reign; the identity of a nation is additionally fissured by region, ethnicity, class, and education."[34] Individual minds, rather, are the repositories of memory. These minds will often remember events differently, even among countrymen. The examples above ought in fact to read "some Kashmiri Muslims," "some Hutus," and "some Germans," but through collective processes large swaths of countrymen will also come to remember similarly, making their memories collective.

Emotions

It is through emotions that memories translate into postures toward present politics. People remember not only the fact of a particular battle, treaty, or system of social stratification, as well as how, why, in whose name, and with what significance it occurred, but they also express a distinct attitude toward it. Two Americans, for instance, might both remember the Battle of Wounded Knee as a massacre, but one intensely resents the U.S. Seventh Calvary and calls for court-martials while another morosely laments the events and proposes that the U.S. government build a monument to honor the fallen Sioux. As mental events, resentment and lamentation are distinct from memories. They are interpretations and propositions that we call emotions—or so argues philosopher Robert C. Roberts. Emotions, he proposes, involve not just feelings, sensations, and tastes but also complex moral assessments of situations in which the holder of the emotion is invested. Anger, for instance, is far more than an upsurge of bile but also involves an offended person's perception that an offender is culpable of a serious wrong against her and is worthy of punishment. Concern-based construals is the definition of emotions that Roberts offers and that I will use here. Every emotion, he argues, involves a defining proposition. This proposition construes a person, event, or a situation in a certain way and prescribes a response. It is not a cold and removed construal but rather involves something that the holder of emotion cares about—a matter of concern.[35]

What is important here is that emotions can arise from political injustices and entail proposals for further violence and conflict. In his study of nationalist and ethnic conflict in twentieth-century eastern Europe, political scientist Roger D. Petersen charts the contributing role of four emotions: hatred, the conviction that the other ethnic group possesses an intrinsic property that makes it the traditional enemy; resentment, the intense feeling that status relations are unjust combined with the belief that something can be done about it; fear, the perception that something valuable to oneself is threatened; and rage, a wish to commit violence that can shift from target to target.[36] Pride, lamentation, shame, guilt, remorse, hatred, joy, sorrow, humiliation, compassion, and many other emotions also influence politics. Like memories, emotions are held individually but shaped through collective processes. Groups of individuals may collectively resent, hate, pity, or love their own government or another people or government.

A temptation is to think of negative emotions as a form of wound that belongs to the preceding list. For instance, psychologists tell us that anger, hatred, and resentment have a way of "eating away" at their holders. This may be true, but it is too hasty to call emotions wounds. Philosophers, theologians, and psychologists, after all, offer defenses of these same emotions. Resentment is a virtue, some argue, through which victims rightly assert their dignity. Anger can sometimes be righteous. Philosophers Jean Hampton and Jeffrie G. Murphy each commend "moral hatred," at least in a qualified way.[37] "Hate what is evil, cling to what is good," Saint Paul wrote in his Epistle to the Romans. Emotions themselves, then, are subject to praise and blame. Whether we are right to praise or blame, however, depends on what moral analysis tells us, an analysis that comes later in this book.

Emotions motivate political behavior insofar as they prescribe action. Imagine Hans, a German shopkeeper and veteran of World War I who, in 1925, finds himself affirming the *Dolchstosslegende*—the claim that Germany lost the war and came to be severely punished in the Treaty of Versailles because it was stabbed in the back by Social Democrats, Bolsheviks, and most of all, Jews. On the basis of this memory, which local militant orators along with some of his buddies at the local beer hall helped him to form, he develops strong resentment toward these events and groups and comes to believe that the Weimar Republic, the government that these traitors formed, ought to be overthrown.

Yet if emotions prescribe action, they do not alone lead to action. In his quieter moments, especially when away from the beer hall, Hans suspects that the legend might be exaggerated and his resentment misplaced and worries, too, about the consequences of so many of his friends believing the legend as strongly as they do. He decides against joining one of the parties advocating Weimar's overthrow. Though emotions both prescribe action and take intense forms, humans also have the capacity to stand back from their emotions, reflect on them, and determine whether or not to act. Of course, Hans could have decided that his resentment was correctly construed and that he should join one of the opposition movements, but this, too, is a further determination that his resentment did not alone yield. Such a determination can be thought of as a judgment.

Judgments

Judgment involves a deeper, more active, more deliberative level of reflection than emotions, Roberts explains.[38] In matters of political morality, judgment involves a determination about the justice of past events, present regimes, and previous efforts to remedy injustice and what sort of actions are to be pursued in response. It involves both principled and prudential considerations. Imagine residents of a Guatemalan village who each witnessed a massacre at the hands of a government Civil Defense Patrol in the early 1980s and who all share the emotion of rage and demand a response. One endorses private vengeance and recommends a vendetta to kill the members of the patrol. Another agrees with the justice of revenge but counsels against it as too risky and costly. Another decides that public retribution, through a trial with due process, then the death penalty, is the best course of action. Still another favors requiring the per-petrators to appear at a public truth commission, giving them a lighter sentence, then forgiving them. Such different determinations made by people with roughly the same emotions illustrate that judgment is both distinct and variable.

As the switchboard that links memories and emotions to actions, judg-ments are important for political reconciliation. If the people of a state collectively judge that a regime is just, they thereby confer on it the crucial legitimacy that it needs. If the people of one state, South Korea, for exam-ple, judge that another state, Japan, is prone to injustice on account of past atrocities that Japan never atoned for, then the climate of opinion between the two states will worsen. Each state will see the other as a threat and adopt hard-line policies toward it, and the elite members of both states will feel pressure from their populations to view the other state's action as an expression of hostility and be more ready to risk war.[39] One of the most important goals of practices of political reconciliation is to change the judgments that people form in response to political injustices and to the wounds, memories, and emotions that injustices leave behind.

Actions

Actions complete the chain from primary wound to secondary wound. Following from judgments, they are behaviors that involve an intention, an end, and a set of means. A person votes for the Nazi Party or joins a guerrilla army; a politician speaks on the floor of a parliament for a truth and reconciliation commission; a government seeks to arrest and try war criminals; a nationalist leader commits war crimes against an opposing ethnic group; a relative of a victim of political murder decides to hunt down and kill the assailant. Most relevant for the discussion of wounds are acts of political injustice. The practices of political reconciliation, though, are also actions—the actions that the ethic of political reconcilia-tion is most concerned with evaluating.

As the many preceding examples should make clear, not all memo-ries, emotions, judgments, and actions multiply, spread, and deepen the wounds of injustice. Injustices do not always or inevitably beget more injustices. Some memories lead to justifiable responses. Some emo-tions, including anger and even "moral hatred," entail just the right con-struals. Some judgments and actions are noble answers to evil. Some responses serve to construct a just peace. Sorting through what emotions, judgments, and actions are the right responses to evils is the job of the ethic of political reconciliation that begins to unfold in the next chapter. Yet as the examples cited in this chapter as well as those of Northern Ireland, Bosnia, Kosovo, Sudan, Algeria, the Basque Country, Iraq, South Africa, Dresden, Hiroshima, China, Korea, and Japan make clear, injustices such as war crimes and the systematic abuses of dictatorship are the sort that frequently lead to memories of cruelty, suffering, and the loss of family, friends, community, and tradition, which then beget emotions of spite, loathing, bitterness, humiliation, hatred, fear, and resentment, which lead in turn to judgments for vengeful retaliation, preemptive military strikes, and disregard for human rights and the laws of war, which then elicit actions such as massacres, genocide, international aggression, torture, or any of the injustices that violate shared human morality, leave woundedness in their wake, and repeat themselves over generations. This chain of events is also common.

Because emotions and memories lead to judgments and actions that involve further political injustice and inflict further wounds, they are rightly the concern of an ethic of political reconciliation. Wounds warrant addressing not only because they directly diminish human flourishing but also because they redound in further wounds. Wounds are the problem that an ethic of reconciliation seeks to remedy.

4

Reconciliation as a Concept of Justice

IN LANDSCAPES OF past political injustice—piled and strewn with bones, rubble, and manifold wounds, emanating hatred, lamentation, revenge, resentment, and despair—what is the meaning of justice? Reconciliation, I argue. That answer will seem strange to some. Reconciliation may be laudable, quixotic, misguided, or conditionally sound, but it is something other than justice, one group of doubters will contend. Others will question not whether reconciliation is justice but whether it is the right kind of justice. They may prefer what conflict specialists call negative peace—a negotiated cease-fire, a peace accord, or even a simple military victory—or else a slightly more ambitious sovereign peace or Hobbesian peace, where a single authority within a territory holds a monopoly on violence.[1] A cessation of violence itself can be a "momentous achievement," insists philosopher David Crocker, a skeptic of ambitious forms of reconciliation.[2] Still others may prefer a more expansive positive peace, a prominent contemporary version being the liberal peace that aspires to replace war or dictatorship with human rights, democracy, the rule of law within states, and adherence to international law.[3]

My argument differs. Reconciliation encompasses peace settlements, human rights, democracy, and other key goals of negative and positive peace. It also includes, for example, the reintegration of a Timorese militant into his village through community service and his confession and apology at a community panel; the provision of truth to an Argentinian mother about the whereabouts of her disappeared son; Chilean president Patricio Aylwin's public apology to torture victims and relatives of dissidents killed during the reign of Pinochet; the German government's reparations to victims of forced labor during the Holocaust along with a public apology and a pledge to tell their story in school textbooks; and the decision of Gordon Wilson of Northern Ireland to forgive the Irish Republican Army bombers who killed his daughter. All of these, I argue, are acts of justice.

This chapter develops a theoretical foundation for this view, making the case that reconciliation, conceived of as a broad restoration of right relationship involving a multiplicity of practices that each redress wounds of injustice in a particular way, is a promising way of conceiving justice. It offers a fuller vision of social restoration, especially in the aftermath of war, genocide, and dictatorship, than other leading concepts of justice, both contemporary and historical.

Reconciliation and Its Critics—and Its Diverse Defenders

In the past generation, talk of reconciliation has emerged from sites of political division across the globe, its promoters differing widely over its meaning as well as its merits. One of the central axes of difference is reconciliation's relationship to justice. Here are the six most common views of this relationship, plus my own (summarized in Table 4.1):

1. Reconciliation sacrifices justice. Some critics view reconciliation as an oppressor's rationale that supplants justice. By reconciliation, what they have in mind is a vision of harmony, national unity, and closure in which former enemies forgive one another and overcome enmity. The justice forgone is that of equality, rights, a fair distribution of wealth, and the prosecution of perpetrators. Reconciliation, for these critics, is usually the cause of the "haves" and the "dids," those who stand to benefit most from saying, "Let's just move on."[4] In the aftermath of the Holocaust, German philosopher Theodore Adorno stated: "Coming to terms with the past" does not imply a serious working through of the past, the breaking of its spell through an act of clear consciousness. It suggests, rather, wishing to turn the page and, if possible, wiping it from memory. The attitude that it would be proper for everything to be forgiven and forgotten by those who were wronged is expressed by the party that committed the injustice.[5]

Similarly, in the Kairos Document of 1985, a coalition of black South African theologians excoriated the "counterfeit reconciliation" proffered

Table 4.1 Seven Relationships Between Reconciliation and Justice

Views Hostile to Reconciliation

1. Reconciliation sacrifices justice.
2. Reconciliation is unjustly paternalistic.

Views Friendly to Reconciliation

3. Reconciliation is a second-best alternative to justice.
4. Reconciliation complements justice.
5. Reconciliation equals the justice of positive peace.
6. Reconciliation encompasses justice.
7. Reconciliation equals justice that entails a comprehensive restoration of relationship.

by a "church theology" that envisioned forgiveness for apartheid officials while all too feebly demanding an end to apartheid:

> In our situation in South Africa today it would be totally unChristian to plead for reconciliation and peace before the present injustices have been removed. Any such plea plays into the hands of the oppressor by trying to persuade those of us who are oppressed to accept our oppression and to become reconciled to the intolerable crimes that are committed against us. That is not Christian reconciliation, it is sin. It is asking us to become accomplices in our own oppression, to become servants of the devil. No reconciliation is possible in South Africa *without justice.*[6]

The authors of the document did not reject reconciliation wholesale but insisted that it could only come in the wake of repentance and an end to apartheid. In other cases, reconciliation allegedly undercuts accountability for war criminals. Human rights advocates remonstrated when, shortly after El Salvador's truth commission published its report in 1993, President Alfredo Cristiani promoted an amnesty law for generals, officers, and death squad leaders with the argument that it was time for national reconciliation. Reconciliation is also seen as sacrificing economic justice. Some critics took the African National Congress to task for negotiating an end to South Africa's apartheid constitution without demanding a dismantling of the economic structures that disempowered racial minorities.[7]

2. Reconciliation is unjustly paternalistic. A related strand of criticism sees the injustice of reconciliation as one of moral overstretch. As one line of argument contends, governments are paternalistic, invasive, and heedless of the boundary between public and private spheres when their representatives ask victims of the worst forms of political injustice to forgive or embrace their perpetrators. Like-spirited detractors see reconciliation as inescapably religious and thus inappropriate for politics. Or else they see it as utopian: bones, rubble, and wounds place a premium on the urgent and the achievable.[8] Political scientist Leigh Payne criticizes a reconciliation of harmony and closure for short-circuiting the vigorous disagreement that makes for healthy deliberative democracy.[9] These critics doubt that reconciliation is a just politics of redress, preferring instead the negative peace of a settlement or the positive peace of liberal democracy.

3. Reconciliation is a second-best alternative to justice. This third view takes reconciliation to mean healing, forgiveness, and often amnesty. It looks on reconciliation as a second-best alternative to the justice of prosecution and restitution where such justice is unavailable. Perhaps the old regime and its armies are still in power or are strong enough to extract an amnesty or even a continued role in government in exchange for peace. Perhaps civil war threatens to return. Perhaps judicial institutions are destroyed or never existed. Whereas criminals ought to be tried and punished during periods of stability, this view holds, in troubled times political orders may instead pursue other practices such as forgiveness in order to achieve national unity and reconciliation.[10]

4. Reconciliation complements justice. A fourth view of reconciliation is also sympathetic to reconciliation and sees it as distinct from the justice of punishment for perpetrators. Yet this view holds that it is possible to have both reconciliation and justice. Reconciliation here involves a number of activities that complement judicial punishment—truth telling; reparations; civil society measures that foster dialogue, healing, and the overcoming of enmity; and perhaps apology and forgiveness—but never at the expense of just punishment. One version of this view strongly decries impunity, holding that reconciliation should never sacrifice justice, but it allows that reconciliation can occur alongside justice.[11] Another version is that of policy analysts who see reconciliation as one of a wide array of practical measures that aid in peacebuilding—the return of refugees, the demobilization of militants, and security sector reform, for instance.[12] This view can also help make sense of the adoption by some countries, including Sierra Leone, Timor-Leste, Germany, and, over the long run, Chile and Argentina, of hybrid approaches—trials combined with truth commissions and other restorative measures.

   5. Reconciliation equals the justice of positive peace. A fifth view is also sympathetic, characterizing reconciliation as not only compatible with but identical to justice—justice that amounts to positive peace. This is the view of David Crocker, who criticizes paternalistic versions of reconciliation but is more amenable to a version that he calls "democratic reciprocity," in which enemies not only cease to commit violence against one another but come to respect and deliberate with one another as fellow citizens. What he decries is a more ambitious reconciliation understood as social harmony—the reconciliation of Archbishop Desmond Tutu, involving compassion, magnanimity, and forgiveness—which he sees as impracticable and heedless of individual freedom, democratic deliberation, and individual accountability.[13] Philosopher John Rawls reasons similarly in endorsing Hegel's *Versöhnung*—or reconciliation—as the outcome of a society's journey from a *modus vivendi* to a stable overlapping consensus on principles of liberty and equality.[14] This concept of reconciliation, then, turns out to be substantively the same as the positive peace of liberalism.[15] It has an international version, too, a condition described by political scientist Yinan He as one of "deep reconciliation," where countries live without expectation of war, recognize one another's sovereignty and territorial boundaries, flourish in their mutual economic interaction, and regard one another's populations sympathetically.[16]

   6. Reconciliation encompasses justice. The sixth view involves a fuller notion of reconciliation, one much wider than positive peace, consisting of a comprehensive restoration of relationship. It conceives of justice, though, much the way that previous views do—as judicial punishment, human rights, and equality. This view, then, sees justice as a component of reconciliation. Reconciliation always includes and never sacrifices justice but is itself something more than justice. Exemplary is the argument of theologian Miroslav Volf, who agrees with the signers of the Kairos Document that reconciliation must include justice in order to avoid being cheap but shuns the conclusion that reconciliation can only be taken up after justice is accomplished. Mirroring God's reconciliation with humanity, Volf's reconciliation begins with victims' will to embrace and to forgive, though victims are not actually to embrace or to forgive until a strong measure of justice is achieved.[17] Like Volf, holders of this view often—though not always—carry a theological outlook from which they derive their view of reconciliation as a wide restoration of relationship.[18]

7. *Reconciliation equals justice that entails a comprehensive restoration of relationship.* Like the sixth view, a seventh view also understands reconciliation as a comprehensive restoration of relationship. Yet it frames justice differently from any of the other views, namely as being inclusive of all of the activities that restore right relationship—for example, the revelation of truth to the Argentine mother, Gordon Wilson's act of forgiveness—and not merely as the rights, equality, and judicial punishment of a liberal, positive peace. Reconciliation, here, does not complement, supplement, balance against, detract from, or encompass justice. Rather, reconciliation *is* justice. This view, I will argue, is a key component of restorative justice and can be constructed from the Jewish, Christian, and Islamic traditions.[19] By building such a view of reconciliation and developing it for political orders, we will arrive at an approach to dealing with past injustice that promotes a distinctively wide, rich, and full vision of human flourishing.

A Concept of Justice

There are two sides to justice. First, justice describes right conduct. Second, justice describes the right response to wrong conduct. Both sides, I argue, appear within a common concept of justice shared by the Bible, the Quran, and writings on restorative justice: comprehensive right relationship.

With respect to right conduct, justice in these sources is the will to live according to the obligations of right relationship in all spheres of life. In the Jewish Bible, for instance, justice is the righteousness, or right relationship, that people practice in the temple, with their families, in the courtroom, and in their business dealings and extend to the king or judge, widows, orphans, aliens, the poor, and most of all, God. Each relationship has its own particular obligations, virtues, and roles: those of a priest, father, merchant, judge, eldest sibling, slave, wife, or king.

As a response to past wrongs, justice is the will to bring a comprehensive repair to the relationships that injustices have ruptured so that the persons involved are once again living according to the demands of right relationship. What is most important about this concept of justice is that it performs this repair with respect to the wide range of wounds that injustices inflict on persons and relationships. Justice, in this sense, restores not an abstract balance of right and wrong, overall utility, political stability, or rights alone but rather the actual wounded persons and ruptured relationships. Again, the idea can be found in the Jewish scriptures, where God's justice involves the liberation of slaves, prisoners, and the inescapably indebted; restitution for victims of crimes; punishment for wrongdoers; acknowledgment of the afflicted; the restoration of justice in governing institutions; and forgiveness for the repentant.

But what about reconciliation? Here we come to the crucial step in the argument for the view of reconciliation defended here. Namely, in the foundational texts of our source traditions and schools, the meaning of reconciliation turns out to be virtually the same as the meaning of justice in this comprehensive, relational sense.[20] Reconciliation, in these traditions and schools, is the restoration of relationships that wrongs have ruptured with the aim of realizing a condition of right relationship, that is, a state of being reconciled. If justice, too, is both a state of right relationship and a process of restoring right relationship following wrongs, then it follows that justice is identical to reconciliation. Put more simply, reconciliation is a concept of justice—the justice of comprehensive right relationship.

Political Reconciliation

What is the meaning and content of right relationship? Is comprehensive reconciliation the proper concern of the political order? The answer to both of these questions lies in the notion of political reconciliation, the kind of reconciliation that I advance in this book. Political reconciliation is a subset of comprehensive reconciliation. It is confined to that portion of relationships that concerns persons as citizens of states and states as members of the international order.

In the political order, the "right conduct" portion of right relationship most centrally involves respect for basic human rights and the rights entailed in international laws governing war. Basic human rights include features of democracy, such as elections, and of the rule of law, such as an independent judiciary. To rights and law can be added citizens' recognition of the legitimacy of rights and their commitment to certain virtues that go along with these rights, including democratic deliberation, civility in this deliberation, and political participation.

The norms that govern right relationship in the political realm are independent of those that govern other spheres of life, such as family, religious organizations, and businesses. True, the political sphere is not isolated from these other spheres. Public laws concern themselves with marriage and divorce, patent and property rights, economic growth, employment, welfare provision, the tax benefits that religious institutions enjoy, and much else. From state to state, from culture to culture, the reach of the state's regulatory authority is constantly negotiated. In the present ethic, though, what is most essential to right relationship in the political order is human rights, their popular legitimacy, and their corresponding virtues. Politically speaking, the condition under which these values are restored is the condition of being reconciled. Governments might sometimes seek to restore something more than this, but they must always stop short of restoring comprehensive justice if they are to remain limited governments, one of the core characteristics of regimes based on human rights and democracy. These limits on the reach of government are what make the present ethic one of political reconciliation. Right conduct in the political realm is little different from the positive peace of liberalism. It is in redressing unjust conduct—the the other dimension of justice—that political reconciliation becomes far more distinctive. Justice, in this sense, involves not merely restoring rights but also redressing the wide set of wounds that political injustices have inflicted on persons and relationships. Political reconciliation takes an interest in a much wider set of wounds than the liberal peace does—namely the full set of six primary wounds described in the previous chapter as well as the secondary wounds that arise from them.

The restoration of right relationship in these many respects is the proper business of the government for three reasons. First, it was agents acting in the name of the political order—governments or opposition movements—who inflicted these wounds and thus rendered them political injustices. It is thus the proper role of authoritative agents of the political order to restore the right relationship that these wounds diminished, insofar as they can. Especially when the state inflicts political injustices, it carries a moral liability.[21] A second, even stronger reason for the state's role is the kind of communication that it uniquely performs. Political injustices involve a distinct disregard for the victim's dignity on the part of those acting in the name of the political order. Restoring the persons and relationships wounded by political injustices requires a countercommunication that nullifies this injustice and recognizes the dignity of the wounded in the eyes of the political order. Such a message can only be voiced by one who speaks authoritatively for the political order: an official of the state. Third, the state's obligation to uphold human rights gives it an interest in encouraging the emotions and judgments that confer popular legitimacy on these rights.

Political reconciliation performs the justice of repair in two ways: through primary restorations and secondary restorations. Primary restorations seek to bring direct repair (increases in human flourishing) to the wounds (diminishments in human flourishing) that political injustices exact on right relationship. These restorations, at least when conducted rightly, are intrinsically just—that is, they are just apart from their consequences for stabilizing social orders and building democracy and peace.

Primary restorations occur through the ethic's six practices—building socially just institutions, acknowledgment, reparations, punishment, apology, and forgiveness—each of which in some way restores individuals and relationships to a condition of comparatively greater human flourishing. El Salvadoran truth commissioner Thomas Buergenthal describes one sort of restoration:

> Many of the people who came to the Commission to tell what happened to them or to their relatives and friends had not done so before. For some, ten years or more had gone by in silence and pent-up anger. Finally, someone listened to them, and there would be a record of what they had endured. They came by the thousands, still afraid and not a little skeptical, and they talked, many for the first time. One could not listen to them without recognizing that the mere act of telling what had happened was a healing emotional release and that they were more interested in recounting their story and being heard than in retribution. It is as if they felt some shame that they had not dared to speak out before and, now that they had done so, they could go home and focus on the future less encumbered by the past.[22]

Through the practice of acknowledgment the community recognizes victims' suffering, affirms their right to restored citizenship, sometimes brings to light information about their suffering, and sometimes encourages perpetrators to acknowledge and feel remorse for their crimes. Other practices work in parallel fashion, bringing restoration to particular wounds in particular ways. Through a collective apology, a head of state delegitimizes the standing victory of those who committed war crimes in the state's name, provides recognition of another state's victims, and invites the members of his community to participate in this recognition. Punishment, reparations, forgiveness, and the building of just institutions help restore relationships in their own ways as well.

Yet just as primary wounds can result in secondary wounds, primary restorations can lead to transformations in people's emotions and judgments so that they view their own or another country's political order more favorably. These secondary restorations can be assessed in terms of their positive consequences for the political community and for relations between political communities. Secondary restorations, too, are fruits of the six practices and involve the four ideal typical parties in political reconciliation. When victims gain or are granted recognition, reparations, an apology, the restoration of their human rights, and a nullification of the standing victory of the perpetrator's injustice, when perpetrators come to feel remorse and to witness the nullification of their own injustice, when members of the community become aware of the crimes that took place during the war or the dictatorship and of the present regime's commitment to deal with them, all of these parties, through all of these practices, are more likely to bequeath legitimacy on a new regime based on human rights. In the international context, a state might be willing to look on a former enemy as a member in good standing of the international order and a worthy partner in economic and political relations. Members of estranged states, factions, ethnic groups, and ideological parties might also come to be more willing to place trust in one another, which is essential to realizing respected citizenship, democratic deliberation, a stable peace between states, and the contracts and exchanges that are required for economic growth.[23] Citizens of a state are more likely to view themselves as a common people, or nation, which in turn makes greater cooperation possible in political, economic, and cultural endeavors.[24] Legitimacy, trust, and national identity can all be seen as forms of social capital—a general "fund" of attitudes that serve to promote aspects of the good such as the stability of just institutions, economic growth, and peace between states.[25]

How the large-scale benefits of legitimacy, trust, and national sentiment—and perhaps their close cousins, patriotism, solidarity, fellow feeling, and commitment to the common good—arise from the restoration of persons and relationships will vary from practice to practice. We can envision Buergenthal's "less encumbered" victims not only wanting to "go home" but also feeling more loyalty to their political order after being acknowledged by the commission. Accounts of truth commissions all over the world, especially those that involve public hearings, have described such revised social judgments. Some accounts also tell of remorseful perpetrators who are then willing to live with a political order that they once fought against rather than join a militia to regain their lost regime. Most directly, the first practice, building socially just institutions that guarantee human rights and the rule of law, helps those who fought for and against a previous regime to feel secure in the justice of a new one, and thereby elicits their loyalty. The practices also can yield positive consequences for relations between states. The Federal Republic of Germany's practice of reparation, acknowledgment, apology, and the building of socially just institutions through both its own constitution and its commitment to European federalism following the Nazi period has fashioned stable and peaceful relations with its erstwhile victims, Poland, France, and Jews living in Israel.

At this point the ethic of political reconciliation can be stated as a definition. It is a concept of justice that aims to restore victims, perpetrators, citizens, and the governments of states that have been involved in political injustices to a condition of right relationship within a political order or between political orders—a condition characterized by human rights, democracy, the rule of law, and respect for international law; by widespread recognition of the legitimacy of these values; and by the virtues that accompany these values. Political reconciliation comprises six practices that each aim to restore persons and relationships with respect to the distinct wounds that political injustices have inflicted on them. These restorations may, in turn, generate emotions and judgments that bequeath on the political order legitimacy, trust, and national loyalty, all forms of social capital that promote the stability of just institutions, economic growth, peace between states, and other social goods. It is also worth summarizing exactly what right relationship means in political reconciliation, namely not only human rights, democracy, the rule of law, and attendant virtues but also a restoration of the six wounds and of trust, national loyalty, legitimacy, and other forms of social capital. Right relationship, when conceived of in this manner, is the goal of political reconciliation.

Elaborating on Political Reconciliation

Five features of the ethic of political reconciliation serve to elaborate it. First, as is clear by now, it involves the governing institutions of the state. Some of today's advocates of restorative justice shun these institutions, viewing the state as an impersonal modern colossus based on an abstract law that has little to do with right relationship among its citizens.[26] Yet the government and its laws are crucial for political reconciliation. In part, this is because officials of the state have the authority to perform the political communication needed to rectify political injustices, but it is also because laws, far from being irrelevant to right relationship, articulate a community's understanding of right relationship. The government of the state is integrally associated with these laws as enforcer, legislator, judge, teacher, and defender. It is also associated, in all of these capacities, with repairing the right relationships that the laws embody. The government's support for the law is crucial to the six practices of reconciliation, in which state institutions (and sometimes international organizations) try and imprison human rights violators, conduct searches and seizures, issue subpoenas, raise and disburse reparations, establish and oversee truth commissions, debar certain wrongdoers from holding office, and issue apologies and perhaps forgiveness on behalf of the community.

Reconciliation is not exclusively the work of governments. Civil society organizations, NGOs, religious communities, and other organizations, too, can promote the restoration of persons and relationships that have suffered the wounds of political injustice. These entities are often able to foster transformations in emotions and judgments that are far wider and deeper than what the state can or ought to effect. Like secondary restorations, these transformations can yield legitimacy, trust, and national loyalty on behalf of the political order. But the state remains indispensable.

A second distinct feature of political reconciliation is its inclusion of punishment. In country after country, debates about the past pit reconciliation against punishment and restorative justice against retributive justice. When it comes to political reconciliation, however, these dichotomies are false. Restorative punishment, a term I borrow from contemporary proponents of restorative justice, is critical to the restoration of right relationship and is one of the six practices of political reconciliation.[27] It defeats the standing victory of the wrongdoer, potentially repairs the disorder in the person of the wrongdoer, seeks his reintegration into the community, sometimes gives recognition to the suffering of victims in the eyes of the community, and through all of these restorations, creates legitimacy for the new political order.

A third distinctive feature is the active participation of the parties to the injustice in the restoration of right relationship. Political reconciliation integrally involves victims, perpetrators, and members of the community who variously accuse, defend, demand, narrate, recognize, learn, listen, affirm, show remorse, acknowledge, forgive, and empathize. True, some aspects of some of the practices involve only meager participation—the establishment and guarantee of human rights through law and institutions, for instance. All of the practices, though, enjoin participation in some way, to some degree. Participation is integral to the redress of most of the wounds that political injustices create and it builds social capital. One of the benefits of public truth commission hearings, political philosophers Amy Gutmann and Dennis Thompson argue, is the creation of patterns of deliberation that can strengthen a new democracy.[28]

Personal participation is most important when the parties undergo transformations of emotion and judgment. Again, changes in outlook do not occur in all aspects of all of the practices. Still, all of the practices in some way seek transformations through which one party who is in some way estranged or alienated from the political order or fellow citizens comes to view the order or these people in a manner that in some way restores what is disordered. In acknowledgment, for instance, a citizen who was previously ignorant or indifferent may come to exercise empathy for a victim by recognizing her suffering, lamenting it, and condemning the injustice that caused it. In some cases, a victim will reciprocate by forgoing her enmity for the political order. Apology involves the empathy and remorse of an offender who was previously impenitent. Forgiveness envisions a victim relinquishing her justifiable anger at a wrongdoer and conferring on him a restored status. All of these transformations require a willed decision to diminish a gap, partition, or fracture sustained by enmity, indifference, ignorance, or refusal and to amplify mutuality and common regard. Replicated, accumulated, and effected in a public context, they can enlarge the sphere of mutual purpose in a riven society.

At this point the ethic risks sounding utopian. A fourth feature—the ethic's almost inevitable partial achievement—addresses that concern. Talk of restoring right relationship may seem to imply that this restoration is expected to be complete, but this is not so. Reconciliation in the political realm will always be partially achieved.

Commending reconciliation does not deny the difficulty of reconciliation any more than advocacy of human rights or economic equality denies that both of these values are massively violated in the world today. One practice but not another will occur in one country while another combination of practices will occur in another country; any given practice will occur in pieces and in parts and will remain imperfect and fragmentary. While the justifications for the practices will show how, in principle, they might be restorative, none of these rationales warrants assurance that these restorations will be successful where citizens have suffered colossal injustices. Political reconciliation will be compromised by the obstruction of the powerful, the destruction of institutions, the chaos of the aftermath of war and dictatorship, and by the simple complexity of the practices.

The incompleteness of reconciliation leads some scholars to argue that if one practice occurs partially or in isolation then reconciliation is not achieved. Some advocates of forgiveness, for instance, hold that forgiveness is not the same thing as reconciliation, which further requires the wrongdoer's apology and the agreement of both victim and wrongdoer to restore their relationship.[29]

The intuition here is sound: One practice alone is not enough; all must work together. Yet it does not follow that reconciliation is not achieved when one practice is not joined by its siblings. As long as a practice involves the will to restore relationships in the political order then it effects some portion of reconciliation, that which is unique to that practice. The process of reconciliation has still occurred and at least some portion of the goal has been achieved. True, it is only a portion and the achievement partial, but the achievement is still real. In the case of forgiveness, a victim wills to relinquish his anger and invites the wrongdoer to remorse and apology. Even when the victim is rebuffed, his invitation and his relinquishment still bring about one portion of restoration with the wrongdoer, one portion of reconciliation. All in all, what can be expected is not full political reconciliation or anything close to it but rather incremental improvement, a movement from less to more, a realization of better relationship among citizens within a state and states in an international order.[30]

Some will protest: Such partiality is precisely the problem. Echoing common criticisms of reconciliation, they might say that when forgiveness is unaccompanied by apology, accountability, or a reformation of unjust structures, it denies justice to victims. Whether or not this critique is true, it does not disprove that forgiveness—or any other orphaned practice—is reconciliation or at least partial reconciliation. The critique is rather an ethical argument about a certain performance of reconciliation. One can allow that a certain practice effects reconciliation without endorsing the way that it does so. Again, reconciliation can be better or worse, practiced rightly or wrongly.

A fifth feature of political reconciliation is the sense in which it involves a return to a previous condition. The prefix *re-* in reconciliation—and in several of its synonyms and components, including restoration, restitution, retribution, redress, rectification, and reparation—evokes a certain puzzle: All of these terms seem to imply a return to a previous condition of justice, but what society has ever enjoyed such a condition? "[I]n this country," writes Antjie Krog of her native South Africa, "there is nothing to go back to, no previous state or relationship one would wish to restore. In these stark circumstances, 'reconciliation' does not even seem like the right word, but rather 'conciliation.' "[31] Before the conquerors arrived, the oppressors took over, and the masters enslaved, there was—what? Few states can point to some halcyon moment in their actual history. What should we make of this puzzle? If what is meant by reconciliation is a return to a condition that existed at a previous point in time, then reconciliation and its fellow *re-* words can be understood metaphorically and analogously at best and certainly not literally. Reconciliation restores a society according to an ideal of justice, but it is an ideal that has not yet existed. It is in the faith traditions, especially Christianity, that reconciliation involves a stronger notion of return, that is, to a condition that once existed, exists outside time, and that will eventually be recovered. Reconciliation, in this sense, is more than metaphorical. Still, it must be balanced by two considerations. First, on this side of heaven it will be highly partial due to sin and human limitations. Second, its proper and just application to politics involves all of the limits on the state's role that I have articulated.

Mercy: The Virtue Animating Reconciliation as a Process of Restoration

The cardinal virtue of reconciliation is mercy. This may sound dissonant in modern parlance, where mercy means "to let one off the hook" by forgoing deserved punishment. The problem of mercy, as many contemporary philosophers frame it, is its tension with justice, meaning retributive justice. Under what conditions, they ask, is a departure from deserved punishment justifiable?[32]

Political reconciliation, though, evokes an understanding of mercy that is older, richer, wider, and more comprehensive than the modern concept. It can be found in the Jewish, Christian, and Islamic scriptures and in the thought of medieval philosophers such as Anselm and Thomas Aquinas. *Misericordia*, the term that Aquinas uses for mercy, is grief for the distress of another, distress that is due either to undeserved suffering or the sufferer's own wrongdoing. Among the virtues that relate us to our neighbor, *misericordia* is the greatest, Aquinas believes.[33]

A merciful action is one whose end is the relief of distress, suffering, and rupture, either the sort that the recipient of mercy has suffered undeservedly or the sort that she has brought on herself through her own wrongdoing. Because mercy seeks restoration, it animates all of the practices of reconciliation. This yields a startling conclusion for modern philosophy, namely that mercy approximates and does not contradict justice when conceived of as reconciliation. More precisely, since mercy involves transformation, it converges with the aspect of political reconciliation that is a response to past injustice. The contrast between the older and the modern concepts is deepened by the older concept's compatibility with punishment. Mercy is reflected in the purpose of restorative punishment—principally, in the restoration of the wrongdoer but also in some aspects of the victim's restoration as well as in the involvement of members of the community. Though restorative punishment envisions forms of penalty other than proportionate imprisonment, it is not a derogation from deserved punishment. Rather, it recommends punishments that are broadly restorative and thus merciful. What reconciliation accomplishes in punishment is not unlike what it performs in all of its practices—a communication that nullifies the injustice of the wrong and seeks the victim's restoration, the wrongdoer's own restoration, and the community's involvement.

My claim is not that the entire concept of justice and the entire concept of mercy collapse into each other so that they become equivalent. The justice that addresses past wrongs is only one side of justice. But this side of justice, at least when conceived of as reconciliation, does indeed overlap with mercy, that which seeks to restore what political injustices have split apart.[34]

Peace: The Goal of Reconciliation

If mercy is the virtue that animates the process of reconciliation, peace is the concept that corresponds to the state of being reconciled. It is a peace of a certain kind, though, one whose comprehensiveness corresponds to the comprehensiveness of reconciliation's justice. Again, it is in the scriptures of Judaism, Christianity, and Islam that such a concept of peace is found. In the Jewish scriptures, it is called *shalom* and connotes rightly ordered relationships in many spheres of life. As with justice, this comprehensive state of affairs is one whose scope exceeds the peace that is proper to the political order. Still, the peace that states may rightfully promote is wider than the negative peace of a settlement or the positive peace of human rights, democracy, and the rule of law and also involves a condition in which right relationship within political orders has been restored (at least partially) with respect to the wounds of political injustice.[35]

When the Allies defeated Nazi Germany in May 1945, they created a negative peace. The federal republic that emerged during their occupation of Germany, a model of the rule of law, was a positive peace. Over subsequent decades the Federal Republic of Germany paid billions of dollars to Israel and to the victims of Nazi crimes; its presidents and chancellors issued numerous apologies and statements of contrition; and its courts brought tens of thousands of Nazis to trial. From the standpoint of political reconciliation, these restorations did not merely cement negative peace and pursue positive peace but also widened the peace to other dimensions—those that are most distinctive to political reconciliation.

Restorative Justice: The First Justification of the Ethic

Thus far I have been describing what it means to conceive reconciliation as justice and how reconciliation involves mercy and peace. Although I have alluded to features that might well commend reconciliation, I have not argued directly for what justifies it or makes it more appealing than alternative concepts. For such a justification, we turn to three religious traditions—Judaism, Christianity, and Islam—and one additional school of thought, restorative justice. I aim to show how each of these sources offers an independent grounding of the ethic and its propositions. In arguing that the justifications of all four separate bodies of thought converge in the propositions, I aim to demonstrate that an overlapping consensus is possible. None of these sources contains the fully developed version of the ethic or grounds it in the same way. Rather, each contains the foundational material to ground the ethic—basic concepts that favor the way of thinking about justice that reconciliation involves. Each tradition and school also contains disagreements and diverse strands. Some of these strands support the ethic of reconciliation better than others. Justifying the ethic from each individual standpoint, then, involves both development of that source and argumentation from within it.

All of this is true for restorative justice. It is not a tradition in the way that Judaism, Christianity, and Islam are traditions, for it has existed—at least in explicit form—only for some three decades. Still, it involves a global network of people who hold common ideas about justice, who carry on disputes about these ideas, and who insist that these ideas have long pedigrees in numerous cultures around the globe. I call it a school. Most members of this school have proposed restorative justice as an approach to reforming criminal justice. Only a few of them have begun to apply it to entire nation-states and to envision it as a panoply of practices, not just punishment or accountability.[36] I join these efforts. The core justifications for restorative justice can also support the core ideas of political reconciliation—its way of viewing justice and its related ideas of mercy and peace. Although proponents have argued for restorative justice in both religious and secular terms, I present it here in secular language in order to show that a secular justification for political reconciliation is possible.

Rooted in abstract law, an impersonal state, and an inordinate focus on incarceration, Western criminal justices systems do little to improve offenders, often hardening them further in their lives of crime. They also do little for victims, whose suffering is rarely acknowledged by offenders or the community and who receive little in the way of repair. Such a critique launched the restorative justice movement, which has now influenced community criminal justice systems in New Zealand, Australia, the United States, Canada, and Great Britain. For their inspiration, advocates of restorative justice typically look beyond modern Western law and justice to the *ubuntu* ethic of sub-Saharan Africa, the rituals of certain native North American tribes and Maori tribes in New Zealand, and certain strands of Christian theology, especially the Mennonite tradition.[37]

Much of the movement's energy is focused on developing practical alternatives to the sequence of trial, sentencing, and imprisonment. These alternatives usually involve gathering all of the relevant parties to a crime and seeking a solution that promotes restoration for as many of them as possible. Since the 1970s, several variants of restorative justice have come into practice. Victim-offender reconciliation processes bring together the victim and offender with a mediator to negotiate a restitution agreement as an alternative to sentencing after the offender has been convicted in a court of law. An expanded version is known as the conference, which adds friends and family of the victim and offender into the mix. Even more extensive are the peacemaking circles of First Nations peoples in North America, which gather victims, offenders, family, friends, and a wide circle of community members to speak about their experience of the crime in a setting of equality, mutual respect, and uninterrupted listening. Criminal courts have come to recognize these circles as a valid alternative to criminal trials, and by 1999 three hundred programs existed in North America and five hundred in Europe.[38]

The central justification for restorative justice is that it promotes wider and fuller human flourishing than competing concepts of justice. This justification is elaborated through three broad claims. First, crime is primarily a rupture of right relationship between victim and offender and between victim and community that involves a range of harms. That is to say, crime is not merely a violation of law, and the state is not the only party harmed by a crime. For victims, crime means the loss of life, injury, property, trauma, and all of the other harms to the person of the victim identified in the last chapter. For offenders, crime wounds their own souls and often deepens their proclivity to commit further crimes. For members of the community, crime diminishes the authority of the law, leaves behind the standing victory of injustice, erodes mutual trust, and reduces security. Crime also inflicts an array of harms on family and friends of both victim and perpetrator.

The second claim is that a response to crime ought to be oriented toward repairing these relationships and the several dimensions of injury and harm that crimes leave behind. Simple trial and punishment through fines and imprisonment is not enough. Measures through which members of the community and, if possible, the offender recognize and acknowledge the suffering of victims ought to be adopted. Victims ought to receive reparations. Punishment ought to be oriented toward repairing the specific kind of breach that occurred between victim and offender. Offenders ought to be encouraged to hear and learn about the hardship that they caused victims and to apologize. Victims may respond with forgiveness. Prominent in the restorative justice community is philosopher John Braithwaite's idea of reintegrative shaming, a form of restorative punishment by which offenders are shamed before members of the community but then invited to rejoin the community—in contrast to stigmatizing forms of shaming, which leave offenders condemned.[39]

I have seen these ideas in action in my own experience as a mediator. One case I mediated involved a teenage boy who had vandalized a retail store, breaking its windows, spraying water into its interior, and causing thousands of dollars' worth of damage. After trying and convicting the teenager, a judge referred the case to the Victim-Offender Reconciliation Program. During the mediation the teenager listened to the store owner recount the damage and anguish that the vandalism had caused him, after which the store owner heard the teenager describe the difficult circumstances of his own life in the presence of his mother, who was also in attendance. After each had listened to the other, the store owner agreed to allow the teenager to repay the damage by working at his store, a form of reparation that would teach the boy the value of work and help him regain a sense of dignity.

That justice involves the active participation of victims, offenders, and members of the community through dialogue, narrative, and negotiation is the third claim of restorative justice. The teenage vandal's acknowledgment of the store owner's hardship, the owner's contribution to formulating a solution, and the teenager's role in restitution were all essential to justice. At the level of the nation-state, one of the best examples of participation in restorative justice was South Africa's Truth and Reconciliation Commission.[40] Through its hearings, which took place around the country and were sometimes nationally televised, members of the community and in some cases perpetrators themselves could acknowledge the testimony of victims. Many perpetrators were publicly exposed for their crimes; some of them came to express remorse. The commission, representing the state, conveyed the values of the community to victims and perpetrators alike.

The same moral arguments that support restorative justice, then, can also support its use on the national level. This concept of justice envisions a fuller notion of flourishing than alternative concepts. Exactly what this flourishing involves and how restorative justice and reconciliation conceive it coming to pass are developed later in the arguments in support of the six practices. For now, we can say that the claims about justice in the restorative justice school also support the concept of justice that I have called reconciliation. Political reconciliation's concepts of mercy and peace are also implicit in restorative justice, which calls for the repair of actual persons and relationships (mercy) and aims at a state of affairs in which this repair has been achieved (peace). The only major core idea of the ethic of political reconciliation that restorative justice does not include is human rights, but there is nothing in restorative justice that prevents human rights from being incorporated into its logic as a standard and a goal.

In Comparison to Other Concepts of Justice

Restorative justice, then, is the first of four traditions or schools that provide a moral defense of reconciliation as a concept of justice and of its companion notions, peace and mercy. The point of extracting these ideas from these sources is that they hold out the promise of a wider, broader, more holistic response to past injustices than alternative concepts do. Political reconciliation is not completely different from these alternatives and shares important commitments with many of them, but it diverges from them, too, usually in the direction of holism.

Consider, first, a classical Western concept of justice, one that finds its most famous formulation in the writings of the Roman jurist Ulpian, made its way into the law code of the Emperor Justinian, and appears in a roughly similar version in the writings of Plato and Thomas Aquinas. Ulpian's formulation is: "Justice is the constant and permanent will to render each person what is his due." Other translations end with "his right," "what he deserves," and "what is owed to him." "Due" could mean that a person is entitled to an action or a good—for example, that the government provides him with health care. Or it could mean that he is rightfully immune from an action—torture, for instance—or that he deserves punishment for his crime. Most of the six practices in the political ethic of reconciliation can indeed be conceived as being "due," making the ethic broadly compatible with Ulpian's famous concept of justice. Reparations, acknowledgment, and the like involve actions that victims are entitled to have performed, goods that they have a right to receive, and actions that other persons or institutions have a duty to perform. Punishment is an action that a perpetrator deserves.

Political reconciliation differs from justice that is due, though, in two important respects. First, the sense in which its component practices perform justice is far wider than the concept of rights and desert alone can describe. Each of the practices does more than respect or realize a right but also redresses a range of additional wounds and harms. The justice of reconciliation achieves something broader, wider, and more holistic. The second difference is that one of the ethic's practices in particular, forgiveness, eludes altogether the concept of due. Perpetrators do not deserve or have a right to forgiveness from victims and victims do not necessarily have a duty to perform it. Still, as I will argue, forgiveness can be thought of as a practice of the justice that restores right relationship.

At least one other concept of justice can be found in the writings of classic Western philosophers, including Plato, Aristotle, Lactantius, Ambrose, St. John Chrysostom, Augustine, and Thomas Aquinas: justice as a general or universal virtue that governs all actions between persons.[41] It extends to the love of neighbors and all actions that promote the common good. Since love of neighbor can involve actions that one's neighbor does not deserve or to which he does not enjoy a strict right, general or universal justice is a wider concept than justice conceived in terms of due and approaches the width of reconciliation. Still, even this wider concept does not express the particular ways that reconciliation brings repair to a wide range of wounds. The justice of reconciliation is far more textured.

Reconciliation also contrasts with a modern concept of justice, utilitarianism, in which a just action or just institution is one that brings about the best outcome or state of affairs. As I argue in the next chapter, a close cousin of utilitarianism, liberal consequentialism, argues that measures to deal with past injustices ought to be adopted or rejected according to whether they further peace settlements and democratic regimes. The present ethic of political reconciliation shares these goals, envisioning them being realized through secondary restorations. Yet it also proposes that some kinds of measures demand to be performed and that some kinds of wounds are rightfully redressed apart from their consequences for stability, democracy, and peace. These measures, primary restorations, are justified not as advancements of general utility but as the particular forms of repair that particular forms of wounds require in and of themselves.

Another concept of justice to which reconciliation will be contrasted in subsequent chapters may be called balance retributivism. One of the most prominent theories of punishment in the modern West, it finds strong expression in Enlightenment thinkers such as Immanuel Kant and is closely associated with the Calvinist tradition. The purpose of punishment, this theory holds, is to establish a balance between wrong and deserved hardship—in and apart from any restoration of persons or relationship. It is this last part, of course, from which the justice of reconciliation differs. Reconciliation, unlike utilitarianism, does not dispense with the concept of deserved punishment. But it does not detach desert from the repair of real diminishments to actual persons and relationships, including the perpetrator. In the practice of punishment, as with the other five practices, it is only such real repair—and no abstract notion such as balance—that grounds the justice of reconciliation.

The Liberal Peace

The most important comparison is with the liberal peace, the globally dominant concept of justice in the age of peacebuilding. What exactly is the liberal peace? It is three things. First, it is a concept of justice, one that springs from the philosophical tradition of John Locke, Immanuel Kant, John Stuart Mill, Woodrow Wilson, and John Rawls.[42] Like all traditions, liberalism contains internal arguments: libertarianism versus welfare state egalitarianism, communitarianism versus its critics, disputes over the role of religion in public life, and competition among philosophical justifications, including Kantianism, utilitarianism, natural law, natural right, antifoundationalism, and others. But like all traditions, liberalism contains unifying ideas, ones that pervade contemporary peacebuilding. Central among these are individual rights and liberties, including most of those that have been elevated to the status of human rights, as well as equality and the rule of law. Over its history, liberalism has come to associate rights closely with electoral democracy as well. Liberalism, like other traditions, stresses judicial punishment but is divided over its rationale, oscillating between retributivism, which justifies punishment as simple desert, and consequentialism, which advocates punishment for its effects, especially rehabilitation and deterrence.

Second, the liberal peace involves actors and institutions that have adopted this concept of justice. Liberal ideas had already been adopted into international law prior to the present age of peacebuilding and later came to propel the third wave of democratization and its attendant efforts to face the wrongs of past dictatorship and then to guide the "United Nations Revolution," the outburst of U.N. peace operations that began around the end of the cold war.[43] Today, the "magisterium" of the United Nations—the secretary general and other top diplomats in the permanent bureaucracy—is arguably the most prominent promoter and espouser of the liberal peace. The manifesto of the U.N. Revolution, former secretary general Boutros Boutros-Ghali's 1992 work, *An Agenda for Peace*, is laced with the ideas of the liberal peace, as are a string of subsequent statements on peacebuilding written or commissioned by the U.N.[44] The same ideas have guided Western governments in their own peacebuilding operations, including the United States in Somalia, Haiti, Bosnia, Kosovo, Afghanistan, and Iraq (early 1990s, 1999, and post 2003); Germany in Afghanistan; and the European Union in Kosovo and the Democratic

Republic of Congo. In the United States, liberal ideas have guided the Department of Defense, the Department of State, and the Agency for International Development in making postconflict reconstruction operations a central mission.

The liberal peace can also be found in a global network of international lawyers, human rights activists, scholars, and journalists who share common ideas about addressing human rights violations, a network that might be called the international transitional justice community. Transitional justice is the broad subject of how to deal with past political injustices. As scholar Paige Arthur documents, though, it can also mean a more particular approach to dealing with past injustices that members of this community, especially in Latin America, developed in the context of transitions from authoritarianism to democracy. The staple elements of this approach include the rule of law, punishment for human rights violators, vetting, truth and transparency, and restitution for victims. Behind this agenda stand commitments to human rights and democracy as well as one belief held with particular emotional force: overcoming impunity. *Nunca mas!*[45]

Third, the liberal peace is a set of activities carried out by actors imbued with these ideas. These activities involve solidifying a cease-fire, a peace agreement, or an end to dictatorship; establishing human rights, free markets, free media, and respect for international law; holding and monitoring elections; returning refugees; delivering humanitarian relief; reforming police and military units; and disarming, demobilizing, and reintegrating combatants. Punishing human rights violators through trials or pursuing vetting policies that disqualify them from holding offices or other jobs is crucial too. Arguably, the signature accomplishments of the liberal peace are the two international criminal tribunals of the 1990s (for Yugoslavia and Rwanda, respectively) and the International Criminal Court.

Some will object that this portrait of the liberal peace and the effort to distinguish it from reconciliation is too neat and tidy. Performers of the liberal peace carry out a wider range of activities than promoting human rights, democracy, the rule of law, and accountability, they will say.[46] Even the activities that I associated with the international transitional justice community are wide in scope and correspond to four of the six practices of the ethic of reconciliation. International lawyers now speak of a "right to truth," while the U.N. General Assembly adopted guidelines for reparations in 2005.[47] Other international lawyers have written of the need for forums for truth telling and accountability at local, national, and international levels.[48] In the U.N. documents cited above, as well as in the secretary general's 2004 report on transitional justice, a movement toward recommending multiple and holistic activities can be discerned.[49] Coordinating diverse actors and activities was also a major motivation behind the Peacebuilding Commission that the UN established in 2005. Has the liberal peace become so complex and holistic that it now differs little from political reconciliation?

The activities undertaken by liberal actors have certainly widened, but the two concepts of justice still differ. Some of their differences involve only certain schools of liberalism or certain dimensions of political reconciliation. Some contemporary liberals, for instance, charge reconciliation with transgressing the private sphere through its soulcraft and the secular sphere through its frequent religiosity. Retributivism and consequentialism, liberalism's classic rationales for punishment, each differ from restorative punishment.

The most important contrast between the two concepts of justice, though, lies in the breadth of what each proposes to restore. Reconciliation is wider than the liberal peace with respect to each of the three claims of restorative justice—wider in the range of wounds that it redresses, wider in the practices through which it redresses these wounds, and wider in the participants that it involves. Reconciliation's concept of restoration is much broader than liberalism's stress on rights. We will see that acknowledgment and reparations, for instance, restore more than can be described by a right to truth or a right to reparations alone and that the other practices, too, aspire to redress a broader spectrum of wounds than the loss of rights alone. Two of reconciliation's six practices—apology and, especially, forgiveness—are found only rarely in liberal thinking. Reconciliation is also more accommodating of transformations in emotions and attitudes, of which liberal thinkers are broadly suspicious. Religious leaders, grassroots initiatives, tribal rituals, community and civil society forums— these and other actors and forms of conduct fit more easily into an ethic of political reconciliation than they do the liberal peace. Even granting that liberal actors now perform a wider set of activities than they did at the end of the cold war—truth commissions as well as trials, reparations as well as human rights—liberal thought still falls short in explaining what goods these many activities bring about or do not; what obligations they fulfill or do not; how the practices integrate with one another or do not;

and how to know the difference. Alone, the liberal concept of justice is too narrow for these tasks.

Skeptics of the foregoing exposition of reconciliation as a concept of justice, peace, and mercy, though, will find other grounds on which to criticize it. To some, reconciliation still forgoes justice. Some see reconciliation as invasive, paternalistic, and illiberal. Still others view reconciliation as utopian. It is to these critics that the next chapter turns.

5

Is Reconciliation Fit for Politics?

REPORTING ON SOUTH AFRICA'S Truth and Reconciliation Commission, journalist Timothy Garton Ash described the following incident:

> [Deputy Chairperson] Alex Boraine told me of a black woman whose husband was abducted and killed, and who now sat listening to his killer.... After learning for the first time how her husband had died, she was asked if she could forgive the man who did it. Speaking slowly, in one of the native languages, her message came back through the interpreters: "No government can forgive." Pause. "No commission can forgive." Pause. "Only I can forgive." Pause. "And I am not ready to forgive."[1]

In this widow's words can be discerned two criticisms of forgiveness and reconciliation that Ash and a phalanx of other commentators have voiced. First, governments are not suited for such tasks: "No government *can* forgive...no commission *can* forgive." Second, governments are morally intrusive when they undertake them: "Only *I* can forgive.... *I* am not ready to forgive." South Africa's Truth and Reconciliation Commission (TRC) and its chairperson, Archbishop Desmond Tutu, are frequent targets for these critics. Their criticisms share a common spirit: Reconciliation in politics is idealistic, utopian, unlikely to succeed, likely to stomp on liberties, disrespectful to souls, prone to boondoggles, guilty of moral overstretch, and contrasts with a more preferable politics that is practical, hard bitten, committed to preserving individual moral autonomy and open-ended deliberation, otherwise modest in its moral expectations, and in general, healthily skeptical.

Philosophically, most of these critics draw from one of two strands of thought. The first suspects that political reconciliation is nothing more than a cloak for power. Belonging to this strand are the realist school in international politics as well as other purveyors of suspicion that behind politics is some more fundamental drive—followers of Karl Marx, Friedrich Nietzsche, and Sigmund Freud, for instance.[2] The second strand is a branch of the liberal tradition of political thought, one that stresses limitations on government power, individual liberty, and autonomy, especially in matters of the soul. It is the view of the liberal critics of Tutu. These "liberal skeptics" of political reconciliation, as we may call them, do not speak for the entire liberal tradition, nor do their commitments represent the entirety of liberalism's commitments. Still, liberal skepticism is important. Several of the transformations of judgment and emotion that the practices of reconciliation seek are just the sort of transformations whose proper place, liberal skeptics insist, lies outside politics: the remorse and repentance of offenders, the transformation of the anger and resentment of victims, forgiveness, healing, and harmony.

Though each of these two strands draws from different commitments, both doubt that reconciliation is fit for politics. Let us turn to the first strand, which suspects the role of power.

Does It All Come Down to Power?

These skeptics hail from a line of philosophers who believe that politics and morality are but emanations of a more elemental drive for power or the accumulation of capital. Again, this sort of skepticism runs deeper than liberal skepticism. Nietzsche, an iconic "master of suspicion," as well as the realist school of international relations thought, where suspicion runs strong, are, after all, inveterate critics of liberalism.[3] In a milieu pervaded by power, any apparent moral progress is unlikely to be more than a coincidental and ephemeral convergence of morality and interest.

Such skeptics might expect power to be especially pervasive during times of transition from war to peace or from authoritarianism to democracy, when the rule of law is fragile and embryonic. Justice is victor's justice, their reasoning runs. The form that justice takes will depend crucially on the distribution of power during the transition. If one party wins a clear victory in a war or prodemocracy forces decisively defeat an outgoing regime, then the transition is likely to involve trials of the defeated.

The rapid collapse of the communist government of East Germany in November 1989 left its leaders with little room to negotiate their way out of trials. Even more extreme was the collapse of Romania's communist government, in which President Nicolae Ceauşescu was shot after a two-hour televised trial. If the transition is a negotiated one, involving the parties' mutual consent, by contrast, then amnesty and the accompanying language of reconciliation can be expected. South Africa's Truth and Reconciliation Commission, for example, sprouted from the constitutional amnesty clause that the outgoing apartheid government negotiated for itself. Outgoing dictators will speak this language because it bars their prosecution while incoming democrats will voice this language as a cloak for their prosecutorial impotence.

Justice is strategic and dependent on relative power. This empirical claim is at the heart of this strand of skepticism. It takes one form for justice between states, another for justice within states. Power lies at the center of what has long been the dominant tradition in international relations thought, the realist school.[4] Beginning with Thucydides, resurfacing in Niccolò Machiavelli and Thomas Hobbes, continuing through twentieth-century Anglo-American voices like E. H. Carr, Reinhold Niebuhr, Hans Morgenthau, George Kennan, Kenneth Waltz, and John Mearsheimer, realists have always agreed on some common propositions. Virtually all have held that states are forced into a competition for military and economic power by the anarchical nature of the international system. Without a common superior, absent a supernational leviathan, states are consigned to a predicament of "self-help" in which they must safeguard their own security. Most realists have also doubted that international law, norms, institutions, or the democratic character of domestic regimes can mitigate this predicament. Virtually no realist, though, has argued that power negates all freedom of action. If states are to some extent free, then they can follow at least a modest ethic, one that counsels moderation, restraint, and stability in their pursuit of power. What states cannot expect to pursue with success are more concrete moral norms, or still less, moral absolutes. On these grounds, realists only naturally expect justice at the end of a war to flow from combatant states' relative power. Thucydides, the first major realist, described the punitive justice that Athens imposed on the inhabitants of the island of Melos in just this way: "[T]he strong do what they can and the weak suffer what they must."[5]

Is realism right about the justice of the past? If so, then it ought to be able to explain war crimes tribunals, a common form of justice that victors of wars have imposed on their enemies. Yet political scientist Gary Bass argues that war crimes tribunals are more than reflections of power. "If a war crimes tribunal is victors' justice," he claims, "it makes a difference who the victors are." Surveying the aftermath of the Napoleonic Wars, World War I, World War II, and the wars in Bosnia and Rwanda of the 1990s, Bass presents a stark correlation: All bona fide tribunals have been pursued by liberal regimes, while none has been sought by illiberal regimes. By liberalism, Bass has in mind the tradition of legalism, espousing the rule of law, retribution through trials governed by fair procedure, and due process. True, liberals will not always prefer tribunals. They will argue over trials at the ends of particular wars and arrive at different solutions in different wars: Contrast the United States' support for the Nuremberg and Tokyo trials after World War II with its opposition to trying Germans at the end of World War I. When liberal states have pursued war crimes tribunals, they always have been selective in prosecuting their enemies' war crimes in overwhelming proportion to their own citizens'. What Bass shows, though, is that power is not as confining and defining as realism claims. It is only a certain kind of state with a certain kind of regime and a certain set of ideas that seeks this particular form of justice.[6]

Most of today's transitions, though, occur within states, not between them, and usually in the wake of civil wars and transitions to democracy. Might victor's justice hold sway in the domestic realm? Focusing on democratic transitions, political scientist Samuel Huntington argues that it does: Outgoing officials who retain enough power to negotiate transitions will prevent trials; leaders of regimes that are overthrown are likely to land in the dock—or go straight to the firing squad.[7] His logic is easily extended to truth commissions, which a power explanation would expect to result from negotiated transitions, where commissions emerge as an alternative to trials and a sop for amnesty. His logic also applies to the context of civil war endings, where relative power can also determine the shape of justice.[8]

Like realism, domestic power explanations do not entirely negate freedom of action or obviate ethical counsel. Huntington advises states to "[r]ecognize that on the issue of 'prosecute and punish vs. forgive and forget,' each alternative presents grave problems, and that the least unsatisfactory course may well be: do not prosecute, do not punish, do not forgive, and, above all, do not forget."[9] However, such explanations insist that choices are constrained. Several of the past generation's institutions for justice faced such constraints. In Argentina, Rwanda, Greece, and Germany, a regime's decisive defeat corresponded to trials and in Romania to swift executions, while in several cases, a negotiated transition or settlement resulted in a truth commission or amnesty, including El Salvador, Poland, South Africa, Peru, Northern Ireland, Guatemala, Chile, and Mozambique.

Yet like realism, the domestic power explanation fails to account for a good deal in the politics of transition. Even sites of trials leave ambiguity. In Argentina, the convictions of five top junta leaders were overturned by a presidential pardon approximately a half decade later, while in Rwanda, it was the UN and leading international lawyers as much as the victors of the civil war who brought about an international tribunal. In other cases where new regimes decisively took power, no trials occurred at all, as in Brazil, or a far weaker practice of lustration resulted, as in Czechoslovakia. By contrast, in some cases trials took place even in the absence of a sharp victory, as in Timor-Leste, Yugoslavia, and Chile, where, eight years after Pinochet departed peacefully from the presidency in 1990, the Supreme Court allowed prosecutions to go forward, resulting in nearly five hundred indictments of military officers and their civilian accomplices.[10] In still other cases—Germany, Argentina, and Brazil—a truth commission actually accompanied victor's justice.

Even in the majority of cases, where truth commissions accompany settlements, it is not clear from a power explanation why exactly these commissions take place: If outgoing regimes exercise power in a transition, why would they agree to a forum that exposes their crimes? The question is all the more salient for truth commissions such as South Africa's, which made amnesty conditional on perpetrators' full confessions. Finally, Sierra Leone, Timor-Leste, Germany, and Argentina were "hybrid" cases that combined trials and truth commissions, a complexity that eludes any sharp prediction of power.

Power cannot be ignored. It partially explains the form of justice that states adopt in dealing with the past. Power enables some partisans to pursue their conceptions of justice but also constrains the entire pursuit of justice so as to leave it compromised and partially realized, as political reconciliation always will be. Yet the suspicion that power is everything cannot be sustained. There is too much that power does not explain. This is true, in part, because the politics of the past is also shaped by actors other than those who wield power (at least in the bald, coercive sense) such as nongovernmental organizations, civil society leaders, including religious leaders, and international organizations like the United Nations. Just as it matters who the victors are, it also matters who these other actors are. South Africa's TRC, for instance, resulted in part from the power of outgoing apartheid leaders to extract amnesty from the incoming African National Congress (ANC), but also from the ANC's promotion of the conception of *ubuntu*—which is much like restorative justice—as well as from the role of parliamentary leaders, human rights groups, and religious organizations in shaping and conducting the commission.[11] Here, as elsewhere, the politics of the past was importantly shaped by ideas.

But Will It Really Work?

In describing Tutu's "ideal of social harmony" as "impractical" and "unrealistic," philosopher David Crocker is not claiming that Tutu's pursuit of his ideal is only a mask for power but rather that in politics such a pursuit is likely to fail.[12] This is liberal skepticism in its typical expression. Liberal skeptics support—and expect—some of the restorations that political reconciliation envisions: rights, the rule of law, democratic procedure, deliberation, reciprocity, and trust, all of which are features of liberal democratic orders. Some of these, like building trust, inescapably involve transformations of judgment. What liberal skeptics seem to doubt is that political orders can effect what they regard as more ambitious transformations: repentance, forgiveness, healing, and the like.

For Crocker, attempts at these transformations of the heart vainly compel agreement in a realm defined by division. Crocker, like political philosopher Rajeev Bhargava, also judges that such transformations can occur only in the long term, whereas political initiatives like truth commissions operate in the short term. In the same spirit, writer Michael Ignatieff doubts that truth commissions can bring repentance: "It is unreasonable to expect those who believed they were putting down a terrorist or insurgent threat to disown this idea simply because a truth commission exposes this threat as having been without foundation. People, especially people in uniform, do not easily or readily surrender the premises on which their lives are based." Tutu's larger mistake, in Ignatieff's view, was thinking that nations are like people, with a single psyche, who will be healed and reconciled once they arrive at a single knowledge of the truth. Ignatieff argues that truth is always contested among victims and perpetrators and knowledge of truth rarely heals entire social orders. In an often quoted passage, Ignatieff writes: "All that a truth commission can achieve is to reduce the number of lies that can be circulated unchallenged in public discourse." Though the statement identifies a potential achievement of truth commissions, "all" asserts limits: Truth commissions can establish facts about when, where, how, and to what extent torture, death, and disappearance occurred but should not be expected to change behavior, beliefs, or institutions. Ash reaches an almost identical conclusion. Liberal skeptics do not necessarily doubt the merit or the possibility of healing, forgiveness, and other transformations in the lives of individuals. Some liberals endorse the value of these goods even as they reiterate that politics cannot bring them about.[13]

The practices that make up the present ethic of reconciliation appear to be guilty several times over of transgressing liberal skeptics' limits on politics. Acknowledgment and reparations aspire to lessen victims' anger, resentment, and hatred and to increase community members' empathy. Apology and forgiveness similarly involve an interior change in outlook on the part of victims and perpetrators. Restorative punishment invites wrongdoers to repentance and apology. These and other transformations may then bring about secondary restorations—a strengthening of legitimacy, trust, and national identity—but they begin with primary restorations that often involve transformations in emotion and judgment.

Is politics indeed ill-equipped for these ends? Liberal skeptics are not precise about when politics goes too far. They identify healing, harmony, repentance, and forgiveness as overambitious, but most of them welcome into politics transformations that bring reciprocity, trust, and assent to liberal orders. Yet what if, as occurred in several prominent cases in South Africa, public censure, hearing the testimony of victims, or even experiencing forgiveness bring top perpetrators not only to express remorse but also to lend their endorsement to the new liberal order?[14] Is such a transformation outside the boundaries of politics? Or is it a welcome gain for trust and legitimacy? In the same piece that he decries political reconciliation, Ignatieff extols the unifying effects of national apologies issued by President Aylwin of Chile and Chancellor Willy Brandt of Germany, criticizes Croatian president Franjo Tudjman for failing to do the same, and appreciates that human rights victims might come to renounce vengeance through coming to know the truth about their past.[15] Why, though, do these not count as instances of healing and reconciliation?

An ethic of political reconciliation does not conceive of the nation as having a group mind or collective psyche. Tutu has never expressed such an idea, nor do most advocates of reconciliation. National identity may be shared by a collective and strengthened through common political measures, but it is always individual citizens who hold—or lose, or recover— the identities and attitudes that make it up. The practices that restore this national identity, the secondary restorations that build this social capital, perform their work through the transformation of individuals. This is how Tutu and I conceive of reconciliation.[16]

What of the central claim of liberal skeptics that government is simply not suited to bring about some of the transformations of judgment and emotion that political reconciliation envisions? The claim is an empirical one and so must be any evaluation of it. The trouble, though, lies in assessing it. The best records of the six practices of political reconciliation are what anthropologist Clifford Geertz once called "thick descriptions": narratives, stories, anecdotes, and case studies, as found in truth commission reports, the accounts of journalists, and the studies of scholars.[17] The strength of such accounts is their documentation of the experience of participants in the practices of political reconciliation. These narratives are replete with refusals, denials, scorn, and revenge but also include stories of forgiveness, repentance, restoration through recognition, and professions of loyalty to political orders run by former enemies. The failures resonate with liberal skepticism; the successes are evidence that liberal skepticism is not the full story. Still, the accounts are susceptible to classic criticisms of thick description. Are they skewed by the author's prior agenda? If someone else had told the story, would the successes still appear as such? How representative are the putative successes?

More objective and systematic studies such as population surveys and comparative quantitative analyses of transitional justice, though, are cumulatively of little help. It is mainly the effects of truth commissions and trials on popular attitudes, peace, stability, and democracy on which such studies have been conducted. Although some of the individual studies are well conducted and yield interesting and significant findings, the collective results of empirical research are mixed and inconclusive, as later chapters will show. If any conclusion about success remains uncertain, however, so must any conclusion about failure. The skeptics' arguments are confronted by some evidence that changes in attitudes occur and are unsupported by the dearth of systematic knowledge about how often they occur. Assuredly, these changes will reflect the imperfect, partial character of political reconciliation, but there is no good reason to think that they do not take place.

But Is It Just?

Crocker deepens his criticism: "Not only is Tutu's ideal of social harmony impractical, but it is problematic because of the way it conceives the relation between the individual and the group."[18] In a separate essay he argues more directly that

> to prescribe [confession and forgiveness] legally would be to compromise the moral autonomy of both victims and perpetrators as well as promote feigned professions of guilt and contrition. More generally, it is morally objectionable as well as impractical for a truth commission or any other governmental body to force people to agree about the past, forgive the sins committed against them, or love one another.[19]

Here the liberal skeptics move from their empirical claim to their moral one. Certain transformations do not justly belong in politics. Ash concludes that "taken to the extreme, the reconciliation of all with all is a deeply illiberal idea." Amy Gutmann and Dennis Thompson echo Ash in their own discussion of state efforts to promote forgiveness, repentance, and other transformations: "[R]econciliation is an illiberal aim if it means expecting an entire society to subscribe to a single comprehensive moral perspective."[20]

Hovering just over the shoulders of these critics are the spirits of John Locke, Immanuel Kant, John Stuart Mill, John Rawls, and Isaiah Berlin, several of whose ideas come through. One is the autonomy of individuals in their "capacity to form, to revise, and rationally to pursue a conception of...[the] good," as Rawls put it. In matters of virtue, religion, the soul, morality, indeed all questions of the good, governments ought to leave citizens free to make their own judgments and instead prioritize matters of the right, like the equal liberties on which liberal regimes are based. When they tell their subjects to forgive, repent, or to be healed, they are promoting the good and exceeding their domain.[21]

For many liberals, autonomy is closely related to a second idea, namely a philosophical position that Isaiah Berlin articulated in several essays over the course of his life, now known as "value pluralism." Value pluralism can roughly be summarized as follows: Beyond core values such as the respect for life and basic liberties, questions of morality and philosophy cannot be resolved according to any single procedure, criterion, or concept of human fulfillment. The political upshot, as Berlin argued in his classic 1958 essay, "Two Concepts of Liberty," is that governments ought to protect the "negative liberty" embedded in basic civil rights but ought never to promote a more ambitious "positive liberty" like Rousseau's general will or the Marxist-Leninist concept of liberation.[22] Value pluralism serves liberal skepticism well. Ash, who elsewhere genuflects, "*Ich bin ein Berliner,*" follows up his comment about the illiberalism of reconciliation with a reminder that "as Isaiah Berlin has taught us, liberalism means living with unresolvable conflicts of values and goals, and South Africa has those in plenty."[23] Ignatieff has written a biography of Berlin in which he averred, "a liberal does not believe in a hierarchy of inner selves (higher, lower, true, false) or believe that there can ever be a political solution to the experience of inner human division," a position that parallels and supplements his view of truth commissions.[24]

A third traditional liberal theme found in liberal skepticism is a close relative of autonomy and value pluralism—democratic deliberation. Not only should citizens be left free to argue, deliberate about, vote on, and most of all, revise their stance on questions of the good, but such argument and deliberation are central democratic virtues. Settlement and imposition are democracy's corresponding vices. Gutmann and Thompson center their own liberal criticism of reconciliation on democratic deliberation:

> Reconciliation of this comprehensive sort is also deeply undemocratic. A democratic society should still seek reconciliation on some fundamental matters of political morality such as freedom of speech, press, and religion, equal political liberty, equal protection under the law, and non-discrimination in the distribution of social offices. But a democratic society that strives for a consensus on such fundamental matters of political morality must still recognize that moral conflict in politics more generally cannot be overcome or avoided. In the democratic politics that the new South Africa seeks, a substantial degree of disharmony is not only inevitable but desirable. It can be both a sign and a condition of a healthy democracy.[25]

For Gutmann and Thompson, as for other liberal skeptics, reconciliation is permissible if it means achieving agreement on fundamental rights, liberties, and democratic procedures and strengthening key liberal democratic values such as reciprocity, trust, deliberation, and respect, but not if it reaches for more.

Political reconciliation again looks guilty. Some of its transformations clearly reach beyond the right to the good, aim to steer selves away from such emotions as anger, hatred, resentment, and fear and promote forgiveness, repentance, and healing. Is this illicit soulcraft? Put more precisely, do governmental efforts to promote transformations of emotions and judgments unjustly stomp on values like autonomy, pluralism, and democratic deliberation that the liberal critics of reconciliation stress?

The most direct response to these critics is that the ethic at hand, while it overlaps with the liberal tradition of thought, does not share all of liberalism's commitments. It converges with the liberal peace insofar as it endorses human rights, democracy, the rule of law, the laws of war, and trials and punishment for human rights violators. However, one can endorse these rights, norms, and institutions without sanctioning such philosophical values as autonomy or Berlin's value pluralism. Human rights, not the whole liberal philosophical package, are indeed all that the ethic demands from the traditions and school that form a consensus on it. It is, after all, a global ethic, one that seeks a consensus from Judaism, Christianity, Islam, and other traditions, such as Confucianism or tribal cultures, that might potentially join a consensus on it. My case for the ethic derives optimism from the fact that many of these traditions contain advocates of human rights, ones who draw from philosophical and theological waters that are relatively unalloyed with Western values such as autonomy, though I also acknowledge the strains on an overlapping consensus posed by differences over even human rights, as disputes between the West and both Islam and Asian cultures have accented. Optimism also emerges from the fact that many actual countries outside the West—African countries, East Asian countries, Israel, and others—practice human rights even while their governments promote attitudes, judgments, and values in regard to the family, sexuality, and religion that Western liberal philosophers, particularly Anglo-American ones, would regard as excessively imposing. Political institutions based on human rights do not call for a privileging of Western notions like individual autonomy or prevent governments from promoting other values—forgiveness, healing, and other transformations of judgment, for instance—so long as this promotion does not infringe on human rights.

Liberal critics might grant that Western liberal philosophy is not the only source of human rights but reply that nevertheless it is their source and they cannot join an overlapping consensus on principles that allow governments to promote what is personal and not political. To this, it may be asked: Does the liberal tradition itself forbid governments from taking an interest in the judgments and outlooks of their citizenry? In his book *Virtue and the Making of Modern Liberalism*, political philosopher Peter Berkowitz argues that it does not.[26] An enduring theme in Western liberal thought is resistance to government's interference in matters of the soul. Complete virtue, the person's final end, and salvation, what ancient and medieval philosophers thought were the chief ends of government, ought now to be supplanted by security, property, and most of all liberty, taught the founding fathers of modern liberalism, including Hobbes, Locke, Kant, and Mill. Yet these pioneers did not discard virtue altogether, Berkowitz argues. Although they may have rejected the political promotion of a full vision of the good life, all of them held that certain virtues are crucial for the health of the political order and indeed for the laws that uphold individual freedom. "Liberalism... can no more do without virtue than a person on a diet can survive without food and drink," as Berkowitz describes their position.[27] Montesquieu, Adam Smith, Alexis de Tocqueville, the authors of *The Federalist*, and Edmund Burke held this view all the more strongly. Many contemporary liberals have not abandoned virtue either. Even John Rawls, who revived a Kantian vision of liberalism centered in freedom and equality in his classic *A Theory of Justice*, stressed the sustaining importance of virtues in the latter, often ignored, part of the book. Such philosophers as William Galston and Stephen Macedo have devoted entire books to arguing for liberalism's dependence on virtues. Galston, for instance, stresses courage, abiding the law, loyalty, independence, and tolerance.[28] To this litany can be added political philosophers such as Yael Tamir and David Miller, who argue, as Mill did, that liberal institutions depend on a common national identity and the communal loyalties that it yields.[29] If virtues are needed to sustain liberalism, then they will be all the more necessary to restore or construct liberalism in settings where citizens are divided, embittered, or disheartened on a large scale.

Liberal skeptics of political reconciliation do not necessarily disagree. Crocker, Gutmann, and Thompson are favorable to reconciliation when it restores respect, trust, the willingness to deliberate, and democratic reciprocity, all of which inevitably involve the transformation of citizens' moral outlooks. But these skeptics implicitly propose a wall that seems to divide transformations of moral outlooks into a politically legitimate sort that involves respect, reciprocity, and trust and a sort that does not belong in politics, like forgiveness, repentance, and harmony. On what basis do they construct this wall? The most plausible reason that can be found in their writings is that the legitimate transformations are ones that promote the goals of liberal political orders, whereas the others do not. Here, though, is where their logic may be called into question.

Recall that the goal of political reconciliation is the restoration of right relationship within and between political orders, defined as respect for and recognition of human rights—a goal that overlaps with some of liberalism's most cherished goals. Yet political reconciliation considers such practices as forgiveness, apology, and restorative punishment, as well as the transformations of emotion and judgment in regard to the political order that they might elicit, to be integral to the restoration of these rights and thus legitimate promoters of liberal goals. The last chapter identified these transformations as secondary restorations—restorations that restore such "public goods" as trust, legitimacy, and loyalty to national identity. To the degree that the practices succeed in effecting secondary restorations, they play a vital role in restoring political orders based on liberal democracy. Persistent emotions of anger, hatred, fear, resentment, vengefulness, the scorn and stubbornness of the wrongdoer, and the indifference of the community are not only wounds but also barriers to people recognizing and respecting one another as legitimate bearers of rights and partners in deliberation. The evidence lies in any number of sites of ongoing strife—Israel and Palestine, Bosnia, Sudan, Sri Lanka, Northern Ireland, Colombia, Kashmir—where regnant hostility makes cease-fires and peace accords precarious.

Certainly, respect, deliberation, reciprocity, and trust are needed, but these are not the sorts of commitments that are likely to generate themselves, at least among people who harbor the strongest of hostile emotions. The absence of these commitments is a symptom. The disease is the emotions that serve as barriers to the realization of these commitments. Tutu's practice of soulcraft in the hearings of the TRC, then, far from being unrealistic or inappropriate, may have advanced liberal democracy. Acknowledgment, restorative punishment, reparations, apology, and forgiveness, insofar as they encourage remorse, recognition, the forgoing of hatred and resentment, and empathetic awareness, which may then create trust, legitimacy, and national loyalty, can be powerful allies of liberal democracy. It is difficult to separate what it takes for embittered enemies to be less embittered and what it takes for them to respect one another in the political order.

Imagine if, in the context of a TRC hearing, Tutu had said to a victim, "your story is heart wrenching and has stirred us all. But in my capacity as an agent of the state, I must make it clear that I cannot speak about your grief, your trauma, or its effects on your family, promote your healing, ask the killer of your son to show remorse for his deeds, or still less even suggest that you might forgive. I can only ask that you respect your fellow citizens and participate in our new democracy." Would such an approach restore either people or politics? The practices that seek to transform emotions help to make liberal politics possible. This may well be what Tutu had in mind when he titled his book *No Future Without Forgiveness*. Nor "without the other practices of reconciliation," we might add. And if this is so, then why cannot the full range of these practices, along with political measures aimed at creating reciprocity, democratic deliberation, and the like, amount to legitimate ends for political institutions? If it is legitimate for governments to cultivate the virtues, attitudes, judgments, and outlooks that sustain political orders founded on human rights and if the transformations in judgment that the practices bring about help to cultivate these virtues, then these transformations are legitimately pursued.

None of this is to deny the difficulty or the likely incompleteness of these transformations. It is only to argue that they have a legitimate place in politics. Still, there is insight in liberal skeptics' reservations. They point to some principled limits on the political practice of these transformations, limits that correspond to the boundaries of an ethic of reconciliation whose nature is political. There are three sorts of limits.

The first set of limits derives from the state's intrinsic connection to the law. Laws are a community's moral norms backed up by the state's sanctioning power. The state thus has a unique mandate to deal with their violation—but no mandate to deal with ruptures other than their violation. The political wounds with which the state concerns itself, then, are only those that result from political injustices. These injustices, by definition, violate some sort of law—if not always the explicit laws of a regime, at least the international law that governs war and human rights. Though the state may address these injustices, it does not seek to restore those relationships, whether they exist between family members, neighbors, or townspeople, that have been fractured by some other event, even one that is somehow related to the war or the injustices of the regime. The same sort of logic applies to the goal of the state's restorative work. It extends only as far as those aspects of right relationship that are governed or promoted by the law. The extent of the state's reach, of course, will differ from regime to regime. In all cases, political reconciliation demands that it extends at least to human rights but no farther than the state's own laws.

A second set of limits also involves the rule of law. They are the constraints posed by the entire body of laws, rights, and procedures embodied in the constitution of the state where political reconciliation is being practiced. The practice of accountability, for instance, whether it involves trials, vetting, or other forms of public censure, must always respect the due process rights of alleged perpetrators. All practices of political reconciliation ought also to respect the complete rights of citizens as well as the boundaries between religion and state as a given liberal democratic constitution prescribes them. Political reconciliation respects laws both because the rule of law is one of its background commitments and because one of its key goals is to restore and strengthen the rule of law in communities where law is lacking or weak.

A third set of limits pertains to the competence of the state. The state should refrain from attempting to perform transformations that it cannot competently effect. Certain constraints govern each of the six practices. The state may significantly restore victims' dignity by publicly acknowledging their suffering, but it cannot provide them with long-term therapy (though it might well provide the resources for it through reparations). It may legitimately promote apology and forgiveness but primarily through exhortation—as Archbishop Tutu did—and, under the right circumstances, by speaking in the name of the community to victims and to other states. Far more often, it will be victims and perpetrators who practice apology and forgiveness. The state should always respect this practice as voluntary. In part, this is because the state cannot begin to understand the range of inner influences that lead a person to determine whether, when, or how to repent or to forgive and so must respect her freedom to decide this. None of these constraints, though, emerges from a strong separation between the public and the private, between those actions that are legitimate and those that are not, but rather from reflection on what sort of actions the state does and does not perform well.

Such borders demarcate where political reconciliation may be practiced. The ethic respects the rule of law, basic human rights, and the just constitutional provisions of the country in which it operates, as well as spheres where individual freedom ought to be respected. But none of these boundaries chokes off the practices.

Is Liberal Consequentialism a Better Ethic after All?

Each of the strands of skepticism recounted in this chapter is suggestive of a certain moral alternative to political reconciliation, one that resonates both with skepticism rooted in power and liberal skepticism and
that might well tout its unique suitability to the rough-and-tumble realm
of politics. Realism's morality of the national interest is a species of this
alternative. The alternative ethic is consequentialism, the doctrine that
the morally best action or institution is the one that maximizes good
outcomes over bad, all things considered. Now, few of the contemporary
writers on the political problem of past evil put forth an undiluted utilitarianism that sets aside all general norms in favor of a pure calculation.
Most all of them hold at least one end as non-negotiable—the rule of law
in a constitutional, liberal democratic regime. Yet for many, once this end
is established, the calculus of consequences takes over. Put simply, societies ought to adopt whatever route best takes them to this destination.
This might include some of the practices of political reconciliation, but
such practices might just as well be omitted, especially when they are too
costly, disruptive, or ridden with bad side effects. We can think of this
ethic as liberal consequentialism.

In arguments about the politics of the past, consequentialism takes
at least two forms. One is the sort that I have just described. It assumes
constitutional liberal democracy as its end and recommends those procedures that, on balance, best achieve it. Political scientist Leslie Vinjamuri
insightfully observes that almost all contemporary arguments about war
crimes tribunals, including the International Criminal Court, whether
they are offered in favor or in opposition, take a consequentialist form.[30]
Proponents argue that such trials deter future perpetrators and establish credibility for the rule of law, among other benefits. Vinjamuri, in
one piece written with her colleague Jack Snyder, is more skeptical, taking the human rights community to task for demanding such tribunals
even while civil wars are being fought. Vinjamuri and Snyder appeal to
a "logic of consequences" in arguing that trials are only likely to be effective once a peace agreement and liberal democracy are already established;
if peace is not yet secure, attempting to apprehend and try combatant war
criminals will only hinder an agreement, prolong the war, and destabilize
liberal democracy. Ethically, they defend a pragmatism that commends
amnesty as part of an "integrated normative vision" for achieving peace
and democracy.[31]

The other sort of consequentialism begins as retributivism. This sort also seeks the rule of law and contends, with the human rights community, that the punishment of past perpetrators builds legitimacy. Yet it is also pragmatic and maintains that retributive principles that hold in conditions of stable peace may prove impossible to pursue in the roiling, impassioned aftermath of war and dictatorship.[32] This is the conclusion that Albert Camus arrived at in a public exchange with his countryman François Mauriac after the French resistance overthrew the Nazi collaborationist Vichy regime in 1944. At first, Camus favored execution for "men of treason and injustice" who had held high positions in the Vichy government. Only capital punishment for traitors could root out the injustice of this period and help France to establish a just regime. Mauriac, a Christian, replied that, instead, the times called for charity, forgiveness, and reconciliation, which meant forgoing trials in favor of reintegrating former enemies. Two years later, Camus came to agree with Mauriac's conclusion. The provisional government's courts had become circuses, meting out death and other harsh sentences to some collaborators while treating far more guilty ones far less harshly. Worse, mobs had executed thousands of real and alleged collaborators summarily in the streets, while maiming, raping, and brutally humiliating many others. Historians compare the period to the Reign of Terror of 1789. Camus did not accept much of Mauriac's reasoning. He was not a Christian and did not agree with much of what Mauriac had to say about divine justice and forgiveness. Rather, he came to reason that, given the consequences of pursuing retributive justice during times when vengeance reigned and judicial structures were shaky, it was better to forgo punishment in the interest of a better future.[33]

The desire to create a better future is consequentialism's strongest claim. Perhaps societies heaped in rubble should not be confined by rigid principles when dealing with the past but ought to focus instead on finding the equipment that best helps them to move on and assemble a just and stable regime. What equipment will work best for any given society is often far from clear. Take the difficult question of amnesty for perpetrators. Do such exonerations help to avoid the pitfalls of retributivism that Mauriac worried about and that Camus came to see? Or do they provoke an outcry about the denial of justice that only further divides a society? Would the pursuit of truth rather than punishment better achieve stability? How consequences balance out is difficult to say in advance. Aryeh Neier makes a similar point about whether trials deter future abuses:

> I do not claim that acknowledging and disclosing the truth about past abuses, or punishing those responsible for abuses, will necessarily deter future abuses. I doubt there is decisive evidence for this proposition. The same can be said of the contrary view, sometimes argued by proponents of amnesties, that an amnesty promotes reconciliation, while if a government making a transition to democracy attempts to punish those guilty of past abuses, it risks allowing those people to seize power again. Either outcome is possible. Whether the guilty are accorded amnesty or punished is only one among many factors that affect the pattern of events in any country.[34]

Uncertain probabilities, multiple possibilities, and unpredictable political pressures similarly apply to virtually any measure recommended for regime construction and make any judgment about its success highly situational. In response, a consequentialist might well recognize this problem but assert its unavoidability. The choices of wounded societies are existential ones, always stabs in the dark. Their best guiding principle is not trials or truth but trial and error.

There is yet a more fundamental problem with consequentialism. Its flaw is quite like that of "thin" reconciliation: It does not deal with the past. Each of the wounds of political injustice uniquely diminishes the human flourishing of the several parties involved in the injustice. The primary restoration of the sufferers of these wounds through practices that seek to restore particular diminishments in particular ways is a good in itself, even apart from the secondary restoration that the practices accomplish. This is the message that one can hear in the plaintive and ordinary voices of those who call for the exposure and punishment of the killers of their loved ones, who plead for knowledge and recognition of the violence that brought them suffering, or who forgive their oppressors. Each in his or her own way draws attention to the particular ways in which he or she has been wounded and the particular kinds of responses that these wounds evoke. Against the impulse to move on, victims cry: "Wait!" A certain kind of justice, redressing certain kinds of wounds, still needs to be performed.

Such justice cannot be expected from consequentialism's blunt, generalized approach. If the only criterion for justice is what best leads a society to liberal democracy, then the sort of justice that addresses wounds in their particularity would be left to chance, dependent on the calculation of consequences in any given situation. For instance, punishment aims not only to deter future perpetrators, create credibility for the rule of law, and promote other goods that benefit a settlement or a democracy but also to communicate censure to the wrongdoer on behalf of the community, invite contrition, and recognize victims. These latter restorations are primary ones, matters of justice whose value is not dependent on the probability that they will promote a certain kind of regime. Political reconciliation pursues these sorts of restorations as well. This is not to say that Snyder and Vinjamuri's argument about consequences can be ignored. There may well be cases in which pursuing punishment is so inimical to securing a peace that it ought to be put aside. Building socially just institutions, after all, is also one of the six restorative practices and may well require a prior peace agreement. Yet, political reconciliation regards such an abjuring of punishment as a sacrifice of justice, even if a justifiable one in some cases. Forgoing punishment, then, would not be simply a factor in calculating the probability of liberal democracy, as it would be in a liberal consequentialist approach to justice. Rather, a presumption for punishment ought to be adopted. If it is possible to pursue peace in a way that incorporates punishment—or any of the other practices—political reconciliation demands that this route be taken.

The argument here runs parallel to the one that defenders of human rights typically make against utilitarianism. Measures that maximize the aggregate welfare of a society may fail to protect dimensions of human dignity that ought never to be violated. Every person matters as an end, not just as a site of pleasure or pain. Likewise, measures that construct a new regime efficiently and effectively may still fail to do justice to every person's past. Consequentialism fails to identify the additional measures that achieve this justice, those that restore.

Another parallel: In a debate about the justice of military intervention in the late 1970s, political philosopher Michael Walzer defended the principle of group self-determination by asking his readers to imagine a painless intervention in which an outsider drops a tablet into the water supply of Algerians that magically turns them all into Swedish Social Democrats. Would this be a just intervention? Walzer objected that in imposing such a solution, painless as it is, outsiders fail to respect the rights of Algerians to determine and bring about the kind of regime under which they want to live.[35]

Imagine similarly that a tablet could magically and instantly transform the embittered and divided citizens of a postgenocide society into avid supporters of a common constitution based on democracy, human rights, and communal harmony, a transition whose consequences appear all good and not at all bad. A problem remains: This society has not dealt with its past. It has not performed the particular kinds of practices that bring about particular kinds of restorations with respect to the particular kinds of wounds that political injustices have left behind. So however smoothly this transition occurs, in profound respects it will not have been just.

Political reconciliation responds to liberal consequentialism in much the same way that it does to other forms of skepticism. Following the logic of restorative justice, it argues for addressing the full range of wounds that political injustices inflict. Liberal skeptics articulate one other related argument for why political reconciliation is not fit for politics: It is too religious. It is to this argument that we now turn. The next chapter makes the case for religion's place in the politics of reconciliation and in so doing inaugurates part 2, on religion and reconciliation.

PART TWO

Religion and Reconciliation

6

Is Religion Fit for Reconciliation?

PRIOR TO ONE hearing of South Africa's Truth and Reconciliation Commission, commission officials confronted Archbishop Desmond Tutu. His conduct of hearings, they claimed, had been too religious. The commission was supposed to be a judicial body. It had been enacted by the new South African constitution, enabled by parliamentary legislation that carefully set forth its legal basis, and carried critical legal consequences, especially for amnesty applicants. Should not Tutu separate his role as head of this legal body from his role as a Christian pastor? Not only did he figuratively wear two hats, but he literally wore full episcopal regalia, including purple robes and a pectoral cross. His interlocutors could do little about his attire. They hoped, though, that he could put to rest the opening prayer, the frequent hymns, and the religious appeals. Tutu assented to begin daily hearings with a moment of silence rather than a prayer. However, as commission official Piet Meiring describes, his concession was reluctant and short lived:

> When the clock struck nine the witnesses and their families were escorted into the crowded hall. Tutu followed with his colleagues. Chairperson shook hands with victims one by one. Then he proceeded to the platform where he took his seat. He asked for half a minute of silence. The first witness was brought to the table and sworn in.
>
> But Tutu could not get under way. He sat down. He moved his papers from side to side. Visibly uncomfortable, he looked at the victims, at the audience in the hall. "No, this won't work! We really cannot start like this," he said over the loudspeakers. "People, close your eyes so

that we can pray!" A long, earnest prayer, followed—to Christ, who is the Truth, and to the Holy Spirit who had to lead us that day. After closing with "Amen," Tutu rubbed his hands together and informed the audience with a disarming smile, "There...now we are ready to proceed."[1]

Opening prayers returned for good.

Tutu did not restrain his religion in other respects, either. At emotional points in the hearings, such as when a victim offered wrenching, teary, and often gruesome testimony, leaving the room speechless and other officials shifting and unsure how to proceed, he would lead everyone in a native hymn, conferring recognition and honor on the victim and respecting the sacred gravity of the moment. In speeches and interviews and in his book *No Future Without Forgiveness*, Tutu described the commission's work in terms of Christian theology. Prior to many of the commission's hearings, crowds of women would gather outside and sing hymns in anticipation of the spiritual ordeal of the testimonies to follow. The commission inaugurated its work with a religious ceremony at St. George's Cathedral in Cape Town. Meiring was also a clergyman and one of several religious leaders and theologians to serve as commissioners or staffers. Religious bodies provided logistical and psychological support for the hearings, recommended the commission's work to their members with religious rationales, and, most directly, participated in hearings where corporate entities testified about their role in apartheid. Many victims and perpetrators, especially ones who experienced an emotional transformation, described their experience in religious language. Cumulatively, the language of faith infused the public conversation surrounding the hearings. In many other countries, too, religious people have contributed their distinctive language and activities to political proceedings that deal with the past. Religious language appears especially strong when these proceedings are sanctioned as acts of reconciliation.

That is the problem, some critics say. Several commentators on the TRC have echoed the misgivings of Tutu's colleagues, reflecting even broader complaints that certain liberal philosophers have expressed in recent years about the political activities of the religious. These criticisms are of a piece with liberal skepticism of reconciliation's appropriateness and effectiveness. Garton Ash sympathetically quotes the complaint of Marius Schoon, whose wife and daughter were killed by the South African security forces, about the TRC's "imposition of a Christian morality of forgiveness."[2] Liberal critics call for a far wider separation of religion and politics and many of them for an ethic demanding that religious concepts be translated into secular language before they enter public debate.

Religion's integral role in the ethic of political reconciliation demands that such skepticism be confronted. This role corresponds to the two tasks of the ethic previously outlined. First, religious traditions provide a ground for the ethic. It is in Judaism, Christianity, and Islam that the concepts of justice, peace, mercy, and reconciliation that form the core of the ethic are expressed most fully and enduringly. Adapted to modern politics, these concepts yield a potent medicine for societies who are dealing with troubled pasts and pursuing stable, legitimate political orders. Fittingly, the Latin word root of religion is *religare*, meaning "to reconnect, to bind together."

The second task is to provide a method for building a principled consensus on the ethic in religiously plural societies. It is with respect to this task that the role of religion evokes the strongest objections among liberal skeptics. Even were they to concede that religion contains potential for reconciliation, they charge that bringing religion into politics is disrespectful and divisive, not binding, reconnecting, or reconciling.

Shortly, I will confront such criticisms. First, though, let us take a look at some of the scenes where religious leaders have brought religious rationales into politics. To be clear, religious actors are not the primary actors who carry out the ethic as I envision it. While the religious contribute to political reconciliation in some instances and civil society actors in general contribute in many instances, the state and its citizens are still the main enactors of the ethic. What religion contributes is conceptual material, a notion of justice. Still, scenes of religious activity testify to the immediate relevance of these rationales and clarify the problems to which liberal skeptics draw attention.

Religion and the Politics of the Past

Prelates and pastors, imams and rabbis have brought distinctive, insistent, hefty, and authoritative voices to political debates about the past in Chile, Brazil, Guatemala, El Salvador, Timor-Leste, Germany, Iraq, Afghanistan, Morocco, Sierra Leone, Poland, Northern Ireland, Bosnia, the Czech Republic, South Africa, and other countries. In several of these places, religious communities and their leaders have promoted truth commissions—they have lobbied for them, helped to negotiate them, and provided them with logistical support and sometimes even commissioners. Tutu stands out as the most prominent example. In some countries, a lay political actor will contribute to this politics as an extension of his religious beliefs, as did Chile's Catholic president Patricio Aylwin, who practiced apology, commended forgiveness, and promoted a truth and reconciliation commission. Even more ambitiously—and dangerously— religious communities have conducted furtive forms of truth commissions under the nose of authoritarian regimes: the Catholic Church in Chile under the Pinochet dictatorship; and a partnership of the Catholic and Presbyterian churches in Brazil during the years of military rule there. Most dramatic of all was the work of the Catholic Church in Guatemala under Bishop Juan Gerardi, who, perceiving weaknesses in official plans for a truth commission to investigate three decades' worth of atrocities during Guatemala's civil war, initiated, formed, carried out, and issued a final report for a separate national truth commission, the Recovery of Historical Memory Project (REMHI). REMHI was impressive for its unique method of investigation. It sent seven hundred "agents of reconciliation" into Guatemalan villages to hear the testimony of victims and to support them emotionally, psychologically, and spiritually. Evidence that REMHI challenged the powerful came two days after Gerardi presented the REMHI report at the Metropolitan Cathedral in Guatemala City in April 1998. In his own garage, thugs operating under military orders bludgeoned him to death.[3]

Religious leaders and communities have also helped to form and lead truth commissions in South Africa, Sierra Leone, post-unification Germany, Timor-Leste, and Peru. Religious leaders as well as faith-based NGOs have promoted reconciliation in civil society as well. In Nigeria, Muslim and Christian clergy have fostered cooperation between their warring communities through public dialogues and rituals in which they quote from one another's texts.[4] In 2002, for the first time, Muslim, Christian, and Jewish leaders in Israel and Palestine signed a common statement, the Alexandria Declaration, appealing for an end to violence and mutual demonization.[5] By building relationships at the grass roots, John Paul Lederach, a Mennonite peace builder, was able to forge a political agreement between Miskito Indians and the Nicaraguan government.[6] Drawing on prayer, friendship, and an ability to connect diverse political players, the Community of Sant'Egidio, a Catholic lay association, was instrumental in negotiating an agreement to end a decade-long civil war in Mozambique in 1992, and, on the reputation of this achievement, was called to negotiate settlements in Kosovo, Algeria, Guatemala, Uganda, Burundi, and Liberia.[7] Cambodian Buddhist leader Samdech Preah Maha Ghosananda, reaching into traditional Buddhist doctrine and practice, created a movement on behalf of forgiveness and compassion as political virtues in the wake of the Khmer Rouge killings of the late 1970s.[8] Religious "militants for peace," as historian R. Scott Appleby calls them, provide leadership for reconciliation efforts with the same ferocity with which religious militants pursue violence.[9]

The religious, of course, can also be militant in the more familiar sense and can be found impotent, sidelined, or even compromised by collaboration in sites of war and dictatorship, doing little either to oppose these injustices or to influence the politics of dealing with past injustices. The hierarchy of the Catholic Church in Argentina was mostly supportive of that country's military dictatorship during the Dirty Wars, which lasted from 1976 to 1983, and exercised little influence over the truth commission that was conducted in its aftermath. Only in 1995 did the Argentinian bishops issue a guardedly worded pastoral letter asking "humbly for forgiveness from God for guilt we can be accused of." In Rwanda, the Catholic and Anglican churches, which were closely linked to the postcolonial Hutu regime, did little to stop the genocide of 1994 or to influence the formation of the international, national, or village level courts that were created to deal with its crimes. At best, they encouraged local parishioners to participate in village *gacaca* courts and supported local reconciliation initiatives.[10] A similar dynamic of collaboration with the state, consensual or forced, and a consequently weak influence on the politics of the past describes churches in the Czech Republic, Hungary, Estonia, Latvia, Cameroon, Uganda, Uruguay, Bulgaria, Romania, Greece, Ukraine, and Russia.

Though the profile of religious actors involved in the politics of the past includes the diffident and the violent along with the dissident and the effectual, religious involvement is global, significant, and in many cases promoting of reconciliation.

Is Religion Fit for Political Reconciliation?

Let us consider now the skeptics who object to religion's involvement in politics. Because of the nature of religion's claims, skeptics fear, it is likely to sow divisions and possibly violent strife among fellow citizens who do not share the same beliefs. If such a wind is allowed through the door of public life, it will destroy the whole house. The most rigorous representatives of this fear are a family of critics who propose a common solution: that religious believers should only support those political policies for which they can provide a "public justification"—that is, a justification that does not rely solely on a religious rationale.[11] Philosophically, these critics—most prominently, John Rawls—are aligned with (and sometimes identical to) the liberal skeptics discussed in the last chapter. When enactors of political reconciliation deploy religious language, they claim, as when they interfere in matters of the soul, they transgress boundaries that are necessary to liberal democracy. Amy Gutmann and Dennis Thompson echo Tutu's irked interlocutors:

> The difficulty [with theological arguments] is that many victims do not share Archbishop Tutu's Christian faith, and even those who do may hold a different view about the appropriateness of forgiveness in such situations. One can grant that on at least some major interpretations of Christian morality, forgiveness may enhance the virtue of granting amnesty and perhaps may even be obligatory. But those who endorse this interpretation should also grant that their interpretation is not shared by many sincere and reasonable Christians. Nor is it shared by many other religious and secular moral understandings that also deserve respect.[12]

"Deserve respect" will prove an important phrase, for respect, philosopher Christopher J. Eberle argues, is the rationale that most strongly ties together arguments for public justification.[13] For Gutmann and Thompson, respect is practiced through a principle of "economy of moral disagreement" by which citizens put forth those justifications for their political positions that minimize moral disagreement with citizens whose worldviews are different from their own.[14] Religious rationales, they claim, are antithetical to this goal.

If religion breeds disrespect and discord, then obviously it cannot act as a reconciling force, however appealing its distinctive concepts of justice, peace, and mercy may be. Are the arguments for public justification correct? Is religion unfit for reconciliation? My answer begins by taking issue with proposals that would forbid or restrict religion's role in the politics of dealing with the past. Not only are such strictures unjustified, but they suppress a balm for restoring societies that have suffered political wounds.

Arguments for Public Justification

What exactly do such arguments for public justification advocate? All proponents of this view present their proposal for religious restraint as an ethical one, rooted in civility and respect, not as a legal one that curtails religious freedom or freedom of speech. Yet they differ over several other matters. One is how much restraint they envision. Viewing religion as a "conversation stopper," philosopher Richard Rorty urges its withdrawal from public argument.[15] Others, such as Robert Audi and John Rawls, call not for its withdrawal but for its accompaniment by a corresponding public rationale—for Audi, a secular rationale, for Rawls, a "political" rationale that is neither philosophical nor theological.[16] Another difference is over what threatens civility and respect. Some focus exclusively on religion as the source of the problem—again, Rorty is a good example. Rawls, by contrast, views all "comprehensive doctrines"—philosophical, moral, or religious—as problematic. Still, for Rawls, as for the entire family of critics, religion seems to be the chief concern. Finally, the critics differ over what they mean by public. Which of the ways in which religious actors have brought their rationales to bear on the politics of facing the past, for example, are public and therefore subject to restraint? Offering one of the most thorough answers, Rawls confines the realm of restraint to the discussion of "fundamental questions of justice"—human rights and liberties—in the "public political forum," meaning the activities of judges, governmental officials, including executives and legislators, and candidates for public office.[17] Others define public more broadly or more narrowly but often less precisely.

The arguments for public justification have given rise to a family of countercritics who defend the unrestricted, unaccompanied use of religious language.[18] Both sides frame their arguments in concepts of liberal democracy: What ethic is most appropriate for this kind of society? Since most of the recent political efforts to address past injustices have taken place in nascent or imminent liberal democratic regimes, and since the ethic enjoins human rights that are foundational to liberal democracy, much is at stake in whether religious rationales for reconciliation are appropriate in this context. The debate is made even more relevant by the fact that most liberal democratic governments

offer some kind of direct support for religion, sometimes even establishing one religion as official. The United States, where the debate
over public justification is most vigorous, is the liberal democracy with
the world's widest constitutional and institutional separation between
religion and state (though accompanied by a strong involvement of religion in politics).[19] Almost inevitably, then, both liberal democracy and
religion will be in play where political reconciliation is practiced. If the
arguments for public justification are correct, then citizens in many
countries will have to appeal to religion far less than they are accus-
tomed to. If these arguments turn out to be problematic, however, then
their provincialism only adds to their flaws.

Arguments for public justification are of the highest importance
for political reconciliation. In their own way, they envision a form of
reconciliation, a way of conducting political debate that will unify, not
divide. Rawls makes the link between public reason and reconciliation
explicit. He follows Hegel in thinking of reconciliation (*Versöhnung*) as
the terminus of a historical evolution from a *modus vivendi*, or truce,
among people whose comprehensive conceptions make them reluctant
to accept the principles of political liberalism to a deep overlapping
consensus in which they endorse these principles as legitimate. For
the religious, argues Rawls, reconciliation means not only giving up
the hope of establishing political hegemony for their faith and endorsing toleration but also agreeing to proceed according to public reason.
When they become willing to proceed in this way, the conflict between
democracy and religion and between religions can be "greatly mitigated
and contained."[20]

Like Rawls, the present ethic of political reconciliation also envisions
a movement from a *modus vivendi*—a peace settlement or an agreement to
end an authoritarian regime—to a moral consensus on principles of justice, a movement that requires transformations of judgment. Right relationship in the political order involves not only the practice but also the
mutual recognition of human rights. Political reconciliation also depends
on an overlapping consensus among holders of differing religious and
philosophical views. Political reconciliation reaches beyond Rawls,
though, in its prescription for how this consensus is to be achieved—
namely, through a wide range of practices that address the wounds that
political injustices inflict. In principle, there is no reason why Rawls could
not endorse such practices. He formed his ideas on reconciliation as the
golden age of truth commissions was only getting under way and ought

not to be faulted for failing to incorporate practices for addressing the range of wounds of past injustices into his theory. Deeper differences, though, lie in the matter of religion. As I envision it, religious reasons may serve as a justification, motivation, and guide for the six practices of reconciliation and, as I shall soon argue, may be publicly articulated without ethical compromise. For Rawls, crucial to reconciliation is the constraint of religion—combustible, fissiparous religion—through public justification.

The Stability Argument

Observing the rise of the religious right and debates over abortion, sexuality, bioethics, and the role of religion in politics in the United States, perceiving religious wars in Bosnia, Sudan, Northern Ireland, and elsewhere, proponents of public justification fear that religion factionalizes and sunders liberal democracy. Eberle quotes legal scholar Martha Minow:

> The central task of liberalism is to guard against the irresolvable political differences generated by diverging religious views. Now I know one should never claim anything is the central task of anything, especially liberalism, but we do seek a political world that would avoid such things as the Thirty Years' War in Europe, the Bosnia conflict, and other disastrous and intractable occasions of violent group collision. I worry that by inviting religion into the public square we risk just such battles, and battles in which force is the only likely result if religious language permeates public debate.[21]

Stability is central to Rawls's *Political Liberalism*, the book in which he first articulated his argument for public reason. Whereas his previous book, *Theory of Justice*, now a classic of political philosophy, aimed to construct a philosophical justification for liberal principles of justice, his aim in the later work is the "political one" of building a stable consensus on a conception of justice among a variety of religious and philosophical views. "[How] is it possible," he poses as his central question, "for there to exist over time a just and stable society of free and equal citizens, who remain profoundly divided by reasonable religious, philosophical, and moral doctrines?"[22] The trouble with religion—as with other comprehensive doctrines—is that its claims are irresolvable and incompatible

with other religious and comprehensive doctrines. A plurality of irreconcilable doctrines, even of "reasonable" ones that accommodate notions
of equal liberties, he claims, is a "normal result of the exercise of human
reason" within free societies.[23] Because religious claims are irresolvable
and irreconcilable, they tend only to undermine a stable consensus on
principles of liberal democracy. Most of the other proponents of public justification reason similarly. Incommunicable, inaccessible, unintelligible, uncriticizable, uncompromising: These qualities of religion,
they say, either stifle political communication or provoke the distinctly
unreflective communication of fisticuffs and firearms.[24]

"The last time we mixed politics and religion, people got burned at
the stake," reads a contemporary bumper sticker. Though typically more
subtle, arguments for public justification commonly follow liberal philosophers of the Enlightenment tradition in invoking the wars of early
modern Europe to caution their fellow citizens about religion's centrifugal
effects. In the introduction to *Political Liberalism* and in the first chapter
of *The Law of Peoples*, Rawls gives strong attention to these wars as well as
to the like-spirited Inquisition and persecution of heretics by the medieval Catholic Church, thus setting the stage for his argument that stable
liberalism is only possible when religious believers become convinced on
principled grounds that modern political orders need not and ought not
rely on theological agreement.[25]

The argument about stability is not just that religion is divisive. By
definition, division arises from any argument in a democratic debate.
Rather, the argument appears to be that religion, irrational and uncompromising, undermines the stability of liberal democracy and courts
violence. Is this true?

The stability argument turns out to be highly selective. Let us grant
its account of the religious wars: they really were fought over irreconcilable, theologically based claims for exclusive religious establishment.
History reveals that we also ought to acknowledge admixtures of economic motives, the competition for power, and the rise of the modern
state, but let us grant the religious account for the sake of argument.[26]
Let us grant, too, that religion has been involved in armed conflict in our
own era, including in Bosnia, Northern Ireland, Kashmir, Sri Lanka, Iraq,
Sudan, and the global surge of Islamic terrorism.

Is it thus proven that that religion undermines liberal democracy?
No. The religious wars were not modern liberal democracy's only historical
incubators. The concept of rights, the separation of temporal and spiritual

authority in Western Christendom, and such innovations as medieval conciliarism all predated the religious wars, contributed to modern liberal democracy, and were themselves rooted in Christian thought, law, and practice.[27] Though the religious wars furthered liberalism, especially religious freedom, they did so differently than today's proponents of religious restraint describe. Historian Perez Zagorin demonstrates that in the array of philosophical proposals for peace the religious wars generated—including religious skepticism and toleration on the grounds of political expediency and exhaustion—it was "profoundly Christian if unorthodox thinkers" who developed principled arguments for religious freedom and did so on theological grounds.[28] If religion had people burned at the stake, so, too, it pioneered the principled prohibition of the same practice.

Subsequent to the religious wars, all of the combatant religious communities have incorporated religious freedom into their teachings—the Catholic Church as recently as 1965—thus rejecting precisely the doctrines inimical to liberal democracy.[29] Stronger still, religious activists, drawing directly on their theology, have promoted and provoked the widening and deepening of liberalism at key historical junctures, including the abolition of the slave trade, then of slavery itself, early feminist campaigns, the American civil rights movement, and numerous democratization struggles of the past generation.

As for violence, the most colossal instances of it during the twentieth century were motivated either by ethnic loyalties or by secular ideologies—Fascist, communist—that sought directly to suppress traditional religious faith. True, some latter-day civil wars and contemporary religious terrorism have been propelled by religious doctrines that deny both the separation of religion and state and religious freedom. Other wars that involve religion, like ones in Bosnia and Northern Ireland, though, are propelled not through the claims of religion but at most through religion's role in shaping the identities of warring communities: They are more like ethnic conflicts.[30] Are there historical and contemporary examples of religious threats to liberal democratic stability? Indubitably. Do religious claims therefore threaten liberal democracy systematically, due to the very fact that they are religious? This the stability argument fails to demonstrate.

A Matter of Respect?

Arguments for public justification seek not just stability but "stability for the right reasons," in Rawls's phrase.[31] Their most central contention is not an empirical but a moral one: Religious arguments fail to respect fellow liberal democratic citizens. Respect is a value that must be taken seriously; liberals are right to invoke it. Gutmann and Thompson argue persuasively that citizens show respect when they deliberate with other citizens, listening to and responding to their reasons and in turn offering counterarguments that they can understand even if they do not endorse them.[32] Deliberative respect is one of the central features of the proposal for religious engagement that I will offer shortly below.

Yet in another sense, it is strange for liberals to argue that respect requires restraining certain kinds of rationales. Classical liberal commitments seem to point in the opposite direction. Both religious freedom and freedom of speech are designed to protect a wide variety of rationales— freedoms that proponents of public justification appear to be asking religious believers to forgo. Liberalism's emphasis on conscience calls citizens to integrate—not to disassociate—their beliefs with their actions and their words. The liberal values of transparency and open deliberation also cut against an ethic that would have citizens employ rationales other than the ones that truly motivate them. Philosopher Jeffrey Stout makes the point:

> If [religious citizens] are discouraged from speaking up in this way, we will remain ignorant of the real reasons that many of our fellow citizens have for reaching some of the ethical and political conclusions they do. We will also deprive them of the central democratic good of expressing themselves to the rest of us on matters about which they care deeply. If they do not have this opportunity, we will lose the chance to learn from, and to critically examine, what they say. And they will have good reason to doubt that they are being shown the respect that all of us owe to fellow citizens as the individuals they are.[33]

All of these arguments, along with the possibility that the demand for respect can be met through an alternative proposal for religious engagement that does not require religious restraint, combine to place the burden on arguments for public justification.

At the heart of the concern about disrespect is the observation that public law is coercive, having behind it the sanction of force. Citizens are legitimately concerned about being coerced, the argument runs. They value the freedom to live according to their conscience and their beliefs. Political society, though, requires laws that coerce. So, when citizens propose laws, advocates of public justification argue, they ought to use the kinds of justifications that respect those whom they are asking to live under these laws.

What makes a justification public? That is, what kinds of reasons are admissible grounds for coercive laws? Philosopher Nicholas Wolterstoff observes that every argument for public justification offers some kind of independent criterion for judging what kinds of arguments are acceptable.[34] In most of these arguments, the criterion is motivated by a concern that reasons be knowable, communicable, and amenable to discussion and debate. Accessibility, in-principle accessibility, intelligibility, reasonableness, rationality, replicability, criticizability, and respect for the beliefs of other citizens are examples of the criteria that the proponents of public justification put forth. It is these criteria, they believe, that religion cannot meet. Are these good criteria?

Eberle argues—convincingly, in my view—that all of the proposed criteria for public justification run into similar problems. A standard for ethical public discourse must be one that is strong enough to prohibit the kinds of reasons that the proponent finds disrespectful—for example, religious ones—yet not so stringent that it rules out the kinds of reasons that healthy democratic debate requires.[35] Consider a set of issues that citizens often debate fiercely in contexts of transitional justice: Should violators of human rights be punished? If so, how? Might they ever be forgiven or granted amnesty? In making their arguments, citizens will appeal, implicitly or explicitly, to ethical doctrines, scientific theories, and shared cultural values that have sophisticated and controversial sets of rationales behind them. The person who says that war criminals must "pay for their crimes" through imprisonment or death appeals to a doctrine that I call balance retributivism. The person who appeals to deterrence—punishing war criminals now will make war crimes less likely in the future—makes a claim whose validity rests on complex social scientific evidence. The advocate of reconciliation who argues that the worst violators ought to be imprisoned while lesser offenders ought to be reintegrated into their communities through local truth commissions rests her claim on something like the moral logic for restorative justice that I have outlined. Even the practical person who says that the costliness of trials detracts from the transition to democracy, as we have seen, is appealing to a doctrine of liberal consequentialism. What is true of all these arguments is that they are laden with theory. Even the ordinary citizen who expresses them in ordinary language is putting forth doctrines whose deep justification involves sophisticated reasoning. All of these arguments are controversial as well, much like the attitudes and beliefs that citizens of Western liberal democracies typically bring to bear on debates about global warming, abortion, environmental protection, economic growth and justice, war and peace, and many other issues.

What possible criterion can rule out religious reasons but admit these other sorts of complex judgments—moral, legal, and scientific—on which citizens typically rely? Say that the criterion is that a reason be one that other citizens of a society find acceptable given their actual convictions. In the United States alone, citizens hold an enormous variety of beliefs—religious, political, moral, and philosophical—and attach to these beliefs a variety of convictions about what it is possible to know and understand. Except for a few platitudinous propositions such as "torturing known innocents is immoral" or "wanton cruelty is wrong," it is hard to imagine claims that everyone will find acceptable and thus worthy of respect. These platitudes are obviously insufficient for confronting the difficult issues of the day.

Other criteria for public justification appeal not to beliefs that citizens actually hold but to standards of what is rational or intelligible. Rawls draws on both kinds of criteria. His idea of public reason is derived from the political culture of actual modern liberal democracies—of the United States, in particular, one strongly suspects—but also has a philosophical content involving a standard of reasonableness. It is reasonableness that separates political conceptions—the notion of free and equal citizens in a constitutional regime or of society as a fair system of cooperation—from comprehensive religious, moral, and philosophical conceptions that he wants citizens to leave out of public debate. Political conceptions are ones that reasonable modern citizens can agree on, whereas comprehensive conceptions are not, in good part because reasonableness is shaped by the "burdens of judgment"—the complexity of evidence, the difficulty of weighing relevant moral considerations, and people's propensity to differ over judgment and interpretation.[36]

Yet if the burdens of judgment are what determine reasonableness, it is hard to see how they could eliminate religious rationales from political contention without also sidelining virtually all of the even moderately complex moral concepts that citizens ordinarily use to reason about difficult political issues. Eberle's conclusion applies again.

Because retributivism, restorative justice, deterrence, and liberal consequentialism all invoke various moral theories and perhaps complex social scientific theories—comprehensive claims about which reasonable citizens disagree—then it appears that Rawls's burdens of judgment disqualify them from political argument. How, then, are citizens supposed to reason about transitional justice?[37] As Eberle points out, even some of the human rights that form the structure of constitutional liberal democracies—like religious freedom—rest on robust rationales that might well fail to meet the standards of the burdens of judgment.[38] As was true for the criterion of actual agreement, it appears impossible to set the justificatory dial strongly enough to rule out what is allegedly inimical to liberal democratic debate but weak enough to allow what is essential to it.

Other criteria for public justification turn out to be no more successful in setting the dial. Let us say that accessibility is the standard. Excluded from political debate then would be most scientific knowledge, which is routinely invoked in debates ranging from global warming to economic growth but which is not understandable to most citizens. Perhaps the standard then shifts to in-principle accessibility, meaning understandable to any citizen with the right level of education. Why, then, cannot citizens with the right amount of education and effort also come to understand religious rationales? Accessibility does not demand their conversion to these rationales but only their effort to understand the reasons why religious people hold their views. It is not possible here to consider every criterion in its full sophistication. I have been persuaded by the opponents of public justification that all of these criteria encounter the same kind of difficulty: In ruling out religious language, they also debar the basic concepts on which citizens rely to carry on normal democratic debate. Because healthy liberal democracy is a fundamental goal of proponents of public justification, this is a large problem for their position.

The Need for an Ethic of Engagement

For all this, public justification advocates may continue to worry that, in some special respect, religious language is incompatible with democratic debate. Perhaps they imagine religious believers arguing solely from fiat—policy X is ordained by the Lord, and that is that! Or maybe from private revelation—the Lord told me policy X, and so it must be! Religious people sometimes argue this way but not necessarily or always. Arguments solely from fiat or private revelation are not amenable to democratic decision making, but their flaws are ones that typify *bad* religious arguments, not religious arguments per se. We do well to remember that there are secular forms of these arguments too. What is needed is an ethic of engagement, not the elimination of religious rationales from public debate. Religious arguments, even ones based on scriptural sources and lacking accompanying secular rationales, are in principle amenable to examination, understanding, consideration, criticism, partial agreement, contradiction, and argument, even on the part of those who do not share their premises, in much the same way as arguments based on ideology, culture, other philosophical or moral doctrines, and science are. In elaborating this point, I now offer a constructive proposal for making religious arguments for an ethic of political reconciliation.

Rooted Reason: A Proposal for Making Religiously Grounded Arguments

If it is ethically permissible for religious arguments to be voiced in public debates, including debates about dealing with the past, more needs to be said about how reconciliation can be constructively advanced through religious arguments, especially in religiously plural settings. The setting for such arguments will vary among a parliament, an official commission, a cabinet, a council of eminent citizens, or the negotiation of a peace agreement between states. In any of these settings, how can leaders offer religious arguments constructively on behalf of an ethic of political reconciliation? Four observations are in order.

The first observation is that there is nothing inherent in religious rationales that prevents them from being the subject of meaningful and constructive conversations about fundamental matters of justice. Leaders from diverse religious or secular perspectives can seek to find an overlapping consensus on truth commissions, trials, and reparations, just as they might seek to find common ground on global warming, reducing their country's debt, or protecting the rights of women. They can reach consensus if they agree to hear and to be heard, to explain their view to others as best they can, to try to understand others' view as best they can, and to find agreement where possible. They need make no prior agreement, explicit or implicit, to express themselves only through reason, natural law, secular language, or any other *lingua franca*, though of course they may draw on any of these modes of reasoning and communication. What makes common ground possible are areas of overlap in the interlocutors' scriptures, traditions, and teachings and, of course, their goodwill and ability to communicate their ideas. The possibility of overlap, of course, depends a great deal on which religious, tribal, or philosophical traditions are involved in the conversation, which representatives of these traditions are involved, and what issue is being discussed. After all, virtually every tradition has an "internal pluralism" of diverse voices.[39] It is impossible to say *ex ante* how much consensus on what issues can be attained, but there is no reason in principle why religious people cannot achieve such a consensus.

A second observation runs in a different direction: The constructive potential of religion is also furthered when religious people (or members of any tradition for that matter) acknowledge a moral obligation to engage the arguments of members of other traditions and views. The value realized through dialogue is respect. In part, it is the coercive nature of law that demands the respect that dialogue promotes, as both public justification proponents and opponents such as Eberle aver.[40] Through dialogue, interlocutors put reasons behind laws and their enforcement. Dialogue also promotes respect in a different sense. In deliberating, democratic citizens respect one another's dignity as beings capable of reasoning, communicating, arguing, reflecting, revising, and acting accordingly. Respect is undermined when a religious believer—or anyone of any point of view—proceeds simply by fiat, feeling, or otherwise failing to put reasons into play.

The moral value of respect implies an obligation to offer reasons to others who are of a different tradition or who may simply disagree. It does not imply an obligation either to agree or to succeed in persuasion. Sometimes democratic deliberation will increase the sphere of overlapping views, but sometimes it will not. It may bring one or both sides to rethink its views in small or in large part. Deliberators must always consider a proposed overlapping view from the perspective of their convictions, asking whether they can endorse it. When they decide that they cannot, they are free as ever to vote, lobby, urge, and bargain according to their beliefs.

In advancing their views of justice, religious advocates will discover benefits in translating their ethic into secular language, not squelching their religious rationales, but accompanying them with a secular rationale—though for pragmatic reasons, not out of strict obligation. This is my third observation. Secular language is not the same as secular philosophy or ideology. It is rather a mode of expression—and not necessarily inimical to religion. Consider scriptural injunctions such as "do not steal," "love your neighbor," and the Quran's "there shall be no compulsion in matters of religion."

All are expressed in secular language, presupposing no claims of a particular faith yet expressing ideas that are situated in particular scriptures. Not all religious claims can or ought to be expressed in secular language; some of these claims secular expression distorts beyond usefulness. At least some concepts can be stated secularly, though, without losing their capacity to be understood in a relatively common way by members of different traditions. The examples cited fit the description, as does a proposition about justice like "the intentional killing of innocent people is prohibited."

There are at least three such benefits that secular language can realize. First, the ethic is strengthened the more widely it becomes the object of an overlapping consensus. In countries whose populations are largely secular or whose populations are mixed between religious and secular, secular rationales may be crucial for building legitimacy.

The second benefit of secular language has to do with the rule of law. Several of the practices of reconciliation are, at least in certain respects, judicial in character. Trials are conducted directly by courts; truth commissions often make decisions of a judicial character; any of the practices could be challenged in a court, just as the amnesty provisions of South Africa's TRC were. Courts are charged with the duty of applying the laws of their respective states' constitutions. The new constitutions of most of the transitional countries of the past three decades are written in secular language. If the judicial processes entailed in certain practices of reconciliation are to be conducted consistently with these constitutions and capable of withstanding judicial challenge, then the justifications that enable them ought to be written in secular language as well. In this limited domain, something like the principle of public justification may apply, not because of any general sense in which religious language is inappropriate to liberal democracy but because of the specific duties of judicial bodies to reason according to concepts and modes found in their constitutions. Perhaps the principle could better be termed judicial justification. It is circumscribed and focused.[41]

The third benefit of secular language is its compatibility with the operation of organizations that often play a key part in promoting the six practices of reconciliation but typically operate in secular language—the United Nations, other international organizations, and NGOs that support transitional justice. Many of these organizations include leaders and staff people who think in secular terms; many, if not most, of their charters, bylaws, public statements, and conduct of daily business are secular. If the religious advocate of political reconciliation hopes that such organizations will support the politics that her ethic demands, she will find great advantage in explaining this ethic in principles that are consistent with their work.

These practical benefits of secular language, of course, can be realized only if the ethic can be expressed in secular language. Some theologians and religious ethicists may be leery of just this possibility. They would share the skepticism of the proponent of public justification about the communicability of religious language, though they would draw the opposite conclusion: Religious believers should not compromise themselves by adopting the logic of secular liberal democracy. Too much is lost in the translation. Shorn of its foundation in the revelation of God as it is written in scriptures, an ethic of reconciliation is likely to be desiccated, denuded, compromised, and stripped of the justifications that it needs for its defense, they might say. It is rather only theological rationales—the sort that appear in the next three chapters—that can sustain the ethic.

To the contrary, I argue that the propositions of the ethic of political reconciliation can be articulated in secular language while remaining compatible with theological rationales. This is my fourth observation. Importantly, the religious proponent of the ethic is not being asked to accept the justification of a secular philosophy that is not his own. He may still endorse the ethic because he thinks that it is rooted in the will, nature, or purposes of God. Nor is it my claim that the secular expression of ethical norms contains all the same meaning as their theological expression or that nothing at all is lost in the translation. The claim is only that the propositions of the ethic are capable of being expressed in secular language without losing their compatibility with theological justifications.

An example from the laws of war will illustrate the point: the prohibition of intentionally killing innocent civilians. A religious ethicist's deep reasons for endorsing this maxim may well be theological ones: The person is made in the image of God; the scriptures contain commandments against murder. Yet the maxim itself is capable of being expressed in secular language. This is not to say that theology is irrelevant for its interpretation. On theological grounds, for instance, an ethicist might argue that the prohibition is an absolute one, whereas an ethicist with a different theology or a secular foundation might be more willing to endorse allowing exceptions. It is only to say that the basic meaning of the prohibition can be conveyed in secular terms, a possibility that facilitates dialogue across traditions.

I offer no general theology or philosophy here that explains which ethical norms, practices, or virtues are amenable to both theological and secular expression. I hold, though, that the propositions of the ethic of political reconciliation are, like the prohibition against targeting innocents, capable of being defended theologically as well as expressed meaningfully in secular language. Whether my contention is supported can be judged simply by whether the arguments in the chapters preceding and following this one are persuasive—the previously stated secular arguments for restorative justice and the theological arguments for political reconciliation in the chapters that follow.

The approach that I have been articulating is, in elaborated form, what I earlier called rooted reason. It is rooted because it invites religious believers (or any other believers) to present their full rationales—untruncated, unsanitized, and unfiltered. Yet it also asks them to enter a dialogue in which they pursue mutual understanding with those of different views. Among the fruits of deep dialogue, particularly important is overlapping consensus. The ethic depends crucially on (empirical) legitimacy: The wider the set of people who endorse it and the more deeply they hold the belief, the more likely it is to succeed. When proponents of an ethic of reconciliation not only offer their deepest reasons for the ethic but also communicate it and seek to win assent for it from people of different religious or philosophical persuasions, the overlapping consensus for it is expanded. In any given country facing past injustices, the search for overlapping consensus will depend greatly on the religious and ideological profile of its population. Which religions are involved? What do these religions teach? What do its citizens believe? Its leaders? Some religions and some belief systems will be more favorable to the core ideas of political reconciliation than others. Deliberation may or may not produce agreement. Perhaps it will produce agreement on some propositions but not others. Perhaps it will result in compromises by which certain of the practices will be realized only partially. Agreement will always be more or less, wider or narrower.

Does Archbishop Tutu Pass Muster?

What, then, of Archbishop Tutu? Given all that I have argued, were his colleagues right in asking him to conduct his leadership of the TRC in solely secular language? Tutu is an important test case for religious rationales. In his capacity as chair of a state-appointed national truth commission, his regalia, rituals, words, and pastoral presence add up to the most publicly authoritative use of religion among the world's political efforts to address past injustices.[42] It was the prestige that Tutu had garnered from his distinctively religious leadership of the antiapartheid movement that moved President Nelson Mandela to ask him to chair the commission. Its mission was to carry out the grand compromise that would end apartheid by providing the truth about the past that blacks and other excluded groups demanded while avoiding the revenge and vindictiveness that might well have driven proapartheid whites to take up arms. The religiously grounded concepts of reconciliation and restorative justice that Tutu and other church leaders proffered helped to broker this compromise. Faith provided a language, rationale, and motivation for victims and perpetrators to speak publicly about the most gruesome of deeds and for other citizens to support the commission in word and deed.[43] In the TRC, religion was a foot soldier, not merely a chaplain providing a sanctifying benediction. Such a role, I have argued, is a legitimate one for religion to play.

Yet Tutu spoke and acted for the state, on behalf of an official body whose judicial decisions conferred heavy material and reputational costs and benefits on citizens, some of whom were not Christians or did not endorse restorative justice. Did he respect them? Did he make an effort, as deep dialogue demands, to reason mutually with those of other faiths and views? Though neither the clause in South Africa's 1993 Interim Constitution nor the 1995 parliamentary legislation that enabled the Truth and Reconciliation Commission was authored by Tutu, both were written in secular language. In the important sphere of constitutional law, they offered rationales that all citizens could readily consider. The five-volume report of the TRC published in 1998, on which Tutu exercised strong influence, was also articulated in secular language, excepting only a cover photograph of Tutu praying over a cross and a short, carefully worded reference to "Judaeo-Christian tradition and African traditional values" as foundations of restorative justice.[44] Both these laws and the TRC report also grounded restorative justice in *ubuntu*, a concept drawn from Bantu tradition and presented as a common one for South Africans. Everyone who testified before the commission was granted the option not to use the words "so help me God." In Tutu's writings, interviews, and speeches about the work of the commission, he often combined Christian theological arguments with both *ubuntu* rationales and secular rationales such as the commission's utility for avoiding civil war. In all of these foundational ways, Tutu and other authoritative bodies justified and explained the work of the commission through secular and other cultural rationales that could speak to the beliefs of all South Africans.

Were there also ways in which Tutu failed to meet the demands of deep dialogue? Arguably, he would have transgressed respect were he to have used religious language to exhort testifiers who did not share his religious convictions, especially in light of the great duress, pressure, and risk that accompanied their appearance before the commission. In fact there is little evidence that he or the other commissioners conducted themselves in this way. In their analysis of the TRC hearings, researchers Megan Shore and Scott Kline found that religious language showed up only in the hearings of the Human Rights Violations Committee (HRVC), where victims and survivors testified, often in an emotional, personal, and heartfelt manner. By contrast, the hearings of the Amnesty Committee, held to determine the truth of perpetrators' testimonies, were more like those of a court-room and were largely devoid of religious language.[45] My own analysis of the HRVC hearings shows that even in that context religious language on the part of commissioners was exceedingly rare. In less than 1 percent of "victim-hearings" (instances in which a victim appeared or two or more victims appeared together) did commissioners use religious language at least apart from Tutu's opening invocations.[46] Victims and survivors used religious language in their testimony more often, but this was by their own volition. It is difficult to argue that the TRC imposed religion.

If religion is a legitimate source for an ethic of political reconciliation, then, can the roots of that ethic be found in religious traditions?

7

Reconciliation in the Jewish Tradition

COMMON TO THE scriptures of Judaism, Christianity, and Islam is the
story of Joseph (in Arabic, Yusuf), the twelfth, youngest—and favorite—
son of Jacob.[1] The story begins with a serious injustice that leaves serious
wounds. When the seventeen-year-old Joseph, "bursting with adolescent
innocence and pride," as theologian Donald Shriver describes him, tells
his brothers of two dreams in which they are bowing down to him, the
brothers become enraged with envy, first intending to murder him, then
resolving to sell him as a slave to traders bound for Egypt.[2] There, Joseph
passes through a serpentine sequence of reversals and successes, first
being thrown into prison after the wife of his powerful master falsely
accuses him of advancing on her, then meteorically ascending the ranks
of the Egyptian court by interpreting dreams, eventually those of Pharaoh
himself, and finally becoming the Pharaoh's second-in-command.
"[W]ithout you, no one shall lift up hand or foot in all the land of Egypt,"
Pharoah instructs Joseph.[3]

The story of Joseph and his brothers then becomes a political one.
Joseph is a thirty-nine-year-old whiz kid—the great Wāzir, as the Quran
calls him—when, twenty-two years after they sold him, ten of his brothers
travel from their home in Canaan to Pharaoh's court in order to plea for
rations during a time of famine. They are directed to Joseph, whom they
do not recognize, and they kneel before him. Joseph recognizes them and
initiates his response to their evil.

Joseph foists on his brothers a series of devious, anguishing rigors. He
makes them prove their honesty by journeying back to Canaan to retrieve
their brother Benjamin, the remaining youngest son, whom their father
adores and is loath to let travel. While they journey, Joseph imprisons

their brother Simeon as collateral. When they return to Egypt, Joseph frames Benjamin for stealing a royal goblet and threatens to enslave him. Is Joseph taking revenge on his brothers? Or is he simply meting out their just comeuppance? Or is this restorative punishment? In neither Genesis nor the Quran are Joseph's rationales entirely apparent. His brothers' interpretation of their plight emerges more clearly. "Alas, we are being punished on account of our brother," they tell one another in the Genesis version. "[W]e looked on at his anguish, yet paid no heed when he pleaded with us. That is why this distress has come upon us."[4]

The outcome of the successive trials is also clear: They are restorative. The brothers come to recognize and repent for their guilt. "How can we plead, how can we prove our innocence?" asks Judah. "God has uncovered the crime of your servants."[5] Judah even offers to become a slave in place of Benjamin. Joseph, too, is transformed. In the Genesis version, he weeps and is "overcome with feeling" in several of his encounters with his brothers.[6] When he at last reveals himself, "his sobs were so loud that the Egyptians could hear."[7] In the Quranic version, Joseph then assures his brothers that Allah will show him mercy. Next, he settles his entire family comfortably in Egypt.[8] In the end, the justice that Joseph administers is nowhere proportionate to his brothers' nefariousness nor does God demand measure for measure. Rather, through the course of the plot, relationships are restored.

For all the weeping and embracing, though, the story remains a political one, especially in the Genesis version. Joseph is a whiz kid but also an *enfant terrible*, prone to lording it over others. As an administrator, he responds to the pleas of starving Egyptians by expropriating their land and reducing them to slavery on behalf of Pharaoh. His brothers' remorse is hardly pure either. After their father dies, they fear that Joseph continues to hold a grudge against them. It is to deflect his retaliation that they tell Joseph that Jacob, before he died, had instructed Joseph to forgive them, and then they prostrate themselves before Joseph, offering to be his slaves. Weeping again, Joseph assures his brothers that they have nothing to fear.[9]

Through all of the politics and the plot, God is working his purposes, as both Joseph and Jacob attest. In the Quran, the last two sections of the story read as Joseph's paean to Allah for Allah's faithfulness through his life's events.[10] In Genesis, Joseph tells his brothers that God has worked through their deeds in order to save lives during the famine, then repeats God's promise to Jacob—whose name is also Israel—that the brothers' descendants will be blessed and eventually brought back to the land of Canaan.[11] In the Genesis version, the story is pivotal to the founding of Israel.

Restoration between victims and perpetrators, involving forgiveness, repentance, and transformation, taking place in a political setting with all of its characteristic messiness, compromise, uncertainty, mistrust, and dynamics of power but ultimately contributing to the building of a nation: The story of Joseph suggests that the core concepts of an ethic of political reconciliation are situated within the three Abrahamic faith traditions. These core concepts—most centrally, reconciliation as a concept of justice that comprises a holistic and interconnected set of practices, but also closely related to principles of peace and mercy—I derive from the narratives, injunctions, theologies, and doctrines through which these faiths describe the character, purpose, and actions of God.

I use the word *derive* deliberately. In none of the *surahs* of the Quran nor in the books of the Jewish Bible or the New Testament can be found a passage that reads "reconciliation is a concept of justice, animated by mercy, entailing peace, which lights the pathway of kings and their minions." Only in the last century or so have theologians and religious leaders advocated reconciliation in the political realm; only in the last couple of decades has reconciliation become a prominent stance. What the scriptures and subsequent centuries of interpretation contain, though, are the materials from which an ethic of political reconciliation for modern political orders can be constructed—certain ways of thinking about justice, mercy, peace, and politics, ones that have not been prominent within the Western philosophical traditions that have shaped the modern state. Neither my interpretation of these concepts nor my fashioning of an ethic from them will command agreement from all within these traditions, but I make my best case, relying on respected interpreters of the concepts' textual meaning. The construction project of derivation, then, begins with disinterment—the unearthing of building materials that have a long history in the scriptures but only a short history in modern politics.

Although my primary sources in the faith traditions are their scriptures, these are not my only sources. In the Jewish tradition, for instance, I look not only to the Bible, known also as the Tanakh, but also to the later tradition of rabbinic interpretation and to Jewish philosophy. I do the same for Christianity and Islam. The Jewish and Christian traditions, of course, also substantially overlap insofar as the Christian Bible incorporates the Jewish Bible as its Old Testament.[12]

Reconciliation in the Jewish Tradition

The Jewish Bible, Rabbi Louis Jacobs points out, contains no word for ethics. Nor does it offer a philosophical argument for the foundations or validity of ethics, the kind of argument found, for example, in Plato or Aristotle.[13] The Jewish Bible, rather, grounds morality in the actions, revelations, and commandments of God, which in turn reflect God's character and purposes. It instructs God's people to follow suit, to "walk in the ways of the Lord."[14] Jewish ethics is an *imitatio dei*.[15] The ethic of political reconciliation that I have been defending reflects the ways of the Lord as portrayed in the Jewish Bible and as later interpreters understood this biblical portrayal.

Reconciliation in the Language of the Jewish Bible

The word *reconciliation* appears rarely if ever in English translations of the Jewish Bible.[16] So in what sense can the scriptures bear out the claim that reconciliation is a concept of justice? Reconciliation, as I have argued, is a state of right relationship and a process of restoration of right relationship. The Jewish scriptures establish the crucial next step in the argument, which is that justice means right relationship, or righteousness. In light of scripture's meanings, therefore, what I have been calling reconciliation can be expressed equally well as a state of justice or a process of restoring justice.

In English, *justice* and *righteousness* typically have different meanings. Justice usually connotes a social virtue and righteousness a personal virtue—the quality of one who is upstanding or even priggish. Commenting on this difference, Bible scholar John Donahue asks us to "[i]magine...people's reaction if we had a national 'department of righteousness' or we talked about 'social righteousness.' "[17] Not so in Hebrew. The two words in the Jewish Bible that are most often translated into English as justice—*sedeq* (or its feminine form, *sedeqah*) and *mishpat*—are also frequently translated as "righteousness." The two terms often appear together in parallel statements or as a hendiadys, a pairing of two terms that expresses a single concept.[18] When they do, *sedeqah* usually means "right" or "righteous" and *mishpat* means "justice." Psalms 97:2 recites, "[d]ense clouds are around him; righteousness [*sedeq*] and justice [*mishpat*] are the base of his throne." Genesis 18:19 speaks of Abraham doing what is "just [*mishpat*] and right [*sedeqah*]." Alone, each of these Hebrew terms is translated in different instances into both right/righteousness and just/justice. English translations of the Bible often differ among themselves as to which way they interpret specific instances of each term. "It is exceedingly difficult to establish the exact difference in meaning of [these] biblical terms," argues Rabbi Abraham Joshua Heschel in his classic, *The Prophets*.[19] In any case, the Jewish tradition has given great status to these terms. The Rabbinic tradition of the second through fifth centuries CE thought that the entirety of the commands of the Torah could be whittled down to the two proffered in Isaiah 56:1: "Observe what is right and do what is just."[20]

Of the two terms, *sedeq[ah]* is the more expansive. It is commonly translated as "righteousness," while the whole family of words with the root *sdq*—which appear in the Jewish Bible 476 times—are translated into English as "righteousness" and a host of related terms: uprightness, straightness, salvation, correctness, truth, prosperity, innocence, vindication, and victory.[21] In the Jewish scriptures, righteousness is a matter of right relationship, between parents and children, priest and worshippers, merchants and buyers, kings and subjects, judge and disputants, members of a community and the widows, orphans, poor, and resident aliens among them, and between each person and God, each living up to the demands of a particular relationship, all of these relationships aggregated into a comprehensive right relationship within an entire community and between an entire community and God.[22] The noted twentieth-century Bible scholar Gerhard von Rad once wrote, "[t]here is absolutely no concept in the Old Testament with so central a significance for all the relationships of human life as that of *sdqh*. It is the standard not only for man's relationship to God, but also for his relationship to his fellows, reaching right down to...the animals and to his natural environment...for it embraces the whole of Israelite life."[23]

Maimonides, the great medieval Jewish philosopher, similarly interprets *sedeq* with regard to its relationship to justice. In *The Guide of the Perplexed* he writes that *sedeq* means "justice," but he goes on to explain that this is not the justice that means "the granting to everyone who has a right to something, that which he has a right to and giving to every being that which corresponds to his merits," the classical concept of justice as the will to render each person his due. Rather, *sedeq* is "the fulfilling of duties with regard to others imposed on you on account of moral virtue, such as remedying the injuries of all those who are injured." Clarifying that this is a meaning of justice, he writes, "[f]or when you walk in the way of the moral virtues, you do justice unto your rational soul, giving her the due that is her right." Collectively, the moral virtues can be understood as righteousness.[24]

Mishpat, the other term that is translated as "justice," is more specific and applied, most often pertaining to courtroom situations and judicial procedures. "The word *mishpat* means the judgment given by the *shofet* (judge); hence the word can mean justice, norm, ordinance, legal, right, law," explains Heschel.[25] Yet *mishpat* is also far closer to righteousness than the English word *justice* is when used in courtroom settings. "While legality and righteousness are not identical, they must always coincide, the second being reflected in the first," Heschel comments.[26] Jewish law codes were oriented around the concept of restoration of right relationship, or righteousness. Like *sedeq(ah)*, *mishpat* can be translated into either "justice" or "righteousness" and enjoys multiple usages in multiple settings, these reflecting the manifold aspects of justice in ancient Israel, which in turn contribute to the comprehensive righteousness of the community.[27] Generally, then, Hebrew makes no sharp distinction between justice and righteousness. Justice means comprehensive right relationship.

Frequently in the scriptures, *justice* and *right relationship* are terms of political and social justice. Bible scholar Moshe Weinfeld devotes an exhaustive study to showing that the hendiadys "justice and righteousness" typically connotes social justice. Justice and righteousness, along with the language of kingship, indeed describe and lend a social and political significance to God's most pivotal covenantal acts—his creation, his disclosure of the law through Moses at Sinai, and the eventual period of universal redemption. Earthly kings and polities are to mimic the pattern. Justice and righteousness define the mission for Israel that God sets forth in his call to Abraham, the father of the nation, and then the mission of the Davidic kings, as the prophets remind them so fiercely and so often.[28]

The politics of justice and righteousness involves core themes in the present ethic of political reconciliation. The concept of justice as righteousness is comprehensive, including but far exceeding judicial norms. It is often expressed conjointly with the pairing of kindness and mercy as well as with salvation. Liberty is a central motif—the freeing of those who are trapped in poverty, debt, and slavery, restoring them to a state of equality. Justice and righteousness are frequently restorative, involving rectifying the plight of the poor and the dispossessed; guaranteeing the rights of the widow, the orphan, and the resident alien; liberating slaves; restoring land to its owners; giving bread to the hungry; canceling the debts of the state and of individuals; rectifying economic injustices such as overpricing and falsification of weights and measures; and, frequently, judging and punishing oppressors. Some scholars have discerned themes of restitution and restorative punishment in scripture's description of the community's norms for dealing with crime. Restoration is also part and parcel of the jubilee year proclaimed in Leviticus 25, when hereditary land is returned to its original owners, slaves are liberated, and debt is forgiven, as well as of the day of fasting described in Isaiah 58, when penitents are to unbind the oppressed, feed the hungry, house the poor, and clothe the naked. Weinfeld comments that "forgiveness and amnesty on the part of the ruler is also called *'doing righteousness and justice.'* "[29]

The righteousness that expresses justice—social, political, comprehensive—is initiated, prescribed, established, sustained, and restored by God. Heschel states: "[R]ighteousness is not just a value; it is God's part of human life, *God's stake in human history.*"[30] It is through covenants with his people that God sets forth the character of right relationship—God's creation of the world, the life that he prescribed for Adam and Eve (and its one stricture), his promises to Noah and Abraham, the commandments that he revealed through Moses, and many other revelations to his people. In the Jewish Bible, covenants are pacts between God and his people. Its terms are set forth and established by God, who promises to sustain and guarantee the blessings of his people unless they violate the covenant, in which case he promises to judge and punish them. Covenant also takes the form of law, which is revealed in the first five books of the Bible, or the Torah. Known also as the Law of Moses, the Torah includes the Ten Commandments as well as scores of *mitzvot* or "commandments"—613 of them, as later tradition would have it—by which Jews are called to live. Law expresses the contours of right relationship and has no meaning apart from it. Fittingly, the language of righteousness appears often in the context of God's covenants. Reflecting his faithfulness to sustaining his covenant (*hesed*), God also restores it after the Israelites have broken its laws. Much in the same way, reconciliation is a process of restoration as well as a state of being restored—a restoration and a state of righteousness, and, we can now say, a restoration and a state of justice.

Peace

The close scriptural resemblance between justice and righteousness is shared also by peace, which is most often translated from the Hebrew word *shalom*. Psalms 85:11 portrays justice (*sedeq*) and peace (*shalom*) kissing. A passage in Isaiah (32:16–17) suggests the close relationship among all three concepts: "Then justice [*mishpat*] shall abide in the wilderness and righteousness [*sedeqah*] shall dwell on the farm land. For the work of righteousness [*sedeqah*] shall be peace [*shalom*], and the effect of righteousness [*sedeqah*], calm and confidence forever." Many other passages suggest a similar intimacy. Peace is not identical to justice/righteousness, for it uniquely emphasizes tranquility, contentment, and quietness, but it overlaps formidably.

One of the most important points of overlap is that peace, like the justice that is righteousness, is holistic. Unlike a negative, Hobbesian peace, "the peace expressed in shalom encompasses far more than the absence of war. Shalom means wholeness, righteousness, justice, grace, and truth; thus all ethical values are found within Shalom," scholars Murray Polner and Naomi Goodman argue.[31] When it characterizes the life of the Jewish community and the relationships that make it up, scripture's *shalom* means health and prosperity, economic and political justice, as well as honesty and moral integrity in relations between persons.[32] Like justice and righteousness, *shalom* is also a quality of God's covenantal relationship with his people. The book of Judges (6:24) speaks of an altar to the Lord that is called Yahweh-shalom, suggesting that peace is a name of God himself. By the third century CE, rabbinic sources took up this designation.[33] If *shalom* is closely resonant with God's justice and righteousness, then it readily follows that reconciliation is not only a concept of justice but also a vision of peace. At least this is true for reconciliation as a state of affairs, if not as a process of restoration. *Shalom*, too, appears to mean a state of affairs— one where right relationship and justice prevail—rather than an act of transformation, though it may well result from a transformation. It is a state of affairs that pervades Jewish writing. Bible scholar Ulrich Mauser finds *shalom* used 235 times in the Jewish Bible.[34] It occurs at least 2,500 times in classical Jewish literature, reports Rabbi Marc Gopin.[35]

Mercy

Still another close sibling in the same scriptural family is mercy, the virtue that animates the transformation of woundedness. Two Hebrew words are most commonly translated into English as mercy. The first, *hesed*, means "steady love," the kind that involves faithfulness to the requirements of relationships as set forth by a covenant. The meaning of *hesed* is probably broader than "mercy," though it includes it. *Hesed* is characteristic of God, expressing his willingness to restore his people after they have been diminished by the consequences of their sin. Daniel Elazar even calls *hesed* "the operative mechanism of *brit* [covenant]."[36] The second word translated as mercy is *rahamim*, a feminine term denoting the love of a mother for her children and often a willingness to forgive. In scripture, mercy is closely related to justice. An important passage in the book of Micah (6:8) commands followers "[t]o act justly and to love mercy and to walk humbly with your God."[37] As with *shalom*, many other passages also link mercy closely with justice.[38] "The Judaic tradition clearly holds that the demands of human justice and the quality of divine mercy are entirely compatible and even integrally related," argues Louis E. Newman.[39] This link between justice and mercy has important implications for these concepts and for reconciliation. The Jewish scriptures, then, sustain the claim that mercy, far from being an exception to justice or a departure from justice in the way that modern Western philosophers view it, in fact promotes justice. Mercy restores justice and realizes it, and, if justice is much like mercy, then it is a matter of restoring people, relationships, and communities, just like the restorative dimension of reconciliation.

Reconciliation in God's Response to Evil

If justice, peace, and mercy are holistic, made up of diverse sorts of right relationships in diverse settings, so, too, evil involves a thorough negation of right relationship, just as systemic injustices in modern political orders involve comprehensive wrongs among a wide range of parties, wounding people, relationships, and communities in variegated and enduring ways. God's intervention in this cosmic tug-of-war is perhaps the most constant and important theme in scripture. The nature, character, timing, and outcome of this intervention tell us much about God's justice.

Evil is always the violation of a moral law or virtue, but in Jewish scripture, it is also the breaking of the right relationships that the covenant and its laws sustain. It involves idolatry, arrogance, rebellion against God, murder, hatred, lust, adultery, lies, corruption, and neglect of the poor. In the Western philosophical tradition, particularly in the thought of Plotinus, Augustine, and Aquinas, evil is a privation of good, a negation of being.

In Jewish scripture, though, it is something more dramatic, personal, and formidable. The force that destroys good and negates being is a "real and active one," one that takes turf, wins battles, and governs realms, admittedly not permanently but not without inflicting wounds that involve immense suffering, lasting injury, and death—the real destruction of real good.[40] Death, sometimes enormous in scale, plagues and other diseases, drought, famine, earthquakes, lightning, the exile and dispersal of peoples, mass confusion, and a global flood are among the consequences of evil that scripture recounts.

Evil is always the product of human sin, choice, and responsibility. In Jewish scripture it is also something more: It is waged by supernatural, superhuman forces. Scholar of Judaism Jon Levenson makes a case that even in the creation of the world God is doing battle with evil, not creating *ex nihilo* but rather combating an already existing, primordial chaos and darkness. Though God is victorious, he does not abolish the chaos and darkness but rather tames and partitions it. Leviathan is still loose, the seas are still wild, and evil persists, subsequent passages attest. Levenson is careful not to deny that omnipotence is an attribute of God, but, unlike the philosophers' unmoved mover who is constantly in control of the universe, the biblical God's omnipotence is dramatically enacted only from time to time and his final victory is postponed—excruciatingly postponed, from the perspective of biblical writers:[41]

> How long, O Lord, shall I cry out
>   And You not listen,
> Shall I shout to You, "Violence!"
>   And You not save?
> Why do You make me see iniquity
>   [Why] do You look upon wrong? –
> Raiding and violence are before me,
> Strife continues and contention goes on.
> That is why decision fails
> And justice never emerges;
> For the villain hedges in the just man –
> Therefore judgment emerges deformed. (Habbukuk 1:2–4)

"How long?" Several Psalms echo this cry.[42] "The possibility of an interruption of God's faithfulness is indeed troubling, and I repeat that I have ventured no explanation for it," Levenson writes. "I might add that I find it especially odd that scholars who lived through the years of the Holocaust and other unspeakable horrors of our century should have imagined that the Jewish Bible consistently upheld a doctrine of God's uniform, uninterrupted kingship, in spite of ample textual evidence to the contrary."[43]

Philosopher Susan Neiman has argued that the problem of evil has been the guiding force of modern thought from Voltaire, Jean-Jacques Rousseau, and Immanuel Kant, through G.W.F. Hegel, Karl Marx, and Friedrich Nietzsche, on to such twentieth-century philosophers as Hannah Arendt, Theodor W. Adorno, and Jean Améry.[44] How can a good and all-powerful God allow evil? Does evil serve any coherent purpose? Does it contain any meaning? Is there a coherent human response to evil? Neiman, though, omits theological or scriptural sources, either premodern or in dialogue with the modern.[45] What can be found in these sources is an approach to the problem of evil that differs sharply from modern philosophers'. The Jewish scriptures offer no overarching explanation; God does not even provide one to Job. Rather they portray God as offering an active response to evil. This is what God's people ask for. "A point usually overlooked in discussions of theodicy in a biblical context," writes Levenson, "[is] the overwhelming tendency of biblical writers as they confront undeserved evil . . . not to *explain* it away but to call upon God to *blast* it away."[46]

God's response to evil is nothing other than the restoration of his covenant—in keeping with his promises, according to his character. The character of this response is complex and sometimes includes irrevocable, overwhelming punishment. Yet over time, with respect to the corporate people of Israel, God's response is restorative. God renews the world after the great flood in Genesis and promises Noah that he will never again destroy the earth. Following the flood, the tower of Babel, and the punishments that they incurred, God makes a covenant with Abraham, promising blessing for his descendants and for all the nations. Saying "I have heard my people's cry," God delivers the Israelites from slavery in Egypt (Exodus 3:7). He restores the Israelites after they build and worship a golden calf. The books of Daniel, Hosea, Job, and several others also contain dramatic descriptions of God restoring his people after they have turned away from him or suffered at the hands of others. It is in the coming of the messiah—expressed strongest in postexilic scriptures—that Jews expect that the covenant will be restored completely and permanently. Just as the wounds of evil are real and lasting, restoration is always a real victory, involving the actual transformation of persons, relationships, and communities—the idea behind restorative justice.

Rabbi Irving Greenberg associates God's restoration of his covenant with *tikkun olam*, a term that appears in Jewish tradition but not in the Tanakh, which he translates as "perfecting the world" and which others have translated as "repairing the universe."[47] The scriptures describe this repair through a succession of metaphors: return to the land; return from exile; a guarantee of life; freedom for prisoners and the oppressed; sight for the blind; comfort for the poor, the widow, and the orphan; defeat of the wicked; and even a restoration of the natural world, where darkness turns to light, dry ground springs up with fertility, thornbushes and nettles turn to cypress and myrtle, and crooked highways are made straight.

"The answer to the suffering of the innocent is a renewal of activity on the part of the God of justice," Levenson writes.[48] The scriptures describe God's renewal of his covenant as justice itself—the restoration of justice. The book of Isaiah (45:8) compares justice with dew and gentle rain, implying renewal, while in Amos (5:24) the waters of justice accumulate to a mighty stream of righteousness, restoring, cleansing, and giving life. The restorative, reconciling concept of justice is perhaps clearest of all in Second Isaiah (roughly books 40 through 60), set in the time of Israel's Babylonian exile, which is its punishment for idolatry, immorality, and indifferent ear to God's call for return. The central theme of the text is God's comprehensive restoration, ultimately through a messianic "suffering servant"—a restoration described again and again through the term *justice,* translated from both *sedeqah* and *mishpat.* Justice, in this section of scripture, is often linked to salvation. One passage reads: "There is no just and saving God but me."[49] What kind of justice, other than restorative justice, could be saving? Several of the relevant terms come together in Hosea (2:21), where, in response to Israel's faithfulness, God makes an intimate promise: "And I will espouse you forever: I will espouse you with righteousness [*sedeq*] and justice [*mishpat*], and with goodness [*hesed*] and mercy [*rahamin*]."

If God's restorative justice is his active response to evil, he enacts this justice not in a singular way but through an array of actions, corresponding to the multiple respects in which evil wounds persons, relationships, and communities—much like the practices of political reconciliation.

Justice in the Jewish Political Community

By keeping the law and, more broadly, living righteously, humans participate in God's justice and hasten God's restoration of justice, ultimately through the messiah. The justice of right relationship is in good part realized through the community's laws and political institutions. For over four centuries these institutions took the form of the Davidic monarchy. In the more than two millennia from the Babylonian exile (597 BCE) until the founding of the modern Israeli state (1948 CE), Jews had to interpret justice and righteousness in a milieu in which they no longer lived under their own sovereign king or government. After the exile, the Jews who returned to Israel lived largely under foreign rule while other Jews lived outside Israel altogether. Then, after the Roman Empire conquered Jerusalem in 70 CE and 135 CE, the Jews became wholly a diasporic people. Even in diaspora, though, during which the Jews were subject to systematic persecutions, they governed themselves as a community and incorporated practices of reconciliation into their common life. Maimonides, for instance, explicated and codified a long tradition of practicing *teshuva*, meaning "repentance," "returning," or "turning toward." As Gopin explains, "[t]here is a covenantal mutuality built into the concept of *teshuva*, and it applies to both the human/divine form of *teshuva* and to the interhuman process of *teshuva* for wrongs done and relationships broken." An interconnected set of practices of reconciliation, *teshuva* involves four stages: 1) restitution; 2) the deep expression of remorse; 3) confession; and 4) the wrongdoer's commitment to change in the future. Gopin believes that forgiveness can be incorporated into *teshuva* as well.[50] Thus, it begins to resemble the practices of political reconciliation.

Whether the founding of an official Jewish state in modern Israel ended the Jewish people's long exile is debated among Jews.[51] This founding did not re-establish the Davidic kingship or the Sanhedrin but rather created a modern constitutional democracy that is governed by Jewish law only in a few areas including marriage, burial, Sabbath practices, and immigration. Jewish ethicists, though, find strong reasons to bring the logic of Jewish scripture and tradition to the law and politics of the modern state, whether it is Israel or a state where Jews live in diaspora. In his book *Covenantal Rights*, scholar of Jewish thought David Novak offers a Jewish defense of the concept of rights both to other Jews as well as to "current political discourse in general," which he believes can benefit from a Jewish perspective.[52]

Novak's defense of rights demonstrates that Jews can endorse—and join an overlapping consensus on—what the ethic of political reconciliation envisions as the central moral and political obligation of modern states. Although no word for human rights is found in the Jewish scriptures or in any ancient Jewish text, the concept of human rights can be found in the scriptures, he argues. He sees rights as correlative to duties. "A duty," he writes, "is something I basically owe to someone else. Hence that person has a right to expect performance of my duty..." In Judaism, duties, in turn, are set forth by God through commandments. To be created in the image of God, according to Novak, is to be the kind of being who performs God's commandments. Some of God's commands are universal. That is, they prescribe duties that Jews owe to all other human beings and that all human beings owe to one another. These duties imply human rights. The Jewish Bible thus offers a rationale for the place of rights in political orders—all political orders, whether or not they are officially Jewish, whether they are ancient or modern.[53]

Are there Jewish scholars who envision the broader incorporation of reconciliation into the modern state? This is the life's work of Rabbi Gopin. "I wonder how powerful a *teshuva* apology process could be on a much larger scale, involving massive injury, murder, or genocide," he writes. He retrieves many other Jewish concepts for peacebuilding and reconciliation in modern politics as well: *aveilus* (mourning), forbearance toward the enemy, the centrality of social justice, and the role of honor, shame, and dignity. In today's Middle East, Gopin argues, Jews as well as Christians and Muslims cannot afford to ignore the peacebuilding potential of traditional religious concepts. His project is to graft these dormant concepts onto the politics of the state—much like the project of political reconciliation. [54]

Yet the problem, Gopin writes, is that "the post-Holocaust scholarly Jewish community has not been much in the mood to mine the sources of Judaism for conflict resolution, especially with gentiles."[55] Is it appropriate to look to the Jewish tradition for an ethic of peacebuilding after Auschwitz? Of the Holocaust, Jewish philosophers and theologians have said variously: God abandoned his covenant, was inexplicably absent, was all knowing but not all powerful, called Jews to suffer for the world, ceased to exist, or was judging Jews for anti-Zionism, for Zionism, or for socialism. Has anyone argued, though, that God was faithful to his covenant?

In his book *To Mend the World*, Rabbi Emil Fackenheim claims that the Holocaust was a rupture like none before, including the destruction of Jerusalem in 70 CE and the Babylonian exile. It was a rupture to all forms of thinking, an event that exceeds the power of historians, sociologists, psychologists, philosophers, and theologians to explain. Fackenheim nonetheless identifies a source of hope that rescues humanity from resignation to meaninglessness: the response of some of the victims. Here he mirrors the idea that God's response to evil is action, not explanation. After describing the atrocities of the concentration camps in merciless detail—Fackenheim was interned in the concentration camp at Sachsenhausen for a short time and his older brother was killed in the Holocaust—he tells of Jews who found strength to resist in some way: Pregnant women who gave birth in the camps, Hasidim who sold precious bread to buy a pair of *tefillin* (objects for prayer), the participants in the Warsaw uprising, and Pelagia Lewinska, an inmate of Auschwitz who simply "felt under orders to live" and to "hold on to my dignity." Fackenheim does not gauge the numbers of such people, present them as representative, or portray their resistance as successful in any material sense. Yet Fackenheim marvels at these performances of the mitzvah *kiddush ha-hayyim*, or sanctifying life. "In an *Unwelt* whose sole ultimate self-expression is a system of humiliation, torture, and murder, the maintenance by victims of a shred of humanity is not merely the basis of resistance but already part of it. In such a world...life does not need to be sanctified: it is already holy." He interprets these instances of resistance as examples of *tikkun*, moves toward mending the world in the middle of a great rupture.[56]

Because *tikkun* was actual then, it is both possible and mandatory today. Further, he argues, Jews may seek *tikkun* with Gentiles, because Gentiles, too, if only a few of them, practiced *tikkun* through resistance. *Tikkun* is even a message for the whole world—*tikkun olam*. In the present, any *tikkun* can only amount to a fragmentary return, but it is a moral necessity to seek it, one that arises from the responses that the rupture could not conquer. These responses point to God: "Did an absolute transcendence *not* become real in the midst of that time and on behalf of our humanity? Heaven forbid that we should say any such thing!" Though it may exceed what Fackenheim wants to claim, it is in the spirit of the present argument to say that these responses were enabled by and are signs of what no less a figure than Pope John Paul II, in his visit to the Great Synagogue of Rome in 1986, called the "irrevocable covenant" between God and the Jews.[57]

8

Reconciliation in the Christian Tradition

THE PHRASE *IRREVOCABLE covenant* comes from the Apostle Paul, who, in his letter to the Romans, compares Gentile followers of Jesus Christ to a "wild olive shoot" that is grafted onto the "holy root" of Israel.[1] The metaphor connotes continuity—consistency, development, an organic connection—and raises a possibility that is highly relevant to the project at hand: that the concept of justice found in the Jewish scriptures will resurface in the New Testament. But does not discontinuity, departure, and cleft arise in the same letter through Paul's teaching that justification—being made just, that is—depends on the believer's faith in Jesus Christ?

Although the New Testament is both discontinuous and continuous with the Jewish scriptures (Old Testament), here, in our search for overlapping consensus, the emphasis is on commonality. The justice that Jesus Christ brings, announces, accomplishes, and embodies—in the startling assertion of some theologians, Jesus Christ even *is* justice—strongly resembles the justice that an ethic of political reconciliation proposes, which in turn strongly resembles justice as found in the Jewish scriptures. The Gospels of the New Testament identify Jesus as the fulfillment of Second Isaiah's prophecy of the suffering servant—the apex of this long narration of God's restoration of justice. The servant "brings justice to victory," the Gospel of Matthew says, quoting directly from Second Isaiah.[2] New Testament scholar N. T. Wright reflects on Second Isaiah as well:

> God's justice is a saving, healing, restorative justice, because the God to whom justice belongs is the Creator God who has yet to complete his

original plan for creation and whose justice is designed not simply to restore balance to a world out of kilter but to bring to glorious completion and fruition the creation, teeming with life and possibility, that he made in the first place.[3]

Wright proceeds to describe how Jesus Christ embodies the same saving, restorative justice. It is a justice that restores right relationships, is animated by mercy, and culminates in a holistic state of right relationship—the New Testament concept of peace. It is a response to evil through which God both sustains his covenant and establishes a new covenant in Jesus Christ.

Reconciliation, Justice, and Righteousness in the New Testament

Reconciliation is "the heart of the Christian message" theologian John de Gruchy declares. While most translations of the Old Testament omit the word, most New Testament translations contain some fifteen instances of *reconciliation* or *reconcile*, derived from the Greek *katallage* and *katallosso*. Twelve of these instances appear in the letters of Paul, who deploys reconciliation as his central metaphor for expounding the Christian gospel and was in turn pivotal in making reconciliation a central concept for the early church, as de Gruchy argues.[4] The two Greek terms can mean either an exchange of goods or money or a transformation of enmity and alienation between persons into a state of friendship and peace—that is, right relationship.[5] Both of these meanings converge in the New Testament, which describes God exchanging places with humanity, taking humans' sin upon himself, and defeating it through his death on the cross, thereby freeing humanity to enjoy right relationship with God and with one another. To this dynamic of exchange and transformation, Eastern Christianity has given the term *divinization*: "God became man so that we might become God," Athanasius summarized it in the fourth century C.E. Exchange and transformation are pivotal, too, in Paul's most developed passage on reconciliation, in his Second Letter to the Corinthians. God "reconciled us to himself in Christ" and "gave us the ministry of reconciliation," a conferral that renders "whoever is in Christ" a "new creation." He closes the passage with "[f]or our sake he made him to be sin who did not know sin, so that we might become the righteousness of God in him," a statement that brings together God's change of place with humanity, transformation ("become"), and, finally, the word that performs the crucial link between reconciliation and justice: *righteousness*.[6]

The New Testament Greek word *dikaiosunē* follows the pattern of the Old Testament Hebrew words *sedeqah* and *mishpat*: It translates into both "justice" and "righteousness." As theologian Christopher D. Marshall explains, in the New Testament the whole family of Greek words that begin with *dik-* (*dikaioō, dikaiōma, dikaiōs, dikaiōsis, dikaiokrisia, dikaios*) commonly translate into the family of English words that begin with *just* (justice, to justify, justly, righteous judgment, and acquittal, which relates to justice) as well as the family of English words that draw on *right* (righteous, righteousness, rectify, requirement, uprightly).[7] The Septuagint, the third-century BCE translation of the Jewish Bible into Greek, uses *dik-* words to translate *sedeqah* and *mishpat*. In the New Testament, too, then, restoration of right relationship is equivalent to restoration of justice. In the letters of Paul, the link between these restorations and reconciliation is made explicit.

To describe the process by which God restores, Paul often uses *dik-* words, most frequently of all, *dikaiosunē*. Words in this family appear sixty-three times in his Letter to the Romans alone. Many of these instances in many translations are rendered as "righteousness," as in the important phrase *the righteousness of God*. Paul also makes righteousness the focus of his more than fifty quotations from the Old Testament in Romans, thus bringing forth into the New Testament the term's meaning in Jewish scripture: a comprehensive right relationship that reflects God's covenants.[8]

Dik- words also express another central concept for Paul, justification. He devotes much of Romans to explaining how justification occurs through Christ's atoning sacrifice on the cross. Because of Adam's act of idolatry, one that subsequent generations have mimicked repeatedly and continuously, all of humanity, Jews and Gentiles alike, is under the power of sin, a debt that it cannot repay, an enslavement from which it cannot break free, whose consequence, or "wages," is death.[9] Keeping the law cannot free humanity from this predicament, Paul stresses. All are guilty and thereby captive to sin. God, then, became man in Jesus Christ, a second Adam who represents all of humanity, and through the suffering of the cross and the resurrection took the curse of sin upon himself, paid humanity's debt, and freed it from the burden of guilt. Through faith, the believer can access this freeing victory, thus becoming justified.[10]

To explain what God has done, Paul uses the language of justice. Admittedly he frequently uses the metaphor of the courtroom, where God pardons the sinner, declaring him not guilty.[11] Clearly a pardon from deserved punishment is one part of how Paul understands the atonement. Considered alone, however, in isolation from the dozens of other images and locutions through which Paul describes justification, the courtroom image is deficient.[12] What it does not explain is that God's justification not only declares but also makes the sinner just. Even God's acquittal is not of the usual sort, merely declaring the prisoner not guilty. Rather, as Bible scholar John Haughey, S.J., writes:

> Not only does God declare persons who deserve the sentence of "guilty" to be declared innocent, but he makes them innocent. Their acquittal does not remain something extrinsic to them as if only their records were tampered with. The acquittal given by God transforms persons at the deepest level of their being. They become "justified."[13]

This transformation occurs because God breaks the enslavement of sin, evil, and death and restores those who were under these powers to the right relationship of God's covenant—a Hebrew concept of justice. "At issue," summarizes Colin Gunton, "is the actuality of atonement: whether the real evil of the real world is faced and healed *ontologically* in the life, death, and resurrection of Jesus."[14]

Such a Jewish meaning informs Paul's use of *just* words. Theologian Kathryn Tanner offers a mini-lexicon of these words based on Old Testament covenantal definitions: "[t]o *justify* someone is to restore that person to his or her proper or rightful place within the relationship, and thereby it involves the restoration or reconstitution of the relationship itself." Likewise, "*[j]ustice* is that way of life...set down by Yahweh, by which Israel is to exhibit its faithfulness to the covenant." Then, to "*do justice* [is to] meet the expectations and demands of the relationship that Yahweh establishes with it." Finally, "to *pronounce judgment* is to act to sustain the justice that this relationship requires."[15] All of these definitions point to the relational character of justice. In Romans as well as Paul's other letters, he enumerates the effects that justification brings: freedom from sin, law, and death (Romans 6–8), the defeat of death (1 Corinthians 15), enslavement to righteousness (Romans 6:18), deliverance from evil (Galatians 1:4), newness of life (Romans 6:4), and much more. Justification comes to its greatest climax, Wright claims, in

Romans 8, where all of creation is renewed and restored.[16] Justification bears communal fruits as well: concern for the weak and the poor, peace and harmony, the mutual bearing of burdens.[17] These achievements of justification, though, are not yet consummated, for evil will not be finally defeated until the last day. What is important in all of this is that justice is actually restorative. For Gunton, the justice of God is "the transformation of the whole created order, as the outcome...of God's loyalty to his creation."[18]

Jesus's redemptive work is itself a demonstration of divine justice. It is in this sense that some theologians identify Jesus himself as actually being the justice of God.[19] Paul speaks of this in his First Letter to the Corinthians when he says that "[Jesus Christ] *became* for us wisdom from God, as well as righteousness, sanctification, and redemption."[20] In this verse, righteousness is translated from *dikaiosunē*, which can, of course, also mean justice. Jesus's justice is also reconciliation. " '[J]ustification'...links [Paul's] understanding of reconciliation directly to God's justice," writes De Gruchy.[21] Reconciliation is the justice that restores right relationships. In his several uses of reconciliation, Paul links it with being "saved by his life" (Romans 5:10), with "peace," and with the destruction of the "dividing wall of enmity" (Ephesians 2:14). Most sweepingly, the Letter to the Colossians says that "all things" are reconciled through Christ, bringing "peace."[22] Most directly, Paul claims in his Second Letter to the Corinthians that, through reconciliation, humans may *become* the *dikaiosunē* (righteousness/justice) of God.[23]

Mercy and Peace in the Language of the New Testament

Just as John de Gruchy announces that reconciliation is the "heart of the Christian message," Pope John Paul II declares in his encyclical *Dives in Misericordia* that "mercy constitutes the fundamental content of the messianic message of Christ and the constitutive power of his mission." Are these claims to centrality incompatible? Not if mercy is the virtue that animates the restoration of right relationships and, hence, reconciliation. In the New Testament, the Greek word for mercy is *eleos*, which translates the Hebrew *hesed*. For John Paul II, mercy is "manifested in its true and proper aspect when it restores to value, promotes and draws good from all the forms of evil existing in the world and in man"—very much the definition of the virtue that animates political reconciliation. At places, John Paul II refers to justice and mercy as being different but complementary. By justice, he often seems to mean equality, rights, just distribution, and deserved punishment—that is, justice as "due"—which he then argues needs to be "corrected" and tempered by mercy. Jesus's sacrifice on the cross, he argues, effects justice by compensating for the sins of humanity but also reveals mercy by restoring man to right relationship, rooted in love, with God and other humans. At times, though, he writes of an even more intimate relationship between mercy and justice, holding that mercy "accomplishes" the justice that in the Old Testament comes to mean salvation, that both mercy and justice "manifest" the love of God, that mercy "restore[s] justice in the sense of that salvific order which God willed from the beginning in man and, through man, in the world," that mercy "reveals the perfection of justice" and "has the power to confer on justice a new content," and that mercy is "the most profound source of justice" and "the most perfect incarnation of justice." Christ himself, he writes, "in a certain sense, is mercy."[24] It is this more intimate compatibility between mercy and justice for which Tanner argues. In Christian justification, mercy and justice are no longer merely juxtaposed but "woven together" and "brought to bear on one another to produce a radically altered sense of both but especially a radically altered sense of justice." It is the covenantal, relational model of justice and righteousness that makes this convergence possible. Mercy is God's refusal to break off covenantal relations with his people, as they deserve, but is also his will to restore them to right relationship. Mercy can even motivate the justice of punishment, Tanner argues, if mercy is understood as an action that upholds the right relationships of the covenant.[25]

In the New Testament, righteousness, justice, and mercy converge to describe the process by which God reconciles his people to himself and then calls his people to reconcile with one another. Two other New Testament concepts describe the state of right relationship that results from this reconciliation: the kingdom of God and peace. Adding another bead to the string of claims about what is central to the Gospel—and without contradiction, for this one coheres with those that de Gruchy and John Paul II stress—Marshall proposes that the "central burden of Jesus' ministry" is the kingdom of God.[26] Scholars differ over exactly what the kingdom of God means, but if we see it as a reign, then we can think of it as the realm of people who live under Jesus's rule according to the ways in which he calls them to live. The kingdom is both a present reality—something "at hand" (Matthew 4:17, Mark 1:15), but also something not yet made complete: "May your kingdom come," Jesus teaches his disciples to pray (Matthew 6:10).[27] In quoting Jesus as saying "[s]eek first the kingdom of God and his righteousness [*dikaiosunē*]," Matthew links the kingdom of God with righteousness and justice and gives it primacy in the message of Jesus's followers. In several other instances, Matthew connects the kingdom with righteousness or right behavior. Righteousness in the New Testament encompasses social justice, similar to the way in which Moshe Weinfeld argues that "righteousness and justice" is a social concept in the Jewish scriptures. In Luke 4, Jesus inaugurates his ministry by announcing a mission of liberation for the poor, the captives, the blind, and the oppressed and refers to the Jubilee year, all themes of social justice that he reiterates many times. The kingdom involves a "radical restoration of God's justice," summarizes Richard Hays.[28]

Still another claim about what is central to the Christian gospel can be made, this one coming from theologian Ulrich Mauser. "The life story of Jesus can be summarized in the phrase 'good news of peace' (Acts 10:36)," he writes.[29] This claim to centrality can also be made without contradicting the others. As with justice, peace is a quality that the Letter to the Ephesians identifies with Christ: "He is our peace."[30] *Eirene*, the New Testament word for "peace," is the Greek translation of *shalom*, and thus carries forth *shalom's* holism and comprehensiveness. Mauser writes:

> Peace, in both the Old and New Testament, is a condition reaching into almost any aspect of human life, communally or individually considered. It is at stake in basic issues of material welfare; it comes to life in physical health; it is expressed in justice and good order; it cannot thrive except in a climate of serious social concern; it provides a home for success and prosperity; it becomes synonymous with salvation; and it is also necessarily linked to harmony and good understanding in international relations.[31]

The Gospels of Matthew and Luke associate *eirene* with events and concepts that entail holistic right relationship: the kingdom of God, the healing of the sick, and forgiveness. The letters of Paul associate peace with the reconciliation—and, hence, justice—that Christ accomplishes on the cross. In the passage in Ephesians in which Christ is declared "our peace," peace is mentioned three other times and linked with the reconciliation that Christ effects between Jews and Gentiles.[32] The Letter to the Colossians presents a poem that recounts God being pleased, through Christ, "to reconcile all things...making peace by the blood of his cross."³³ "All things," states an earlier verse, include "thrones," "dominions," "principalities," and "powers," which were both created and reconciled in Christ.

An analysis of New Testament terms, then, reveals that the reconciliation that comes through the life, death, and resurrection of Jesus Christ is a comprehensive restoration of humanity to a state of right relationship, a work of justice that is closely linked with mercy, peace, and the kingdom of God. Though the terms do not carry identical meanings, each converges so closely with God's work of reconciliation in Christ that any of them can justifiably claim to express the central theme of the Gospel story.

God's Response to Evil Through Jesus Christ

In the New Testament, as in the Old Testament, God responds to evil mainly with action, not explanation.³⁴ In Jesus Christ, God brings restoration to woundedness: standing in solidarity with and bringing healing to victims; judging and defeating evil; calling sinners to repent and be restored; forgiving; and renewing all creation, including its political orders. These many parts of restoration all reflect the justice—and peace and mercy—that is achieved through God's work of reconciliation.

Most important for our purposes are several of Jesus's actions, teachings, and parables depicting God restoring of his own initiative, without demanding prior punishment or payment, so as to transform the one restored. The Gospel of Luke features a series of restorative parables in its fifteenth chapter, beginning with the shepherd who rejoices in finding the one lost sheep he left behind ninety-nine others to seek, followed by the woman who similarly exults in finding the one lost coin for which she scoured her home, culminating in the famous parable of the prodigal son, who, after squandering his inheritance and desperately deciding to turn home, is welcomed by his father, who runs to embrace him and prepares a feast for him. When the older son protests his own failure to receive a feast despite his faithfulness, his father reassures him that "everything I have is yours" but insists that "now we must celebrate and rejoice, because your brother was dead and has come to life again; he was lost and has been found." In the Gospel of Matthew, Jesus likens the kingdom of God to a king who forgives the unbearable debt of a servant who, in turn, refuses to forgive the debt of a fellow servant, thus incurring the king's lasting punishment.³⁵ In the Gospel of John, Jesus saves an adulterous woman from a judicial sentence of death by stoning at the hands of scribes and Pharisees, then tells her to go and sin no more.[36] In these and other Gospels, he heals people from debilitating illness, forgives their sins, and raises Lazarus from the dead.

The restorative justice of Jesus culminates in his death and resurrection: "[H]is entire preaching, beginning with the manifesto of the Sermon on the Mount, has that 'hour' as its goal, not only ethically but theologically," remarks theologian Hans Urs von Balthasar.[37] Over the centuries, Christian theologians have reflected on this hour and its meaning using a variety of theories, metaphors, models, and doctrines. We must beware what theologian H. A. Hodges called the "tyranny of the theories," which can trap us in logical systems that are themselves dwarfed by the "hour's" own depth of mystery.[38] Neither the Catholic Church, the Orthodox Church, nor most mainline Protestant churches have proclaimed any single official theory of the atonement or reconciliation. Rather than theories, Gunton argues, we understand God's reconciling work best through metaphors, none of which captures the entire mystery but the most apt of which depict an important dimension of it: "[W]ith the metaphors of the atonement we propose to refer to the action of God by the use of words which are customarily used to refer to something else."[39]

Paul used several metaphors to describe the atonement. The author of the Letter to the Hebrews uses the image of sacrifice rituals. The church fathers of the first millennium adopted victory, as in a battle, as their prevalent metaphor. Connoting the crushing stranglehold of sin, evil, and death and the even more dramatic and thorough unshackling and restoration accomplished by God, the victory image serves the construction of an ethic of political reconciliation particularly well. St. Athanasius conveyed it most enduringly in his treatise, *On the Incarnation*, of roughly 318 CE; other churchmen such as the second-century figure Irenaeus of Lyons also expressed it vividly. In choosing to sin, Athanasius's account runs, humans become separated from God, in whom they enjoy happiness and flourishing, and come under the dominion of sin, the powers of this world, and, as the early church fathers often stressed, the devil himself. This captivity involves corruption that leads to death. Such corruption is thorough, Athanasius describes, infecting even cities and nations through war and division. It is a condition from which humans cannot escape through their own efforts, even through repentance.[40]

God has a dilemma, explains Athanasius. It is unworthy of him, contrary to his honor, that his creation should be destroyed. Yet God must also be true to his word that death is the consequence of sin and abolish the actuality of death and corruption in order to re-create the world. God's solution is an exchange. Out of love, at his own initiative, he entered the world through the corporeal body of his son, and in solidarity with humanity he took on and abolished death. It is to describe this idea that the early fathers, perhaps others more so than Athanasius, use the language of battle, especially with the devil. Athanasius echoes the scriptural language of Christ paying a penalty, making a sacrifice, and becoming a ransom and a curse but uses it to describe the price that Christ paid to defeat death, "trampling death by death," in the words of an Eastern Orthodox hymn. Christ is not making a payment or sacrifice to God the Father. By the same act, though, Christ restored "the whole nature of man" and gave people the hope of resurrection. Other church fathers stress all the more strongly the thoroughness of this restoration. Irenaeus uses the term *recapitulation* to describe the restoration and perfection of the entire creation, including society and nature.[41]

It was Anselm's *Cur Deus Homo* ("Why God Became Man") that decisively diverged from interpreting Christ's death and resurrection as a restorative victory and inaugurated several centuries of interpretation of these events in harsh, abstract, legalized, transactional, calculating, retributive terms. Or so runs the charge leveled by his most vituperative critics, beginning immediately with Anselm's contemporary Peter Abelard, continuing through latter-day feminist and liberation theologians, and resonating in the assaults of centuries of Eastern Orthodox theologians. Today, Anselm has begun to make a comeback. More recent theologians have reinterpreted him as being less retributivist and more restorative, more consistent with such church fathers as Athanasius and Irenaeus, than his venerable line of critics have made him out to be.[42]

Cur Deus Homo was one of the first attempts to systematize the atonement into a theory.[43] Anselm sought to explain through reason, rather than through scripture, why God became human. Every rational being was created by God for happiness, Anselm argues, and this requires obedience. Disobedience, or sin, is a failure to render to God what is his due and thus dishonors him. Justice requires that humanity restore this honor. Were God simply to remit the penalty for dishonor, he would be compromising his own justice—eliding distinctions between the guilty and the innocent and failing actually to remove the sin that creates disorder. Yet humanity, whose sin is an infinite offense, cannot satisfy God's justice. God, though, is able to satisfy justice, either through restoration or through punishment. Since his goodness and honor demand that he be faithful to the purposes of his creation, he mercifully chooses restoration. So that humanity can restore honor, God graciously becomes human, all the while retaining his divinity. By surrendering his infinitely valuable life, Christ renders satisfaction. God is then willing to remit the debts of humanity. Humanity can take part in salvation by approaching God through Christ, especially in the sacrament of the Eucharist.[44]

Unquestionably, Anselm's account is more legalistic than Athanasius's. Justice means that when humans have defaulted on their obligations, they must provide satisfaction either through a penalty or another means of compensation. God remits debt only when Christ renders satisfaction. There seems to be little sense here of Christ acting in solidarity with humanity. Yet Anselm is more interested in restoration of right relationship than his detractors have allowed. God's honor, a central idea for Anselm, means his commitment to upholding the *ordo universi*, that is, the beauty, order, and design of the universe, including its social structures. Honor is not so different from right relationship. Justice, the restoration of honor, is the restoration of this *ordo*—right relationship—just as satisfaction is making right what sin has disintegrated. The God who chooses restoration out of his character, purposes, and loving initiative is a God who is faithful to his covenant.[45] Anselm holds that God's son paid humanity's debt but he never asserts that the Son paid this debt directly to the Father or that the Father demands such a payment from his Son. Rather, Christ dies out of obedience to the Father and renders his death as a gift to the Father. Because Christ's life is infinite in value, it exceeds all of humanity's debt. It is upon accepting the gift that the Father remits this debt. Christ, then, renders satisfaction and makes a sacrifice, but it is a payment that at the same time restores. For Anselm, mercy and justice converge in much the way that Tanner suggests. God is merciful in his willingness to restore; in restoring, he satisfies justice—a holistic recapitulation.

It was Anselm's successors whose views far better fit the description of legalistic, transactional, and retributive, and far more squarely departed from the victory metaphor. Building on the legal elements and propensity for systemization in Anselm's thought, they developed from it something quite different—what has come to be known as the penal substitution theory of the atonement. Protestant reformers developed the theory most starkly. Some of its defining themes can be found in the thought of Martin Luther. The theory grows louder in the works of John Calvin and especially in his chain of successors, who have influenced Protestant theology and indeed criminal justice in England, the United States, and elsewhere. Today, the penal substitution theory remains "one of the main bastions of . . . orthodoxy" among many Protestant Christians.[46]

In holding that sin incurs a penalty, a debt, and alienation from God and that God pays this debt and overcomes this condition through his Son, Jesus Christ, penal substitutionists differ little in their thinking from Anselm and the early church fathers. It is the logic behind this action that they understand differently. Two broad themes in the thought of the fathers of the Reformation help pave the way for a justice that is mostly payment and hardly at all restoration.

The first theme is found strongest in the thought of Martin Luther: that God's justification of humanity is an act completely separate from God's sanctification—or actual restoration—of humanity. Contrary to Athanasius, for whom the same atoning act both defeats sin and restores humanity to life, Luther taught that justification is solely to be thought of as God's imputation of righteousness to the sinner, a verdict of not guilty that the sinner can receive through his confession of faith alone. Justification, then, is a legal declaration, not a transformation of the order of God's creation and covenant. True, Luther's gospel is not without restoration. It is only apart from and following justification, though, that God is willing to restore and sanctify humanity. Justification and sanctification, then, are distinct processes. If justification is God's justice then we are left with a notion of justice that involves no restoration.[47]

The second theme, also a departure from previous tradition, is the claim, especially strong in John Calvin, that Christ himself is punished for humanity's sin at the hands of God the Father. Recall that Anselm thought that God faced a choice between punishment and satisfaction and chose the latter. Calvin, though, held that God the Father actually imputes humanity's guilty verdict to his Son, Jesus Christ, and that this transfer is the condition of humanity's acquittal. Calvinists stress that God has become angry with humanity, an enemy of humanity, and cannot accept humanity in its sin. Only Christ's expiatory death appeases him, placates him, and changes his mind.[48] God the Father does not send his Son on a restorative mission so much as he waits with arms folded until the penalty for sin is paid before taking any restorative action. This view, however, is difficult to support through scripture, despite the reformer's insistence on "scripture alone." Though some English translations refer to Christ's death with the terms *propitiation* and *expiation*, several others do not use these terms at all, and none describes this action as Jesus paying a penalty that God the Father demands from him or inflicts on him.[49] True, Paul makes clear that sin carries the penalty of death for humanity and that Jesus suffered that penalty.[50] This is different, however, from saying that Jesus bore punishment from God. As Marshall explains:

> Christ suffers the penalty of sin not because God transfers our punishment onto him as substitute victim but because Christ fully and freely identifies himself with the plight and destiny of sinful humanity under the reign of death and pays the price for doing so. The thought is not one of legal imputation of guilt to Christ but of Christ's solidarity with humanity in its shameful and culpable situation. Christ takes our guilt in the sense that, as our "representative substitute," he accepts the deadly consequences of our guilt...

Rather than "penal substitution," redemptive solidarity—a far more restorative concept—best sums up atonement, Marshall argues.[51] The loving initiative through which God the Father sends his Son to redeem humanity is also worth stressing. Such active agency is expressed in many scriptures, most poignantly in the parables of Luke 15 involving the shepherd, the coin seeker, and the father of the prodigal son. It can be found in the letters of Paul, who continually stresses God's initiative in restoration: "But God demonstrates his own love for us in this: While we were still sinners, Christ died for us."[52]

In fairness, Calvin's writings are complex and also contain passages that moderate these tendencies. For instance, he also writes of the cross as the initiative of God, of Christ's victory over death, and Christ's donation of righteousness to the believer. Yet despite the leavening effect of these passages, they are hard to reconcile with the passages that define justification as involving much in terms of payment and little of restoration. Nor is the argument here an indictment of all Protestant thought on justification, justice, and atonement. Earlier in the chapter I drew heavily on Protestant theologians to make the case for reconciliation as a concept of justice in Christian theology, and shortly I shall go on to describe the rise of theologies of political reconciliation in the twentieth century, many of which are Protestant. It remains the case, though, that the reformers' articulation of justification as declared, imputed righteousness influenced ensuing generations of Protestants.

As long as atonement theorists have followed Anselm in his legal turn, so too have critics answered with softer, more irenic models that do away with satisfaction, appeasement, expiation, and blood payments and reconceptualize Christ's life and death as an example of sacrificial love. Peter Abelard responded thus to Anselm, as did sixteenth-century Italian theologian Faustus Socinus to the Calvinists of his day, as did many others, energizing debates over theology and criminal law well into the twentieth century.[53] What these critiques rightfully stress is the power of the cross to inspire and shape persons and societies. Exemplary approaches, however, hardly encourage a restorative ethic of political reconciliation either. They lack the actual decisive, victorious, response to evil on which such an ethic is built.

Far more promising is the twentieth-century revival of thinking akin to the early church's victory approach, with an encouraging twist: a more explicit application to the social and political realm. De Gruchy traces the rise of modern theologies whose understanding of justification and atonement includes the transformation and reconciliation of political orders. In the 1870s, German theologian Albrecht Ritschl argued for Christ's reconciliation as an effective transformation of the world. Reacting to the sulfurous carnage of World War I, scandalized by the complicity of modern theologians in the cultures of nationalism that bred its battles, theologians such as Scotland's P. T. Forsyth and Switzerland's Karl Barth rejected Ritschl's optimistic liberal theology but adopted the idea that Christ's justification begets the transformation and reconciliation of political orders. Barth came to believe that the Christian gospel was a source of analogous principles for politics.[54] He even saw the state as an order of reconciliation. Out of these convictions, he became one of the few Christian leaders to speak out against Germany's Nazi government and because of that was forced to resign his academic chair in Germany and return to his native Switzerland. German theologian Dietrich Bonhoeffer reasoned along similar lines about reconciliation; he, too, opposed the Nazi government and was eventually executed for his complicity in a plot to kill Hitler. Other theologians of the mid-twentieth century also held that salvation involved political reconciliation, including the Czech scholar Jan Milic Lochman, whose ideas influenced the struggle against apartheid in South Africa.[55]

All of these theologians are Protestant. De Gruchy might have included Catholic sources.[56] Though John Paul II's *Dives in Misericordia* of 1984 is one of his lesser-known encyclicals, its final section includes a call for forgiveness and reconciliation as political principles, a revolutionary idea in Catholic social thought that he would reiterate in 1997 and again in January 2002, when, shortly after the attacks of September 11, 2001, he appended to Pope Paul VI's maxim "no peace without justice" the corollary "no justice without forgiveness." John Paul II was not entirely original, for Pope Benedict XV had similarly appealed to nations to practice forgiveness and reconciliation at the close of World War I.

Other theologians of the late twentieth century and early twenty-first century added new dimensions to the same line of thinking. Jürgen Moltmann, a German Protestant theologian who wrote in the aftermath of the Holocaust, contributed the idea of solidarity: In enduring the suffering and rejection of the cross, Jesus acts in solidarity with the tortured, the murdered, the poor, the marginalized, including the victims of Auschwitz, and even with the perpetrator. In his influential book, *The Crucified God*, he recalls Elie Wiesel's image of God dying on the gallows at Auschwitz but interprets it as the presence, not the disappearance, of God. "Even Auschwitz is taken up into the grief of the Father, the surrender of the Son and the power of the Spirit." If theology is to have anything to say to the world after Auschwitz, he reasons, it must say something in Auschwitz. "God in Auschwitz and Auschwitz in the crucified God—that is the basis for a real hope which both embraces and overcomes the world, and the ground for a love which is stronger than death and can sustain death."[57] Still other theologians have, like John Paul II, Benedict XV, and Benedict XVI, developed theological arguments for apology and forgiveness in politics.[58] Together, apology and forgiveness, solidarity, the redemption of social structures, and other themes such as restorative punishment begin to suggest the possibility of a holistic theology of political reconciliation, one that integrates several practices into a common concept of justice.

I am sympathetic to Barth's idea of analogy. Imitated in modern political orders, God's victory in Christ as well as biblical concepts of justice, peace, and mercy may guide restoration and rebuilding. A long tradition in Christian theology, though, holds that Christ's victory is not yet consummated. The doctrine of original sin undergirds the reality that efforts at reconciliation will be met with partial achievement and periodic failure. If the twentieth century saw the rise of theologies of political reconciliation, so, too, it hosted theologies like that of Reinhold Niebuhr, who urged his readers to remember that strivings for justice would meet with ironic failures, unintended effects, and the parrying punches of power.[59] Evil still controls turf, and in politics this has never been more evident than in the twentieth century. Still, what the twentieth-century theologies of political reconciliation claim is that to work for reconciliation in settings where injustices have occurred is to participate in the victorious redemptive work of God.

The project of reconciliation in the political realm might arouse the worries of two sorts of skeptics. One is the secular person for whom all talk of the kingdom of God or a political analogy of Christ's redemption begets a worrisome vision of modern crusades, inquisitions, and expulsions that leaves little room for dissent and promotes anything but reconciliation. Can a religion that sees Christ's redemption as holistic accept the boundaries that liberal constitutional governments impose and that the ethic of political reconciliation endorses? Within Western Christianity today, support for human rights, including religious freedom, democracy, a strong differentiation in function between church and state, and an openness to the expression of these principles in secular language by state constitutions, enjoys strong theological and philosophical support.[60] In the case of human rights, this support usually rests on the inherent worth and dignity of the person as a being created in the image of and loved by God. Nothing in these liberal institutions or in the idea of rights poses a barrier to religious bodies and citizens promoting an ethic of political reconciliation, whether through persuading, cajoling, protesting, resisting, contributing, helping to form and lead truth commissions, providing recognition and material assistance for victims, and, as has become more common recently, apologizing and seeking forgiveness for their own complicity in past injustices.

The other sort of skeptic's worries complement those of the secularist. They are the worries of such theologians as Stanley Hauerwas, William Cavanaugh, and John Howard Yoder, who think that when the church involves itself in modern secular society, it all too easily contracts out its soul and marginalizes its message. Cavanaugh, for instance, calls the state a "parody" of the church that seduces Christians through its parallel liturgies and loyalties.[61] The complicity of the church is at its worst, all these thinkers hold, when the state wages war. In political orders dominated by violence—as are today's liberal democracies, they believe—the church is a "resident alien," a pilgrim who preaches a message from the outside. The true mission of the church is simply to "be the church."

How might these critics regard the project at hand, which aims to retrieve a logic of justice from religious texts and traditions and graft it onto modern political orders based on human rights and international law? I suspect that they will be more favorable to the retrieval than to the grafting. A difficulty with their writings is their failure to make clear whether all political orders or just liberal political orders are inimical to the way of Christ and the church, and if liberal orders are the problem, whether entire liberal orders or only certain features of liberal orders are the source of the trouble. Hauerwas seeks to clarify: "I have no interest in legitimating and/or recommending a withdrawal of Christians or the church from social or political affairs. I simply want them to be there as Christians and as church."[62] Still, it remains unclear in the writings of these theologians what sort of activities are authentically those of Christians and the church and what sort are not. Several features of the current project might trouble them. I envision an ethic of reconciliation practiced in the context of political orders based on human rights, democracy, and constitutional government. Is this too compromised? I advocate that religious actors, without silencing their distinctive rationales or language, also pursue an overlapping consensus by forming alliances with actors from other traditions and sometimes adopting secular language to do so. Does this marginalize their message? I envision the church as a civil society actor that is separate from the state but active in influencing it. Does this overly confine the church? In places, I endorse natural law as a foundation for portions of the ethic. Is this too much of a departure from distinct theological sources? These questions I leave open, an invitation to conversation.

9

Reconciliation in the Islamic Tradition

SINCE THE ATTACKS of September 11, 2001, Westerners have conducted a vigorous and often rancorous debate about Islam. Some view Islam as intrinsically militant in its texts and teachings, opposed to genuine dialogue, unified and constant in its hostility to the West, and inhospitable to human rights and democracy—a religion against which the West must prepare to defend itself. For others, Islam is diverse, open to dialogue, capable of historical change, and contains large populations open to human rights and democracy—a religion with which the West can cooperate. Long before the attacks, Muslims also debated what sort of civilization the West is. Millions have wanted to adopt Western political structures, economic systems, and culture; millions of others have viewed the West as a source of imperialism, cultural decadence, and threats to Islamic lands and holy sites. Gradations and nuances, corollaries and qualifications, and, all too often, prejudices and misconceptions abound on all sides.

Not incidental to these debates is the question of Islam's relation to Christianity and Judaism: Are these three faiths siblings in an Abrahamic family? The difference between Islam and its two putative siblings is in some ways greater than the differences between Christianity and Judaism that we encountered in the last chapter. Islam does not claim to grow organically from Christianity in the way that Jesus claimed to fulfill the Jewish law. Then again, Muslims and Jews commonly reject the divinity of Jesus and the doctrine of the Trinity—an idolatrous, polytheistic teaching, the Quran says. All three faiths espouse a single creator God, numerous similar moral teachings, a shared line of prophets, and an expectation of judgment at the end of time. The Quran speaks of Jesus some thirty-five times, revering him as a prophet, teaching his virgin birth from Mary, and predicting his return at the end of time. Crucial to the question of resemblance among the three siblings is their perspective on their putative father: Abraham, the great patriarch himself. These perspectives are complex, argues theologian Karl-Josef Kuschel in his balanced book, *Abraham: Sign of Hope for Jews, Christians, and Muslims*.[1] The scriptures of each faith, he shows, contain passages that seem to claim the great patriarch exclusively as their own as well as passages that share his paternity with all of humanity.

It is not my ambition to resolve these grand controversies here. I aim to pose for Islam, as I did for Judaism and Christianity, these questions: Do Islamic texts and traditions contain the materials for the construction of the ethic of political reconciliation that I am proposing? Can Muslims, on the basis of their religious convictions, join in an overlapping consensus on such an ethic? My answer to both of these questions is yes. Islam differs from Judaism and Christianity on any number of doctrines, but the method of overlapping consensus demands not that religions and philosophies carry an equivalent understanding of reconciliation but that they contain teachings that, when drawn out and developed, can support the ethic. My investigation of Islam begins with its basic concepts of justice, reconciliation, peace, and mercy, proceeds to its understanding of God's response to evil, then looks briefly at Islamic criminal law. The strongest Islamic support for an ethic of political reconciliation, though, comes from traditional Arab Muslim tribal rituals for dealing with crimes in the community, rituals that approximate the principles of the ethic better than any similar communal practice that I have found in Judaism or Christianity. The greatest dissonance between the Islamic tradition and the ethic, by contrast, lies in the skepticism of certain factions of Muslims toward the modern sovereign state, human rights, and international law—the context in which I envision the ethic taking place. Still, I argue, substantial support for these institutions can be found in Islam as well. Though not as skeptical about Islam as some, neither do I share the easy optimism of others. What the possibility of convergence requires is an argument.

Justice and Reconciliation in Islam

The Arabic words that translate to justice in the Quran do not translate as easily and fluidly into righteousness as their Hebrew and Greek equivalents do. Yet a case can be made that justice in the Quran means something much like righteousness—living in right relationship in all spheres of life, according to the norms, obligations, and expectations that each sphere demands, as set forth by God.

Several words translate to justice in the Quran, each expressing a different aspect of justice, explains scholar of Islam Majid Khadduri in his thorough and important work, *The Islamic Conception of Justice*. These words appear in almost one hundred expressions. The Quran likewise cites two hundred admonitions against injustice, expressing this concept as well through an array of terms. Next to the existence of God, justice is stressed more than any other principle by the Quran and the ensuing traditions of interpretation, Khadduri claims.[2]

The most common word translated to justice is *'adl*. Closely related is *qist*, the quality of a just action.[3] Both terms mean "to give someone his or her full portion," according to another scholar of Islam, Rashied Omar.[4] A somewhat different slant comes from lexicographer Ibn Manzur, for whom the core meaning of justice is "the thing that is established in the mind as being straightforward," as Khadurri quotes him as saying.[5] *'Adl* can also mean fairness, equality, balance, or a golden mean. Its antonyms develop its meaning further. The term *injustice* is most commonly translated from *jawr*, which means to be partial, biased, and unfair, as well as from *tughyan* (tyranny), *inhiraf* (deviation), and *zulm* (wrongdoing). The latter term, *zulm*, originally means "to take something out of its proper place," implying that justice means to restore the proper order of things.[6] The word from which *'adl* is derived is the verb *adala*, whose meanings, according to Khadduri, include to straighten, to amend or modify, to deflect from one (wrong) path to another (right) path, to be equal or to equalize, and to balance or be in a state of equilibrium. Other sources show *adala* to mean moral probity and righteousness. That this action word also translates to justice shows that justice is not only a condition where things are right but also a process of making things right.[7] Stressing the connection between justice and righteousness even further is the adjective *'aadil*, which is closely related to *'adl* and denotes the quality of one who speaks truthfully and is therefore *sadiq* (*saduq, siddiq*)— truthful, righteous, upright. Finally, in at least one *surah* (5:8), the Quran associates justice closely with *taqwa*, the righteousness that comes from being pious and fully conscious of God.[8]

In the Quran, just as in the Bible, justice is comprehensive, applying to the whole of life. "Used in the broadest sense to include moral and religious values," justice "indicates for men the paths of right and wrong" and of "happiness" and has "universal application to all men," Khadduri explains.[9] Recall that "straightness" was also the essential meaning of the Hebrew term *sedeq(ah)* yet could connote by analogy the terms of right relationship in all spheres.[10] Terms such as *full portion, equality,* and *balance* may at first seem to apply mainly to those goods that can be meted out according to a scale of measurement: wealth, property, commerce, and punishment. These terms also find application in a whole variety of relationships, including those in which vice might arise through excesses and shortfalls of some kind, just as Aristotle's golden mean applied to a whole range of virtues, not just ones involving calculation or distribution. Omar confirms that justice in the Quran governs orphans and adopted children, marriage, contractual matters, all economic dealings, legal affairs, relations between religions, and relations between enemies. He quotes renowned fourteenth-century CE Islamic jurist Ibn Qayyim al-Jawziyyah: "God has sent his Messengers and revealed His Books so that people may establish *qist* [justice], upon which the heavens and the earth stand. And when the signs of justice appear *in any manner*, then that is a reflection of the *sharia* and the religion of God."[11] To act justly is to submit to God—the very meaning of Islam—and to trod the path of salvation. "Be just: that is / Next to piety," *surah* 5:8 commands.[12]

Both the Quran and a long tradition of interpretation regard justice as being realized not just in the lives of righteous Muslims but in communities. A collective of Muslims living righteously according to God's covenant is called *umma wasat*, where *wasat* denotes moderation and balance. "Thus have We made of you / An *Ummat* justly balanced. / That ye might be witnesses / Over the nations," *surah* 2:143 states. A long succession of commentary on this phrase interprets it as referring to a thoroughly just community, explains scholar of Islam Asma Afsaruddin.[13]

Virtually all major schools of interpretation have affirmed that justice is established by God and pervasive in its relevance to human affairs, even as they have disagreed over how God established justice and how humans can know its content. These very issues, part of a much larger dispute over reason and revelation, were taken up by Muslim intellectuals during the rich period of ferment and interpretation that spanned the centuries from Mohammed's death in 632 CE to the writings of Ibn Rushd, known in the West as Averroes, in the twelfth century. What can the ordinary person know through the light of his reason alone? What can be known solely through God's active revelation of his will, recorded in the holy scriptures and interpreted by the most authoritative religious scholars, the *ulama?* These are not unlike questions that Jewish and Christian theologians have pursued for centuries.

The first major school of Islamic interpreters, the Mu'tazilites, held that truth, morality, and justice existed objectively and were not solely emanations of God's will (though they were surely also that), and that humans could apprehend these realities, at least in part, through their reason (though surely through revelation as well). Their opponents, known as Ash'arites, countered that truth, morality, and justice existed only insofar as they derived from God's will and command and could be known only through God's revelation in the Quran as well as through the Sunnah, the words and deeds of the Prophet as recorded by his companions. A common, though not wholly accurate, belief held today is that during the tenth and eleventh centuries, the "gates of *ijtihad*," or interpretation, closed up.[14] What is indisputable is that by the twelfth century, in part for political reasons, the Ash'arite view had become orthodox among jurists in the majority Sunni community, who then partially stifled subsequent developments in Islamic philosophy. Borrowing heavily from Plato and Aristotle—and largely responsible for reintroducing them to the Latin West—such philosophers as Ibn Rushd continued to innovate, in his case stressing the capacity of reason to discern justice and morality. Shii Muslim philosophers continued to produce great works as well, even after Ibn Rushd.

Whatever Islamic theologians, philosophers, and jurists thought the status of justice was and however they thought humans could know it, none disputed that it depicts the right relationships that God calls humans to practice in every dimension of life. As Ibn Rushd made clear, even Aristotle taught that justice is the central and highest virtue, the one that perfects all other virtues.

If justice in Islam is a matter of comprehensive right relationship, then it spurs the same syllogism that it does for Judaism and Christianity. If reconciliation is a process of restoring relationships to a condition of rightness and if justice is also right relationship, then it follows that reconciliation is a matter of what Islam calls justice—a process of restoring justice and a state of justice. The Quran corroborates the conclusion. The word most often translated to reconciliation is *sulh*, which means "settlement" or "conciliation" but not only in the narrow sense of a mere contractual agreement or an end to fighting but a deeper, more thorough restoration. The active form of the word, the verb *islah*, supports this interpretation, meaning "to make good, proper, right, to reconcile, or settle." *Surah* 49:10 speaks of reconciliation in terms of the brotherhood between religious believers: "The Believers are but / A single Brotherhood: / So make peace and/ Reconciliation between your / Two (contending) brothers; / And fear Allah, that ye / May receive Mercy." Another verse, *surah* 4:114, places conciliation on a par with charity and justice: "[I]f / One exhorts to a deed / Of charity or goodness / Or conciliation between people... / To him who does this, / Seeking the good pleasure / Of Allah, We shall soon give / A reward of the highest (value)." *Surah* 4:128 implores believers to maintain their marriages, even if it requires providing economic incentives to a difficult husband: "[S]uch settlement is best." Some translations of this verse render "settlement" as "reconciliation." All of these instances describe restoring right relationship and achieving justice.

Mercy and Peace in Islam

Of the ninety-nine names for Allah, *merciful* is considered by Muslims the most important. *Rahma*, the word for "mercy," and its derivatives appear 326 times in the Quran.[15] The phrase *bismillah, al-rahman, al-rahim*, meaning "in the name of God, the most gracious, the most merciful," begins all but one of the Quran's 114 *surahs*.[16] *Surah* 21:107 describes Muhammad's mission as *rahmatan lil 'alamin*, one of compassion and mercy to the world. *Surah* 40:7 also describes mercy in sweeping terms, saying that the Lord "[embraces] / All things, / In Mercy and Knowledge."

According to the famous lexicographer Imam Raghib al-Isfahani, the meaning of the term *rahma* is a "softening of the heart towards one who deserves our mercy and induces us to do good to him/her."[17] *Rahma* closely resembles the Hebrew word *rahamim* and carries its connotation of feminine compassion. The companion term *rahim* also means "merciful" or "compassionate," depicting the actions of God as well as humanity.[18] Characteristic of God, involving an impulse to do good toward one in a position to receive mercy, the Quran's mercy is, like mercy in the Bible, far more sweeping and restorative than the modern concept and thus serves well as the animating virtue of the process of reconciliation.

Likewise, *salam*, the Arabic word for "peace," refers to the condition that reconciliation produces—a general state of justice, not just a cessation of hostilities. Scholar of Islam Mohammed Abu-Nimer resounds this holism: "Peace in Islam is understood as a state of physical, mental, spiritual, and social harmony, living at peace with God through submission, and living at peace with one's fellow human beings by avoiding wrongdoing. Islam obligates its believers to seek peace in all of life's dominions."[19] The very word *Islam* stems from the root *slm*, which it shares with *salam*, and connotes living in a right and peaceful relationship to God—the peace informed by justice that characterizes a state of reconciliation.[20] Peace in Islam is not merely to be realized among individuals but is also meant to characterize entire social orders.

Islam's Response to Evil

Evil in Islam does not hold humanity captive or engage in a great battle with God, as it does in Judaism or Christianity. The Quran also describes the sin of the Garden of Eden and even the presence there of the devil—known as Iblis or Shaytan—but this sin, though the fruit of human folly and feebleness, is not a fundamental rebellion or the fall of humankind. In Islam, then, God's atoning sacrifice is unnecessary. According to the Quran, Jesus was not crucified, but sin still brings harm to the sinner (*zulm al-nafs*) just as it does to its victim.[21] In all cases, sin rejects *fitra*, the inborn disposition of humans to be good, just, and living in right relationship with God. Thus, evil still creates a problem that requires a solution.

The solution that the Quran prescribes again and again is repentance, in response to which God forgives and shows mercy. Like the Jewish Bible, the Quran describes repentance through the metaphor of turning. It most frequently does this—more than sixty times—through the verb *Ta'ba*, meaning "to turn toward someone in penance."[22] As in Judaism, repentance is a condition for forgiveness, but once the wrongdoer performs repentance, God's forgiveness is generous and merciful. In the case of Adam, the Quran says: "Then learnt Adam from his Lord / Certain words and his Lord / Turned towards him; for He / Is Oft-Returning, Most Merciful" (2:37). God is willing to forgive any person just the same. *Surah* 6:54 says, "verily, / If any of you did evil / In ignorance, and thereafter / Repented, and amended / (His conduct), lo! He is / Oft-Forgiving, most Merciful." A separate verse reads "Say: 'O my servants who / Have transgressed against their souls! / Despair not of the Mercy / Of Allah: for Allah forgives / All sins: for He is / Oft-forgiving, Most Merciful'" (39:53). Many other verses run similarly.

The Quran also speaks of God inflicting harsh judgment and punishment on the unrepentant, but in these teachings we can discern some of the core ideas of restorative justice. It would be impossible to make sense of God's willingness to forgive in the Quran if dealing with sin required an equal, proportionate punishment, a balancing of the scales. Rather, as I have begun to argue for Christianity and Judaism, punishment is God's way of preserving his covenant and is thus compatible with his mercy. Drawing on the thought of Fazlur Rahman, theologian Carol LaHurd comments on the Quran, "God's mercy is obvious in creation, in God's gift of the prophets and their messages, and in God's judgment—as God's way of guiding humanity in the covenant of obedience to God as sovereign."[23] Forgiveness, too, arises from God's desire for restoration. "For such the reward / Is forgiveness from their Lord, / And Gardens with rivers / Flowing underneath, /An eternal dwelling," says *Surah* 3:136.

Reconciliation in Islamic Criminal Justice

What guidance does Islam give for dealing with evil through earthly human institutions? Can the core ideas of restorative justice also be found in Islam? Any answer must lie in both the Quran and in *fiqh*, the Islamic tradition of jurisprudence. Islam contains several traditions of law: four schools of interpretation in Sunni Islam—Hanafi, Shafi'i, Maliki, and Hanbali—and yet another school, Jaafari, in Shii Islam. Generally, Islam has classified crime and punishment into three categories: Hudud, Qisas, and T'azir. Hudud crimes are ones for which Islamic texts mandate a specific punishment. The most serious crimes, they include theft, adultery, slander, drinking alcohol, highway robbery, rebellion, and apostasy but, interestingly, not murder.[24] All types of murder as well as physical assaults that result in injury and death make up a second category, Qisas crimes, which are infractions against public law but not ones for which a specific punishment is prescribed in advance. A third category of crimes, T'azir, are ones that are not serious enough to be Hudud or Qisas and do not carry a specific penalty.

The evidence for restorative justice in these categories is admittedly mixed. It is muted in the rather unrestorative penalties of Hudud: death (for apostasy), death by stoning (for adultery), amputation (for theft), and whippings (for drinking alcohol). Some modern Islamic societies try to minimize the application of these penalties by raising the evidentiary standards that these punishments require to prohibitive heights, though this does not change their underlying rationale of retributive balance.

Just as it is surprising to find murder and assault in a middle category of crime, it is surprising to find the Quran flexible—and arguably encouraging restoration—in the punishment that it prescribes for these crimes. A central text is *surah* 2:178:

> The law of equality / Is prescribed to you / In cases of murder: / The free for the free, / The slave for the slave, / The woman for the woman. / But if any remission / Is made by the brother / Of the slain, then grant / Any reasonable demand, / And compensate him / With handsome gratitude. This is a concession / And a Mercy / From your Lord.

The verse seems first to set forth a balancing retributive logic of punishment but then to allow a surviving relative of the victim to opt for a "remission" whereby the offender pays him compensation. In Islamic jurisprudence, compensation takes the form of a payment that is determined by a court of law. *Surah* 5:45 carries a similar structure: "We ordained therein for them: / 'Life for life, eye for eye, / Nose for nose, ear for ear, / Tooth for tooth, and wounds / Equal for equal.' But if / Any one remits the retaliation / By way of charity, it is / An act of atonement for himself." How is the justice of "life for life" compatible with the justice of remission? Clearly, the justice in play cannot be one that requires a balancing punishment; otherwise, remission would make no sense. In his widely respected translation of the Quran, Abdullah Yusuf Ali comments in a footnote on the first verse in the passage quoted above (2:178) that the "law of equality" was meant to limit the disproportionate revenge of pre-Islamic Arabic cultures. The point of the verse, he suggests, is to limit punishment, not to mandate its degree. When compensation is chosen, it seems to enact something much like restorative justice. Some translations of verse 2:178 even render "remission" as "forgiveness." Either way, the verse associates the concession that it speaks of with the mercy of Allah. Forgiveness and mercy, then, are combined with reparations for the victim's family that function as a punishment for the offender, a punishment that he is called to accept through remorse and repentance.

The route of forgiveness and compensation, though, always remains optional for the victim, who can also demand the punishment of "the law of equality," including execution. This somewhat weakens the case for an underlying logic of restorative justice for crimes of Qisas. If optional, however, the route of compensation and forgiveness is also recommended, suggest two other verses in the Quran: "If thou dost stretch thy hand / Against me, to slay me, / It is not for me to stretch / My hand against thee / To slay thee: for I do fear / Allah, the Cherisher of the Worlds" (5:28) and "[t]he recompense for an injury / Is an injury equal thereto / (In degree): but if a person / Forgives and makes reconciliation, / His reward is due / From Allah: for (Allah) / Loveth not those who / Do wrong" (42:40). The Quran, it seems, favors restoration in cases of murder and bodily assault.[24] For an ethic of political reconciliation that is meant to be enacted in modern states facing large-scale injustices of precisely this form—murder, torture, injury, impairment—this is quite significant.

T'azir, the third category of crimes, Islamic legal scholar Nawal Ammar argues, is the most amenable to the approach of restorative justice. Meaning "chastisement," T'azir is aimed at the public good, resembling the communication of censure that is the central justification of restorative punishment. In the Hanafi school of jurisprudence, the key aim of T'azir punishments is rehabilitation. For T'azir crimes, the forgiveness of victims and the repentance of offenders can each reduce or abolish the level of penal sanctions.[25] For T'azir crimes, as for Qisas crimes, Islam puts forth a logic of restorative justice.

Rituals of Reconciliation in Arab-Muslim Culture

If, in Islamic jurisprudence, we can find concepts that resemble the core principles of an ethic of political reconciliation alloyed, as they may be, with dissonant concepts, in another strand of the Islamic tradition we can find principles and rituals of reconciliation that are richer than any other public or communal practice that I have found in the three faiths considered in this book: rituals of reconciliation practiced by tribes in Lebanon, Jordan, Palestine, Egypt, other parts of North Africa, and perhaps elsewhere in the Arab world.[26] Though some of these practices date back to pre-Islamic Bedouin cultures, all of them came to be rooted in *sharia*, or Islamic law. Arab Islamic societies have employed them— much as I envision the ethic of political reconciliation being practiced— both to make peace between tribes and to bring repair to those affected by crimes, including murder, within tribes. Today, the governments of Jordan, Lebanon, and Israel still allow these practices on the local and village level. Known as *sulh*, which, as we have seen, is a notion of deep settlement, and *musalaha*, which translates to "reconciliation," these rituals involve an interconnected set of practices that embody the kind of justice—and peace and mercy—that I have been arguing for, justice that restores persons, relationships, and entire communities with respect to the specific kinds of injuries that they have suffered.

As political scientists George Irani and Nathan Funk and scholar of Islam Mohammed Abu-Nimer suggest, the principles of *sulh* and *musahala*— often referred to together simply as *sulh* or *sulha*—can be understood in contrast to the principles undergirding the modern Western field of conflict resolution.[27] Having become a specialized field, Western conflict resolution theory stresses incentives, interests, needs, and the bargaining dynamics that result from configurations of actors, power, and authority structures. *Sulh* rituals, by contrast, draw on a community's traditional understandings of the obligations that go with relationships, ones governed by the values of honor, dignity, shame, and respect. Western conflict resolution approaches treat the individuals and parties to a settlement as isolated free agents in a negotiation governed by judicial procedure, while *sulh* treats them as enmeshed in webs of relationships with family and community. While in Western conflict resolution approaches, settlements are based on a just outcome denominated in terms of compensation, punishment, rights, and fairness, *sulh* seeks a broader restoration of right relationships among victims, offenders, families, and community members—a justice of righteousness. With Western theories, settlements are achieved through bargaining and mediation; *sulh* involves a portfolio of practices that, like the ethic of political reconciliation, include acknowledgment, reparations, apology, forgiveness, and rituals of settlement. The mediators who conduct these processes are, in the Western approaches, trained specialists in a field, often with a legal background, who act as neutral, third-party mediators, arbitrators, or judges, while *sulh* is conducted by community and village elders with traditional bases of authority for whom impartiality is surely a virtue but who are much more closely related to the parties involved in the negotiations. Western practices conclude in a signed agreement; *sulh* concludes with a ritual of *musafaha* (handshake) and *mumalaha* (breaking bread together). Western conflict resolution theory is typically secular, whereas *sulh* is based on religious faith, both in its justifications and procedures. These contrasts should not be drawn too sharply. Western conflict resolution theory is itself diverse, with some of its strands taking into account some of the values stressed by *sulh*.[28] Yet the core enduring themes of the Western field remain different from the essentials of *sulh*.

Sulh rituals are sophisticated. Those described by Irani and Funk begin with the offense, one resulting in injury, death, or some other grievance. To fend off vengeance, a family member of the offender then contacts respected local leaders, who respond by establishing a *jaha* (delegation) to investigate the case. Next, the *jaha* hears the grievances of the victim, if he is alive, as well as the victim's family members, and seeks their authorization to arbitrate. Upon consenting, the family forswears retaliation and assents to a truce (*hudna* or *'atwa*), and *sulh* formally begins. After a period of mourning (often forty days), the *jaha* determines the amount of *diya*, or blood money, to be paid as compensation. Then, the families come together for *musahafa*, a ritual of shaking hands. Often, the offender will bear a knotted white flag that symbolizes peace. In response, the family of the victim shares bitter coffee with the family of the offender as a gesture of forgiveness and *musahala* (reconciliation). To conclude, the two groups break bread together in a meal served by the family of the offender to the family of the victim known as *mumalaha*. The main ritual of reconciliation can vary from culture to culture. Abu-Nimer tells of Awlad Ali tribes in northern Africa that ask a convicted murderer to lie on the ground beside a sheep as a symbol of his surrender and then invite a member of the victim's family to symbolically make the choice of killing either the offender or the sheep, a decision that confers honor and dignity on the victim's family by allowing it to demonstrate that it chose mercy when it could have done otherwise.[29]

Sulh rituals are a high-yield commodity for the ethic of political reconciliation, combining acknowledgment, apology, forgiveness, and a form of reparation that can also be interpreted as restorative punishment. Victims, offenders, community leaders, and family members all participate in these restorative practices, ones that together address several dimensions of woundedness, including the lost dignity and honor of victims and family, damage to the soul of the offender and the honor of his family, and the breaking apart of the entire community, which might easily unravel through cycles of revenge. The rituals have a public political dimension, occurring under the auspices of respected community leaders, and they are rooted in faith. Abu-Nimer witnessed a set of *sulh* rituals in a Palestinian village in which passages from the Quran and the Hadith, authoritative Islamic texts, were read at every stage.[30]

The analogy between *sulh* rituals and political reconciliation is far from perfect. Occurring within a tribe's hierarchies of wealth, gender, and authority, such practices will scarcely satisfy a critic of the unjustness of these structures—the concern that motivates political reconciliation's practice of building socially just institutions. *Sulh* rituals also depend on consent, the absence of which enables the retributive option in the case of Qisas crimes. The setting for *sulh* differs from the setting of political reconciliation as well. When practiced within a community, *sulh* usually deals with a single crime at a time, not injustices that span the entire community. When practiced between tribes, *sulh* rituals may model political reconciliation between states, but then a larger dilemma arises: Can *sulh* be transposed to the modern state? In part, this is a question of scale. Does the personal, face-to-face aspect of *sulh* prevent its enlargement? This question will be confronted in subsequent chapters. Yet for Islam, a deeper question arises: Is the modern state, particularly a liberal democratic constitutional one, even a legitimate entity?

Islam and the Modern State

I have been arguing all along that a modern state based on human rights and principles of international law is a fundamental principle of political reconciliation. Human rights and international norms of war define the content of political injustices. Building state institutions based on these principles constitutes one of the six practices of the ethic. More generally, the modern state is the setting in which the practices take place. Restoring human rights is integral to restoring right relationships in or between communities. The compatibility of Islam with these principles, then, is crucial if Muslims are to share in an overlapping consensus on them—in Morocco and Sierra Leone, where truth commissions have taken place, in Sudan, whose civil war begs for efforts to address the past, or in any international conflict in which Islamic states have participated. To what degree can today's Muslims join in an overlapping consensus on the state, human rights, and international law?

Today's Muslims, of course, are a rather large category: 1.5 billion people living in a wide range of countries and cultures. Islam has no single voice that commands authority among the *umma* in matters of doctrine, so we must appeal to indicators of beliefs. Certain strands of Quranic interpretation stress that justice, righteousness, and peace are obligations as well as possibilities for all persons and communities, not just Muslims. Afsaruddin points to both premodern and modern interpretations of the Quran that consider Christians and Jews as belonging to righteous and just communities.[31] What about specific principles? Virtually every majority Islamic state is a member of the United Nations and has accepted the charter's principles of nonaggression, noninterference, the sovereign equality of states, and its broad commitment to human rights. Fifty-six states belong to the Organization of the Islamic Conference, which is based on a strongly similar set of guiding principles. Today, the two countries with the world's largest Muslim populations—Indonesia and India—are democracies; Muslims widely support democratization in Turkey as well. Opinion polls show strong support for democracy among Muslim populations throughout the world; one shows 85 to 95 percent of Muslims in favor.[32] Among the world's Muslim scholars and jurists, Hashmi claims, "[w]hile there is a small fraction of Muslim theorists and activists who deny the compatibility of Islamic law and public international law, the vast majority of Muslim scholars and all Muslim-majority states generally accept prevailing international norms, in both theory and practice."[33]

Other indicators, however, point to weaknesses in the Islamic consensus on human rights and international law. As late as 2006, Freedom House reported that only three out of forty-seven Muslim-majority countries—Mali, Senegal, and Indonesia—fit the category of "free," an indicator of their governments' conformity to standards of human rights.[34] To be sure, not all of these regimes are based on Islamic principles. Since World War II, most Arab regimes have fashioned themselves far more on the principles of the French Revolution—equality, economic modernization, nationalism, and the tight control of religion—than on the Quran. Other Islamic states, though, have adopted the religious authoritarianism of the Iranian Revolution. In the last quarter century, most Muslim states have signed the Universal Islamic Declaration of Human Rights (1981) and the Cairo Declaration on Human Rights in Islam (1990), both efforts to create an alternative version of the Universal Declaration of Human Rights that is based on a notion of *sharia* that carries far weaker protections for women, non-Muslims, and accused criminals.

Generally, Hashmi argues, Islamic political thought about the state and the international system falls into three broad categories. The broad middle ground is occupied by what he calls Islamic internationalists—modernists who accept the state as a legitimate entity but only if it is based on and promotes Islamic principles. Internationalist thinkers tend to favor international organizations that unite Muslims, such as the Organization of the Islamic Conference. Internationalists are particularly good candidates for joining an overlapping consensus for political reconciliation, combining an openness to the state with a commitment to the traditional Islamic principles that ground the core principles and the six practices. Whether all internationalists endorse the full spectrum of human rights in the global international legal documents, though, is unclear. Religious freedom, for instance, remains a disputed issue. Hope for consensus lies in the arguments of liberal and modernist Muslim scholars for full religious freedom on the basis of Quranic verses such as 2:256: "Let there be no compulsion / In religion." By these scholars' standards, religious freedom involves the right of Muslims to alter their religion and considers the historical system of protected minority status for Christians and Jews (*dhimmitude*) to be unjustly discriminatory.[35]

Flanking internationalists on the secular side are what Hashmi calls statists, Muslims who fully endorse the modern state but on largely secular grounds: Western concepts of equality, economic progress, socialism, and nationalism (the French Revolution model). Islamic statists are most common in the West and among the modern nationalist regimes that have dominated the Arab world since World War II, many of them patterned after Kemal Atatürk's Republic of Turkey. Hashmi divides statists into two strands, one that attempts to incorporate Islam into the public sphere but only within defined boundaries, and the other viewing Islam as a threat to modernization and nation building that ought to be thoroughly privatized. Quintessentially, statists support the state, and in principle they might also support international law and human rights. In practice, though, the authoritarianism of these regimes belies any deep commitment to these principles. Often, their suppression and co-optation of Islam amounts to a denial of religious freedom. Statists' lack of a strong commitment to Islam weakens their potential for endorsing the principles of political reconciliation on the basis of their faith.

On the radical side are what Hashmi calls cosmopolitans. They view the state and the state system as imperial, European impositions and nefarious partitioners of the *umma*, the global body of Muslims. Some proponents, such as Ayatollah Khomeini of Iran and Abu al-A'la Maududi of Pakistan, came to embrace the state reluctantly, viewing it only as a base of operations for creating a worldwide Islamic order. Cosmopolitans view most of the present Islamic world as a *dar al-nifaq*, "an abode of hypocrisy." Today, cosmopolitans rule governments in Iran, Sudan, twelve states of Nigeria, and Saudi Arabia, have left their imprint on the constitution of Pakistan, and advocate their cause through such transnational organizations as the Muslim Brotherhood and Jamaat-e-Islami.

Cosmopolitans might also be called radical Islamic revivalists. Their founding fathers were intellectuals and activists of the early and mid-twentieth century like Maududi, the founder of Jamaat-i-Islami, Egypt's Hasan al-Banna, the founder of the Muslim Brotherhood, and Sayyid Qutb, also of Egypt, who commonly held the conviction that Islam was trapped in a centuries-long, global descent into *jahiliyyah*, a state of barbarism. This decline was thorough, they thought, involving not only moral and spiritual dimensions but also social and political ones. Having been dominated by Western colonial powers, Muslims must not only pursue moral and spiritual renewal but must reassert their governance. Revivalists disagree over the form that this governance ought to take—whether it involves a caliph, for instance. They accept the state only provisionally and always with a demand that it be governed by a strongly restrictive form of *sharia* law, one that often involves Hudud punishments, discrimination against women with regard to marriage, divorce, inheritance, and educational opportunity, and restrictions on the religious freedom and other opportunities of non-Muslims—all significant departures from the leading international human rights instruments.

What does this array of opinion mean for an overlapping consensus on the ethic of political reconciliation? Again, assessing the beliefs of 1.5 billion Muslims, still less determining the grounds of these beliefs or the depth to which they are held, is not an easy task. Yet recall the complexity and flexibility of the overlapping consensus. People may endorse the ethic for different reasons, for instrumental reasons, and even for dubiously constituted reasons and still participate in its practices. They may endorse some of the practices but not all of them or not every aspect of each one—the full panoply of human rights, for instance. Instances of partial consensus will result in partial achievements of the ethic.

Consensus will be strengthened, though, the more that those Muslims who do not share in the consensus today can come to join it on the basis of, not through an abandonment of, their beliefs. The best opportunity for this widening and deepening comes through Hashmi's internationalists, who wish to adapt Islam to the modern state based on human rights and membership in a community of states governed by international law.[36]

The travelers of this route are today's Muslim reformers. Each pursues reinterpretation through a separate strategy. One of the most compelling of these strategies is that of Islamic legal scholars Abdullah and Hassan Saeed, who seek to ground the human right of religious freedom in the Quran, the Hadith, and other prominent sources in the Islamic tradition.

Another is that of Sudanese legal scholar Abdullahi Ahmed An-Na'im, who attempts an Islamic defense of the array of human rights found in the international legal instruments, especially those that prohibit religious and gender discrimination and body-impairing forms of punishment. Still another Islamic legal scholar, Khaled Abou el Fadl, takes a somewhat different tack, arguing that the modern state is not the promoter of divine law that Islamic jurisprudence envisions, nor is it an entity in which the concept of *dhimmitude* finds sound application. Muslims governing in modern state institutions ought rather to seek consensus and avoid treating people as second-class citizens. El Fadl, too, is a strong Muslim supporter of human rights as they are found in modern international law. The ranks of Islamic reformers also include Abdulaziz Sachedina, Fazlur Rahman, Farid Esack, AbdolKarim Soroush, and many others.[37] What their collective labors promise is a genuinely Islamic justification for the constitutional state, human rights, and international law which, once it has been fashioned, can be fastened to Islamic justifications for the other principles and practices of political reconciliation, forming an integrated Islamic groundwork for the ethic.

PART THREE

Practicing Political Reconciliation

Four Practices: Building Socially
Just Institutions, Acknowledgment,
Reparations, and Apologies

OVER THE PAST several chapters, I have sought to develop and ground the core ideas of an ethic of political reconciliation—reconciliation as a concept of justice, mercy, and peace—in Judaism, Christianity, Islam, and restorative justice. It is the six practices that actually enact political reconciliation: 1) building socially just institutions; 2) acknowledgment; 3) reparations; 4) apology; 5) punishment; and 6) forgiveness. Part 3 charts these practices, showing how they both reflect the core ideas of the ethic and giving them concrete application within and between states.

Each practice aims to achieve some measure of justice by redressing the direct wounds that political injustices inflict: primary restorations. Table 10.1 summarizes the wounds that each practice addresses and the kinds of primary restoration that it brings about. All of the practices might also effect secondary restorations—increases in legitimacy, trust, identification with the nation, respect for other states, willingness to engage in democratic deliberation, and other forms of social capital.

The practices complement one another, complete one another, and weave together. Each effects reconciliation uniquely and irreplaceably. A surfeit of one practice cannot make up for a deficit of another. Were one of them absent, so would be an important dimension of the justice of reconciliation. Some practices are a response to another's call. Apology, for instance, invites forgiveness. Even if one practice does not beckon another, it may still affect another. Some victims who have testified before truth commissions have reported that public acknowledgment of their suffering led them to drop

Table 10.1 The Practices and How They Restore

Practices	Dimension of Woundedness Addressed	Primary Restoration
Building Socially Just Institutions	Violation of victims' human rights	Community creates laws and institutions guaranteed by the state that establish and enforce human rights, democracy, the rule of law, and related goods as well as legitimacy for these goods and the virtues that attend them.
Acknowledgment	Lack of acknowledgment of victims' suffering	A spokesperson for the political order—and hopefully other members of the political order—confer upon victims awareness of, sympathy for, and a will to restore the suffering of the victim.
	Ignorance of the source and circumstance of political injustices	Processes of acknowledgment bring to light truths about political injustices that were previously unknown to victims and to the public.
	Standing victory of the perpetrator's injustice	By bringing to light truths about injustices that were previously suppressed and naming them as injustices, political processes of acknowledgment can serve to denude these injustices of their legitimacy or bring down their "standing victory."
	Harm to the soul of the perpetrator	At times, public acknowledgment can inspire contrition in perpetrators.
	Violation of victims' human rights	By adopting and proclaiming human rights as their standard, processes of political acknowledgment contribute to the public legitimacy of human rights.
Reparations	Harm to the person of the victim	Reparations seek to repair the actual harm to the victim—physical, economic, psychological—in a way that restores the victim to the status quo ex ante as much as that is possible.

	Lack of acknowledgment of victims' suffering	The state, acting on behalf of the political community, bestows reparations upon victims as a way of recognizing their suffering and restoring them to full citizenship (or, if victims are members of another state, the restoration of their full human rights).
	Violation of victims' human rights	In publicly identifying victims as objects of injustices, reparations proclaim and fortify the legitimacy of human rights, both those of the victim and those of the entire community.
	Standing victory of the perpetrator's injustice	In publicly identifying victims as objects of injustices, reparations delegitimate the standing victory of political injustices.
Punishment	Standing victory of the perpetrator's injustice	Through the state's communication of censure to perpetrators—as well as to victims and members of the community—punishment brings down the standing victory of political injustice.
	Lack of acknowledgment of victims' suffering	Punishment confers recognition of victims' dignity.
	Ignorance of the source and circumstance of political injustices	Punishment often yields information on the source and circumstances of the suffering of victims.
	Violation of victims' human rights	Punishment redresses the violation of the victim's basic rights insofar as it expresses, reaffirms, and thereby strengthens human rights as the legally valid values of a state or of relations between states.
Apology	Standing victory of the perpetrator's injustice	When a spokesperson for a political order apologizes for a political injustice he contributes to the defeat of its standing victory.
	Harm to the soul of the perpetrator	A perpetrator's apology can initiate the repair of her own soul.

(continued)

Table 10.1 (continued)

Practices	Dimension of Woundedness Addressed	Primary Restoration
	Lack of acknowledgment of victims' suffering	By conveying moral respect for the victim, acknowledging his humanity, and endorsing his full restoration into the political community, a political apology serves to repair social ignorance of his suffering.
	Violation of victims' human rights	Political apology reinforces the legitimacy of victims' human rights.
Forgiveness	Standing victory of the perpetrator's injustice	In naming and condemning the perpetrator's injustice and in willing to construct a future where the wrong no longer has standing or efficacy, a victim helps to bring down the standing victory of the perpetrator's political injustice.
	Harm to the person of the victim	In willing to construct a new relationship, a victim regains his agency and potentially overcomes long-term debilitating effects of anger.
	Harm to the soul of the perpetrator	In cases where a perpetrator has apologized, in forgiving, a victim ratifies this apology, thereby releasing the perpetrator from guilt, and gives the perpetrator new freedom and strength to continue in a restorative direction.
	Violation of victims' human rights	In practicing constructive forgiveness, a victim wills a relationship between herself and the perpetrator that is characterized by mutual respect for human rights and sets an example for others in the political order to practice a similar relationship.

their demand for retribution. Other times, one practice will contain what another lacks. Punishment, for instance, calls the wrongdoer to account for his deeds in a way that none of the other practices does.

That the ethic of political reconciliation centers on practices rather than purely on principles corresponds to the sense in which reconciliation is a process of restoration, not merely a goal. It follows the school of virtue ethics in prescribing a set of activities that, each in their own unique way, bring about an excellence or a dimension of flourishing.

Incomplete and partial, the practices are ongoing and may even occur years or decades after the injustices themselves. Even in the 1990s the German government was redressing the events of the Holocaust, just as in the early 2000s Spain began debating remembrance of its civil war of the 1930s. The six practices are not intended to be accomplished serially or in any particular order and always will be tailored, adapted, and configured in unique combinations according to the contours of a given landscape of political injustice.

I present for each of the six practices: an overview of its role in the age of peacebuilding; an account of how it uniquely reflects reconciliation as a concept of justice, mercy, and peace; in some cases, a contrast with the way that other concepts of justice view the practice; a description of how the practice performs primary and secondary restorations; and an exploration of additional moral dilemmas that are unique to the practice. Space constrains the attention that I can give to each practice. The ethics surrounding any of these practices merits, and in several cases has been treated in, a volume at least the size of this one. I select punishment and forgiveness for deeper treatment because they garner the most heated controversy, both in their own right and in the eyes of those who view them as being in tension with each other, and thus merit the most extensive ethical development. In this chapter, I turn to the first four practices.

Building Socially Just Institutions

Since 1974, some ninety societies across eastern Europe, Latin America, Africa, and East Asia have sought to replace dictatorships with democracies.[1] With this trend has come new constitutions: "By some estimates," report Erin Daly and Jeremy Sarkin, "fully 60 percent of the constitutions in effect by the early 2000s were adopted since 1989."[2] Since the end of the cold war, a similarly intense global wave of peace operations sponsored by the United Nations—what I referred to earlier as the United

Nations Revolution—has sought to foster human rights and democratic institutions in states that have seen civil war. Between 1987 and 1994, the U.N. Security Council increased its resolutions fourfold, tripled its peacekeeping operations, multiplied by seven its economic sanctions, increased its military forces in the field from 10,000 to more than 70,000, and raised its budget for peacekeeping from $230 million to $3.6 billion.[3] Eighty percent of the peace operations undertaken since 1945 began after 1989.[4] These operations have burgeoned not only in number but in ambition. They have come to include humanitarian relief, election monitoring, refugee resettlement, the disarmament of military factions, reform of police and military units, the construction of judicial institutions, and, in some cases, the assumption by international authorities of states' sovereign powers over their military and police.

Building institutions based on human rights and democracy is, of course, at the heart of the liberal peace. The global outburst of these efforts can be attributed to the wide and rapid spread of democracy as a political ideal; a human rights revolution promulgated through international law, international organizations, and the rise of NGOs dedicated to the cause; and the end of the cold war, which allowed renewed cooperation in the U.N. Security Council. Is building socially just institutions also a practice of reconciliation? Many would not think so. Reconciliation contradicts, complements, or is a second-best alternative to human rights and democracy, skeptics say. But if political reconciliation is a form of justice that seeks to restore right relationship, then building socially just institutions is entirely fittingly a component of political reconciliation.

The main primary wound that this practice redresses is the lack of respect and legal guarantee for human rights. I argued earlier that this lack of respect and guarantee is itself a wound to persons and right relationship. Violations of human rights are not simply assaults on the persons and goods that these rights protect—life, bodily integrity, economic livelihood, and the like—but are also violations of a respect that citizens owe to other citizens (both within and outside their own state) and that governments practice when they enshrine rights in their laws and enforce them. Human rights are a form of right relationship that involves complex claims between citizens, between citizens and state institutions, and between the institutions of one state and the citizens and institutions of other states.

What does the enshrinement and guarantee of human rights involve? It first and foremost entails laws, institutions, and enforcement measures that protect against the most egregious political crimes: war crimes, crimes against humanity, genocide, military aggression, torture, rape, and forced displacement. It also involves protections against other crimes that are characteristic of dictatorships: surveillance, illegal detention, and the restriction of expression, assembly, religion, and movement. As articulated in international law and understood in political practice across the globe, human rights include and are themselves sustained by features of democracy such as elections, legislative institutions, the right to vote, participation, and representation. Guaranteeing human rights also requires the rule of law: judicial institutions that provide fair trials and criminal procedures, humane and proportionate punishments for valid crimes, equal protection under the law, and other related values. Essential, too, are basic economic provisions such as the right to form unions, to own property, and to enjoy the means of subsistence, a fair wage, and safe working conditions. In sites of civil war and genocide, providing and guaranteeing rights requires not only sound institutions but also the range of activities that U.N. peace operations have come to undertake. To human rights can be added the obligations of states in international and humanitarian law, especially the prohibition of military aggression.

When citizens see that human rights have attained the status and force of law, they will more readily regard the institutions that uphold these rights as legitimate and adopt the kinds of virtues that attend democratic deliberation, such as civility. These attitudinal changes are secondary restorations, though they reinforce the rights and institutions that primary restorations construct. It is the prospect of this virtuous cycle that leads theorists and practitioners alike to insist that once violence has stopped, building at least minimally just institutions is the most urgent task of peacebuilding.

Building socially just institutions is where the liberal peace and the ethic of political reconciliation converge most clearly. The rights, institutions, and laws for which liberals find justification in the writings of Locke, Kant, Mill, and Rawls are also ones for which religious traditions provide justifications and which an expanded version of restorative justice can readily adopt. Political orders characterized by human rights and democracy are the goal of political reconciliation and the core of a just peace. Constructing such orders enacts mercy in the wide sense that the ethic defines mercy.

To say that building socially just institutions is ethical is not to say that it is easy. Transitions to democracy are often tumultuous and reversible. U.N. peace operations are burdened with complexity, lack of funds, local opposition, and the sheer scale of the conflicts that they aim to transform. Some of these difficulties involve controversy. Political scientist Roland Paris, for instance, has criticized U.N. peace operations for rushing to conduct elections, promote a free media, and open up markets without first building stability. Institutions must come before liberalization, he counsels, arguing that such key Enlightenment rights theorists as Hobbes, Locke, and Kant support his position.[5] As important as Paris's argument is, it has more to do with operations than with deep ethics. Even he does not question the basic values that peace operations promote.

Other criticisms of the contemporary practice of building socially just institutions, though, run deeper. Some critics charge that in some cultures promoting the whole panoply of human rights is morally overambitious and even imperialistic. After the United States overthrew the repressive Taliban government in Afghanistan in 2001, for instance, a heated debate occurred between Afghan leaders and Western human rights advocates as well as within the U.S. government over whether the laws of the new Afghan government would have to match the full standards of the international human rights conventions, especially in matters of religious freedom and women's rights. The United States eventually consented to a constitution that was far weaker in these matters than what human rights advocates wanted.

How does the ethic approach such issues? Via the two tasks outlined in chapter 1. The first of these is to set forth the meaning of justice in the wake of massive injustices. Here, the ethic calls for the wide range of human rights, including religious freedom and the rights of women. The second task involves forging overlapping consensus in contexts of deep religious and cultural disagreement. In this case, it would favor strains of Islam that are more favorable to religious freedom and the rights of women. Such strains exist in Afghanistan, even if they are not dominant. Where constitutions and laws fail to reflect a consensus on these rights, the ethic judges them less than fully just, though sometimes they are the best that can be obtained.

If some critics charge the ethic with forcing too much, others worry that it demands too little. One school of contemporary transitional justice criticizes approaches that focus on political and civil human rights while ignoring gross economic and gender inequalities.[6] Such inequalities are not only intrinsically unjust, they argue, but are also one of the chief causes of the armed conflict to which transitional justice responds. Although reparations to human rights victims are a common feature of transitional justice, it is not individualized compensation but far more systemic measures that this school calls for. Its recommendations range from truth commissions that devote greater attention to economic and gender inequalities to schemes of economic redistribution that attempt to flatten out inequalities.

Should political reconciliation involve a greater measure of economic justice? A holistic approach can hardly omit such justice, it seems, but cautionary notes are in order. It is clear that armed conflict occurs disproportionately in countries at low levels of economic development, but economic inequality contributes to armed conflict in different manners and degrees in different places. Economist Paul Collier has argued that it is not the broad "grievances" of impoverished masses that cause conflict but rather the "greed" of small armed groups that seize and extract rents from a country's raw materials assets—mineral wealth in central Africa, for instance.[7] Similarly disputed is the best route to economic development. Advocates of an economically reformist transitional justice criticize the reigning orthodoxy of economic development, a close cousin of the liberal peace known as the Washington Consensus, which stresses free markets, low barriers to trade, commerce, and investment, and reduced public sectors. While the Washington Consensus may have weaknesses and has come under fire from globally prominent economists, strongly interventionist schemes of redistribution have hardly achieved a consensus either.[8] Continual controversies and rapid evolution in theories about both the economic origins of conflict and the best route to economic development make these theories difficult to integrate into a general ethic of political reconciliation.

Some proposals of the critics of inequality, though, merit incorporation. Truth commissions ought to investigate and expose economic and gender injustices, especially ones that result from structures that cause and perpetuate inequality and structures that stem from corruption, crimes, exploitation, and human rights violations. South Africa's apartheid, with its legal confinement of ownership, residency, and rights of movement to certain races, stands out as an obvious example. Admirably, some truth commissions—including those in Peru, Guatemala, Sierra Leone, and Timor-Leste—have given attention to the economic dimension of injustice. Building socially just institutions ought also to involve guaranteeing those rights that best promote greater equality: the rights to own property, move about freely, form unions, and enjoy education and health care. Finally, even if there is no consensus about the best route to economic development, recognizing the role of development in peace-building is essential. Radical inequalities, malnutrition, unequal access to resources, corruption, restrictions on the rights of women, and the weak states that result from lack of revenues are all intrinsically unjust and all contribute to conflict. Increasingly, U.N. peacebuilding operations are recognizing the importance of economic development.[9] So should an ethic of political reconciliation.

A final issue of ethics surrounding building socially just institutions is the role of armed struggle in this practice. What place does war have in an ethic of political reconciliation? Building socially just institutions requires defeating the dictatorial regimes and aggressor states that stand in their way. This was the Kairos Document's point: True reconciliation must involve an overthrow of apartheid. The ethic of political reconciliation, then, honors the just war tradition—both its criteria for when war can be fought (*jus ad bellum*) and for what sort of means are just within war (*jus in bello*)—whose basic commitments can be found in international law, natural law reasoning, and each of the religious traditions that inform this book. Disappointingly, contemporary just war thought has little to say about civil war, the most prevalent kind of war in the past half century. The broad outlines of a theory of just civil war would allow a "right of revolution" in cases where governments egregiously violate or fail to uphold human rights, where the challenging party represents a markedly more just alternative, and where the gain in justice can be judged to be proportionate to the loss of life. These criteria, especially the last, may well render most of the world's civil wars of the past half century unjust, but in those cases where war, either international or civil, is justified, it may be thought of as a dimension of establishing socially just institutions.

When armed struggle is necessary, it must be pursued in a way that brings not merely the victory of one side but also a peace characterized by justice. That the very purpose of a just war is a just peace can be found in the writings of such classic just war thinkers as Augustine and Aquinas. Even during the antiapartheid movement's struggle to overthrow South Africa's regime, it held out the prospect of a peace in which blacks would live together with whites as equal citizens. Nonviolent movements manifest particularly vividly the possibility of struggling against injustice while holding out the prospect of a just peace. Human rights scholar Adrian

Karatnycky has demonstrated that nonviolent opposition to dictatorial regimes is not only possible but also common. By his count, about fifty of the sixty-seven transitions to democracy between 1972 and 2005 were driven by "people power." Strikingly, transitions to democracy driven by nonviolent struggle were significantly more likely to produce sustainable freedom than ones wrought by violence.[10] Though nonviolent movements will not succeed under all conditions and against all opponents—a view that even Mahatma Gandhi held—the moral logic of reconciliation demands that the possibility of nonviolence be pursued.

Reconciliation also demands efforts to achieve peace once the struggle is over. A plethora of U.N. peace operations as well as U.S. interventions in such places as Kosovo, Afghanistan, and Iraq have led just war theorists to envision a *jus post bellum* that would define the moral responsibilities of victorious forces.[11] Do states that have intervened or achieved victory in stopping aggression have a responsibility then to undertake statebuilding in the way that the United States and its allies undertook in Japan and Germany after World War II? This question, too, deserves more treatment than I can offer here. Broadly implicit in the practice of building socially just institutions is a *prima facie* duty to contribute to such construction, though it must surely be qualified by the criterion of "probability of success," a simple idea that admittedly conceals the complexity of the tasks that peacebuilding operations involve. A consensus of scholars agrees that, to date, these operations have had mixed success.[12] Mixed, though, implies that the results are in part positive and worth improving on.

Acknowledgment

Even when rights are restored in laws and institutions, instances of their violation may well remain forgotten, ignored, or suppressed. Redressing this social ignorance is the goal of the second practice: acknowledgment. Acknowledgment is the action by which a political official or body of officials, speaking on behalf of the political order, recognizes victims as having suffered a political injustice, as having been wounded by this political injustice, and as being full citizens again. Acknowledgment is amplified when other citizens join in this same recognition.

During the age of peacebuilding new forms of acknowledgment have proliferated, the most prominent being the truth commission, an officially sanctioned body that is tasked with investigating the injustices of a specified place and period of time.[13] Political scientists Kathryn Sikkink and Carrie Booth Walling have demonstrated a sharp increase in truth commissions since the 1980s.[14] Truth commissions in Latin America in the 1980s, especially in Argentina and Chile, were the first to attract global attention. These inspired the most famous truth commission to date, South Africa's Truth and Reconciliation Commission of the mid-1990s, which in turn became the standard for other truth commissions around the world, including ones in Sierra Leone, Timor-Leste, Peru, and elsewhere. Some forty truth commissions have appeared since 1974.[15] The vast majority publish a public final report. Otherwise, though, they vary markedly. Some involve public hearings, others do not. Some identify the names of perpetrators, others do not. Some involve international commissioners, others only domestic personalities. They vary in their authority to compel testimony. A few commissions lack the official status that bona fide truth commissions enjoy but perform much the same kind of investigation, as did Guatemala's Recovery of Historical Memory (REMHI) Project, which the Catholic Church established and conducted.[16]

Other forms of acknowledgment have abounded, too. Germany's effort to make available to victims the files that the Stasi, or East German secret police, had kept on them during the period of communist government is one example. Older and more common types of acknowledgment include memorials, monuments, museums, days of commemoration, and public rituals. A wave of memorials and museums to Holocaust victims swept over Germany following a national debate about its Nazi past in the 1980s. Public school history textbooks make the acknowledgment of past injustices part of the education of children and are often the subject of great controversy.

Revealing the truth about injustice is a standard component of the liberal peace as well. A campaign for a legal "right to truth" is now afoot among international lawyers. What, in their view, is the purpose of revealing truth? To expose the lies that officials tell about the past; to prevent these same officials from retaking power; to establish a new regime or a peace agreement on a basis of integrity; to identify perpetrators and promote their accountability; to facilitate reparations, trials, the rule of law, and the reform of courts and other government institutions; and to honor victims.[17] Contemporary liberals tend to be skeptical of more ambitious aims for acknowledgment. They doubt that public truth telling can or ought to pursue the healing or transformation of victims.

The ethic of political reconciliation goes beyond the acknowledgment that liberalism envisions. Acknowledgment of past injustice not only reduces the lies that circulate in public discourse, as Michael Ignatieff put it, and helps to establish the rule of law and the like—what I call secondary restorations—but also, more directly, it aims to achieve intrinsically valuable primary restorations, redressing wounds that are wider and deeper than is often recognized. In an ethic of political reconciliation, the transformation of relationships through the redress of wounds is a pursuit that is properly political, though in some ways also properly limited by the political. Mutual recognition is not only a feature of the justice of right relationship in the present but a mode of repairing right relationships that past wrongs have wounded. In willing the improvement of what is broken, these restorations are also matters of mercy. The resulting condition is one of greater peace.

Primary Restorations

The failure of the surrounding political order to acknowledge victims' suffering is itself a wound, the wound that acknowledgment most strongly and directly addresses. This sounds simple to the point of tautology, but it is in fact more complex.

Recall the distinctive nature of a political injustice. A perpetrator—a Chilean torturer, a Serbian officer at Srebrenica—acts in the name of a political program or ideal and treats his victim as little more than an enemy or obstacle to this agenda. The resulting wounds diminish the victim not only personally—psychologically, economically, bodily—but also by severing his right relationship with the perpetrator and with the political order in whose name the perpetrator has acted. In part, the severance of right relationship with the political order is restored by the first practice, building socially just institutions that guarantee and uphold human rights. Yet even if victims' rights were restored, a failure of the political order and its members to recognize their wounds constitutes still another wound. The nature of this wound is difficult to describe in precise terms, but it can be understood as the political analogue of the plight of one who suffers alone in a hospital, say from a disease or from the wounds of a crime, yet receives no attention, encouragement, or help from loved ones. Her isolation itself is a wound. The victim of political injustices is isolated, too, though in her case it is from the members of the political order in whose name the injustice was committed.[18]

What acknowledgment accomplishes is a political version of solidarity with the suffering. A spokesperson for the political order, hopefully joined by other members of the political order, confers awareness of, sympathy for, and a will to restore the suffering of the victim. When the victim receives this recognition, her condition of social isolation is alleviated. One South African torture victim, Mzykisi Mdidimba, expresses that her testimony at the Truth and Reconciliation Commission "has taken it off my heart.... When I have told stories of my life before, afterward, I am crying, crying, crying, and felt that it was not finished. This time, I know that what they've done to me will be among these people and all over the country. I still have some sort of crying, but also joy inside."[19] Mdidimba is clear: It is because her suffering has been made known "among these people and all over the country" in a forum that has bestowed sympathetic public acknowledgment on her that this suffering has been taken "off her heart."

As Mdidimba's statement suggests, acknowledgment is a form of social interaction in which officials of the political order invite victims to think anew about the injustice that wounded them—not to forget it but to view the political forces behind it as having been defeated, superseded, and nullified. When their wounds are seen as part of past injustice, victims are encouraged by their surrounding social order to think of themselves as no longer victims. In this way, their memories may be transformed.

The political character of the practice of acknowledgment is crucial to what it can do—and what it cannot. Critics sometimes take truth commissions to task for not bringing about long-term psychological healing. Such a criterion, though, is not only overly stringent but also misplaced. Truth commissions cannot and ought not to be expected to effect long-term healing. They can only redress the public, political dimension of injustice, which is integral to but not exhaustive of the wounds that the injustice has inflicted.

Is there evidence that public, political acknowledgment is truly restorative? Mdidimba's testimony speaks favorably. But what should we make of the findings of the Trauma Centre for Victims of Violence and Torture in Cape Town, South Africa, that 50 to 60 percent of victims who gave testimony to the commission experienced difficulties after testifying or expressed regret for having testified, or of reports of women who suffered sexual violations being traumatized by having to tell of this violence at nationally televised hearings?[20]

In his study of South Africa's TRC, political scientist David Backer compared the commission's effect on victims who participated in hearings, victims who did not, and the public at large. Victims are "generally satisfied" with their decision to take part, he reports. Almost identically with the general public, about three-quarters of victims applaud the TRC process as a whole. More individuated questions, though, show dissatisfaction with parts of the process. Backer surveyed victims' perceptions of the justice of the TRC on eight dimensions—acknowledgment, voice, truth, apology, accountability, punishment, reparation, and systemic change—and finds that only with respect to acknowledgment did they carry a positive view. Though this finding is broadly negative, it is a positive one for the practice of acknowledgment. Among the negative judgments, most of them arguably stem from factors that were beyond the control of the commission or were related to the negotiation of its founding: the lack of punishment, reparations, or redress of socioeconomic inequalities. Judgments are more favorable toward the most distinctive accomplishments of the TRC itself.[21]

Given these mixed results, what forms and features of public acknowledgment are most effective? What seems to make the most difference is personalism—direct and empathetic attention to the individual victim. The most reparative forms of acknowledgment are those in which political officials and onlookers exercise the highest degree of empathy for the victim, provide support for the victim in any trauma that public acknowledgment may provoke, offer long-term support for the victim's healing, and encourage integration of the victim into a community from which he may have become alienated.

Truth commissions vary in their level of personalism. Final commission reports document thousands of violations, giving acknowledgment to a broad range of victims but offering little personal recognition. In some commissions, acknowledgment occurs when victims give their statement behind closed doors. The Chilean Commission on Truth and Reconciliation displayed a flag on every desk where testimony was given, thus conferring the government's imprimatur on the victim's words. Other commissions, such as those in South Africa, Sierra Leone, and Peru, involve public hearings in which victims appear before commissioners, loved ones, other citizens, and sometimes even perpetrators. In South Africa, some hearings were televised nationally, creating an audience of observers that spanned the citizenry but whose empathy was mixed and remote. Many commissions have provided counseling for victims both prior to and following their testimony. Still other commissions, like Timor-Leste's, have involved community forums in which victims tell their story before members of their village as well as perpetrators, who were thus brought to hear the impact of their deeds.

Among the best practitioners of personalism was Guatemala's REMHI. Beginning in 1995, REMHI sent eight hundred volunteers out to investigate the civil war's massacres, the vast majority of which occurred in rural Mayan villages at the hand of the government's Civil Defense Patrols. Known as *animadores* or "agents of reconciliation," the volunteers were trained to interview applicants with emotional, spiritual, and psychological sensitivity, learning how simply to be quiet and listen, react when people cry, and remain as long as people need to tell their stories. They performed all of this in seventeen local Mayan languages. They paid particular attention to gender, bringing to light sexual violence and the burdens borne by women victims in caring for their families and communities. Through 7,000 interviews, they recorded the stories and facts surrounding the massacres. REMHI planned to follow up, too, through a popularized version of the truth commission report and village-level workshops. Personalism was also manifested in Guatemala by initiatives outside REMHI: communal exhumations of graves, memorials, monuments, and commemorations, all at the village level.[22]

The capacity of practitioners of acknowledgment to redress and transform the wound of indifference is echoed in Judaism, Christianity, Islam, and restorative justice. The three faith traditions point to a God who actively hears the cries of the poor and the oppressed, who comforts and relieves them by his communication of awareness and love, who calls members of the religious community and political rulers to join in this recognition, and associates this recognition with justice. In condemning "mighty men" who cause "the cries of the poor to reach [God]" and in describing God as one who has "heard the plea of the afflicted," the Book of Job proffers a concept of justice that the Jewish Bible repeats frequently.[23] In training its volunteers, REMHI appealed to two verses that link acknowledgment to social restoration, one from Genesis, in which God asks Cain, "Where is your brother?" and the other from Nehemiah, expressing a call to rebuild "the city of your fathers, which lies in ruins." In the Christian tradition, the justice of acknowledging the poor and victims of oppression is strongest in the writings of theologians who view Christ's death on the cross as an act of identification with the forgotten. "Through his own abandonment by God, the crucified Christ brings God to those who are abandoned by God," claims Jürgen Moltmann.[24] In the social thought of the Catholic Church, acknowledgment is a dimension of solidarity, which, Pope John Paul II explains, is exercised when members of a society "recognize one another as persons" and show awareness of the poor. Solidarity is specifically Christian, he says, when one's neighbor is seen as the living image of God.[25] In Islam, acknowledgment is manifested in Allah's commands to remember the poor and to refrain from the injustice of forgetting the needy and the oppressed.[26] One of the restorative justice movement's persistent criticisms of Western systems of justice is that they confer little recognition on victims of crime. When the community and the perpetrator confer such acknowledgment, a dimension of restoration and of justice is achieved. Restorative justice's stress on participation also reflects the virtue of personalism.[27]

Acknowledgment also redresses other wounds of political injustice by, for example, bringing to light crimes that were previously unknown to victims and to the public. The Final Report of Peru's Truth and Reconciliation Commission, for instance, revealed the number of fatalities in the war between the government and the Sendero Luminoso to be some three times the number that both human rights organizations and the government were citing.[28] Knowing the truth about how and at whose hands one was blinded or lost a loved one can sometimes reopen old wounds, but victims have also reported that such knowledge can bring healing. When a political process renders a judgment about the justice of these facts, knowledge starts to become acknowledgment and is more likely to be restorative.

Acknowledgment can also offer repair with respect to wounds that are closely associated with perpetrators. By bringing to light truths about injustices that were previously suppressed, political processes of acknowledgment, such as processes of punishment, can strip these injustices of their legitimacy, that is, bring down their standing victory. At times, truth commissions can also inspire contrition in perpetrators (the wounded soul of the perpetrator being one of the wounds of political injustice). This is infrequent, though, and occurs mostly when perpetrators take part directly in hearings or community forums.

A final primary wound that acknowledgment addresses is the lack of human rights. Acknowledgment assists in building socially just institutions by encouraging recognition and legitimacy for human rights. When governments make human rights the benchmark for truth commissions, textbooks, or memorials, they also declare these rights, with the full force of their authority, as a standard for their people to live by.

This is the problem, according to certain critics: moral overreach. They argue, first, that it is naïve to think that a single notion of truth about the past can attain common agreement. Second, when a government commends a single truth for an entire nation, they claim, it violates the norms of liberal democracy, one of the basic purposes of which is to preserve space for debate about truth, justice, and collective values. Timothy Garton Ash thus applauds the South African Truth and Reconciliation Commission for its revelation of repression and violence but questions its assertion of "truth with a capital T" and hears an Orwellian ring in the term *truth commission*.[29] Michael Ignatieff recommends that truth commissions pursue "factual truth" about what happened rather than "moral truth" that explains why the events occurred and who was responsible.[30] Political philosopher Andrew Schaap calls into question truth commissions' goals of seeking to establish a "redemptive narrative, a collective memory" and sees truth commissions instead as a vehicle for recovering the possibility of disagreement among citizens.[31] In the wake of a dictatorship or civil war, civic disagreement alone is a priceless achievement.

Even knowing factual truths about the past is far from simple, several of these critics argue. About this, they are right. Any attempt to know what happened at a village massacre or in a torture chamber will be hindered by conflicting accounts, memories fogged by time and trauma, problems of selection among a mass of detail, and lies. Assessing the motives, levels of duress, and other circumstances behind violations is all the more challenging. The difficulty of these problems varies from episode to episode but rarely can they be overcome altogether.[32] Does it follow, then, that we ought to give up seeking moral truth?

The moral truth that ought to govern political acknowledgment is human rights: no more and no less. No more because a more ambitious standard risks becoming partisan, the agenda of this or that party, a value that ought to be open to debate, deliberation, and voting, not fixed as common for everyone. No less because human rights are the standard that gives truth commissions and other public forms of acknowledgment form and direction. It is difficult to imagine a truth commission operating without first answering: the truth about what? If truth commissions are mainly platforms for establishing democratic contestation, then by what standard should they conduct their work of investigating and publicizing acts of injustice?

The problem with contestation as the grounding rationale for truth commissions goes deeper. It asserts that contestation ought to be preferred over other values as the common standard for a society. On what basis, however, should we prefer contestation over, for instance, the values of public order and safety proclaimed by a dictator or, more plausibly, such values as human dignity, the prohibition of torture, and the right to life? If one argues that contestation trumps values as the governing standard for political acknowledgment, one must either make the case that contestation is truer or better than these values or else one simply asserts it by fiat. Yet to adopt either of these strategies is to refute oneself, for then one is arguing—impossibly—that the value of contestation is to be considered beyond contestation. It is difficult to reject the idea that some value or set of values ought to govern the proceedings of political acknowledgment.

The positive argument for human rights is that they are integral to the justice of right relationship as well as intrinsically valuable. Liberal democracies around the world have incorporated human rights into their constitutions and regard them as beyond debate. They are central to the U.N. Charter and many other international legal documents. Judaism, Christianity, and Islam commonly offer endorsements for human rights (though Islam contains more divisions and reservations), restorative justice readily adapts to human rights, and the Thomistic natural law and Kantian traditions of ethics are well-resourced to defend the concept. Skeptics are still entitled to be skeptical; I cannot establish the truth of human rights definitively here. The overlapping consensus, though, is formidable.

Secondary Restorations

Acknowledgment can also bring positive changes in broad popular attitudes that benefit democratic regimes and peace settlements—a form of social capital I have called secondary restorations. There are several ways this could happen. One is that when governments bring to light injustices in the past, they demonstrate their commitment to justice in the present, thus leading citizens to view new institutions or a new peace settlement as more legitimate. Second is Ignatieff's mechanism: Exposing the lies of the previous regime drains it of popular support. Third, more directly, truth commissions produce recommendations for reform.

It is also possible that acknowledgment will backfire, producing negative secondary effects. The public debate that truth commissions (as well as monuments, memorials, and other public commemorations) provoke may turn out not to reinforce institutions and settlements but to exacerbate division. In some countries, public conversation is choked off by decisions or events—in El Salvador, for instance, by an amnesty law that the government passed almost immediately after the release of the truth commission's report. Truth commissions may also raise public expectations about social change, accountability, and reparations and then leave citizens more disappointed when these fail to materialize.

Evidence for the kind of secondary restorations that acknowledgment produces comes in two varieties. The first comes from social scientists who, taking advantage of the large number of truth commissions to date, have investigated how they correlate to increases in democracy. The results have been mixed. Political scientists Hun Joon Kim and Kathryn Sikkink show that truth commissions correlate positively with improvements in human rights practices.[33] Sikkink and Walling find that countries with both truth commissions and trials had better human rights scores than countries with trials alone.[34] Tove Grete Lie and her colleagues find that, when peace settlements are accompanied by progress toward democracy, truth commissions contribute to these settlements' durability.[35] A separate trio of researchers, however, discover that when truth commissions occur alone, in the absence of amnesties or trials, they are associated negatively with democracy and human rights. It is only when they occur in combination with both amnesties and trials that positive correlations result.[36] Still another researcher, Eric Brahm, finds that societies that adopt truth commissions are no better or worse than societies that do not adopt them.[37] Taken together, these studies yield uncertainty about the secondary restorations.

A second form of evidence consists of surveys that measure directly the attitudes that secondary restorations bring about. The most systematic surveys come from South Africa. Political scientist James Gibson's nuanced and multitiered survey of 3,700 South Africans in 2001 showed that among whites, Asians, and coloureds (all racial classifications of the apartheid regime) learning the truth about the past decreased animosity and increased the sense of being reconciled, though the hostility of blacks neither increased nor decreased.[38] Backer's surveys also measured the reaction of the general public to the TRC. Among victims, 89 percent of respondents were of the view that TRC was necessary to avoid a civil war in Africa, while the general public was more mixed but still positive, with 54 percent agreeing with the proposition. When the general public was asked to evaluate the TRC on the whole, 24.3 percent of respondents "strongly supported" it and 52.2 percent "supported" it—an overwhelmingly positive response. When asked how well the TRC has done in "providing a true and unbiased account of South Africa's history" 41.2 percent of the public said "excellent job" and 42.5 percent said "pretty good job."[39] In these surveys, the secondary restorations of truth commissions, or at least one of them, fare better: Commissions can garner the positive evaluation of the general public. Unproven, though, is whether this esteem translates into increased support for democracy.

Reparations

Reparations, the third practice, are often defined widely enough to include such forms of acknowledgment as memorials, textbook revisions, and apologies. All of the six practices in the ethic of political reconciliation can be thought of as reparations in the sense that their central rationale and aim is reparative or restorative. Here, though, reparations are defined far more narrowly and distinctly as a transfer of money, goods, and services to a victim in response to the political injustices that she suffered. Both governments and individual perpetrators can supply reparations, but I will focus on the governments. Recipients can include individuals but also large groups and their representatives. Reparations as conceived here include most of the types outlined in the Basic Principles and Guidelines approved by the United Nations General Assembly in 2005.[40] They are, first, restitution, which involves restoration, to the degree that it is possible, of liberty, human rights, citizenship, property, and employment to the condition that the victim enjoyed prior to the violation of the human rights; second, compensation in the form of financial payments for any "economically assessable damage"; and third, rehabilitation, which includes medical care and psychological, legal and social services. A fourth type of reparations, satisfaction, includes measures that I categorize as other practices, including guarantees against recurrence of the human rights violations, the exposure of truth, and public apology.

Like truth commissions, reparations settlements have sharply expanded during the age of peacebuilding, beginning in the 1980s with Argentina's comparatively generous reparations to victims of the Dirty Wars. The historical prototype for these settlements, though, arose a generation earlier in Germany, the same country whose injustices elicited the historical prototype of international tribunals, the Nuremberg Trials. The Luxembourg Agreement of 1952, in which the German government pledged 3 billion

Deutschmarks to the state of Israel as reparations for survivors of the Holocaust, was the first major payment granted by a national government to its (or, more accurately, to its predecessor regime's) victims and remains the largest reparations payment to date. Germany has continued to pay reparations for Nazi atrocities, by now some 70 billion dollars.[41] In addition to Argentina, other major reparations have included Chile's for the victims of Pinochet's crimes; the United States' payment of 1.2 billion dollars to Japanese Americans the U.S. government interned during World War II; Germany's agreement in 2001 to provide payments to forced and slave laborers during the Holocaust; and the efforts of post-transition governments in Poland, the Czech Republic, and Hungary to compensate for property that previous communist governments had confiscated.

During this same period, reparations have also risen in their standing in international law. Even earlier, reparations—or closely related concepts —had established a place in the Universal Declaration of Human Rights, the American Convention on Human Rights, the International Covenant on Civil and Political Rights, the Torture Convention, and the European Convention on Human Rights. In Latin America, reparations took a major leap forward in the Inter-American Court of Human Rights' decision in the Velásquez-Rodriguez case of 1988, which set forth the state's duty not only to investigate and punish human rights violations but also to make reparations to victims. The United Nations' Basic Principles and Guidelines of 2005 stands as a major commitment to reparations in international law.

What is the moral rationale for reparations? One is punitive. The most memorable application of this rationale once again involved Germany but this time as the provider of gargantuan and crippling reparations to the Allies at whose hands it was defeated in World War I. Reparations might also serve as a punishment imposed on individual perpetrators of political injustices. Whether reparations can be justified on punitive grounds depends on the validity of those grounds and their compatibility with the justice of reconciliation-the subject of the next chapter.

Another rationale is distributive justice, that branch of justice that concerns itself with a just allotment of wealth, offices, and opportunities. Distributive justice judges the morality of this allotment apart from whether acts of wrongdoing brought it about. In a country where massive wealth is concentrated in the hands of a few and the masses live in poverty, for instance, proponents of distributive justice judge this distribution to be unjust independently of how it came into being. Sometimes advocates of reparations appeal to distributive justice. Proponents of property restitution in postcommunist central Europe, for instance, saw it as a means of privatizing the economy and thereby increasing overall wealth as well as a means of righting wrongs. Opponents meanwhile questioned why, especially given scarce resources, property claims should be privileged when most people living under communist regimes suffered deprivations of a wide variety. "If everyone suffered, why should only some be redressed?" queried Czech Republic president and former dissident Václav Havel.[42]

Distributive justice, however, is not the proper rationale for reparations, the aim of which is to redress victims of identifiable acts of wrongdoing, not to rectify inequitable distributions of wealth. As I argued earlier, distributive justice is important in its own right and has a place in an ethic of political reconciliation. Distributive justice may compete with reparations claims, as it has in central Europe, but it is not the reason for reparations. Of course, acts of political injustice may sometimes take the form of economic discrimination and deprivations, as in the creation of the apartheid state in South Africa. In response to these injustices, reparations may be warranted, but this warrant arises from wrongful acts, not simply an inequitable distribution of wealth.

The liberal tradition offers still another rationale for reparations: They restore the victim, as much as is possible, to her condition prior to the injustice. This rationale is often phrased as *restitutio in integrum*. The German word for Holocaust reparations, *wiedergutmachung* ("making good again"), captures this idea, too. The same rationale underlies tort law in the Anglo-American tradition and, broadly speaking, reparations in international law.[43] The phrase *as much as possible* is important. The loss of life and limb, along with trauma and other injuries, is not easily rectified, advocates realize, but where restoration is not possible, compensation may be. The Inter-American Court of Human Rights, for instance, has devised elaborate formulas for calculating compensation for various kinds of suffering. Behind *restitutio in integrum* are several liberal commitments: a stress on individual freedom as the value to be restored, the rights of victims, deserved punishment, and deterrence of future crimes.[44] What should be made of this rationale for reparations?

How Reparations Bring Restorations

The ethic of political reconciliation enfolds liberalism's rationale but calls for something wider. The ethic justifies reparations according to what they repair—persons and relationships that have suffered the wounds of political injustice. With respect to one primary wound, in particular, political reconciliation converges with liberalism's aim of restoring the status quo *ex ante*. This wound is the one that I have called harm to the person of the victim—bodily, economic, emotional, and psychological. Both liberalism and reconciliation want to put back what the victim lost—again, as much as is possible. When harm to a person occurs through political injustices, it is up to the state to ensure the payment of reparations. This payment ought to occur as widely as possible given the resources available (which are often scarce). Reparations fall short when they overlook or exclude an entire faction or class of victims in a given site of political injustice—victims of sexual violence, for instance.

As a justification, repair of the harm to the person of victims is not without problems. One problem arises with respect to a particular variant of reparations claims, namely those made by descendants of victims of political injustices who are no longer alive. As such claimants assert, had not my great grandfather been enslaved, his land seized, or he and his community massacred, I would be better off today and so am entitled to reparations.

In a widely cited article, political philosopher Jeremy Waldron voices profound skepticism of such claims, which he associates with the native peoples of his own New Zealand and with similar groups in Australia, Canada, and the United States.[45] In part, he argues, these claims depend on dubious historical counterfactuals. How does the claimant know that he would be better off had his grandfather's land not been seized? Had his grandfather kept the land, he might have gambled it away, farmed it in a manner that destroyed the soil for future generations, or sold it out of the family. The descendant has no way of knowing how history—and thus his own fate—would have differed. If his grandfather had been massacred prior to having children, the descendant would not even exist.

Waldron goes on to raise a related argument, that historical injustices may be "overtaken by events in a way that means their injustice has been superseded."[46] Imagine a grassy plain, he proposes, where several groups of people each own water holes from which they derive sustenance. One of these groups seizes the water hole of another group unjustly, out of greed. Now the victim group has a just claim to restitution of its water hole. Then an ecological disaster occurs that causes every water hole to dry up except for the victim group's water hole. The circumstances of this new scenario require the victim group to share its available water. It no longer has a claim to have the status quo *ex ante* restored. It still suffered an injustice, Waldron argues, but new justice claims have now superseded this injustice. What counts most, he says, are the justice claims of the people who presently live on a given piece of land apart from how they or their forebears arrived there.[47]

By Waldron's own allowance, his objections do not erase all reparations claims made by descendants. Can subsequent events supersede previous injustices, though, as he claims? Let us allow that such events yield new considerations of justice, usually ones of distributive justice, that compete with claims to restitution. Still, why must we then conclude that the previous injustices have been superseded, at least if *superseded* means "canceled"? To be sure, given the competing claims, full restitution of land may not be the right solution. It has not ceased to be the case, however, that the group that lost its water hole has suffered an injustice or that its members are entitled to compensation in some form.

As for whether a descendant's condition would be different if his forebear had not suffered an injustice, such a counterfactual assertion may be difficult to know in many cases, as Waldron suggests, but in other cases the connection between historical events and the fate of subsequent generations may be clearer than he allows. Many historical injustices cannot be described as one-time events that leave their victims and their victims' children free to proceed on their randomized historical pathways. Often, rather, injustices leave pernicious legacies that follow descendants into the future. Consider African Americans, for instance, who, even after they were freed from slavery in 1863, continued to suffer from Jim Crow laws that sustained slavery's legacy and who, even after the civil rights movement of the 1960s, continued to be hindered by generations of educational and economic disadvantages. In like fashion, seizures of Native Americans' land in the United States left legacies of economic disadvantage and cultural despair that continue to affect the lives of descendants. None of these considerations makes claims for reparations, for these people or for others, simple or straightforward. The degree to which descendants suffer palpably from injustices committed against their forebears varies from situation to situation. In many instances, the connection will be too fuzzy and indirect to make a strong case; certainly the connection will become fuzzier and more indirect as time passes. The claim here is only that, in principle, on the rationale of *restitutio in integrum*, descendants may proffer just claims to reparations.

Similar complexities attend property claims of the kind made in central Europe after the fall of communism.[48] Property that was once seized may have changed hands later and be inhabited by a new owner at the time that reparations claims are made. In some places, properties were seized in a succession of historical episodes: What point in history should serve as a baseline? When original owners are no longer alive, complexities deepen: Properties were not always bequeathed, and it is not always clear who the recipients ought to be if restitution is otherwise justified. Here again, these considerations complicate but not do eviscerate reparations claims. Especially when the possibility of compensation rather than full restitution is admitted, the legacies of wrongs can be addressed with flexibility and cognizance of diverse circumstances.

The largest problem facing reparations in cases of large-scale political injustice is the unavailability of resources. Most of the injustices in the past generation have taken place outside the developed world, in countries where resources are scarce and needed for tasks like rebuilding the economy that will seem far more urgent. Scarcity does not negate the rationale of repairing harm to the person of the victim, but it magnifies the "as much as possible" clause. If reparations can be awarded at all, they can be done so only in part. In many poor countries the sole hope that victims have for adequate reparations is from outside contributions.

Reparations may also redress wounds of political injustice other than direct harms to the person. In these cases, the ethic of political reconciliation moves beyond liberalism. The manner in which political reconciliation deals with these other wounds is much the same as the manner in which acknowledgment does. Reparations are acknowledgment fortified materially. Like acknowledgment, for instance, reparations aim to heal the wound of social ignorance. The state, acting on behalf of the political community, bestows reparations on victims as a way of recognizing their suffering and their restoration to full citizenship (or, if victims are members of another state, the restoration of their full human rights). Reparations operate in these instances by communicating a message. The material transfer fortifies this message, lending it credibility and sincerity. On this justification, the exact amount of reparations is not important. It is not dependent on calculations of how much the victims suffered or on historical counterfactuals. Broadly, reparations as recognition ought to be proportioned to the scale of harm suffered, but this proportion need not be exact. Let us call this principle soft proportionality.

Reparations function similarly to acknowledgment—again with material fortification—in redressing other primary wounds as well. In publicly identifying victims as objects of injustices, reparations proclaim and fortify the legitimacy of human rights, both those of the victim and those of the entire community. Through the same public message, reparations delegitimate the standing victory of political injustices. When victims receive reparations, they are more likely to view a new regime or peace settlement as legitimate, to place trust in it, and to forge bonds of trust and commitment with their fellow citizens—all secondary restorations.

Reparations have a strong grounding in the traditions we have been examining. One of the strongest refrains in restorative justice is that traditional criminal justice does nothing to restore victims or to elicit perpetrators' commitments to restoring victims. Reparations are designed to do both. Material restitution aimed at promoting *shalom*, the peace of restoration, was the core principle for dealing with injured parties in the law of Israel as set forth in the Torah, argues Bible scholar John Hayes. In the postbiblical tradition, the Mishnah prescribed five kinds of harm resulting from injury for which perpetrators are obliged to provide compensation. The perpetrator's restitution also constitutes the first stage in the performance of *teshuva*, or repentance, in Jewish tradition, according to Rabbi Marc Gopin.[49] Likewise, the Islamic tradition of jurisprudence allows relatives of murder victims to choose compensation as a possible punishment for perpetrators. In *musalaha* rituals, the payment of compensation is a crucial step in reconciliation. In the Christian tradition, reparations, paid by sinners to their victims as a penitential gesture toward the restoration of right relationship, date back to the earliest years of the church. "One must do what is possible in order to repair the harm (e.g., return stolen goods, restore the reputation of someone slandered, pay compensation for injuries)," the *Catechism of the Catholic Church* explains.[50] All of these traditions view reparations as a component of the restoration of right relationship following sin, crime, and injustice.

Reparations' material transfer and their redress of harm to the person of the victim make them unique among the six practices and place them in a symbiotic relationship with the other practices. When reparations occur without apology, they risk being branded as blood money. Ambassador J. D. Bindenagel, who helped negotiate a $5 billion settlement in which Germany would compensate those who were slaves and forced laborers during World War II, stresses that without both apology and a financial settlement the agreement would not have been possible.[51] More stalwart were the mothers of the disappeared in Argentina, who continue to refuse compensation because they regard it as the government's strategy to buy their silence.[52] Conversely, apology without reparations can seem empty. Truth telling, an expression of acknowledgment, is another activity whose credibility is fortified by reparations. Lisa LaPlante and Kimberly Theidon found in their interviews with victims who had participated in Peru's Truth and Reconciliation Commission that, while they broadly reported that testifying before the commission was a positive experience, they also had conditioned their participation on the hope of securing material reparations from the government. These reparations have been slow in coming, thus threatening the positive secondary restorations that they might bring.[53] Finally, reparations can foster victims' willingness to forgive. When victims have received acknowledgment, apology, and reparations, they are more willing to exercise the restorative will to forgive. The six practices work together.

Apology

One of the defining differences among the foregoing practices is the respective role that they give to the four idealized actors in the ethic: the state, the community, perpetrators, and victims. In building socially just institutions, the state is the lead actor, though each of the other actors plays supporting roles. Acknowledgment and reparations involve the state and victims as lead actors and the community as a supporting actor, with perpetrators sometimes entering the stage and playing an important role. In apology, the fourth practice, the lead role shifts to the perpetrator.

An apology requires the perpetrator to admit that he performed the deed, recognize that it was wrong, display regret for having done it, communicate this regret to the victim, accept responsibility for it, and pledge not to repeat it. Like all of the other practices, apologies performed in political contexts have grown in frequency. "The Age of Apology," legal scholar Roy L. Brooks calls our time.[54] Psychiatrist Aaron Lazare locates the outbreak of political apologies in the 1990s and finds a sharp increase in them over the course of the decade. Despite this expansion, though, apologies remain dwarfed by the scale of political injustices themselves.

Apologies are rare from those who commit political injustices and especially rare from high-level officials, but they do occur. The most senior official to issue an apology is probably the last president of apartheid South Africa, F. W. de Klerk, who, speaking before the Truth and Reconciliation Commission, said "apartheid was wrong" and apologized for the harm that it did. In subsequent questioning before the commission, however, he denied knowledge of specific crimes committed by members of his government and insisted that they were not official policy, thus emptying his apology of credibility in the eyes of many victims and onlookers.[55] Remarkably, President Nelson Mandela also apologized for crimes that the African National Congress committed in its struggle against apartheid. Apologies came from several other senior and midlevel apartheid officials as well. There was the prominent public confession of retired Argentine navy captain Adolfo Scilingo and the chain reaction of confessions that it set off in Argentina. To these examples of remorseful perpetrators might be added one from my own experience, that of the commander of a Kashmiri Muslim militant force who, after being captured and jailed by the Indian government, came to feel remorse for deaths that he had caused and sought to make amends.

More common, though still rare, are apologies performed by heads of state for injustices committed by past governments. Here again, Germany takes the lead.[56] "The Germans: unsurpassed both at the crime and at repenting it," wrote journalist Daniel Vernet in *Le Monde*.[57] Chancellor Konrad Adenauer's statement of responsibility upon signing the Luxembourg Treaty of reparations of 1952 was the first major executive statement of responsibility and remorse, delivered at a time when Germany was largely still mired in amnesia. Chancellor Willy Brandt fell to his knees before a memorial to victims of the Nazis in Warsaw in 1970. Federal republic president Richard von Weizsäcker's speech to the Bundestag in 1985, in which he was "specific and unflinching," as Lazare puts it, in describing the crimes of the Third Reich, was the climax of this trend.[58] Though an intense national debate over how to remember the Nazi past took place during the 1980s, it ended in the victory of a "culture of contrition" that was shared across almost the entire political spectrum.[59]

Analysts often contrast Germany's remorse with the impenitence of Japan. Japanese leaders have apologized far less and far later in history than German leaders have, though in the 1990s Japanese heads of state conducted an outburst of apologies: for Japan's aggression during World War II; for its treatment of prisoners of war; for its soldiers' treatment of foreign comfort women, or sex slaves; and for its colonization of South Korea. Unlike in Germany, though, such contrition sparked an enduring backlash from conservative nationalists and was accompanied by the continued omission or misrepresentation of Japan's past crimes in history textbooks and by a pattern of commemorating Japanese victims over foreign victims, symbolized most acutely by prime ministers' repeated visits to the nationalist Yasukuni Shrine commemorating Japanese war dead.[60]

The place of apologies in the liberal peace is small. Though it appears briefly in a couple of international law documents, apology is not one of the standard practices that the "transitional justice community" has advocated or that Secretary General Kofi Annan enumerated in his 2004 statement on transitional justice.[61] In Judaism, Christianity, and Islam, by contrast, repentance is pervasive and restorative. The Jewish Bible repeatedly calls the sinner to repent and promises God's response of acceptance and restoration. The Jewish tradition developed rituals of *teshuva*, or "turning," involving remorse, confession, restitution, and a commitment to reform. The corresponding Arabic term for repentance, *tawbah*, also means "to return" and appears (sometimes in derivative form) eighty-seven times in the Quran.[62] The Quran and several Hadiths indicate that Allah is mercifully willing to forgive the repentant. Islam, too, has developed rich rituals of repentance involving awe for Allah, remorse, resolve to reform, and restitution. Repentance is a critical part of restorative rituals of *sulh* and *musalaha*. Repentance is central in Christianity too. "Repent, for the kingdom of heaven is near," John the Baptist says in announcing Jesus's ministry. Repentance is essential for the sinner's receipt of forgiveness and restoration of relationship to God. The Catholic sacrament of reconciliation calls for genuine remorse, full confession, and a firm purpose of amendment. Finally, theorists of restorative justice also view the offender's repentance as a crucial step in the holistic restoration of right relationship. Do these traditions tell us how apologies ought to be performed in politics? Strands within all of them conceive of apologies taking place communally, but few voices have given sustained thought to apology in the modern nation-state.[63]

Collective Apologies

When heads of state apologize they sometimes do so for their own acts or omissions. U.S. president Bill Clinton, for instance, apologized for acts as disparate as his failure to intervene in Rwanda and his sexual misconduct in the Oval Office. Yet, more often heads of state apologize for deeds for which they bear no personal responsibility. Often these deeds are those of a previous head of state, perhaps even one who ruled under a different regime or constitution. Adenauer, Brandt, and Weizsäcker apologized for the deeds of Hitler and the Nazi regime; U.S. president George H. W. Bush apologized for the deeds of President Franklin Delano Roosevelt and his administration. Sometimes heads of state apologize for the deeds of lower-level officials—commanders, soldiers, administrators—of previous regimes, as when Clinton apologized to the victims of the Tuskegee experiments on African Americans that the U.S. Public Health Service conducted between 1932 and 1972. At other times, leaders apologize for actions that one of their own subordinates committed but for which they bear no direct responsibility. Let us call these apologies—performed by a head of state (or other top official) for deeds that she did not herself commit—collective apologies.

Collective apologies and, as we shall see, some performances of political forgiveness give rise to a problem of vicariousness or representation in a way that the other practices do not. When the state stages a truth commission, builds a memorial, or pays reparations, its authority to act in the name of the political community is not disputed, but apology, skeptics will claim, is the sole prerogative of the perpetrator of the political injustice. No one else may speak in his name. Can collective apologies be justified?

I believe they can. To see why, consider the definition of *political injustice*—an injustice committed in the name of a political regime, program, or ideal. Consider further that any political injustice has two dimensions, an individual dimension and a collective dimension. All political injustices are committed by individual perpetrators, people who acted deliberately, freely, for a reason. To be sure, agents at different levels of command, from a private up to the head of state, will bear varying degrees of responsibility and culpability for the injustice depending on to what degree they initiated or planned the injustices and what level of duress they were under. Still, every individual who commits or helps to commit a political crime bears responsibility and guilt for her actions.

But political injustices also have a collective dimension. Perpetrators of political injustices act under the authority of, in the name of, and in cooperation with the political order and its purposes. This is readily apparent when the perpetrator is a head of state, but it is also the case that anyone who acts under the authority of an army or a bureaucracy shares its purposes. When she commits a crime, the collective also commits a crime. Certainly this is how her crime is manifested to the victim. Contrast how the torture of a Chilean dissident by an agent of Pinochet's regime differs from a nonpolitical maiming, for example, one committed in the course of an armed robbery. The victim of the political crime is violated doubly, not only through harm to his person but also through the denial of his right to live under a government that establishes and enforces his human rights—a denial inflicted by an agent of the same government whose duty it is to uphold justice. The same is true if the crime is committed by a domestic armed opposition group, which carries a duty to fight a just revolution, or a foreign army, which is morally bound to fight a just war in a just manner in pursuit of a just peace. The collective dimension of political injustices, then, derives from the just purposes of a political order and the authority of all those who act in its name. Because this collective is invoked in the crime, it is involved in the crime.[64]

I have identified the standing victory of the injustice as one of the wounds of political injustices and defined it as the moral fact of the injustice that persists in the minds of all who are aware of it. This moral fact is sustained over time by the memory of a people. In this standing victory, in this memory, both dimensions of political injustices, collective and individual, can be found. The persistence of the collective dimension can be seen most readily in cases of historical injustices that people view as looming large long after these injustices have been committed. For instance, many people today believe that the Armenian genocide that took place in Turkey in 1915 is an atrocity that cries out to be addressed through an apology, or at least a statement of acknowledgment and regret, on the part of the government of the Republic of Turkey, even though both perpetrators and victims have long passed on. The genocide stands victorious.

It is the collective dimension of a standing political injustice for which a head of state (or similarly high-placed official) may apologize even though he himself did not actually commit or authorize this injustice. His apology is valid because he has the standing to speak for the political order that is obligated to uphold the human rights of its citizens (and of citizens of other states with whom his state is engaged). This standing is conferred on him by the constitution and laws of his own state. Thus it is he who may apologize for the political injustices committed by agents of that same political order. "I dare—as President of the Republic—to assume representation of the entire nation in begging forgiveness from the victims' relatives," declared Chilean president Aylwin when he apologized to Pinochet's victims on behalf of all Chileans.[65]

The link between an apologizing head of state and previous perpetrators may not be strong. The apologizer may preside over the same collective people as the perpetrator but govern in a new administration, in a successor regime, or under a new constitution. Alternately, the identity of the governed people may have changed. Between 1949 and 1990, for instance, the Federal Republic of Germany, whose presidents and chancellors voiced apologies for Germans, did not include millions of Germans who had lived under the Nazi regime yet, through the events after the war's end, ended up living in East Germany, Poland, or Czechoslovakia. These political metamorphoses do not negate the authority of subsequent leaders to apologize. Even if the boundaries and inhabitants of a political association change over time, we may still think of a people as constituting an ongoing association. That Germany's boundaries and population shifted did not mean that Germany ceased to exist as a nation or a political association. The federal republic could still speak for many Germans, even if not for all Germans.[66] Even if regimes and constitutions change, the fact that any given association of people is entitled to a government that upholds the human rights of its members, along with the correlative duty of any government to uphold these human rights, together place a successor government in a kind of continuity with its predecessor government: Both constitute the political authority that possesses universal duties of justice toward this particular group of people. It is this standing, again derived from the fundamental purposes of political association, that gives a head of state authority to apologize for the collective dimension of political injustices.

As for the individual dimension of injustices, only the perpetrator can apologize for them. This is a simple implication of moral agency. Because the person who chose to commit (or abet, or authorize) a wrong bears responsibility for his actions, only he can disavow this responsibility. If he does not, the responsibility remains with him. When the perpetrator dies so, too, does the possibility of apology, at least for the individual dimension of the injustice. Since the collective lives on, however, qualified authorities may apologize for the injustice committed even after the actual perpetrators have died. The two dimensions of injustice, then, yield two forms of apology, individual and collective. In principle, each may be performed separately. Only in the case when a leader of a collective apologizes for an injustice that he performed in the name of the collective do the two forms of apology converge in the same act.

What about the victim? Can apologies be directed only to victims who are alive? Many apologies are delivered to living victims, such as Clinton's apology to survivors of Rwanda's genocide for not intervening on their behalf. Yet even in this example, and all the more so in other instances, apologies are directed either to a combination of living and deceased victims or to living representatives of victims who are deceased. Germany's apologies to Jews for the crimes of the Holocaust, for instance, have been directed both to Jews who have lived through these events as well as to those who died.

What makes such apologies morally possible is the fact that political injustices carry both individual and collective dimensions with respect to victims just as they do with respect to perpetrators. Most political injustices kill and wound victims not only in their person but also as members of groups. This is perhaps most obvious in the case of genocide: People are killed because they are Jews and Tutsis. States also commit political crimes against members of dissident groups or opposition forces on account of this membership. When one state attacks the troops of another in an act of aggression, it kills these troops as agents of the target state. Once these victims are dead, nobody can apologize to them for what they have suffered, but one could apologize to members of the same collective—living Jews, living Armenians, children of disappeared Chilean dissidents—for the shared dimension of their suffering, that is, the sense in which their collective was attacked. Philosopher Trudy Govier usefully distinguishes among primary victims, those who are directly harmed by a crime; secondary victims, friends and family members; and tertiary victims, who are members of the same communal group—national, ethic, religious, or the like.[67] It is tertiary victims, including ones of future generations, to whom an apology may be directed on account of their communal tie. Here again, we have a problem of fluid boundaries. Because of intermarriage and complex histories, not all African Americans today are direct descendants of slaves, but here again, the fact that collectives have fluid boundaries does not negate their existence. Many living African Americans are indeed descendants of slaves; to them, an apology can be directed.[68]

A final point about collective apologies: If the leader of a collective may voice an apology on behalf of his collective, the members of that collective are themselves free to endorse or to oppose that apology. This freedom is best realized in a democracy, where the right to dissent is protected. Many apologies or proposed apologies have indeed provoked debate. Conservatives in Japan have criticized their government's apologies for Japan's crimes in the Second World War. In America, proposals for a U.S. government apology for slavery are polarizing. Lack of popular support in no way detracts from the authority of heads of state to issue apologies, just as they have the authority to sign treaties, command armed coercion, and conduct foreign policy even though these actions may be unpopular. A lack of popular consensus, however, may well detract from the restoration of relationship that a leader hopes to achieve.

The Restorations that Political Apologies Bring

Much of this analysis can be applied to an argument for how apologies perform restorations. First let us consider primary restorations. One of the wounds that the practice of apology most distinctively addresses is the standing victory of a political injustice. Few acts undo the legitimacy of a crime more effectively than a perpetrator's renunciation of it. When a spokesperson for the political order decries the collective dimension of the injustice, she brings the legitimacy of her office to bear in defeating this injustice's standing victory. On this score, a good apology will be one in which the apologizer takes direct responsibility and communicates genuine contrition, rather than, for example, simply expressing regret that the victim suffered.

Just as an act of injustice harms the soul of the one who commits it, a second wound of political injustice, so, too, the perpetrator's apology, his renunciation of his attachment to it, can initiate the repair of his soul. This primary restoration is especially strong in the religious traditions and restorative justice. Apology also addresses social ignorance of the victim's suffering, a third wound, by conveying moral respect for the victim, acknowledging her humanity, and endorsing her full restoration into the political community. Apology, especially when performed by a head of state, reinforces the legitimacy of the victim's human rights, disrespect for which constitutes a fourth wound.

As for secondary restorations, victims who receive apologies, like those who receive acknowledgment or reparations, might come to look on their political order as more legitimate and worth supporting. They may also become less desirous of revenge. When victims who are minorities receive apologies, other citizens might become more likely to endorse the victims' full membership in the political community.[69] Apologies might also promote normal, peaceful relations between states.

These secondary restorations, though, are far from inevitable. Some scholars caution that when apologies are unpopular they can deepen divisions within and between states. Political scientist Jennifer Lind's study of the effects of apologies on Germany and Japan's relations with their neighbors in the decades after World War II ends with a sober conclusion: Apologies are not necessary for reconciliation and can even set it back. The United States reconciled with both Germany and Japan in the 1950s in the absence of substantial apologies from either country. When German leaders began to apologize in the 1970s, they only reinforced this reconciliation, but when Japan turned contrite in the 1990s, the resulting domestic backlash obstructed reconciliation with its neighbors, she argues. To be clear, what Lind calls reconciliation between states corresponds to a form of what I call secondary restorations: normal, peaceful, international relations. My own concept of reconciliation also includes primary restorations, which have value independent of secondary restorations. Still, Lind's analysis stands as a warning that apologies will not always beget secondary restorations. Wisely, she counsels leaders to balance the effects on foreign and domestic audiences when considering apologizing and, whenever possible, to conduct apologies to other states through multilateral or bilateral forums in which apologies are mutual and less likely to provoke a backlash from unrepentant patriots.[70]

Apology also bears important relationships to the other practices. Accompanying reparations can render apologies more than empty words. Acknowledgment also strengthens apology. In the rare examples of high-level perpetrators who apologized, most did so in conjunction with a truth commission that brought to light both their deeds and their victims' suffering. Among the other practices, it is forgiveness that is most naturally paired with apology. Not only do prior apologies often make victims more willing to forgive, but often they also explicitly involve a request, and thus create the occasion, for forgiveness.

Each of the four practices discussed here reflects reconciliation as a concept of justice. For the two remaining practices, I offer a more extensive consideration.

II

Punishment

LIKE THE OTHER practices, judicial punishment for violators of human rights has expanded sharply over the past three decades. There have arisen two international criminal tribunals; a permanent international court; national-level trials in Argentina, Chile, Rwanda, postcommunist Germany, and elsewhere; hybrid courts combining international and domestic authority in Sierra Leone, Kosovo, Timor-Leste, and Cambodia; trials involving universal jurisdiction whereby Rwandans are tried in Belgium and Yugoslavs are tried in Denmark; numerous "vetting" arrangements that disqualify past perpetrators from holding positions in government and business; and local community forums in Rwanda and Timor-Leste that try perpetrators in the presence of victims and members of the community.

The liberal peace echoes loudly in all of these forums, more loudly through punishment than through any of the other practices. It is the international legal and human rights community that fiercely advocates international tribunals and national courts and liberal justifications that most typically explain the moral logic behind trials. Occasionally these are retributivist, holding that punishment is simply deserved. Far more often, they are consequentialist, stressing punishment's potential for deterring future human rights violators and promoting peace, democracy, and the rule of law. Yet it is not just the logic but also the passion of the liberal peace that pervades trials. Placing Yugoslavia's Slobodan Milosevic, Liberia's Charles Taylor, or Argentina's General Jorge Videla in the dock, backers insist, accomplishes what the Nuremberg Trials did when Rudolf Hess, Hermann Goering, and Joachim von Ribbentrop were tried two generations ago: bring justice to the perpetrators of the worst sort of crimes humanly imaginable.

Critics take proponents of trials to task for their excessive moral ambition; for their obliviousness to the ways that trials can undermine, not promote, peace and democracy; and for their unquestioned faith that trials deter major human rights violations. These detractors charge that proponents want to pursue justice even should the heavens fall—and that the heavens often do fall: Trials inflame revenge, communal rivalry, and cynicism. The debate has evolved into one about effects. Do trials deter? Do they encourage harmony between warring ethnic factions? Do they help fashion the rule of law in places where judiciaries have been destroyed?

How does reconciliation fit into this discussion? The concept flies about in the melee. Critics of trials claim that they subvert reconciliation by inflaming divisions. Proponents of trials argue the opposite. In 1994, then U.S. ambassador to the UN Madeleine Albright argued that "establishing the truth about what happened in Bosnia is *essential* to—not an *obstacle* to—national reconciliation."[1]

Who is right? By embracing punishment as one of the six practices, I endorse the aims of these trials, broadly speaking. I differ, though, from most proponents—and most critics—in my arguments for punishment, in my view of punishment's relationship to reconciliation, and in the forms of trials that I advocate.

The type of punishment suitable to the ethic of political reconciliation might best be called restorative.[2] Punishment may be justified as the state's communication of censure to a perpetrator on behalf of the community's values. Such a censure invites a broad restoration of the persons and relationships that the perpetrator has wounded through his act of political injustice. Understood restoratively, punishment is a dimension of the justice that is embodied in reconciliation, animated by mercy, and aiming at peace. Restorative punishment figures prominently in the Jewish, Christian, and Islamic traditions and is the central concept of restorative justice. Contrary to consequentialism, restorative punishment is not justified simply for its effects, though they are surely important. Rather, restorative punishment preserves the widely shared idea that punishment is simply deserved for crime. Yet unlike versions of retributivism that justify punishment as an abstract balancing of harm and punishment, restorative punishment seeks an actual restoration of human flourishing among victims, communities, and perpetrators. Restorative punishment aims for both primary restorations—in which punishment directly accomplishes reconciliation—as well as secondary restorations, which correspond to consequences.

A Global Explosion of Judicial Punishment

Historically, judicial punishment for political injustice is rare. This rarity makes all the more noteworthy the sharp global expansion of trials at the end of the twentieth century. Sikkink and Walling demonstrate that the number of new trials initiated by countries around the world accelerated markedly beginning in the mid-1980s and continuing through 2004. Leslie Vinjamuri shows that 61 percent of the tribunals that have taken place between 1945 and 2007 occurred since the end of the cold war in 1989.[3] Other scholars caution that, as a percentage of countries in transition, trials actually have decreased since the 1980s.[4] It is important to remember, too, that in most sites of injustice the scale of human rights violations far outstrips the number of convictions and prison sentences—as with apologies. Still, the sharp growth in the number of trials over the past generation makes this trend a representative part of what I have called the age of peacebuilding.

The driving force behind this trend is a global network of officials and activists who advocate for the liberal peace and can be found in human rights organizations, the global guild of international lawyers, the UN, the European Union (EU), Western governments, and Western-oriented sectors of governments elsewhere. In an age in which a high concentration of political transitions creates a demand for dealing with the past, the members of this network come willing and equipped to supply their solution—trials based on Western judicial procedures. This network has in turn encouraged what could be called a demonstration effect in which trials inspire copycats.

The *ur*-source for dreams of judicial punishment is the International Military Tribunal held at Nuremberg just after World War II. Although controversies over the trials persist, Nuremberg retains vast prestige as the first major internationally constituted tribunal to try individuals for atrocious political acts. It also set important precedents for international human rights law by invalidating such defenses as following the orders of a superior and obedience to domestic laws.

Over the next four decades, the cold war rivalry placed prospects for international tribunals on ice. Few trials for major human rights violations took place within domestic states either. A major exception was Germany, where, between V-E Day on May 8, 1945 and the mid-1980s, 90,921 people were officially accused of committing war crimes and crimes against humanity during the Nazi era, with 6,479 of them receiving convictions.

Admittedly these grand totals conceal a bumpy history. Eighty percent of these prosecutions occurred between 1945 and 1951, when Germany was still under Allied control. Amnesty laws passed by the Bundestag between 1949 and 1954 slowed prosecutions greatly until West German courts resumed them in the 1960s. By 1986, the number of cases closed without convictions had reached 83,140.[5] Even so, the German record is impressive in comparison to other countries with mass atrocities in their pasts. Aside from a few other countries' trials for the crimes of World War II and the Holocaust, the only major domestic trial of perpetrators of large political injustices during this period was Greece's prosecution of its military junta from 1967 to 1974.

The modern wave of judicial punishment began in Argentina, following its transition to democracy under President Raúl Alfonsin in December 1983. There, national courts tried nine and convicted five leaders of the junta that ruled during the Dirty Wars of 1976 to 1983 and forced the disappearance of some 30,000 political opponents. This was a case where a truth commission, the National Commission of the Disappeared (CONADEP), worked hand in hand with courts conducting trials, supplying them with vital information. However, as prosecutions were primed to expand, the military became restive and threatened to bring down Argentina's delicate democracy. In 1987, at Alfonsin's urging, the National Congress brought prosecutions to a halt through its Full Stop and Due Obedience laws. Then, in 1990, Alfonsin's successor, Carlos Menem, pardoned the five convicted generals, though the story does not end there. One of these generals, Jorge Videla, was convicted again in 1998, this time for kidnapping children during the war. In 2003, the National Congress repealed the Full Stop and Due Obedience laws, and in 2006 prosecutions resumed. High-profile domestic trials also took place in Chile, Germany, Ethiopia, and Rwanda.

Resurrecting the legacy of Nuremberg even more fully were three international courts created in the 1990s: the International Criminal Tribunal for the former Yugoslavia (ICTY), the International Criminal Tribunal for Rwanda (ICTR), and a permanent International Criminal Court (ICC). The U.N. Security Council created the first two, while the ICC, a standing court with wide jurisdiction, was created through a treaty in 1998 and came into being in 2002. Today, more than one hundred states are members, though the United States, China, Russia, and India, three of whom are permanent members of the U.N. Security Council, are conspicuously absent. At the time of this writing, the ICTY had indicted 161 persons, including such top leaders as Slobodan Milosevic, Radovan Karadzic, and Ratko Mladic, and convicted forty-eight; the ICTR had convicted twenty-nine, including former interim prime minister Jean Kambanda; the ICC had indicted fourteen people in four conflicts.

In addition to these international tribunals, there have been a number of hybrid courts, created by agreements between the UN and a national government, composed of international and national judges, and combining international and national criminal law in their proceedings. To date, hybrids have been created for Timor-Leste, Sierra Leone, Kosovo, and Cambodia. Similarly mixing the international and national are trials conducted under universal jurisdiction, whereby a court in one country (such as Belgium) tries the citizen of another country (such as Rwanda) for human rights violations. The most celebrated case of universal jurisdiction was the trial of Nazi official Adolf Eichmann in an Israeli court in 1961. The practice has become more common since the mid-1990s and includes the well-known case of a Spanish judge's indictment of Chile's Pinochet in 1998.

Arguably falling under the practice of judicial punishment is also vetting, sometimes called lustration, which prohibits certain officials of a previous regime or armed conflict from enjoying some benefit or position, either in the post-transition government or in such private sector institutions as businesses or universities. The best-known cases took place in Germany and eastern Europe following communist rule, as well as in Iraq, where the United States imposed a formidable sweep of Ba'ath Party members from the Iraqi government after its invasion of 2003. Although punishment is not the only or even the most important role of vetting, it is unavoidably one of these purposes.

In certain respects, truth commissions perform punishment, though not strictly judicial punishment. Commissions that publicize the names of perpetrators bring public shame on them, often destroying their reputation as respected citizens. This effect is especially pronounced in those commissions that hold public hearings, where perpetrators have their deeds exposed before the commissioners, the victim(s), an audience of onlookers, and sometimes a radio, television, or newspaper audience. In several countries, including Timor-Leste, Argentina, Sierra Leone, Germany, and Chile, truth commissions occur in addition to and sometimes supplement the work of trials.

A final form of judicial punishment has received less attention than the others but is, in theory, the most promising for an ethic of political reconciliation: community justice forums. The two most important of these are the *gacaca* courts of Rwanda and the Community Reconciliation Panels (CRPs) of Timor-Leste. Both countries' governments touted these forums as ones of reconciliation—in Rwanda through a national network of billboards. Both countries' forums sought forms of punishment that encouraged confession and apology from perpetrators, the reintegration of perpetrators into their communities, the acknowledgment of victims, the practice of forgiveness by victims, and the broad participation of members of the community. Both were also born of political necessity, viewed by each government as a solution to an overwhelming caseload facing its national courts. In Rwanda, as late as 2000, 125,000 suspected *génocidaires* festered, diseased and dying, in overcrowded prisons built to house only 15,000.[6]

Each of the two systems also employed traditional justice practices. *Gacaca*, a Kinyarwandan term meaning "justice on the grass," is a set of practices for resolving disputes within a village, in which the victim, perpetrator, families, and community members gather before a set of elders. When used to try alleged perpetrators of crimes in the genocide of 1994, *gacaca* courts incorporated international human rights standards, elements of Western jurisprudence, and fairly harsh punitive standards, the latter in part the result of pressure from Western donors and human rights monitors.[7] In Timor-Leste, too, village dispute resolution practices were formalized, modified, and to some degree westernized by the Timorese state. Both sorts of community forums are also embedded in a tiered system of judicial punishment. In Rwanda, those suspected of planning genocide, "notorious" murders, torturers, and rapists were kept out of the *gacaca* system and tried in more traditional courts, while the "biggest fish" were sent to the ICTR.[8] Timor-Leste sent murder, rape, and torture suspects to its Special Panels for Serious Crimes (SPSC), a hybrid UN-national tribunal, and its investigative arm, the Serious Crimes Unit (SCU), while reserving the CRPs for those suspected of beatings, arson, and stealing livestock.

Community forums of this sort carry a special potential for embodying the holistic justice of restorative punishment and the ethic of political reconciliation. Yet they are not without flaws, ones that reinforce this book's persistent reminder that reconciliation is always partial and imperfect.

The most common practice in the aftermath of atrocity, though, is no punishment at all: amnesty. Legal scholar Louise Mallinder has shown that more than 420 amnesty processes have been initiated since

World War II, with a sharp increase beginning in the mid-1970s. Amnesty is part and parcel of the age of peacebuilding.[9] Not all amnesties are blanket amnesties; some are conditional on the perpetrator's confession, apology, acceptance of a democratic transition or peace settlement, or even exile. Amnesties range from complete to partial in the crimes and in the perpetrators that they cover. All amnesties, though, forgo punishment to some extent.

How Is the Global Explosion of Punishment Justified?

With the explosion of judicial punishment has come an explosion of arguments, often vituperative, for and against. What is striking about these arguments is the great extent to which they focus not on the intrinsic value of determining guilt and punishing criminals but on the consequences of punishment.[10]

"The fulcrum of the case for criminal punishment is that it is the most effective insurance against future repression," writes legal scholar Diane Orentlicher. By "insurance," she means deterrence: "By laying bare the truth about violations of the past and condemning them, prosecutions can deter potential lawbreakers . . ."[11] Deterrence holds great prestige. The preamble to the Rome Statute of the International Criminal Court declares the court's aim to "put an end to impunity for perpetrators of these crimes and thus to contribute to the prevention of crimes."[12]

The rule of law is the second most prominent rationale for judicial punishment.[13] Orentlicher writes: "Trials may, as well, inspire societies that are re-examining their basic values to affirm the fundamental principle of respect for the rule of law and for the inherent dignity of individuals."[14] When a newborn democratic regime in Argentina places its dethroned generals in the dock, it is argued, Argentinians are inspired to believe that this regime promotes the rule of law, leading them in turn to bequeath support and legitimacy back to the regime, thereby strengthening the rule of law all the more.

Proponents of trials cite other benefits as well. Trials stem the cycle of revenge by taking retribution out of the hands of citizens and placing it in the hands of authorities. They assuage enmity between warring communities by convincing one group of citizens that the other's masterminds of murder are being brought to justice. Even more directly, punishment sequesters behind bars those who are most likely to fan belligerent passions and instigate further violence. Causal effects such as these are what such proponents of punishment as Madeleine Albright seem to have in mind when they say that lasting peace is not possible without justice.[15] Sometimes proponents link these effects to reconciliation, as did the U.N. Security Council resolution that established the ICTR.[16] Others, such as Orentlicher, fear that reconciliation is a "watchword for impunity" and caution that it should not hinder trials in promoting peace and the rule of law.[17]

Skeptics doubt every one of these claims about the fruits of trials. There is little evidence that deterrence occurs, especially across borders, they aver.[18] Nor is it clear that trials promote the rule of law. Sometimes trials can even undermine the legitimacy of a regime or a peace settlement, particularly when they are seen as the tool of one side of a conflict or of a remote international community. Skeptics expect trials to have little effect on peace and stability or else to undermine it. Provoking their doubt most are trials during civil wars. Critics charge the ICC's indictment of Uganda's Lord's Resistance Army leader Joseph Kony, for instance, with keeping him away from the negotiating table and thus leaving refugees to languish in camps, preventing child soldiers from returning home, and perpetuating a war in which thousands have been killed, raped, and mutilated. When skeptics of punishment invoke reconciliation, it is usually as a constructive alternative to punishment. People on the ground, they say, need measures that bring an end to their ambient pandemonium and that repair their quotidian environments.[19]

For all of these consequentialists, among them both proponents and opponents of trials, the question of justice is an empirical one, the sort that can be assessed through data and measurement.[20] Yet to many such arguments seems strange and stunted. They would seem strange to Dragica Levi, a tolerant, multicultural Jew who remained in Sarajevo during the war of the early 1990s and who told political scientist Gary Bass: "With war criminals walking free—they must pay.... If you lose your husband and the killer is walking free, you must have hate in your heart. If you did something you have to pay for it. It is normal."[21] This is the core insight of retributivism—that punishment is justified because it is deserved, apart from its consequences.

Some sort of retributivism is implicit, even if seldom acknowledged, in any argument for trials and courts that judge defendants according to concepts of guilt, deserved punishment, and proportionality and not primarily according to the utility of punishment. Yet retributivism is rarely found in debates over judicial punishment for human rights violations, despite its prominence in Western philosophy, criminology, and penal practice, where it has made a comeback over the past generation.[22]

To simplify greatly, in the century and a half prior to 1970, at least in the Anglo-American world, utilitarianism had supplanted retributivism. Such early utilitarians as Cesare Beccaria and Jeremy Bentham argued that punishment ought to be adopted only for its effects—the rehabilitation of the criminal and, far more importantly, deterrence. Utilitarian criminology, though, eventually fell out of favor, in part because rehabilitation programs did not work but even more so because it was hard pressed to answer deeper questions about its theory of punishment. If the effects of punishment are all that matters, why not give extra punishment to a famous person who is popularly thought to be guilty—or even punish one who is innocent—in order to achieve a deterrent effect? Or why not incarcerate and give treatment to a person who is statistically likely to be a criminal but who has no actual criminal record? In truth, utilitarians did not favor these fearsome scenarios but rather advocated leniency. Yet leniency, retributivists insist, does not solve the fundamental problem: Utilitarianism ignores punishment's core moral purpose of delivering to the guilty the hardship that they deserve. Deterrence had deeper problems as well. Hegel charged that it treats a criminal like a dog, a mere means to the social end of lowering the crime rate. Deterrence also provides no reasons for respecting proportionality, leaving punishment without any principled upper limit. For its part, rehabilitation mistakes a guilty person for a sick person, treating him as someone to be improved rather than as a moral agent who is responsible for respecting the laws of the community.[23]

Do not all of these objections apply as well to rationales for the punishment of human rights violators that appeal only to deterrence or to the rehabilitation of shattered states? Slobodan Milosevic, Charles Taylor, or Joseph Kony, claims the retributivist, should not be conceived as a mere tool of deterrence or rehabilitation, apart from whether the tool is effective.

Again, the retributivist's core claim is desert. Everyone who is guilty of committing an act that the law justly renders a punishable crime ought in principle to be made to experience hardship. Deserved deprivation is a sufficient justification for punishment. Several corollaries pertain. Those who are punished ought to be punished only for the crime that they commit and only in proportion to its magnitude and to their culpability. No one should be punished for a crime that she did not commit. Guilt should be determined through fair legal procedure, ideally conducted by the courts of the state. Retribution is not revenge, retributivists often insist. Philosopher Robert Nozick offers five factors that differentiate the two: 1) Retribution responds to an actual wrong, while a victim may seek revenge for an injury, harm, or slight that is not necessarily a wrong; 2) retribution respects proportionality, while revenge is limitless; 3) an agent of retribution may have no tie to the victim of the wrong, while revenge is always personal; 4) retribution takes no pleasure in the suffering of the guilty, while revenge does; and 5) retribution is committed to general principles, desiring just punishment for everyone in similar circumstances, while revenge has little concern with generality.[24] Finally, a sophisticated retributivist does not necessarily reject consequentialist reasons for punishment, which might be added to the core rationale of desert. When desert is missing or compromised, though, punishment is seriously misguided.

If retributivists are right, then Milosevic, Taylor, and Kony, along with Pinochet, Eichmann, and Pol Pot, ought to be punished primarily and sufficiently because they deserve to suffer for their terrible crimes and only secondarily because punishing them might promote deterrence, peace, or democracy. But are retributivists right? Justifications for retributive action come in a wide variety of forms. At the core of them all are the concepts identified above: guilt, desert, proportionality, and a fair trial. Asserting these concepts, however, does not establish their validity. Why, for instance, do criminals deserve punishment?

One answer is that desert is a property of morality that needs no further justification. That is, it cannot be denied by anyone who thinks about it carefully and honestly. It is self-evident.[25] Yet is the retributive idea in fact self-evident? Skepticism is warranted. Denying the idea entails no logical contradiction or self-undermining assertion. Nor is it clear what compelling answer meets those who would deny it. The actual reactions of thousands of ordinary people to crimes, including the political injustices of war and dictatorship, further a sense of skepticism. My own reading of the literature on transitions as well as my own experience in speaking with scores of people involved in violence in Kashmir, Burundi, and elsewhere reveals a striking diversity of desires for the treatment of perpetrators among victims. Some adamantly demand retribution or revenge; others are willing to forgive or to allow amnesty upon a perpetrator's acknowledgment, confession, or apology; others favor reparations over imprisonment; others are willing to forgive from the outset. A study of more than one thousand victims in eleven postconflict or conflict regions conducted by three researchers at the Max Planck Institute in Germany is more systematic. Only 42 percent of victims supported imprisonment; 39 percent supported monetary reparations for victims. Regions varied: only 10 percent of Afghans supported imprisonment, for instance. In some areas, support for monetary payments exceeded support for imprisonment. Among those who supported punitive action against perpetrators, rationales differed. The most frequently cited main purpose of punishment, voiced by 69 percent, was establishing the truth about what happened. Only 25 percent said that taking revenge on perpetrators was a main purpose.[26]

Empirical evidence alone does not refute the self-evidence of a good or an idea. However, unless it can be demonstrated that denying the concept of desert is self-contradictory or otherwise mistaken, it is hard to override the fact that a large proportion of people, including victims of human rights violations, respond to crimes through rationales other than retributivism.

Another argument for retributivism, perhaps its most common justification, sees punishment as an act of balancing and may thus be called balance retributivism. It is symbolized by the blind Greek goddess of justice, who holds scales in her hand, and is echoed in such common phrases as "he must pay his debt to society." A famous passage by Immanuel Kant stands as history's purest expression of the idea:

> Even if a civil society were to be dissolved by the consent of all its members (e.g., if a people inhabiting an island decided to separate and disperse throughout the world), the last murderer remaining in prison would first have to be executed, so that each has done to him what his deeds deserve and blood guilt does not cling to the people for not having insisted upon this punishment; for otherwise the people can be regarded as collaborators in this public violation of justice.[27]

Virtually all versions of balance retributivism hold that the hardship of punishment balances out either the gain that the perpetrator has won or the harm that he has inflicted: evil for evil, harm for harm. A crucial feature of balance retributivism is that the balancing of scales occurs in and apart from any actual restoration.

Is this a morally satisfying solution to crime? Philosophers John Braithwaite and Phillip Pettit doubt that punishment balances criminals' gains. They offer the example of the burglar who breaks his leg in a robbery and of a rapist who contracts syphilis—are these in fact gains?[28]

And does the rapist's sordid sexual act benefit him in any intelligible way? I argued earlier that crime disintegrates the soul of its perpetrator. If the objectively disintegrating soul of a triumphant drug kingpin sitting by his swimming pool affords small consolation, recall that other perpetrators experience their disintegration palpably, such as a person who murders out of passionate anger and shortly thereafter comes to be wracked by guilt. The point is not to generalize about the effects of crime on criminals, some of whom do gain, perhaps most clearly when the gain is material. It is rather that we cannot generalize that violating the law is a gain. So we cannot accept a theory claiming that gains are what punishment quintessentially counterbalances.

A retributivist might reply that punishment actually balances harms, not gains, but this merely raises another conceptual problem: the notion of an equivalence between punishment and either the gains or harms of crime. In what sense is twenty-five years in prison equivalent to the hardship suffered from rape? How are we ever to assess the comparability of such different forms of suffering? In the case of such massive human rights violations as genocide or even a smaller scale war crime, that which is supposed to serve as a balancing punishment is beyond all imagining. As philosopher Hannah Arendt wrote to her former teacher Karl Jaspers,

> [t]he Nazi crimes, it seems to me, explode the limits of the law; and that is precisely what constitutes their monstrousness. For these crimes, no punishment is severe enough.... This guilt, in contrast to all criminal guilt, oversteps and shatters any and all legal systems. That is the reason why the Nazis in Nuremberg are so smug.[29]

Arendt did not oppose executions for Nazi leaders. "You must hang," she concluded her book about a different Nazi trial, *Eichmann in Jerusalem*.[30] Rather, she doubts that hanging Nazi SS leader Ernst Kaltenbrunner could somehow balance out his killing of several million innocent people. In what currency is balancing denominated?

Ultimately, we must ask: What precisely does balancing do that provides satisfaction? Quite literally, what good does it do? It certainly does not undo—that is, bring the murdered back to life, heal the leg broken by the mugger, or reverse the trauma suffered by a rape victim. Is some ledger of good and evil in the universe being balanced? Or some tally of evil inflicted and evil suffered? If so, where does such a ledger or tally exist, and who is keeping it?

None of these arguments warrants a rejection of retributivism's core commitments of desert, guilt, and proportionality, but they call for a stronger justification of these commitments.

A Restorative Justification for Punishment

Restorative punishment holds that the purpose of punishment is the repair of persons, relationships, and communities with respect to the harms that crime, or in this context, political injustice, inflicts on them.[31] The central form of harm that a political injustice (or any crime) causes is the wound that I have called "the standing victory of the wrong-doer's injustice." Restorative punishment's main purpose is to defeat this standing victory by communicating censure.

Understood in this way, punishment seeks to redress a real wound. The defeat of the standing victory of injustice, though, is not a consequence of punishment. Rather, the communication of censure itself defeats the message of injustice. The restorative rationale also differs from consequentialism in preserving the idea of desert. Just as the perpetrator created the standing victory of his message of injustice through his act, so, too, does the defeat of this message occur through a censure of this same person for this very deed and only for this very deed.

Restorative punishment manifests the larger ethic of political reconciliation for which this book argues. The justice of reconciliation is a justice that redresses the range of wounds that injustices inflict. The practice of punishment performs this justice by redressing most centrally the standing victory of the political injustice but also, at least potentially, each of the other five wounds of injustice. Because all such redress occurs through punishment's communication of censure and not as a further consequence of punishment, it falls into the category of a primary restoration. As with retributive theories, though, restorative punishment can also bring good consequences in addition to its central task—deterrence and the promotion of peace and stability. The value of these goods need not be dismissed. They are secondary restorations. Whether these restorations actually occur is an empirical matter. Even if punishment never achieves deterrence or peace, though, it may still perform its primary restorations. The positive consequences of trials ought to be welcomed but are not alone enough to justify them.

Restorative punishment also contrasts with most contemporary discussion of trials in how it relates punishment to reconciliation. It does not equate reconciliation with social peace or see reconciliation solely as a consequence that punishment succeeds or fails in promoting. To an even lesser degree does it view reconciliation as an alternative to punishment. Instead, it sees reconciliation as involving any restoration of right relationship that punishment brings about, either of the primary or the secondary kind. In its primary restorations, restorative punishment does not so much effect reconciliation as it performs—that is, brings about—the justice that is reconciliation. From this follows the surprising claim that punishment also performs mercy—the mercy that wills the restoration of all that is broken. Finally, punishment furthers peace—not merely the social stability that might (or might not) result from punishment but also the peace of right relationships that is constituted in part by the primary restorations that punishment performs.

Restorative Punishment in the Four Traditions

The justice, mercy, and peace that restorative punishment embodies reside in each of the traditions that make up the overlapping consensus on the ethic. Restorative punishment is the signature idea of restorative justice. The tradition's three main components—harms to persons and relationships as the key object of redress, measures that restore these harms, and the participation of a wide array of parties—are at the heart of restorative punishment.

Can support for restorative punishment be found in the Jewish tradition? One might not think so if one focuses on stories in which God destroys those he punishes and even entire nations.[32] These actions appear not to be restorative and may well surpass our moral categories, but if they do, they hardly hand a victory to balance retributivism, which, after all, touts the rationality of desert and proportionality. Still more inconsistent with a measure-for-measure paying up are the many episodes in which God explicitly refrains from doling out to wrongdoers what they deserve. The scriptures repeatedly describe God as "slow to anger, abounding in loving kindness," or something quite close to this. In at least four passages God vows to punish and then comes to think better of it.[33] God repeatedly restores his covenant without any evidence of an equal paying up on Israel's part. If balance retributivism best describes God's purposes in punishment, God would appear to be a poor keeper of the balance.

Is there a common purpose to be found both in God's harsh destruction and in God's tender restraint? God's will to restore his covenant with the people of Israel comes closest. This may not account well for how each individual is treated, but most acts of punishment in some way aim to "purge the evil from your midst," as Deuteronomy repeatedly states, and to bring Israel as a community closer to *shalom*.[34]

That restorative punishment was practiced in Israel's law courts during the time of the judges will vex one who thinks first of the *lex talionis*: eye for an eye, tooth for a tooth. Yet the Torah describes a judicial punishment whose aim is to restore the integrity of the covenant law among Israelis. This restoration occurred primarily through restitution—an actual reparation of what was lost to the one who lost it.[35] *Shillem*, the Hebrew word for "restitution," is a close variant of *shalom*, connoting restoration and the act of making full.[36] Though restitution for theft sometimes amounted to several times the value of what was stolen, the added amount was designed to communicate the seriousness of the offense. What, then, of the eye for an eye passages, which appear in three places in the Torah?[37] Their point was mainly to limit retribution by keeping it proportionate and equitable, thus constraining the blood revenge typical of local tribal practice.[38] This interpretation prevailed in postbiblical times as recorded in the Mishnah and other Talmudic texts.[39]

Most difficult to square with restorative punishment are texts in the Torah that mandate the death penalty, which they do for more than twenty crimes, including adultery, homosexual behavior, striking a parent, and idolatry. Not only did these practices not survive into modern times, but they did not survive in strong form even into the time of the Mishnah in the second century, when rabbis sought to place such burdensome procedural constraints on the death penalty as to make its practice rare.[40] More importantly for the present argument, the purpose of the death penalty, even as prescribed by the Torah, was not to restore a balance but rather to purge and cleanse the community and to restore covenantal relations.[41] Here, too, what is directly applicable to modern nations are not the specific punishments of the Jewish Bible but rather their underlying principle—a restorative one.

Commenting on the *lex talionis*, Jesus offered:

You have heard that it was said, "Eye for eye, and tooth for tooth." But I tell you, Do not resist an evil person. If someone strikes you on the right cheek, turn to him the other also. And if someone

wants to sue you and take your tunic, let him have your cloak as
well. If someone forces you to go one mile, go with him two miles.
Give to the one who asks you, and do not turn away from the one
who wants to borrow from you.[42]

A counsel of nonviolence? Of nonresistance? Disputes continue. My view is
that Jesus was forbidding something very much like balance retributivism.[43]
Several scholars agree that the offenses that he enumerates were judiciable
ones. Jesus seems to have had judicial punishment in mind.[44] Earlier in this
sermon, he had made clear that he did not intend to abolish the Jewish law.
If my preceding argument is correct, this law already contained a restorative
logic of punishment. Jesus now extends that logic—and perhaps renders it
redundant—by saying: Do not just limit retribution, rather do not seek it at
all. If one—an individual, a disciple—is wronged, then he ought to love his
enemy and do good to him. The restorative logic is thus deepened.[45]

Is Jesus abolishing law courts? Neither he nor Paul advocates such
a thing. Judicial punishment is the business of government. Under what
rationale is the government supposed to carry out punishment? After
repeating Jesus's injunction not to repay evil with evil in Romans 12,
Paul writes in Romans 13 that the governing authority is "God's servant
to do you good. But if you do wrong, be afraid, for he does not bear the
sword for nothing. He is God's servant, an agent of wrath to bring punishment on the wrongdoer." The Greek word for God's wrath, a concept that
Paul brings forward from the Tanakh, is *orgē*, meaning "an expression of
anger." So the government may inflict punishment as an expression of
anger (censure) or as a deterrent to wrongdoers.[46] Neither the government
nor a wronged individual, however, ought to aim to repay evil for its own
sake or for the sake of a balance.

It is not just the teachings of Jesus and Paul, of course, but the death and
resurrection of Jesus Christ that inform Christian views of punishment.
Views of the atonement beget views of reconciliation, which in turn beget
views of punishment. The Calvinist notion of penal substitution readily
supports balance retributivism; the holistic reconciliation of Athanasius
and of several twentieth-century theologians supports restorative punishment. Today many Christian churches advocate something much like
a restorative view of punishment. "The primary effect of *punishment* is to
redress the disorder caused by the offense.... [It] has a medicinal value: as
far as possible, it should contribute to the correction of the offender" says
the *Catechism of the Catholic Church*, for instance.[47]

The case for restorative punishment in Islam appeared earlier, embedded in the larger case for reconciliation in Islam. To recount it briefly, the prescribed punishments for Hudud crimes are admittedly not restorative. In the jurisprudence for Qisas crimes, which include murder, however, a restorative logic can be found in the victim's option for compensation and forgiveness and in the Quran's commendation of this option. Crimes of Ta'zir, especially as the Hanafi school treats them, are ones that call for a restorative response of restitution, repentance, and forgiveness. Finally, practices of *sulh* and *musalaha* model the restorative rationale quintessentially.

Each of the traditions and schools, then, can support a view of punishment that, reflecting the justice of reconciliation, aims to bring repair to the real harms that crimes inflict. How can punishment best address these real harms? By addressing the widest range of wounds, involving the widest array of participants, and complementing the other practices in the ethic of political reconciliation.

Primary Restorations

The Standing Victory of the Injustice

Unless and until it is defeated, a political injustice continues to stand victorious as a "moral fact"—in the perpetrator's eyes, in the victim's eyes, and in the eyes of the members of the community. As long as the injustice stands, the victim still remains a victim and the perpetrator in some sense remains victorious. Judicial punishment is a communication of censure whose purpose is to defeat, or to bring down, decisively the standing injustice. It is morally essential that this communication be performed by the state or a legally constituted international authority, for such an authority, at least when it is governed by the rule of law, has the legitimacy to vindicate, uphold, and restore the laws of the community.

To whom is the communication directed? Above all, to the perpetrator, of course. The physical aspect of punishment is not something added to the communication but is itself a part of it. Just as an injustice involves an action, not mere words, so, too, does the message of punishment. Only imposed deprivation can communicate commensurately the gravity of a crime. If a perpetrator should choose to accept a punishment, then the hardship becomes his participation in the defeat of the evil he committed—much like a penance.[48] Hardship or deprivation, then, are goods and not a return of evil for evil, harm for harm.

The communication is also directed to victims, who were most defeated by the injustice, and to the members of the community, whose laws are vindicated. The hope of the communication is that its targets will receive and accept it. When they do, their reception serves to defeat the injustice. The validity of the communication, though, is not strictly dependent upon anyone's reception. A perpetrator may remain stalwart—in political contexts, most do—and even popular in his community. Despite this, assuming that he is guilty and that his trial was fair, the communication that occurs through punishment is still delivered and still inflicts a defeat to the message of injustice.

By defeating the standing victory of injustice, judicial punishment addresses a real harm—a moral fact—and not an abstract balance. Yet it does not leave behind the core commitments of retributivism. Restorative punishment insists that a certain perpetrator deserves a certain punishment because he is guilty of a certain corresponding crime. Thus, the essential connection among deed, guilt, and punishment that desert embodies is retained. What about proportionality? Like retributivism, restorative punishment holds that, all else being equal, greater crimes deserve greater punishment. The veracity of a communication of censure demands that it speak to the magnitude as well as the wrongness of a crime. Yet because punishment does not aim at a strict balance, it does not require an exact quantification of punishment denominated in years spent in prison or money paid in fines. Such a drive for equivalence suffers from the same problem that plagues the balancing justification in general: How is the wrong of a murder or torture to be appraised? Pettit and Braithwaite point out that punishments for murder have varied dramatically from culture to culture and from period to period. In Japan, for instance, 27 percent of prison sentences for murder are suspended, often because a judge decides that a murderer's deed can better be addressed by a family or community.[49] Restorative punishment instead applies the principle of soft proportionality, allowing punishments to be adapted to the range and kind of harms done and the kinds of restorations that need to take place within a given political community.

What kind of judicial punishment effectively communicates a defeat to standing political injustices committed during war, genocide, and dictatorship? One that bears two qualities: strong legal authority and popular participation.

Since a communication that defeats injustice is also one that delivers a victory to just laws, it must be delivered by an authority who speaks for the law and who determines guilt and punishment in a way that reflects the law's justice—namely, a court. In this regard, restorative punishment approves of trials and parts ways with advocates of reconciliation who reject judicial punishment. International tribunals are especially promising for their authority when human rights violations are involved, for they can claim best a warrant to speak for humanity and convict perpetrators of crimes that are recognized as crimes by all of humanity.

The principles that fall under the heading "rule of law" are crucial for the fair determination of guilt and punishment and hence for the authority of a court's communication. Their importance is seen best in their absence. Rwanda's *gacaca* courts are a prime case and an unfortunate one since their designers had reconciliation in mind. Although no final report had yet been published at the time this book was written, several recent accounts of the courts' performance, based on systematic surveys and observations of trials, reveal an egregious lack of due process protections, damaging the fairness of punishment as well as the prospects for reconciliation. Judges, usually respected village elders, received only minimal training. Though they were required to be literate, many were not. Neither defendants nor their accusers had lawyers. Sometimes people were tried in large groups, as were nineteen people in the village of Sovu. Witnesses, the sole source of evidence, were often unreliable in their testimony and subject to violence or the threat of violence by accused perpetrators and their families and friends. In 2008, for instance, Rwandan police addressed 794 cases of violence against survivors and witnesses. Reports of false testimony abounded, some of it given by innocent people who confessed in order to avoid the risk of a much longer sentence if judges disbelieved them. Sentences were inconsistent and unsystematic. All of this sharply compromised a just communication of censure.[50]

Other judicial responses to large-scale basic human rights violations in the past generation have carried much higher standards, including courts in Argentina, Chile, and Germany as well as the international criminal tribunals and the International Criminal Court. One of the chief accomplishments of these standards is what international lawyers call "the individuation of guilt," an idea restorative punishment embraces through its stress on desert. Punishment's communication is directed at an actor for an action and not a general social problem like instability.

Individuation is denied when a collective is instead blamed. This happens in two ways. One is exoneration, where defendants plea that they

were a cog in a complex bureaucratic machine that complicated and dif-
fused responsibility, that they acted under superior orders, or that their
actions were legal under the laws of their country. One of the great precedents of the Nuremberg Trials was their nullification of such invocations
of collectivity. The other form of appeal to collectivity is blaming an entire
nation for the crimes of a portion of its leaders and citizens. The Treaty of
Versailles held all of Germany responsible for World War I. Serbs blame
Croatia and all Croatians for atrocities and vice versa. Not only is such
blame unjust toward the innocent, but it fuels further conflict. One of the
conclusions generally shared by genocide scholars is that these events are
carefully and even meticulously planned and are not spontaneous may-
hem. This is not to deny the complexity of individuation. If the duress of
superior orders or the bureaucratic diffusion of responsibility do not exon-
erate, they might reduce culpability. The consensus in the international
legal community is that the leaders who conceived, planned, and ordered
atrocities rank highest in culpability; others rank lower. These are just the
kinds of distinctions that good judicial procedure is capable of making
and communicating.

An authoritative and just communication of punishment must also
be distributed impartially to all perpetrators of crimes. A failure to do
so is what is known as victor's justice. The ICTY has succeeded admirably in trying Serbs, Croats, and Muslims proportionately to their crimes.
Argentina's trials of the 1980s can be credited with placing leftist guerrilla leaders as well as Dirty War generals in the dock. Conversely, the
Nuremberg Trials were accused of victor's injustice insofar as they con-
sisted only of judges from Allied powers and ignored these powers' own
possible war crimes in Dresden, Hamburg, and cities across Japan.
Because these trials were balanced by formidable moral and legal accomplishments, they rightly maintained prestige. Faring far less well were the
Tokyo trials of the same years, which were more widely perceived as a tool
of the conquerors.[51] Problematic, too, is the postgenocide government of
Rwanda, which, blaming rival Hutus for almost the entire genocide, has
allowed very few violations committed by members of the Tutsi Rwandan
Patriotic Force (RPF) to be tried. By a wide consensus, analysts now hold
that the RPF was responsible for tens of thousands of Hutu deaths, both
in its reinvasion of Rwanda during the genocide and in its incursions into
Congo after the genocide.[52] The Rwandan government's partiality is both
intrinsically unjust and contradicts the message of reconciliation through
which it commends the *gacaca* trials to its people.

All of these factors are widely recognized as features of a fair trial. Participation is much more distinctive to restorative punishment. By participation, I mean the active involvement in the judicial process of those drawn into the web of the crime's effect. Occurring most directly through an actual assembly, participation was a main idea behind the *gacaca* courts in Rwanda and the Community Reconciliation Panels in Timor-Leste.

Participation adds dimension and depth to punishment's communication and meshes punishment with other practices of reconciliation. By hearing the story of victims, perpetrators come to understand the harm they have wrought and thus the meaning of their punishment. In hearing the story of perpetrators, victims come to understand the circumstances surrounding perpetrators' actions, including mitigating factors, duress, and, in some cases, the perpetrators' own history of suffering. In civil wars, after all, perpetrators are often also victims. Several of the victims who participated in Timor-Leste's CRPs reported to interviewers that they became willing to relax their demand for punishment when they came to understand that perpetrators were pressured by superiors in the context of war. This is not to say that victims will or should abjure punishment, especially for crimes that are grave and intentional. When victims are integrated into the proceedings, though, they may well come to favor communally restorative modes of punishment. In telling their story before the perpetrator and the community, victims gain acknowledgment, contribute to the formulation of a fitting punishment, and are more receptive to this punishment when it is delivered. In the CRPs in Timor-Leste, victims commonly dropped their demand for punishment when they believed that perpetrators had experienced shame and had offered a sincere confession and apology.

The community members who attended the CRPs—an impressive 30,000 to 40,000 over the two years of their operation—heard both sides. As in a truth commission, they conferred recognition on the victim and heard the story of the perpetrator. Present for the judges' verdict, they served as recipients of the punishment's communication and thus helped to defeat its standing victory within the community in a way that also served to integrate. By adopting the traditional Timorese reconciliation mechanism, known as *nahe biti* (meaning "stretching or rolling the mat"), which community elders and religious leaders customarily directed, the CRPs enhanced the legitimacy of the panel process, helping its verdicts to stick. The verdict delivered by the judges communicated a reconciling form of punishment, involving the perpetrator's payment of money or symbolic items to victims, his help in repairing their houses, or his performance of community service such as building a school, church, or road. The process concluded with a traditional feast and often acts of forgiveness on the part of victims. Midpoint interviews with participants showed 90 percent of them citing positive results. A large proportion of them also wanted the CRPs to continue.[53]

Popular participation also epitomized—and was integral to all that was successful in—Rwanda's *gacaca* courts. This emerges clearly in the most thorough study of *gacaca* to date, that of Phil Clark, a scholar of transitional justice. Clark spent fifteen months observing the courts over nearly their entire lifespan, from 2003 to 2010, observing sixty-seven hearings and conducting 459 interviews from high government officials to ordinary participants, including suspects and survivors of the genocide alike.

What Clark concludes from his study corresponds well with the case for restorative punishment advanced here and with the overall argument of this book. He challenges the views of human rights and legal scholars— the liberal peace—who criticize *gacaca* for its low due process standards and its one-sided prosecution of Hutus. The problem with such views, he argues, is that they focus too much on *gacaca's* formal design and not enough on its lived reality. Giving shape to the courts were the participation of ordinary people—suspects, survivors, and bystanders—and the cultural and religious views that they brought to the grassy spaces where they met to tell and hear stories of murderous crimes. What emerged, he maintains, was far more than a judicial proceeding but rather a hybrid of peace, justice, healing, forgiveness, reconciliation, and the more urgent and pragmatic tasks of clearing out and improving inhumanely over-crowded prisons. Adjusting for differences between Clark's and my own usage of the terms *peace, justice,* and *reconciliation,* I conclude from Clark's analysis that *gacaca* involved a form of accountability that incorporated or complemented several of the practices and the primary and secondary res-torations that an ethic of political reconciliation entails: acknowledgment, reparations, apology, forgiveness, and a change in the attitudes of survi-vors and suspects that enabled them to live in the same village, which, in thousands of cases, they had little choice but to do. Corresponding also with the present argument, Clark finds that, to the degree that par-ticipants took on this holistic approach, they did so out of a culture that stresses communal identity and out of a Christian theology that stresses confession, forgiveness, and the restoration of relationship.

Clark is careful not to overstate his case. *Gacaca's* various achieve-ments were realized by some more than others and to different degrees—reconciliation's partiality. Clark reports that, in many cases, hearing the truth about the crimes of the genocide retraumatized victims, though in many of these same cases it brought healing in the long run. Reconciliation between enemies that began at *gacaca* will still require years of effort. The greatest tension was between reconciliation and punishment. Long-term imprisonment conflicted with the goal of reconciliation, Clark observes.

Even noting Clark's cautions, it may be questioned whether, at least in one respect, his view of *gacaca* is overly positive, namely his view that its legal standards for determining punishment were far more sound than the human rights lawyers have allowed. Arguably Clark's defense leaves many of the lawyers' objections—which I detailed earlier in the chapter—unanswered. What Clark succeeds in showing, though, is that whatever *gacaca's* problems as a judicial procedure, it was far more than a judicial procedure, amounting to a restorative form of punishment that elicited a wide range of restorations through the participation of thousands.[54]

Such restorative processes of judicial punishment are difficult to achieve in a conventional trial, which is not conducive to a full, fluid, or empathetic hearing of victims' and perpetrators' stories. In the case of some courts, the communicative value of punishment is undermined by the courts' remoteness from the community in which the crimes took place. A survey of Rwandans conducted in 2002 showed that 87.2 percent claimed to be either "not well informed" or "not informed at all" about the ICTR.[55] If conventional trials are less participatory, though, they are better able to guarantee the rule of law than such community forums as the *gacaca* courts. The Timorese CRPs also involved low due process stan-dards, though with far less deleterious results than the *gacaca* system.

Strong legal authority and participation, then, appear to stand in ten-sion. Can they be balanced? The different performance of the *gacaca* and the Timorese panels can be explained in part by the fact that *gacaca's* loose due process was combined with its judgment of serious crimes and its deliverance of very long prison sentences, while the Timor-Leste pan-els tried arson, beatings, and theft but not murder, rape, or mastermind-ing atrocities, which were supposed to be tried in the Special Panels for Serious Crimes, a higher court that combined national and international judges. This higher court secured eighty-one convictions before its dis-solution in 2005, though most of these were of lower-ranked perpetra-tors. The high-ranking officials involved remained largely sheltered by the

Indonesian government. That the CRPs dealt with less serious crimes made victims more amenable to such restorative punishments as community service. Even then, some complained that their spirit of forbearance at the panels was predicated on their expectation that high-ranking perpetrators would be convicted at higher levels—an expectation that was largely unfulfilled.

Generally, trials of high-level perpetrators in which a potentially long prison sentence is at stake require a level of legal rigor that is hard to square with strong participation. It is forums that promote accountability for low-level perpetrators that provide the most opportunity for popular participation, though these, too, demand important features of the rule of law. The optimal combination of legal authority and participation will differ from country to country and from circumstance to circumstance. Different levels of courts and different combinations of institutions for different levels and kinds of crime will almost always be part of the solution. Legal authority and participation, though, are the criteria that arise from addressing the wound of the standing victory of political injustices through restorative punishment.

The Wounded Soul of the Perpetrator

The wounded soul of the perpetrator, one of the six wounds that political injustices inflict, is obviously relevant to the practice of punishment. Skeptics will object: Of what concern is the soul of Adolf Eichmann, who organized the killing of millions of Jews and other victims? Of course, not every murderer or violator of human rights is Eichmann. Consider also the anonymous Tutsi who killed his Hutu boyhood schoolmate during a time when white-hot revenge suffused the nation but who later comes to regret it. His soul is of concern in part because, if neglected, it might lead him to commit future crimes. In addition, this man and thousands of other Tutsis must eventually return to his village and live peaceably with others, especially since Rwandan jails cannot hold them for long. These concerns, though, relate to secondary wounds and are consequentialist in form. Is there also intrinsic value to restoring the perpetrator's soul?

The three religious traditions that form an overlapping consensus, strands of the restorative justice school, as well as other sources (Plato, for example) say that it is the perpetrator who is damaged most by his crimes. This in no way diminishes what the victim has suffered. Their claim is rooted in the idea that the soul is the most important part of the person, the center of his worth. So when a person flouts a fundamental and universal norm and disregards the dignity of another, he wounds himself; when he commits such actions on a mass scale, he wounds himself in the worst way possible. "His soul is in jeopardy as his victim's is not," writes philosopher Herbert Morris.[56]

Through punishment the community invites the restoration of the perpetrator in the hope that he will repent and accept his punishment as a sincere expression of this repentance. "You gotta participate in your redemption," Sister Helen Préjean said when she counseled death row inmate Matthew Poncelot to repent for his crimes, as portrayed in the film *Dead Man Walking*.[57] Again, the perpetrator's punishment would be valid even if he did not repent, but restorative punishment seeks and invites his transformation and accountability.

Is the state's interest in the perpetrator's soul overly paternalistic? No more paternalistic than the law is in coercively asking people to comply with its moral demands, replies philosopher Jean Hampton. Imagine if a rapist were to protest that a police officer, the judge, and the guard outside his prison cell were paternalistic for confining him to jail. He may rightly be told that he is being confined because he contravened the law and the morality that it embodies. Yet if that is the case, then why should not that same morality be communicated to him in the hope that he will come to accept it? If that is paternalistic, then why is not the law against rape itself paternalistic? Punishment seeks only to convince the perpetrator of the rightness of the law, of her obligation to keep it, and of her duty to make amends for breaking it, but it compels no more than this. Keeping with retributivism's rightful emphases, the state may justly inflict no more than the punishment that is deserved and proportionate in its effort to communicate the message of punishment.[58]

If some consider restorative punishment too heavy handed, others will consider it impossible. Consider again Eichmann, a bureaucratic orchestrator of the Holocaust. His Israeli captor reports having found him to be a man without a conscience.[59] What does that mean? The implication is that the person is beyond repentance, incapable of ever grasping that what he has done contravenes a moral law. Imagine how naïve it would be for a moralist to argue with such a person. If a perpetrator is indeed beyond repentance, then any change in his soul is a hopeless prospect.

Yet what does it mean to be beyond repentance? People certainly exist who have lost permanently the capacity for moral awareness and decision, but others exist who retain this capacity yet have so thoroughly turned off their conscience that it remains only a dim wisp. What is the difference? The first sort is a psychopath, one who has reached insanity, a robot who is programmed but does not reflect, or King Kong, a monster whose end is destruction and whose deliberation is only instrumental. The second is someone much like Eichmann, who, Arendt writes, "had a conscience," allowed it to function, though "within rather odd limits," for four weeks in 1941 and was then "troubled by no questions of conscience" from January 1942 to fall 1944, when the Final Solution took place. During this time, as for most of his former career, he gave his conscience over to the Führer, whose word he considered law, so much so that it would have bothered his conscience had he not heeded the Führer's commands.[60]

The first sort of person has lost her free will, her capacity for rational reflection, or what philosophers Charles Taylor and Harry Frankfurt have each called a second order desire.[61] A first order desire, they explain, is unreflective: Angela wants a cheeseburger. A second order desire is the ability to reflect on the first order desire and decide whether one wants to pursue it. Worried about her cholesterol, Angela thinks again and concludes that she does not want the cheeseburger. Second order desires do not amount to conscience, which involves an awareness of the moral law, but their existence denotes a capacity to reflect on and possibly change one's beliefs, including one's moral beliefs. The first person—the psychopath, the robot, King Kong—no longer possesses this capacity. The second person, however much she may have immersed herself in evil, however unlikely a change in her outlook might be, still retains it.

So there are indeed some people in whose case moral change is an impossible expectation, but their existence should not blot out the hope that a judicial process could elicit change in other perpetrators. The one incapable of moral change is just the sort of person who should not be involved in a judicial process at all. He is unfit to stand trial. A trial, after all, is a communicative enterprise. If it is to be fair, then the defendant must be able to hear, consider, and respond to the charges against him and to offer reasons and arguments in his defense. To do these things, then he must have the (second order) ability to reflect on his actions. One cannot hold at the same time that a person has lost his conscience and that he ought to be tried. If he is a psychopath, he ought to be placed in an institution, if King Kong, in a cage, and if a robot, in the hands of technicians who can deprogram him. It is only if he has some reflective abilities that he should be placed in the dock. If he does possess such abilities, then a possibility always remains that trials or imprisonment might change his outlook.

One might grant that a trial presupposes a capacity for change yet still object that repentance rarely occurs, especially among those who commit major human rights violations. The reason lies not in a lack of conscience but in a conscience committed stalwartly to injustice. It is naïve to expect that the apartheid official who has built his whole life around white superiority, for instance, will abandon his beliefs easily.

In my discussion of apology, I offered several examples of remorseful perpetrators, ones whose stance may not be typical but is nevertheless plausible. Might they be faking it to avoid punishment? Such suspicion does not fit most of the cases. "Neither timing nor institutional arrangements cause, predict, or explain remorseful confessions," writes Leigh Payne.[62] The designers of the TRC pointedly avoided making apology a condition for amnesty, requiring only a full confession of deeds. Some perpetrators offered confessions that were clearly unremorseful and were granted amnesty nonetheless. South African defense minister Magnus Malan's apology came after he was acquitted by a court. Captain Scilingo and the other confessing Argentine officers were protected by the Due Obedience law during the mid-1990s, when they confessed. In Scilingo's case, it was his personal disintegration and subsequent religious conversion that prompted his apology. The Kashmiri militant of my own experience practiced and enacted his apologies on his own and was not required to make them by the Indian government.

Most of these apologies did not occur in the context of judicial punishment. Only the Kashmiri militant and Eugene De Kock came to their remorse through trial and imprisonment. Still, these cases may well hold lessons for judicial punishment. The thread running commonly through all of them is that remorse occurred in contexts in which perpetrators came to reflect on the suffering of victims. The remorseful perpetrators in South Africa heard victims recount such suffering in the context of the TRC. Policeman Eric Taylor cites the film *Mississippi Burning* and Nelson Mandela's autobiography as the spurs of his turning. For Thapelo Mbelo, a black man who collaborated with the apartheid police, it was the testimony of the mothers of the men that he had conspired to kill that led him to apologize to them. In Scilingo's case, it was an incident in which he nearly fell out of the plane out of which he was pushing Argentine dissidents that prompted him to reflect on their fate.[63] Is there a way that judicial punishment can encourage such reflection and thus perhaps the perpetrator's remorse?

We are led back to Timor-Leste and Rwanda. Among 941 *gacaca* court defendants observed by Avocats Sans Frontières between October 2005 and December 2007, 352 confessed to crimes of which they had been accused.[64] The confessions were, understandably, highly strategic, formulated in response to strong incentives for sentence reduction. Often they were heavily qualified. Defendants, for instance, admitted to being present at the site of a killing but, in order to secure a light prison sentence, insisted they had not done the deed.[65] This strategy did not always succeed. Max Rettig's report of the *gacaca* courts in Sovu shows that 40 percent of the time judges rejected confessions as incomplete and imposed prison sentences that averaged twenty-five years. The strategic imperatives created by this "confession game" severely undercut prospects for sincere remorse and, still more, the possibility that others would believe even earnest remorse. Rettig reports that 70 percent of nonsurvivors and 90 percent of survivors of genocide agree that people lie during *gacaca*.[66] These gloomy findings may seem at first to stand in tension with Clark's more positive view of *gacaca*, but even he considers the prospect of imprisonment one of the greatest sources of tension in *gacaca*. It is despite this tension, not in ignorance of it, that Clark nevertheless considers *gacaca* a success.[67]

Timor-Leste's Community Reconciliation Panels fared better. Here, too, victims and perpetrators aired their stories in front of the community, but perpetrators conveyed sincerity in reporting their experience of confession, claiming that it helped them to integrate back into their communities and that it freed their children from blame by association. Their apologies and expressions of remorse were common. Victims reported a far higher rate of satisfaction in what they were hearing from perpetrators. The incentive structure of the CRPs encouraged this. Although a confession and an admission of responsibility were required for a settlement, judges did not scale the quantity of punishment to the quality of confession. Punishment took the form of community service, not lengthy prison sentences. In few cases were confessions not accepted or did an agreement fall apart. The process was adjourned in only thirty-two cases, compared to 1,371 successfully completed.[68]

Again, the incentive structure of the CRPs as well as their success can be attributed in part to the fact that they did not address murder, torture, rape, or the officials and leaders who planned human rights violations. Higher Timorese courts of the Western legalist variety were supposed to have tried these more serious criminals but did so only to a limited extent and tried few of the high-ranking perpetrators. The CRPs did not face the gargantuan task of trying more than 100,000 murder suspects, as the *gacaca* courts did. Must we conclude, then, that the remorse of perpetrators is unlikely in a courtroom procedure, when lengthy prison sentences are at stake and the worst sorts of crimes are involved? Must we conclude that remorse is only somewhat more likely when perpetrators are contemplating their deeds from a prison cell? Is remorse likewise far more probable when the procedures and the punishments are restorative in nature, as in a community forum like those of Timor-Leste? Perhaps so, but three points must be kept in mind. First, as we have seen, high-ranking officials as well as ordinary murderers sometimes do come to express remorse even in traditional courtrooms. When they do, their souls begin to mend and their injustice is publicly renounced. Second, in situations in which fair judicial punishment through trials and imprisonment for murderers and other perpetrators of serious crimes is not feasible, community forums are a second-best solution. In such a setting, a perpetrator's remorse is more likely, but victims may well feel shortchanged. Third, in sites of past injustice, those following the orders to carry out injustices are far more numerous than those issuing the orders. If community forums are best able to handle less serious crimes—though still quite serious ones—the remorse they bring about still contributes to restoring a great number of souls, not to mention the people who must live with them again.

Four Other Wounds

There are four other primary wounds of political injustice to which judicial punishment can bring primary restorations. These wounds are: the lack of acknowledgment of victims' suffering, ignorance of the source and circumstances of political injustices, harms to the victim's person, and the violation of the victim's human rights.

In their relatively rare expressions of retributivism, advocates of judicial punishment argue that punishment upholds the dignity of victims. "Punishment is the absolute duty of society to honor and redeem the suffering of the individual victim," human rights activist Aryeh Neier says. Stressing the difference between his view and consequentialism, he adds, "I want to quarrel with the assumption that a principal reason for seeking justice, or criterion for evaluating its efficacy, should be the future stability of a reconstituted democracy."[69]

If honoring and redeeming the victim is not the central purpose of punishment in the present ethic, it is certainly one intrinsic purpose. Much like the practice of acknowledgment, punishment confers recognition on the victim's dignity. A political injustice does not take away a victim's dignity, at least in an ethic that understands dignity as an objective worth that no person or crime can destroy. Yet the injustice does demean, or show disregard for, a victim's dignity, a defilement that stands as part of the same moral fact as the victory of the injustice. When the state's communication of punishment defeats the standing victory of injustice, then, it also hands a victory to the dignity of the victim. Lead prosecutor of the ICTY Richard Goldstone made the point well when, upon hearing that Serbian war criminals Radovan Karadzic and Ratko Mladic might be given amnesty, he exploded in public: "What politicians have the moral, legal or political right to forgive people charged with genocide and crimes against humanity—for the deaths of tens of thousands of people—without consulting the victims? I just find it abhorrent."[70] This victory of the victim is enhanced all the more when members of the community recognize it. As trials of deposed Iraqi president Saddam Hussein and his collaborators were being considered, an Iraqi Sunni cleric declared: "The trials should be public, in front of the people, so that they feel that they have truly been liberated and that their rights have been returned to them by those who stole them."[71] Similarly, victims who testified in Timor-Leste's CRPs reported that they came to feel more respected by their community.[72] Community forums are well suited to confer such recognition.

Judicial punishment often yields information on the source and circumstances of the suffering of victims as well. When perpetrators deny great crimes, they deprive surviving victims of the knowledge of how, by whom, and for what reason their family members were killed or they themselves were injured. After Japan's defeat in World War II, Japanese military officers lit massive bonfires to burn the records of police, military units, and the cabinet; killed witnesses to war crimes; and, in a thousand instances, took their own lives, all serving to block the exposure of atrocities.[73] Thus, Michael Ignatieff writes that "[t]he great virtue of legal proceedings is that rules of evidence establish otherwise contestable facts. In this sense, war crimes trials make it more difficult for societies to take refuge in denial."[74]

Yet trials also have limits in exposing crimes. Rules of evidence and procedure, Drumbl points out, favor the exposure of "logical and microscopic" truths over context and texture. Sometimes, too, he explains, the exposure of truth is interrupted or terminated. It is halted because of procedural flaws; it is prolonged for years and occurs in sporadic stops and starts; or, as with Slobodan Milosevic at the ICTY, the defendant dies before the verdict can be delivered.[75] By and large, truth commissions and judicial community forums such as Timor-Leste's CRPs paint the truth of atrocities in a far more pointillist and personalist fashion. Still, because trials have the ability to seize and subpoena information and elicit the testimony of witnesses and defendants, they are sometimes able to root out information that other forums cannot.

When judicial punishment includes reparations, it contributes to redressing harms to victims. The moral logic here is much as it is for reparations. Western-style criminal trials normally do not issue reparations to victims, a key complaint of restorative justice advocates. It is instead civil trials that deliver settlements to victims, but these are not usually the sort of trials that take up the cases of human rights violations. A major stride in a restorative direction is Article 75 of the Rome Statute, which empowers the International Criminal Court to order reparations to be paid either to individuals or to groups, with the payment coming either from the perpetrator herself or from a Trust Fund for Victims that the Assembly of State Parties set up in September 2002. National courts in Rwanda also added civil liability to their criminal convictions, ordering defendants to pay damages to victims. Though defendants, often indigent, frequently could not pay, the damages arguably still carried symbolic force. *Gacaca* courts sometimes required perpetrators to work to restore damaged property, a punitive reparation that was more economically realistic but challenging to monitor.[76] The CRPs of Timor-Leste included reparations and the repair of houses, buildings, and roads as a part of their reconciliation agreements, although in these cases as well, monitoring was difficult.

Finally, in practicing judicial punishment, a state redresses the violation of the victim's rights insofar as it expresses, reaffirms, and thereby strengthens human rights as the legally valid values of its realm or of relations between it and another state. What is not meant here is the sense in which the populations of a state or of several states will become more supportive of human rights or the rule of law in reaction to a favorable verdict—this is a secondary restoration. Rather, it is the sense in which a court empowers standards of human rights and the rule of law by simply enacting them through its procedures and its verdicts and through the very fact that it has brought serious perpetrators to trial.

Secondary Restorations

Although consequences are not the only or primary criterion for judging trials and punishment, they still matter for justice. Consequences are equivalent to what I call secondary restorations, transformations in people's emotions and judgments in relation to their own or another political order. When positive transformations occur, they strengthen democracy, the rule of law, and peace. Today's debates over tribunals are heated, though, because their detractors argue that not only do trials fail to bring about secondary restorations but they actually make things worse.

If the destructive effects of punishment turn out to prevail vastly over its restorative effects, what are the implications for an ethic of political reconciliation's view of punishment? Because punishment brings about primary restorations, the ethic poses a presumption in favor of it (either Western-style trials or community forums). Primary restorations are enough to justify punishment; no secondary restorations are needed. Yet if punishment brings about substantial setbacks for peace or democracy, the moral case for pursuing it is lessened. If the setbacks are strong enough, they override the presumption in favor of punishment.

Is a decision not to pursue punishment in sites of human rights violations a failure of justice? Absolutely. Restorative punishment holds that anytime perpetrators fail to receive the justice that they deserve an injustice occurs. Still, it is justifiable for states to refrain from apprehending, prosecuting, and trying every perpetrator in a given setting. Prosecutors make such decisions all the time, whether they work for a city, a county, a nation-state, or the International Criminal Court. Societies justifiably balance pursuing criminal justice with such other goals as national defense, health care, and other worthy pursuits. These competing goods have moral value as well. In settings where efforts are being made to bring war or dictatorship to an end or to preserve stability in the wake of a peace agreement or political transition, the goods of peace, democracy, human rights, and the rule of law can override the presumption for punishment. Thousands of lives or the possibility of the rule of law could be in the balance. Building socially just institutions is also one of the six practices of reconciliation and ought to be honored.

Do the supposed negative consequences of judicial punishment override its benefits? As with consequentialist arguments in general, the question of secondary restorations is an empirical one.

Does Judicial Punishment Deter?

Recalling the amnesty granted to the Turkish officials who massacred more than one million Armenians nearly a quarter century earlier, Adolf Hitler argued to his general staff in 1939, "who after all is today speaking about the destruction of the Armenians?"

ICTY prosecutor Richard Goldstone argued that the international community's failure to prosecute Pol Pot, Idi Amin, Saddam Hussein, and Sudan's Mohammed Aidid encouraged Serbs to undertake ethnic cleansing in the early 1990s.[77] Does judicial punishment have a deterrent effect? Does punishing or threatening to punish a human right violator induce him or another to refrain from committing a future human rights violation?

Little systematic evidence exists. There is some indication that harsher punishments deter certain crimes, but there is little evidence for such an effect on major human rights violations.[78] There are also logical reasons to doubt deterrence. When leaders or rank-and-file soldiers have undertaken to slaughter members of another ethnicity, nationality, or political persuasion and decided that this goal is worth risking their own lives, they are unlikely to be deterred by time in jail. If they are committed strongly enough to such a goal, they may even be willing to jeopardize military victory or effective occupation, as Nazi military leaders did when, at great military cost, they systematically massacred civilians in the Soviet Union and southeastern Europe. When legal threats do come along, as they did in the war in Yugoslavia in the 1990s, war criminals often have already committed massive crimes and have little additional punishment to fear from committing further ones.[79] In dictatorships, leaders and underlings perceive little threat as long as their regime appears strong. If their regime weakens, they might make a strategic decision to commit crimes in order to save it. In genocides like Rwanda's, people sometimes carry out massacres because they fear being killed if they do not. True, some analysts claim evidence that indictments from the ICTY in The Hague deterred war crimes in Yugoslavia.[80] Yet such claims are vastly overshadowed by the Serb massacre of approximately 8,000 Bosnian men and boys at Srebrenica in July 1995, with The Hague standing idly by. Serbs committed further massacres against Kosovar Albanians despite the ICTY's indictment of Milosevic and other top Serbian leaders. Advocates of trials claim that if Western powers had been more willing to use force, the ICTY's deterrent effect would have been far stronger. The possibility cannot be dismissed, but the day when outside powers can be counted on to hunt down and arrest war criminals in conflicts in which they do not already have a large stake is still far away. If deterrence were to occur, it would certainly enhance the justice of judicial punishment, but there is little evidence that it occurs.

Does Judicial Punishment Promote the Rule of Law?

There are at least three ways in which judicial punishment might advance the rule of law. One, the legitimacy effect, holds that citizens become more supportive of a new regime or a peace settlement when they see human rights violators brought to justice. A new regime's trials of the old regime's leaders serve as a down payment on democracy.[81]

Second, the judicial institution effect holds that trials do not (merely) convince citizens of their regime's commitment to human rights but actually teach them the meaning of law and human rights. A society that has been living under a dictatorship as long as anyone can remember has forgotten, or simply never learned, what the rule of law and human rights mean. Fair trials teach judges and lawyers what it means to enact justice. Especially when trials are publicly visible, as they are when former top leaders are the defendants, they also model the rule of law to the people and, at least when a favorable verdict is rendered, give prestige to the courts. In her widely read book, *Legalism*, political philosopher Judith Shklar extols the Nuremberg Trials for establishing a strong ideology and practice of the rule of law in postwar Germany.[82]

A third version of the rule of law argument might be called the democratic discourse effect. Legal scholar Mark Osiel argues that, while the central purpose of trials is retribution and deterrence, the trials of top perpetrators also serve as "show trials" in that they create public debate. Unlike the show trials of totalitarian regimes, though, they do so within a fair process. Debate and contest—and not shared national values—are the best effect that can be hoped for from trials, this argument claims. Insofar as such controversy is civil and nonviolent, it teaches and enacts the habits of democracy.[83]

Do trials promote the rule of law in any of these ways? Kim and Sikkink offer evidence that they do. Surveying one hundred states that have made transitions to peaceful democracy, they find that states where trials have occurred have experienced lower levels of human rights violations than states where no trials have taken place. They also find that trials have no significant negative effect on human rights violations. What explains this? They offer an intriguing answer by contrasting the effects of truth commissions, which, having no power to deter through imprisonment, fines, or vetting, are also associated with lower levels of human rights violations. This suggests that trials improve the rule of law by increasing popular support for it, by teaching judicial norms to the population or by eliciting civil public debate. Kim and Sikkink also show that polities with neighboring states that have conducted trials are likely to have lower levels of human rights violations, which they cite as evidence that trials communicate norms.[84]

Far more ambivalent about the effects of trials is a separate study of transitional justice conducted by political scientists Leigh Payne, Tricia Olsen, and Andrew Reiter that also looks at the impact of transitional justice institutions on human rights and democracy in a large number of countries. They show that trials do a better job than truth commissions, state-administered amnesties, or the *de facto* amnesty of no transitional justice at all in improving human rights and democracy scores. In their statistical regression analysis, however, which evaluates the impact of trials side by side with other factors, the significance of trials disappears. It is only when trials take place in combination with truth commissions and (limited) amnesties that they regain statistical significance as a positive contributor to human rights and democracies. A holistic approach appears to have an impact, then, but not trials alone.[85]

Other studies are less conclusive and support the finding that transitional justice has neither harmful nor beneficial effects. In their book *Can Might Make Rights?* Jane Stromseth, David Wippman, and Rosa Brooks examine four countries whose war criminals were tried in international tribunals or hybrid courts—Yugoslavia, Rwanda, Timor-Leste, and Sierra Leone—and found that, while these trials were effective in disempowering organizers of atrocity, they were less effective in establishing the capacity for local judicial punishment (the judicial institution effect) or convincing populations that accountability was being achieved (the legitimacy effect).[86]

There is evidence at least in some locales that populations welcome trials as an advance for justice. Surveys of Rwandans taken during the early stages of the *gacaca* courts showed high levels of support for them. In one survey, 74.4 percent of respondents agreed that *gacaca* was "doing a good job of delivering justice."[87] Even as late as 2004, fifteen years after the fall of communism, the demand for lustration processes was still high in

Poland, Hungary, and the Czech Republic.[88] Though isolated, such surveys show that trials and the idea of justice they contain can command popular support.

All in all, the evidence that trials strengthen the rule of law is significant but not overwhelming. The effect of trials in any given case is even less certain. Paradoxically, it is in part the rules that make trials fair that also make them unpredictable. Not only might the guilty be acquitted but they may well use trials as a platform for vindication.

The features of trials that make people more likely to perceive them as just are likely to be the same ones that deliver an effective defeat to the standing victory of injustice: They are conducted according to the rule of law; if a conflict is two sided, they try the criminals from both sides; and they are conducted as close to the people as is compatible with the other criteria. A 2002 survey that showed more than 80 percent of Rwandans favorable to the *gacaca* courts (which were still in their pilot phase at the time) also showed only 30 percent positive about the ICTR, which was being held in neighboring Arusha, Tanzania, and 30 percent positive about the trials in Rwandan national courts. A full 85 percent "agreed strongly" or "agreed" that gacaca courts ought to be used "to demonstrate that Rwandans can solve problems consistent with Rwandan traditions."[89] Rwandans were much more likely to sympathize with courts that were close to home.

If, however, the evidence is not overwhelming that trials advance the rule of law, neither is there systematic evidence for the opposite effect.

Does Judicial Punishment Promote Peace?

Many recent trials have taken up crimes committed during civil wars. Most commonly these trials occur in the period after civil wars are formally settled but when peace remains precarious. In the last decade or so, it has become more common for trials to take place during civil wars, as in Kosovo, Liberia, Uganda, and Sudan.

Advocates of judicial punishment claim that trials bring peace and reconciliation between former enemies. In part this occurs through a version of the legitimacy effect: People are more likely to endorse a peace settlement if it is accompanied by the justice of trials for perpetrators—especially the other side's. So, too, they are less likely to pursue revenge and are more likely to live peacefully with members of the opposing group, perhaps even in their own village. The ability of trials to individuate guilt restrains entire collectives from blaming one another. Most simply, punishment places behind bars those whose beliefs and judgments are most likely to continue to fuel war and war crimes.

Skeptics expect the opposite. When courts try perpetrators of human rights violations in conjunction with a peace settlement, they argue, the perpetrators and their allies will see it as an unjust imposition and will spoil the process. When courts try perpetrators unevenly or are perceived to try them unevenly (victors' justice), perpetrators and members of their community will seek further revenge, thus perpetuating the cycle of violence. In contrast to the supposed achievement of placing top-ranked perpetrators behind bars, in cases where a conflict is still raging, indictments and threats of arrest also keep leaders away from the negotiating table.

Who is right? Broadly speaking, neither side. In most cases it is difficult to show that trials contributed to peace, but in only one case have they been arguably counterproductive.

The ICTY, created in 1993, hindered neither the agreement that ended the war in Bosnia in December 1995 (the Dayton Accords) nor the war in Kosovo in 1999. What about the effect of the ICTY on the consolidation of peace in the years after Dayton? One commentator argues that the ICTY was a boon, sidelining virulent nationalists without sparking public protest, and encouraging moderates.[90] Certain focused events, though, like the assassination of Serbian prime minister Zoran Djindjic in March 2003 by killers working for government officials who feared being turned over to The Hague, the attempted assassination of Chief Prosecutor Carla Del Ponte, and a popular protest involving 40,000 people in Split, Croatia, in response to the arrest of Croatian general Gotovina in December 2005, stand as episodic evidence that trials interfered with the consolidation of peace. There were not many such episodes in Yugoslavia, though, and there was a reason for this, argue Vinjamuri and Snyder: The ICTY and Western powers refrained from arresting and prosecuting precisely in those circumstances in which such actions threatened stability—evidence that trials could undermine peace even when they do not. The ICTY has remained unpopular, especially with Serbs and Croats, who view it as unfairly focused against them.[91] The ICTY, then, has not contributed demonstrably to peace, but neither has it undermined it more than sporadically.

In Rwanda, the strongest evidence for a positive effect of trials on peace lies in the reported attitudes of citizens. Strong majorities of Rwandans perceived the *gacaca* courts as helpful for ending violence and promoting reconciliation (the latter effect asserted by 79 percent).[92]

Among those who were aware of the ICTR's work, a majority considered it successful and conducive to reconciliation.[93] While perceptions alone do not make a stable peace, these surveys can be taken as modest evidence of a positive effect.

Today, Uganda's unresolved civil war is the site of one of the world's sharpest debates over the effect of punishment. The war has been fought since 1986 between the Lord's Resistance Army (LRA) and the Uganda People's Defense Forces (UPDF), the army of President Yoweri Museveni. The LRA is led by Joseph Kony, who claims to be a "spokesperson of God" and fights for a government that is based directly on the Ten Commandments. It has forcibly conscripted 85 percent of its troops, abducted more than 30,000 children and forced them to be become soldiers, displaced 1.6 million Ugandans into camps, and committed thousands of brutal war crimes and crimes against humanity. The UPDF has committed crimes as well, though not as many.

The Acholi Religious Leaders Peace Initiative (ARLPI) is a coalition of high-level religious leaders who urge a peace agreement that integrates combatants back into their villages through reconciliation, forgiveness, and the practice of traditional restorative rituals. The ARLPI also vociferously advocates amnesty. At its urging, the government passed the Amnesty Act of 2000. Human rights groups and their allies within Uganda, including, at least for a while, President Museveni, opposed the ARLPI, urging judicial punishment and strenuously objecting to amnesty, though not all of them reject forgiveness and local reconciliation. They place their hope in the new court, among whose first indictments were five leaders of the LRA, including Kony.

Proponents of the ICC claim that its indictments will isolate and weaken the LRA's leadership, build confidence in the possibility of peace between the north and the south, serve as a deterrent to future crimes, stigmatize criminals, respect traditional rituals, and weaken Sudanese support for the LRA, and that the court's allowance of mitigating circumstances provides an incentive for LRA leaders to come forward.[94] Opponents retort that indictments will choke off any incentive for LRA commanders to leave the bush, undermine traditional rituals, and encourage the government to return to its failed military solution.[95]

In favor of the ICC indictments, the peace process that began at Juba, Sudan, in 2004 continued to make strong progress well after the ICC announced the arrest warrants. A series of cease-fires and agreements on four major issues were achieved between August 2006 and February

2008, including an agreement on accountability and reconciliation that called for trials of perpetrators of "the most serious crimes" along with practices of truth telling, reparations, restitution, rehabilitation, apologies, memorials, and commemorations. A call for "alternative penalties" raised suspicions of impunity among Western human rights groups. Still, in March 2008, Museveni, reversing his position, indicated that traditional rituals and national tribunals could together replace trials at The Hague. The parties did not conclude a peace settlement, though, failing to reach agreement mainly on the demobilization of soldiers.

On the side of the opponents of the ICC, Joseph Kony still insists that he will not sign an agreement as long as his indictment stands. In December 2008, he and his army crossed into the Congo to maraud civilians and thus demonstrate their continued power. Kony's indictment, then, seems to stand in the way of his signature.

Ugandan public opinion of the trials is mixed. A 2007 survey of northern Ugandans shows that 60 percent of respondents had heard of the ICC and that, among these, 71 percent believed the ICC "had contributed to reducing the violence," while 64 percent agreed that "the ICC has assisted in pressuring the LRA into peace talks." Yet 64 percent of respondents who had heard of the ICC also said that the court should now revoke arrest warrants or suspend them until after the talks are completed, while 76 percent said that pursuing trials could endanger the Juba peace process. Whereas a 2005 survey showed 66 percent of respondents wanting trials and punishment for LRA leaders and 22 percent favoring forgiving them, the 2007 survey showed only 41 percent preferring punishment while 54 percent favored forgiving and integrating them upon their confession and apology. Perhaps most tellingly, while the 2005 survey showed 53 percent preferring peace with trials over peace with amnesty, in 2007 a striking 80 percent preferred peace with amnesty.[96] Ugandans appear to have moved toward dropping a demand for judicial punishment, at least prior to or as a condition of a peace settlement.

Has judicial punishment in Uganda delayed peace? The ICC's indictments have certainly kept Kony away from the table, at least during part of the peace process. Yet any strong general conclusion against judicial punishment is weakened by the partial success of the Juba talks, especially on the crucial issue of accountability, as well as by the contingent nature of Kony's obstruction. At certain points in the negotiations, had talks gone differently, Kony might well have signed a settlement agreement.

Amnesty

In the present ethic of political reconciliation, the presumption for trials amounts to a presumption against amnesty. When the achievement of peace or democracy warrants overriding this presumption, amnesty ought to be pursued so as best to promote other dimensions of reconciliation. There are different kinds of amnesties, after all. Least satisfying are blanket amnesties, either explicit or *de facto*. Far better are amnesties that make immunity from prosecution conditional.

Conditional on what? One condition is the acquiescence of all parties to peace and the rule of law—the practice of building socially just institutions. In South Africa's transition from apartheid, amnesty forestalled the punishment of most apartheid officials. What it brought about instead was no small achievement: a transition from one of the most unjust regimes in the world to a multiracial democracy with one of the most progressive constitutions in the world.

Amnesty can also be granted in exchange for the truth—the practice of acknowledgment. As the South African parliament gave shape to the amnesty decreed in the 1993 interim constitution, it linked amnesty to the perpetrator's full revelation of truth. The result was the hearings of the TRC and a five-volume report that made public the thousands of crimes that the regime had committed (as well as those that the ANC had committed). Amnesty was not dispensed easily—complete amnesty was granted to 1,167 of the 7,112 petitioners. Still, the process had its shortcomings. Some received amnesty without confessing fully, while few of those denied amnesty were prosecuted.[97] Another exchange of (partial) amnesty for truth is Colombia's 2005 Justice and Peace Law, which offers reduced prison sentences to 3,200 paramilitary fighters (among 30,000 who had demobilized) who had committed serious human rights violations in exchange for the full confession. Here, too, the process tended to favor perpetrators. Human rights groups have criticized the law for not allowing authorities adequate time and resources to investigate crimes and for providing little in the way of reparations and support for victims.

Amnesty can also be conditional on the exile of dictators, a vetting process of sorts. This was the case with Haitian general Raoul Cédras, whom the United States forced to relocate to Panama when it reinstated democratically elected President Jean-Bertrand Aristide in 1994. Other countries have reduced the punishment of perpetrators in exchange for community service, as Rwanda did for some perpetrators in its *gacaca* courts. Amnesty might also be granted in return for public apologies or reparations to victims. In Mozambique, amnesty was combined with local rituals of integration. Its peace accords of 1992, ending a sixteen-year civil war that killed more than a million people, gave amnesty to both government and opposition fighters. Though the amnesty was unconditional, fighters were integrated back into their home villages at a remarkably high level through rituals drawn from the traditional culture as well as ones conducted by the Catholic Church. The settlement has garnered high and lasting public support.[98]

When amnesties must be unconditional, they ought to be restricted in their scope as much as possible. Negotiators, for instance, might agree to forgo prosecuting the leaders of a departing dictatorship or armed faction yet allow room for a court to undertake prosecution at some future date. The International Criminal Court or a foreign national court might also undertake prosecution if it judges perpetrators' immunity to be contrary to international law. International lawyers generally agree, although not without debate, that the crimes enumerated by the 1949 Geneva Conventions (war crimes in war between states), the Genocide Convention, and the Torture Convention require prosecution by states that are parties to them. In civil war, though, amnesties are allowed by a protocol of the Geneva Conventions—explicitly for the purpose of reconciliation—and are arguably not prohibited by any convention for crimes against humanity.[99]

A final way to restrict amnesty is to focus on prosecuting top perpetrators in cases in which it is only possible to prosecute a limited number of crimes. The International Criminal Court, the ICTY, the ICTR, and the Special Court of Sierra Leone (SCSL), for instance, focus only on the top leadership of political, military, and bureaucratic units who carried out human rights violations.

Amnesty is allowable in an ethic of political reconciliation, but it is a second-best solution to punishment and the primary restorations that it performs. At times the value of peace and a transition to democracy and the rule of law—and the human costs of the failure of peace or democracy—warrant overriding the presumption for punishment. But how often? Vinjamuri, writing with political scientist Aaron P. Boesenecker, counts eighty-seven amnesties since the end of the cold war and notes that, of seventy-seven peace agreements between 1980 and 2006, thirty included amnesty mechanisms.[100] Did these amnesties encourage peace and successful transitions? Snyder and Vinjamuri argue that they did so in Namibia, Mozambique, El Salvador, Macedonia, Cambodia, and Afghanistan.[101] Juan Mendez, though, argues that amnesty was unnecessary for El Salvador's transition and points to the limited scope of amnesty in Haiti and Guatemala as evidence that peace does not require it. Sierra Leone's amnesty of 1999 is one that several analysts, including Snyder and Vinjamuri, believe to have been a terrible mistake, only emboldening the rebel forces of Foday Sankoh to renew their violence. Even if an amnesty is justifiable at a given point in time, a presumption against amnesty also demands keeping open the possibility of reversing or curtailing it later, as happened in Chile eight years after Pinochet's departure from power in 1990. Again, my conclusion may seem distressingly inconclusive: Amnesty must be evaluated case by case. Still that conclusion is significant in one sense: It leaves intact the presumption for punishment.

Conclusion

Punishment is integral to reconciliation. An ethic of political reconciliation does not reject what the liberal peace is most proud of—the expansion of trials for the perpetrators of the worst crimes imaginable. Yet the ethic justifies punishment differently than liberalism's twin schools of punishment, retributivism and consequentialism, do. It proposes an alternative, restorative punishment that redresses a range of harms.

What sort of judicial punishment does this view favor? Some of its criteria are little different from those of the liberal peace, especially rule of law standards. Still, it is distinctive in favoring most those forms of evaluating guilt and carrying out punishment that best communicate censure to the perpetrator and among the community, those that offer the best possibility of restoring the soul of the perpetrator, and those that acknowledge the suffering of victims, reveal the truth about suffering, help determine reparations, affirm the value of human rights and the rule of law, and beget emotions and judgments that reinforce peace and stability. By and large, it is community forums that carry the greatest promise for this combination of restorations.

There are admittedly some good reasons why community forums do not enjoy wider use, including their sometimes low standards of the rule of law. Especially when such crimes against humanity as murder, torture, and rape are involved, when high-ranking perpetrators are being tried, or when lengthy prison sentences are at stake, due process considerations become crucial. It is Western-style courts that perform best here. The principles of restorative punishment dictate that courts ought to be as close to the people and as participatory as possible without compromising due process standards.

Restorative punishment also suggests that community forums for judicial punishment ought to be expanded to more conflicts, especially those where perpetrators are numerous and will be returning to live in their communities of origin. This expansion could take place more easily if rule of law standards for these forums were strengthened so as to provide greater training for judges, perhaps legal representation for victims and defendants, and protection for witnesses. The challenge will be to incorporate these insights from Western judicial procedure into community forums without destroying the forums' organic, free-flowing communication. An international set of standards for local justice could prescribe such reforms and thereby encourage the expansion of community forums.

For the top political, military, and administrative officials who most intentionally and systematically conduct the planning and execution of crimes, the International Criminal Court, international criminal tribunals, and hybrid international-national courts are the most appropriate setting for trials. Their international status makes them best suited to communicate a message of censure that will carry the gravitas and international publicity appropriate to crimes that "shock the conscience of mankind." These courts are also most likely to prosecute evenhandedly, though they will sometimes be accused of practicing victor's justice even when they are balanced in their indictments and arrests. Hybrid courts, which have the advantage of being closer to the inhabitants of the country where the crime took place, and are thus better able to deliver a communication that will be received by them, are particularly promising. Sierra Leone's hybrid court demonstrates that trials with an international imprimatur can successfully prosecute high-ranking perpetrators.

For perpetrators of serious crimes—murder, torture, and rape—who are not the originators or architects of the injustices, Western-style courts, with all of their protections, are the most appropriate forum as of now. Even under soft proportionality, prison sentences are needed in most cases to communicate the gravity of the offense to the perpetrator, and when sentences are at stake, due process is especially crucial. In some cases, though, serious crimes might be tried in community forums. In countries where perpetrators of these crimes are numerous and Western-style courts are unable to try them, community forums could be adapted. Because of their limitations, these forums ought to confine their punishment to short sentences or reintegrative community service. Although to many this will seem to fall far short of proportionate justice, it is preferable to delivering long sentences to innocents on the basis of unreliable testimony, and it helps people to live together in places like Rwanda where they have little alternative but to move back to their village. Another situation favoring community forums is one in which the culpability of perpetrators of serious crimes is low—for instance, the many Ugandan children the LRA abducted, made into soldiers, and trained to commit war crimes. Here, too, the need for community reintegration was great.

Gradations of courts and combinations of institutions are best suited to restorative justice. The complementary principle of the International Criminal Court, which allows states to try perpetrators when they are able and willing, reflects this approach. States with combinations of truth commissions and trials—such as postunification Germany, Sierra Leone, and Timor-Leste—offer the possibility that a perpetrator could face both kinds of forums, with all of the restorations that each institution effects. Here, the challenge is for each institution to conduct its work so as not to undermine the other institution. For instance, perpetrators must face incentives such that giving testimony before a truth commission will not incriminate them at their trial, perhaps through being granted immunity for their testimony to the truth commission.

It is these gradations, innovations, and creative combinations that restorative justice proposes. Like the ethic of political reconciliation in general, it incorporates and builds on important institutions and commitments of the liberal peace. Yet by offering an alternative concept of justice, it also recommends principles and practices that aspire to a more holistic restoration.

12

Forgiveness

THE MOST SURPRISING, controversial, and dramatic development in the age of peacebuilding is the growth of forgiveness. It is embodied far less than the other practices in global norms and institutions. Punishment is supported by international law, an international criminal court, national courts, and large communities of officials and activists. Human rights and democracy have even stronger support among activists and in international law. Acknowledgment has its truth commissions and its memorials. Reparations and apology are practiced and enacted by presidents and legislatures. Not so forgiveness. It has practitioners and proponents, but arguments for it are generally not found in speeches and statements coming from the United Nations, Western governments, or other advocates of the liberal peace.

With surprise comes controversy. In South Africa, Timor-Leste, Uganda, and Germany furious debates have pitted forgiveness against punishment, amnesty against accountability, mercy against justice, and release against resentment. Of the six practices, forgiveness is the one most criticized by liberals. It is also the practice that is most disproportionately and distinctly—though not solely or unanimously—advocated by religious leaders and their followers.

The sheer unexpectedness of forgiveness contributes to its drama. Advocates of forgiveness sometimes speak of it as an interruption or a reversal. It is enacted by the victim, the one whom a political injustice has rendered a defenseless object of assault. It is not something that the victim owes or to which the perpetrator has a right. In forgiving, the victim raises a dissident voice against revenge. Like all dissidence, forgiveness purports both to destroy existing injustice and to construct a better politics.

These constructive possibilities are what make forgiveness a practice of reconciliation and a tool of peacebuilding. As is true for each of the other practices, forgiveness employs a unique configuration of parties to address certain wounds of political injustice in distinct manners. In doing so, it advances justice, contrary to the common view that places forgiveness and justice in opposition. Forgiveness is at its most ethical when it occurs in conjunction with the other practices—punishment included. Forgiveness versus punishment is thus a false choice.

Though forgiveness of political injustices has contributed to peace, its practice in politics stands in need of development, both practically and theoretically. Only a handful of philosophers and theologians have written systematically and deeply about its political expression.[1] Their works are dwarfed by books and articles on trials, truth commissions, reparations, and apologies. Already political forgiveness has drawn a wave of critics who pointedly draw attention to its difficulties and its abuses, sometimes arguing that it is impossible. Forgiveness can indeed be difficult, sometimes excruciatingly so, and is liable to dysfunction. Its dysfunction, though, is not inevitable but rather instructive. What it demands is an ethic of forgiveness, one that explains how the practice can succeed but also how it can go awry. Because the criticisms are sharp, let us begin with them.

The Critics

"[F]orgiveness is pitiless," writes Cynthia Ozick. "It forgets the victim. It negates the right of the victim to his own life. It blurs over suffering and death. It drowns the past. It cultivates sensitiveness toward the murderer at the price of insensitiveness toward the victim." Disputing that vengeance is brutal, she counters: "It is forgiveness that is relentless. The face of forgiveness is mild, but how stony to the slaughtered."[2] Francine, a victim of the Rwandan genocide, relates her own perspective:

> Sometimes when I sit alone in a chair on my veranda, I imagine this possibility: one far-off day, a local man comes slowly up to me and says, "Bonjour Francine, I have come to speak to you. So, I am the one who cut your mama and your little sisters. I want to ask your forgiveness." Well, to that person I cannot reply anything good. A man may ask for forgiveness if he had one Primus too many and then beats his wife. But if he has worked at killing for a whole month, even on Sundays, whatever can he hope to be forgiven for?[3]

Another respect in which forgiveness stands out among the six practices is that its critics are the most vituperative. Virtually none of these critics, and indeed no philosopher I know of except for Nietzsche, rejects forgiveness in personal life. In the case of massive political injustices, though, they find forgiveness "pitiless," "impossible," and "obscene."

One of the most thorough and thoughtful critiques can be found in philosopher Thomas Brudholm's tellingly titled book, *Resentment's Virtue.* Forgiveness, Brudholm believes, has become a "growth industry," touted by professors, pastors, and therapists, frequently the theme of academic conferences, and enjoying "near hegemonic" status in writings on reconciliation and transitional justice. Yet too often this advocacy amounts to unreflective boosterism. The problem lies, first, with those who urge forgiveness on victims. Brudholm devotes the first part of his book to the South Africa Truth and Reconciliation Commission, whose commissioners, he says, often manipulated victims by presenting forgiveness as the preferred response to their suffering. Tutu praised victims for their "extraordinary willingness to forgive" and often "marveled" at those who forgave, but many victims did not think forgiveness marvelous. "[I]f [the perpetrators] come to you and ask for forgiveness would you be prepared to sit down with them, shake hands with them, and reconcile with them?" one commissioner asked a mother whose son had been murdered. The mother refused. Brudholm amasses evidence of many other similar experiences: Commissioners strongly commend forgiveness, and victims object. The commission also linked forgiveness to the government's grant of amnesty, thus asking victims also to renounce judicial punishment. What the commission denied victims was their autonomy, their right to make up their own mind about how to view their suffering.[4]

But Brudholm's criticism of the commission's approach runs deeper than issues of agency and autonomy. The commission's message, he argues, denied the moral validity of anger and resentment. In therapeutic fashion, advocates of forgiveness pathologize these emotions, diagnosing victims as traumatized, resentful, and vindictive and recommending that they move on, seek closure, and undergo transformation. Yet these negative emotions have an important moral component, Brudholm claims. They are a form of protest that draws the world's attention to the dignity of the victim and to the validity of the moral order. Forgiveness and bloodthirsty, destructive revenge are not our only choices. For a notion of resentment that both refuses forgiveness and mounts a moral protest, Brudholm turns to the essays of Holocaust survivor Jean Améry. Key to understanding Améry's resentment—or *ressentiment*, as Brudholm argues it should be rendered—is the society in which he wrote: West Germany during the two decades following World War II, which proceeded to achieve an "economic miracle" and technological advancement while granting amnesty to Nazis, forgetting victims, and calling all of these things forgiveness. To this, Améry responds with "a morality of revolt and resistance" whose central message is not so much trials and retribution as it is refusing to forget victims and what they have suffered. Persistent acknowledgment and remembrance, for Améry, represent the beginning of an ethically sound basis for moving forward.[5]

Running through Brudholm's analysis, as through much criticism of forgiveness, is the conviction that forgiveness is advocated and sometimes practiced too easily, heedless of what victims have suffered. "Such systematically organized mass atrocities leave behind a measure of devastation that is hard to fathom," Brudholm writes.[6] Does forgiveness have no place, then, in the wake of mass atrocity? Or can it be salvaged—advocated respectfully and practiced ethically? In a separate essay, Brudholm declares that he "does not argue or conclude that it is morally impossible to advocate post-atrocity forgiveness in any form and on any level whatsoever" and leaves open "the possibility of a kind of advocacy in which the given problems and reasons for caution have been appropriately dealt with."[7] Yet his skepticism is dominant. "After crimes that shock the conscience of humanity, 'healing' appears like a fantasy and complete forgiveness might neither be possible nor desirable," he concludes.[8]

Hearing the Forgivers

Brudholm's argument cannot be ignored. The victims whose voices resound in his quotations of them will not allow it. Advocacy of forgiveness, then, also begins best with the voices of victims.

In Kashmir, the disputed land that straddles India and Pakistan, war has taken between 40,000 and 100,000 lives since 1989 (the numbers are hotly disputed). Through my own work there, I have come to know Bashir, a Muslim man who grew up as a truck driver in a small mountain village known as Baramullah on the Indian side of the border. In 1994, a band of Muslim militants assassinated Bashir's father, a politician. Not long after, they killed his brother. Then, one day, they came to the house where he was staying, murdered his uncle, and then sprayed

Bashir with bullets, an assault that he miraculously survived but that left him marred by the scars. For the next seven years, Bashir pursued a vendetta, determined to hunt down and kill the murderers.

Then, in June 2001, having reflected on the meaning of forgiveness, especially in his Islamic tradition, Bashir chose to forgive. The murderers were not present; several of them, it turns out, had by that time been killed in the conflict themselves. Still, with tears streaming down his face, he forgave from his heart, dropping his vendetta and resolving to adopt a new attitude toward them. Bashir has since dedicated his life to victims of the violence, particularly widows and orphans. He has found children of the murderers and has helped them to get an education. He established a humanitarian NGO and works actively for reconciliation in his hometown, a historic center of militancy. To this day, he continues to speak of his act of forgiveness with great conviction, claiming that Allah made it possible.

On November 8, 1987, Gordon Wilson, a legislator in Northern Ireland, and his daughter Marie, a twenty-year-old nurse, attended a ceremony in honor of Great Britain's war dead at the Enniskillen War Memorial. During the ceremony, a bomb planted by the Irish Republican Army exploded. As Wilson later described:

> We were both thrown forward, rubble and stones and whatever in and around and over and under us. I was aware of a pain in my right shoulder. I shouted to Marie was she all right and she said yes. She found my hand and said, "Is that your hand, Dad?" Now remember we were under six foot of rubble. I said, "Are you all right?" and she said yes, but she was shouting in between. Three or four times I asked her, and she always said yes, she was all right. When I asked her the fifth time, "Are you all right, Marie?" she said, "Daddy, I love you very much." Those were the last words she spoke to me.

Sixty-three people were injured and eleven were killed in the explosion. Afterward, Wilson told the BBC, "I have lost my daughter, and we shall miss her. But I bear no ill will. I bear no grudge.... Dirty sort of talk is not going to bring her back to life." He said that he forgave her killers and added: "I shall pray for those people tonight and every night." His words had a wide impact. Loyalist paramilitaries forswore revenge for the bombing. British parliamentarians and Queen Elizabeth II commended him. Wilson traveled through Ireland, speaking of his loss and the need for reconciliation, but he continued to grieve. A pastor who heard him speak six years after the event recalls him stumbling through his address, halted frequently by tears. In 1995 he died at the age of sixty-seven "with a broken heart."[9]

When Eric Lomax was a young British officer army during World War II, the Japanese Army captured him, brutally tortured him, and held him in prison under inhuman conditions for three-and-a-half years. After he returned to his home in Edinburgh in 1945, he married his fiancée and began a career but was traumatized, not yet understanding "that there are experiences you can't walk away from, and that there is no statute of limitations on the effects of torture."[10] He had no self-worth, could not trust people, and lived withdrawn. He carried a burning hatred for the Japanese and yearned for revenge, especially against the interrogators at the prisoner of war camp where he had been tortured.

In the mid-1980s, following his retirement, he began a historical investigation of his war experiences and came to learn that one of his interrogators, Nagase Takashi, was alive in Japan, had repented for his wrongs in the course of a conversion to Buddhism, had lived a life of charitable works, including building a Buddhist temple along the Siam-Burma railway, and was even offering to help British veterans learn of their past. Lomax was skeptical that such repentance could be anything but a "fraudulent publicity stunt" and remained committed to revenge.[11]

In 1987, Lomax visited the Medical Foundation for Victims of Torture in London, whose director, Helen Bamber, helped him to address his history and begin to overcome his trauma. "The idea of revenge was still very much alive in me," he recounts, even as friends suggested that he ought to forgive. "The majority of people who hand out advice about forgiveness have not gone through the sort of experience I had; I was not inclined to forgive, not yet, probably never."[12]

Buoyed by her husband's healing, Lomax's second wife, Patti, wrote Nagase a letter. Nagase replied, describing his conversion and expressing compassion. In later letters, Nagase continued in the same spirit even after hearing of Lomax's reserve. "In that moment I lost whatever hard armour I had wrapped around me and began to think the unthinkable: that I could meet Nagase face to face in simple good will. Forgiveness became more than an abstract idea: it was now a real possibility."[13]

Lomax and Nagase met in person in 1998 in Kanburi, Thailand, the site of the prison camp. Nagase trembled and cried, repeating "I am so sorry, so very sorry." Lomax accepted his apology:

I could no longer see the point of punishing Nagase by a refusal to reach out and forgive him. What mattered was our relations in the here and now, his obvious regret for what he had done and our mutual need to give our encounter some meaning beyond that of the emptiness of cruelty. It was surely worth salvaging as much as we could from the damage to both our lives. The question was now one of choosing the right moment to say the words to him with the formality that the situation seemed to demand.[14]

It was not until they traveled to Japan and had spent several more days together that Lomax read to Nagase a formal letter of forgiveness. They eventually became good friends. "Sometime the hating has to stop," Lomax concluded.[15]

Nelson Mandela practiced forgiveness even during the twenty-seven years that he was imprisoned on South Africa's Robben Island. He showed decency to his white warders, seeking to make friends with them. When one especially brutish warder, Piet Badenhorst, was about to be transferred off Robben Island, he called Mandela to his office, where they wished each other good luck. Mandela even learned Afrikaans, the language of the dominant people. He remained open to negotiating with the apartheid government and called President F. W. de Klerk "a man of integrity" after his release. He later reflected on his experience: "In prison, my anger toward whites decreased, but my hatred for the system grew. I wanted South Africa to see that I loved even my enemies while I hated the system that turned us against one another."

Later, he made reconciliation and forgiveness major themes of his presidency. He invited three of his former warders to sit in the VIP section at his inauguration. He held a luncheon for the wives of former apartheid presidents and prime ministers as well as of leaders of liberation movements. Betsie Verwoerd, widow of Prime Minister Hendrik Verwoerd, known as the architect of apartheid, declined to attend, politely telling Mandela to drop by for tea sometime—which he did by showing up at the door of her house in a remote white enclave. Similar was his handling of the 1995 rugby World Cup games, involving a sport that had long symbolized white unity, and a team, the Springboks, that had long been the pride of South African whites. When the Springboks reached the finals, Mandela showed up at the stadium wearing their team jersey, eliciting the wild applause of the largely white audience. "Personal bitterness is irrelevant," he wrote to the TRC in the early stages of its work. "It is a luxury that we, as individuals and as a country, simply cannot afford."[16]

On November 16, 1989, a death squad of the El Salvadoran military murdered six Jesuit priests, their housekeeper, and her daughter. In 1991, a military tribunal tried nine soldiers for these murders, acquitting seven and convicting two, both of whom were released following the passage of El Salvador's amnesty law in March 1993, which in turn came on the heels of the report of El Salvador's truth commission. None of the high-level planners of these murders was ever brought to justice or acknowledged his role in the crimes.

Jesuit José Maria Tojeira, rector of the University of Central America in San Salvador, at first favored amnesty for criminals who told the truth about their crimes. Then he and the Jesuit community of El Salvador revised their position so as to favor an *indulto*, a legal pardon that would come after perpetrators were tried, convicted, and publicly recognized the crimes they committed. "We have never harbored hate toward these people, and we have extended Christian forgiveness to them from the beginning." They had offered Christian forgiveness in a moral and spiritual sense, as they saw it, but they still demanded that the murderers repent for their deeds and be held accountable. On March 27, 2000, the Jesuits of the Central America Province proposed that the case of the murders be reopened in the hope that the perpetrators and planners of these deeds be convicted.[17]

These are anecdotes. They involve various configurations of victims and perpetrators, persons and institutions, individuals and groups, the short term and the long term, living and dead, religious and secular. Nobody knows how frequently forgiveness takes place. Circumstantial evidence for the practice can be found in a public discourse of forgiveness— advocacy, debate, testimony—in South Africa, Rwanda, Uganda, Timor-Leste, Sierra Leone, Northern Ireland, Poland, El Salvador, Chile, and the former Yugoslavia. Surveys of popular attitudes in Uganda, Rwanda, and Iraq show support for forgiveness of political injustices that is significant but complex, often coupled with demands for accountability.[18] The anecdotes, the survey evidence, and a comparison of forgiveness to other practices reveal that victims forgive perpetrators of gross political injustices but also that forgiveness nowhere comes even close to being "near hegemonic." Should forgiveness now become a more common political practice? A tool of peacebuilding? Or are Brudholm and other critics right to warn us away from forgiveness in contexts of massive political injustices? An answer begins with a prior question: Just what is forgiveness?

What Is Forgiveness?

Perhaps forgiveness is simply a relinquishment: The victim of a misdeed forgives when he cancels the payment that a perpetrator owes him. This may well be part of forgiveness, but this cannot be the whole of it or even its essence. Imagine that James, a small-business owner, is swindled by a competitor and possesses overwhelming evidence of it. Outraged and financially compromised, he considers pursuing prosecution, which would likely return him his losses along with extra for his pains. Immersed in other profitable deals, however, he decides he does not have time to pursue the matter and eventually forgets about it almost entirely. Clearly James has relinquished what is owed to him. Has he exercised forgiveness, though? Not in any meaningful sense. He has dropped the matter and moved on. Forgiveness must involve something more.

In political contexts, the relinquishment of something owed or of prosecution rightly pursued is better thought of as judicial mercy or pardon. Judicial mercy is a decision by a judge to reduce or eliminate the punishment of a defendant who has been found guilty. It is narrower than and may not at all correspond to the notion of mercy defended in this book. It is possible that it could involve no will to restore. A pardon is a decision to grant immunity from prosecution and punishment to a person for a crime. Amnesty for known or highly probable human rights violators is a species of pardon. I have argued that amnesty—forgiveness as relinquishment—could be adopted justifiably when punishment demonstrably detracts from peace and stability and when it is administered so as to promote other restorative measures. I also argued, however, that amnesty is a second-best measure and always sacrifices a dimension of justice. In the same way, forgiveness as relinquishment is especially vulnerable to the criticisms put forth by Brudholm, other critics, and victims of massive political injustices: It sacrifices justice insofar as it falls short of taking seriously the dignity of the victim and the validity of the moral order.[19]

The "something more" that true forgiveness requires is a will to construct. In what sense? Jean Hampton points the way in saying that forgiveness involves "overcoming a point of view."[20] A victim decides to revise her enduring view of a perpetrator in a fashion that is restorative. More specifically, she wills and communicates that she no longer counts the perpetrator's misdeeds against him and that she views him as a person in good standing. Forgiveness is a proactive, constructive effort on the part of the victim to view a perpetrator in a new light.

What does it mean not to count a deed against someone and to view him in good standing? In part it involves relinquishment, namely of revenge or of any kind of punishment understood as an exaction of payment to the victim.[21] Bashir gave up the payback he had previously desired. Crucially, forgiveness further involves an internal relinquishment, a forgoing of anger, resentment, and the victim's active construal of the perpetrator as one to be condemned and brought low for his deeds. "We have never harbored hate towards these people," the Salvadoran Jesuits asserted. True, anger and resentment can be dogged, but forgiveness involves at least a will to work at overcoming them.

The constructive dimension of forgiveness involves the victim's further affirmation that he sees the perpetrator as being in good standing. That is to say, he does not speak against the perpetrator or urge others to condemn, excoriate, or bring her down. The victim speaks and acts so as to will restoration. Each of Mandela's acts of forgiveness involved an active effort to reconstrue his enemies as fellow citizens in good standing. Through these actions, the victim regards the perpetrator as one who is more than—and can be better than—her deeds. If the perpetrator has apologized, the forgiver acknowledges and accepts this renunciation of her misdeeds. In cases in which the perpetrator has not apologized, the forgiver wills that she do so. Forgiveness is clearest when it involves the words *I forgive*, but it still takes place when all of these deeds occur even in the absence of the utterance.

Forgiveness may not come quickly or suddenly. Psychologists Robert Enright and Catherine Coyle have constructed a model of twenty steps in forgiveness that cluster into four phases, including: 1) an "uncovering phase," involving a growing awareness of the wrong and its effects; 2) a "decision phase," involving a change of heart and the consideration of forgiveness; 3) a "work phase" involving a reconstrual of the offender; and 4) a "deepening phase" when the forgiver finds new meaning and purpose through the act of forgiveness.[22] Frequently, advocates of forgiveness cite empathy with the offender as a pivotal step. In reality, some victims may forgive far more quickly, as Wilson and the Jesuits did, while others never get past the uncovering phase. Perhaps Lomax best illustrates Enright's stages of forgiveness, having first uncovered his anger and trauma through counseling, then becoming aware of his perpetrator and his repentance, only gradually coming to feel empathy, then expressing forgiveness at an even later stage, and still after that living his reconstrual as a new reality. Mandela's forgiveness, by contrast, appeared to be a way of life, practiced over many years. Acts of forgiveness continue to unfold dynamically after they are performed, in both crescendo and diminuendo. Wilson continued to grieve. Bashir translated his forgiveness into service. The reconstrual that forgiveness involves can be swift, delayed, staggered, repeated, and subject to evolution.

Forgiveness always involves a form of reconciliation but may well fall short of achieving full reconciliation. Right relationship is restored in one significant way by a victim's decision to reconstrue her view of a perpetrator and is thus furthered by every act of forgiveness. In some cases, little more will occur. Sometimes forgiveness will involve no reciprocal apology, acceptance, or even acknowledgment on the part of the perpetrator. Again, in Bashir's case, some of the perpetrators were likely dead. Wilson did not know the perpetrators' identity. Sometimes the exercise of other rights, such as self-defense, will truncate the reconciliation that results from forgiveness. An abused wife might forgive her husband but justifiably refuse to live under the same roof with him; one nation-state might forgive another and yet maintain its defensive armaments. Those granting forgiveness will vary, too, in how much reconciliation they are prepared to undertake. A wife might forgive her ex-husband for his misdeeds but not want to remarry him. A victim of arson in Timor-Leste might forgive the arsonist yet remain unable to muster anything more than respectful coexistence toward him. Other times, as with Lomax and Nagase, more will be possible.[23]

How might forgiveness promote reconciliation in the political realm? Political forgiveness both addresses a certain kind of crime—a political one—and involves a certain dimension of the reconstrual that forgiveness involves, namely a victim's revision of his view of the perpetrator's political status. Prior to forgiveness, the victim viewed the perpetrator as one whose political cause and deeds should be fought—in short, as an enemy. Upon forgiveness, he comes to view the perpetrator as a fellow citizen in good standing, a member of a common legitimate political order, and a person to be reasoned with and respected in all the ways that citizenship merits. The case of Mandela may be most paradigmatic. Each of his acts of forgiveness involved a communication to a member of former opposition forces that he or she was now a bona fide fellow citizen.

A definition of forgiveness, including political forgiveness, must also identify what forgiveness is not. Forgiveness does not necessarily mean forgetting. To forgive sometimes might mean to forget, especially in matters small and personal, but neither logically nor morally does it always mean to forget. Political forgiveness does not supplant the memory that memorials, commemorations, reparations, and revised textbooks sustain nor hold that victims ought to forget deeds or perpetrators, even if that were possible. How can a victim both remember a perpetrator's deeds and no longer count these deeds against her? He can do so, I propose, by thinking of his perpetrator not as someone who never committed wrongs but as one who now has a new status. When Lomax came to see Nagase as his friend, he did not forget that Nagase had been his torturer or come to think of Nagase as little more than a friend he had met while touring Thailand. It was his construal of Nagase as an enemy who had been transformed that gave their friendship its special meaning and power.

Forgiveness also does not mean condoning. In a genuine act of forgiveness, Pamela Hieronymi argues, the victim judges that 1) the act in question was wrong, 2) the wrongdoer is a member of the moral community and can be expected not to commit such a wrong, and 3) she herself ought not to be wronged.[24] If forgiveness were lacking any of these elements, it would not simply be morally compromised; it would not be forgiveness at all. If a wrong is no longer a wrong, then there is nothing to forgive.

All of these features of constructive forgiveness help to make clear a final feature—its relationship to resentment. Resentment is an emotion that construes a wrong as a wrong, a victim as deserving repair, an offender as deserving to be punished, and violated values as meriting reassertion and re-elevation. In the past generation, resentment has gained great ground among Western philosophers.[25] Far from being petty and sniveling, as Nietzsche considered it, or pathological, as therapists render it, resentment is an important moral assertion, they claim. It is a form of protest, as Hieronymi argues, demanding that others take seriously the dignity of victims, the validity of the moral order, and the dignity and soul of the wrongdoer.[26] Resentment can even be motivated by care and concern. The value of this protest, they say, is what advocates of forgiveness too easily forget.

For many philosophers, forgiveness is the renunciation of resentment.[27] Renouncing resentment is also a component of forgiveness as articulated here, but it is crucial to understanding constructive forgiveness that we not draw the distinction between resentment and forgiveness too sharply. Not only does constructive forgiveness not condone or necessarily forget evil but it takes evil seriously in the same ways that resentment does. It names, confronts, and draws attention to the evil, asserts that the victim has been the target of evil, and wills that the perpetrator renounce the evil. The difference between constructive forgiveness and resentment is the manner in which they seek this defeat. Resentment seeks it by actively asserting the perpetrator's evil against him, denouncing him for his deed, and perhaps drawing others' attention to it. Forgiveness seeks this defeat by willing a world in which the perpetrator has rejected the evil and in which the evil has been transformed and overcome.

Brudholm argues that resentment is, or at least can be, a virtue, whereas I conceive of it as an emotion. Resentment can indeed be a justifiable emotion. Insofar as it construes a perpetrator's injustice as a wrong that is worthy of condemnation, accountability, and redress, resentment can be endorsed as a valid protest. Forgiveness, though, which leaves behind the protest dimension of resentment, is also warranted in principle and is often to be commended. This places forgiveness in an interesting relationship with resentment insofar as both are justifiable yet one may rightly supersede the other. A victim could justifiably resent and then at some point forgive. The question then becomes: When and on what grounds should a victim move to forgiveness?

What Warrants Forgiveness?

A perpetrator apologizes, leading his victim to believe that the wrong has been overcome. A victim, wronged by a friend, views their friendship as worth repairing. A victim sees that a perpetrator is suffering from his misdeed and wants to relieve him. A perpetrator's history of good deeds outweighs his misdeed and encourages a victim's forbearance. A victim reflects that she is a sinner, too, and is thus disposed to lift up her fellow human being. Forgiveness breaks the cycle of violence.

All of these are good reasons to forgive. Some of these reasons will make more sense in interpersonal relations than in politics. If a massive political injustice has been highly asymmetric (say, the Nazi genocide), it would be appalling to ask victims (the Jews, for instance) to forgive on the grounds that they are sinners too. Rarely will prior friendships be in play in major political injustices. None of these, though, is the central reason why victims ought to forgive, either in personal relations or in politics.

The core moral rationale for forgiveness is justice. In modern Western thought and at sites of past injustice around the world, forgiveness and justice are normally seen as being at odds. Yet if, as I have been arguing, the three religious traditions and the school of restorative justice are correct in thinking of justice as reconciliation or restoration of right relationship, then forgiveness can be viewed as an act of justice. Forgiveness achieves justice if it is constructive forgiveness, the sort that elicits greater right relationship out of a condition of woundedness. It is the justice of reconciliation—and not, as critics of forgiveness judge it, its emotional or therapeutic benefits or the need to end cycles of violence—that serves as the primary moral reason for forgiveness.

Primary Restorations

The Standing Victory of Political Injustice

Like most of the other practices, forgiveness helps to defeat the moral fact that I have called the standing victory of injustice. Yet if other practices also conspire in this defeat, what is left for forgiveness to contribute? Apology, in particular, might seem to render forgiveness redundant. If the perpetrator has renounced his wrong genuinely and thoroughly, then what more is needed from the victim? The answer lies in relationship. A wrong is not simply committed by one person but is committed by one person against another. In the case of political injustices, one person violates the respect that he owes another as a bearer of human rights. When a perpetrator apologizes, he condemns his own role in the political injustice and thus helps to defeat its standing victory from one angle. Yet the victim retains his own freedom to decide how he will respond to the perpetrator and thus retains a measure of control over whether the standing victory of the injustice is defeated. As the object, or recipient of the injustice, he plays a crucial role in the ruptured relationship that the standing victory of the injustice signifies. He may decide—independently, from his own standpoint as an object of the injustice—whether to accept the apology, deciding not to count the perpetrator's deed against him and to view him in a new light; reject the apology, continuing to count it against him; or do nothing at all. In some cases, like all of those previously cited except for that of Lomax, victims might forgive unilaterally. But in all cases the victim's decision determines to what degree the relationship is restored and the standing victory of the injustice is nullified.

When the victim chooses to exercise forgiveness he helps to bring down the standing victory of the political injustice. His act of forgiveness does this first because it names and condemns the wrong. In some cases, this condemnation may be implicit. There is little doubt, for instance, that Mandela saw apartheid as an evil. In other cases, it is crucial that the naming and condemning be protracted and forceful. One example involves someone we met earlier: Thapelo Mbelo, the black man who had worked as an *askari*, or stooge, for the apartheid police. A documentary about the South African Truth and Reconciliation Commission, *Long Night's Journey into Day*, closes with a scene following an amnesty hearing in which Mbelo meets with mothers of the Gugulethu Seven, black activists the police had murdered with Mbelo's cooperation. Mbelo is repentant and asks for forgiveness. Forgiveness, though, does not come easily. One mother declares:

Oh, you feel bad? How much worse do you think the parents of those children feel? Do you see what size I am today? Wait, let me stand up, do you see how thin I am? I used to be fat. Do you see how I look? I used to be fat. It's clear to me that you have food, because you're getting money for selling out your own blood. How do you feel about selling out your own blood instead of defending it? And to think you did it just for the money! Selling your blood for money. I'll stop there.

Another concludes, "I have no forgiveness for you." Several other mothers dress down Mbelo and refuse him forgiveness. Only then does one mother, Cynthia, who had delivered her own blast only moments earlier, decide to turn:

Just a minute, my son. Doesn't the name Thapelo mean "prayer"? I see what your name means, and I don't know whether you follow it or not. Speaking as Christopher's mother, I forgive you, my child. Because you and Christopher are the same age. I forgive you my child, and the reason I say I forgive you is that my child will never wake up again. And it's pointless for me to hold this wound against you. God will be the judge. We must forgive those who sin against us, even as we wish to be forgiven. So I forgive you, Thapelo.

I want you to go home knowing the mothers are forgiving the evil
you have done, and we feel compassion for you. There is no place
for throwing stones at you, even though you did those things....
I forgive you, my child. Yes, I forgive you.[28]

Forgiveness here is no mere moving on.

The standing message of the injustice is defeated further by the victim's decision no longer to hold the perpetrator's wrong against him and
to view the perpetrator as a person in good standing—to "go home knowing the mothers are forgiving the evil you have done." This decision, as
I have argued, involves a will that the wrong be left in the past. The victim no longer regards the wrong as relevant to her relationship with the
perpetrator and wills that the perpetrator become a better person than
he was when he committed the wrong. The victim is willing a future in
which the wrong no longer has force or efficacy and where, in the political realm, both victim and perpetrator respect each other as full citizens
with full human rights. After Mandela was freed from prison, his acts of
forgiveness helped to bring down the authority of apartheid even beyond
the dismantling of the apartheid regime. In forgiving, he willed a relationship with his oppressors in which their wrongs would have no force or
relevance and would be overcome. Is this not a unique way to defeat the
standing victory of injustice?

Harms to the Person of the Victim

Advocates of forgiveness often speak of its benefits for the victim. Anger
and resentment, they say, gradually corrode the soul and even the body.
Brudholm and his allies challenge this. Anger and resentment are not
pathologies but rather important expressions of morality, especially in cases
of mass atrocity, they reply. Forgiving can be traumatizing, they add, especially when practiced hastily, unreflectively, or under pressure. My response
to this serious challenge is to argue for forgiveness on grounds of morality
and justice rather than healing and therapy. Yet in an ethic where justice
involves the redress of real harms that political injustice causes, part of the
justice of forgiveness is restoring the victim with respect to the wounds that
she has suffered. Here, justice and the therapeutic blur.

One of the most devastating ways in which political injustices harm
victims is to objectify them, robbing them of their agency and of their ability to pursue their own and others' flourishing. Most objectifying of all is

torture, which often seeks a thorough erasure of the victim's humanity. If forgiveness is indeed a constructive act, one that defeats a wrong, then it initiates a profound reversal in the relationship between the victim, the perpetrator, and the surrounding community. Namely, it re-empowers the victim as an agent, as something other than the recipient of an assault. As psychologist Pumla Gobodo-Madikizela describes:

> The victim in a sense *needs* forgiveness as part of the process of becoming rehumanized. The victim needs it in order to complete himself or herself and to wrest away from the perpetrator the fiat power to destroy or to spare. It is part of the process of reclaiming self-efficacy. Reciprocating with empathy and forgiveness in the face of a perpetrator's remorse restores to many victims the sense that they are once again capable of effecting a profound difference in the moral community.[29]

This is perhaps most evident in the life of Bashir, who was controlled by his vendetta but then, through the commitment to service that arose from his act of forgiveness, came to define the social and political reality around him.

Closely related to the re-empowerment of the victim's agency is his liberation from anger and resentment. While critics of political forgiveness may rightly claim the moral validity of resentment, they also underestimate the corrosive effects of retaining anger and resentment. For four decades after World War II, Lomax suffered from the classic traumatic symptoms of inward withdrawal, nightmares, and a restricted ability to relate intimately, especially in his two marriages. Through counseling and then forgiveness, this condition sharply improved. Psychological research, much of it conducted by Enright and his colleagues, confirms that forgiveness decreases depression and anxiety and increases hope and self-esteem.[30]

Other Wounds

Another wound to which forgiveness can bring a restorative dynamic is the wounded soul of the perpetrator. In my discussion of apology I argued that, by expressing remorse, a perpetrator helps to defeat the standing victory of the injustice, detaches himself from the wrong, and desires that the effects of the wrong be diminished. In forgiving, the victim ratifies this apology. Far from merely letting the perpetrator off the hook, by seeing

the perpetrator as a person (and citizen) in good standing the victim col-
laborates in the restorative work that apology initiates. By not counting the
perpetrator's deed against him the victim releases the perpetrator from
guilt and gives the perpetrator new freedom and strength to continue in
a restorative direction. Nagase received something much like this from
Lomax, who wished to free Nagase from guilt both in his present life and
in the afterlife that Nagase, a Buddhist, believed he would face.

There are two other wounds that constructive forgiveness potentially
transforms, especially if it is conducted publicly. One is the lack of recognition of the victim's suffering. Because forgiveness involves naming and condemning the wrong done against her, the victim who forgives publicly can
gain broad acknowledgment and sympathy for her suffering. When Wilson
forgave his daughter's killers, he gained such sympathy from both sides of
the conflict in Northern Ireland. Another wound is the violation of human
rights, which are rightly enshrined in law and enforced by the state. By practicing constructive forgiveness, a victim wills a relationship between herself
and the perpetrator that is characterized by mutual respect for human rights
and sets an example for others in the political order to do likewise.

Secondary Restorations

Critics of forgiveness decry those who argue, like Bishop Tutu, that "there
is no future without forgiveness" or that forgiveness is the only way to
avoid cycles of revenge. I argue for no such necessity. The moral case for
forgiveness, as for the other practices, hinges not on its consequences but
on the primary restorations that it performs. That said, these primary restorations may produce further benefits for political orders. The dramatic
reversal of forgiveness carries the potential to break the cycle through
which primary wounds beget secondary wounds. The victim's reconstrual of the perpetrator is itself an act of judgment, often spurred by the
emotions of compassion and empathy, that might well beget social capital
for political orders: legitimacy, national identity, and devotion to the common good. In the individual case, forgiveness begins to create this capital
through its primary restoration: One victim comes to view one perpetrator as a fellow citizen rather than as an enemy. The social effect of forgiveness is magnified when others follow suit or respond in kind. Forgiveness
carries special credibility in beckoning others because it is enacted by the
victim, the one who might be least expected to act restoratively. Wilson's
forgiveness is said to have induced loyalist paramilitaries to refrain from

retaliating against the Irish Republican Army (IRA) in Northern Ireland. Although it is impossible to prove, it is entirely plausible that Mandela's acts of forgiveness and general spirit of reconciliation helped to avert a violent backlash among conservative whites in South Africa and a corresponding counter-retaliation among blacks—exactly the civil war that, only a few years earlier, so many South Africans thought would be the only route to the end of apartheid. Forgiveness can beget further forgiveness.

Through all of these primary and secondary restorations, forgiveness brings about the justice that is defined as reconciliation. In the political realm, this means a condition in which citizens respect one another as citizens in a way that they did not previously. Forgiveness achieves reconciliation best when performed in partnership with the other five practices. Améry's denunciation of forgiveness in postwar Germany, at least as Brudholm presents it, was mostly for its forgetting the victims of Nazi crimes. He wrote at a time when Germany seemed to him swept up in a spirit of moving on, had done little to remember Jews and others who had died, had granted amnesties to Nazi war criminals, and then, during the 1960s, was engaged again in a debate over trials. If forgiveness were to be accompanied by acknowledgment, punishment, apology, and repentance, which remember and address the past with respect to both victims and perpetrators, it would suffer far less from the bane of amnesia. It is when the past is rightly remembered that victims are best positioned to transform it in the way that forgiveness uniquely does.

Reasons Not to Forgive

Some will persist in skepticism, especially when massive political injustices are involved. Their objections might take several forms.

Radical Evil

Hannah Arendt, who recommended forgiveness as a resource for politics, also thought that some forms of evil are so great they "[transcend] the realm of human affairs and the potentialities of human power" such that they can be neither punished nor forgiven.[31] Are some evils too colossal to be forgiven?

Some of the reasons offered against the forgiveness of massive political injustices are similar to considerations that we encountered in our discussion of punishment. One was the incorrigible moral monster.

How, it might be asked, can someone be forgiven who has not only committed massive evil but is so given over to evil that he can never change? I argued earlier that we should think of the moral monster as a person without reflective capacities. This lack, I maintained, makes him unsuitable for a just trial, which is a communicative enterprise. So it goes for forgiveness, which places hope for the remorse and reform of the perpetrator at the core of its logic. Similarly, it will not do much good to advocate resentment as the proper emotion directed at such a creature, for this emotion, too, as philosopher Peter Strawson has argued compellingly, is intelligible only in the context of interactive human relationships.[32] The moral monster cannot intelligibly be punished, resented, or forgiven, but, as with punishment, we must ask who fits the description of the moral monster. Many an architect of heinous deeds can be said to be "given over" to evil, such that their remorse is quite unlikely, yet they show no evidence of being a robot, a psychopath, or King Kong. If that is the case, then it is not impossible, though it may be unlikely, for them to receive or accept forgiveness.

Another objection is rooted in balance. On what grounds, the skeptic might ask, could or should accounts ever be cleared for deeds of such magnitude? As I argued in the last chapter, though, the ethic of political reconciliation rests not on the logic of payment and balance but on the logic of restoration. If punishment does not seek to right a balance, forgiveness should not be criticized for failing to right a balance.

Perhaps restoration is not possible in cases of mass atrocity for a different reason: forgiveness of such deeds is simply beyond the psychological capacity of victims. I have come across no instance of a surviving victim forgiving or being asked to forgive Adolf Hitler, Pol Pot, Saddam Hussein, or Joseph Stalin. Still, not all political murderers or torturers are wrongdoers of this magnitude. Each of the five stories that open this chapter involves a perpetrator who participated in a large-scale human rights violation and whose victim found it possible to forgive and to live out this forgiveness robustly. True, in all of these cases, the perpetrators were not planners or directors of atrocity, except perhaps for de Klerk, whom Mandela forgave, though even de Klerk did not invent apartheid and consented to its peaceful dismantling. Then again, a widow of a victim of Eugene de Kock was willing to forgive this high-level orchestrator, just as some Ugandans are willing to forgive leaders of the Lord's Resistance Army and of the Ugandan government's army. It may well be that no one has ever forgiven or ever will forgive a Hitler or a Pol Pot, but if forgiveness has limits, it is exceedingly difficult to demarcate exactly where these limits reside.

Impunity

With political realities making judicial punishment of Indonesian generals highly unlikely, Timor-Leste's president and foreign minister have advocated forgiveness and reconciliation. When South Africa granted amnesty to high-ranking apartheid officials as a condition of their departure from power, it was justified as forgiveness. Both actions have been criticized for sacrificing just punishment.

Political realities may well force the abjuration of judicial punishment in some cases, but in principle forgiveness and judicial punishment need not be incompatible. Forgiveness need not be a second-best alternative to punishment nor is it merely amnesty. The Salvadoran Jesuits stood on solid ground in demanding the conviction of the same murderers whom they forgave.

It is the restorative justification of each practice that enables the moral compatibility of punishment and forgiveness. In forgiving, the victim defeats the perpetrator's injustice by naming and condemning it, asserting her own dignity as a subject and enactor of justice, and inviting the perpetrator also to name, disclaim, and show remorse for it. In willing punishment, the victim claims that the defeat of the perpetrator's injustice also requires the hard treatment of punishment, both as a communication from the community and, should the perpetrator accept it, the perpetrator's own communication of penance. Such a will for punishment in no way contradicts the victim's will to forgive. In her own eyes, the perpetrator is in good standing. It is from the standpoint of the community and its laws that the perpetrator's injustice stands victorious. The victim asserts no payment owed from or resentment against the perpetrator but rather his desire to see the standing victory of the injustice defeated. Just as apology did not cancel the need for punishment, neither does forgiveness. The fact that the state carries out the punishment furthers its compatibility with forgiveness even more. Acting on behalf of the community and its laws, the state is best situated to communicate the values behind the law to the wrongdoer. It can also, of course, ensure other important aspects of ethical punishment such as a fair trial, due process, and proportionality. In this scenario, victim, perpetrator, and state each defeat the message of wrongdoing from a different direction in a restorative division of labor. Such is the logic of restorative justice, which involves many parties in diverse roles.

Apology

An absence of remorse and apology on the part of a perpetrator is one of the strongest reasons not to forgive, in the view of both skeptics and qualified advocates of forgiveness.[33] Others, though, support the possibility of unilateral forgiveness, even of great injustices.[34] Four of this chapter's five exemplary stories—Bashir, Wilson, Mandela, and the Salvadoran Jesuits—involve unilateral forgiveness, unprompted by apology. Were all of these acts unjust or misguided? The main conceptual and emotional roadblocks to unilateral forgiveness are ones that I have addressed: Forgiveness condones evil, fails to take evil seriously, precludes resentment, forgoes payment owed, and is little more than a yielding up of claims in the face of injustice. As I have argued, though, forgiveness amounts to none of these things, and a lack of apology does not change this picture. The way is clear, then, for unilateral forgiveness. Far from being indifferent to a perpetrator's remorse or to the wounds caused by injustice, unilateral forgiveness invites the perpetrator's apology (if he is still alive) and seeks a world in which the wrong is overcome, transformed, and divested of force. A lack of prior apology even adds drama to these restorative thrusts. If the apology continues to be lacking, of course, reconciliation will remain sharply limited, but it is still partially achieved through the victim's will to reestablish right relationship.

At the same time, because a lack of apology is a lack of justice, it constitutes a valid reason for a victim to adopt resentment instead of forgiveness. In an atmosphere in which apology is disdainfully lacking and amnesia prevails, a victim may decide that persistent protest is warranted. This protest also invites apology and wills the defeat of injustice, but through a different strategy. Unilateral forgiveness, then, is justifiable though not required.

Is Forgiveness an Obligation?

That last argument raises a more general question: Is forgiveness of political injustices ever required? Let me first offer an answer to this question on grounds of natural reason; below I consider religious answers. That forgiveness is justice may seem to make it a duty, for justice is a set of obligations that constitute right relationship. Yet there are other aspects of my case for forgiveness that argue against it being required. If it is morally legitimate for victims to remain in resentment and if victims can be psychologically unready for forgiveness, then they cannot be required to undertake forgiveness. Were forgiveness seen and promoted as an obligation, it might force victims back into the position of being an object, again manipulated by a perpetrator, and thus undermine victims' recovery of their agency. Should forgiveness, then, be regarded as conditionally justified, a gift but not an obligation, or perhaps an aspect of justice that is not obligatory?

Reconciliation encompasses but exceeds justice that is understood as rendering another his due. Were forgiveness to be due, then for a victim to fail to perform it would be a wrong. Forgiveness is not justice of this sort. Perpetrators do not have a right to forgiveness and neither they nor any other person can demand that victims perform it. Yet the justice of reconciliation, involving the conduct of right relationship and the restoration of right relationship, involves more than what is due. Earlier I discussed several premodern philosophers—Aristotle, Augustine, Aquinas—who thought of justice as a general virtue, one amounting to all love between persons. This sort of justice is still an obligation, much in the sense that "love your neighbor" is a command in the Jewish and Christian scriptures but an obligation that is not due. Unlike the obligation not to kill or steal, this obligation does not involve a just claim on the part of its recipients or something strictly deserved. It resembles what philosophers call wide obligations, ones whose performance is required but whose manner of performance is open-ended. One may have an obligation, for instance, to practice benevolence or to improve the lot of others but not to perform any particular action in doing so.

Forgiveness, I argue, falls under this wide sort of obligation of justice. Insofar as forgiveness widens the sphere of right relationship in political orders—and, for that matter, in the personal ream—forgiveness promotes justice. It is not morally required, though, in a strict sense. Rather, it is one way in which justice can be pursued. It comes closer to being a specific obligation when a genuine apology is proffered, but even here psychological readiness can be lacking and the victim's autonomy to decide for or against forgiveness must be respected.

Forgiveness matches the justice of reconciliation even more closely in that it addresses the real harms to right relationship that political injustices inflict. The justice that aims to bring greater flourishing from the actual diminishment of right relationship in the past also converges with mercy, the will to restore all that is broken. Forgiveness, then, is an act of mercy, as it is usually thought to be. What is more surprising is that it is an act of both mercy and justice—a possibility created by the ethic of political reconciliation.

Religious Justifications for Forgiveness

A forgiveness that enacts both justice and mercy, constructively restoring right relationship, is found distinctively in Judaism, Christianity, and Islam.

The Jewish Bible reveals God's most central traits to be compassion and a willingness to forgive, both reflections of his mercy, argues Rabbi Louis E. Newman. Again and again, God forgives both individual sinners and the people of Israel, not without rebuke and punishment, to be sure, but always returning to look on Israel anew, much in the manner of reconstrual. The Day of Atonement, a ritual that priests perform, enacts this forgiveness, cleansing the people's sins and restoring right relationship among them. Newman holds that God's forgiveness has no limits with respect to the severity of the offense. God's purpose in forgiveness is to restore the right relationships of his covenant.[35]

God's forgiveness is the model for forgiveness between members of the community. Such horizontal forgiveness, as it is often called, is taught not primarily in the Torah but rather in rabbinical sources, most prominently the second-century Mishnah and the writings of Maimonides. It reflects God's covenant and is central to reconciliation between God's people and God himself. In the ethic that emerges, the initiative for repairing wrong lies with the perpetrator. Provided that he practices *teshuva* genuinely— and recall Maimonides' view that this was rigorous—the victim has an absolute duty to forgive. Forgiveness is not condoning—the rabbinic tradition commends the expression of outrage—but is rather a repair of the relationship that a wrong has ruptured.[36]

"The forgiveness that vanquishes hatred and anger is a prized virtue in Islam," writes Mohammed Abu-Nimer.[37] The texts of the Quran and the Sunna, classical Islamic jurisprudence, and the modern writings of Islamic intellectuals all endorse forgiveness. The word *forgive* (or *forgiveness* or *forgiving*) shows up 128 times in the Quran, sometimes describing the character of God and sometimes involving exhortations for humans to forgive.[38] "O my Servants who / Have transgressed against their souls! /

Despair not of the Mercy of Allah: for Allah forgives / All sins: for He is / Oft-Forgiving, Most Merciful" says the Quran.[39] God forgives especially those who are repentant and those who are merciful to others, the Quran says elsewhere.

Muslims are called to forgive even when they are angry or have the ability to take revenge. Sometimes the Quran exhorts forgiveness in the case of apology, but other times it makes no reference to prior apology. The Hadith contain an example of the Prophet forgiving his persecutors even without their contrition, an example of Mohammed forgiving his enemies, and a further instance of Allah commanding Mohammed's companion Abu Bakr to forgive one who deserves punishment for murder.[40]

As we have seen, Islamic jurisprudence, drawing on passages in the Quran, both allows and favors forgiveness for Qisas crimes, including murder. Forgiveness is also a component of *musalaha* rituals, taking place when the family of the victim offers bitter coffee to the family of the offender. Today, forgiveness is prominent in the thought of such Muslim spiritual writers as Fetullah Gülen, who advocates it as an imitation of Allah and as a means of repair and restoration—much as in the present ethic of political reconciliation.

Most interpreters of Christianity find its ethic of forgiveness to be even more expansive. Here, too, forgiveness is grounded in the action of God. "As Jesus told us when he was on the cross, forgive those who sin against you," said Cynthia, the mother who forgave Thapelo Mbelo. God's central action of forgiveness takes place through Jesus's death and resurrection, through which God liberates humanity from the burden of its sin and makes possible a union with Jesus that involves real and complete restoration. The promise of forgiveness through Jesus is a "new covenant" in which right relationship is restored.

Those theologians who espouse the most robust practice of forgiveness connect it closely with this atoning action of God. Viewing forgiveness between persons as a participation in God's forgiveness, Alan Torrance calls for an ontology of forgiveness—that is, a view grounded in the character and actions of God—rather than an ethic of forgiveness.[41] Gregory Jones advocates forgiveness as a way of life that shares in the life of the Trinity.[42] Unilateral forgiveness, for these theologians, is much to be commended (and is even required), for it imitates God's own initiative of forgiveness, and might well bring about *metanoia*, or transforming repentance, in the heart of a perpetrator. Just as "God bore our sin and condemned it in Jesus Christ...not out of impotence or cowardice, but

in order to free us from sin's guilt and power...we should absorb the
wrongdoing in order to transform the wrongdoer," Miroslav Volf writes.[43]
All of these theologians share the view that forgiveness is not just a relinquishment but also a construction.

Those Christian theologians who put forth a more cautious and
qualified view of forgiveness tend to focus on the explicit injunctions of
Jesus.[44] Several times, Jesus strongly commends forgiveness to his followers: "If you do not forgive men their sins, your Father will not forgive
your sins." He tells his disciple Peter to forgive "seventy times seven
times." In cases in which a sinner repents, Jesus holds forgiveness to
be an obligation. "If your brother sins, rebuke him, and if he repents,
forgive him. If he sins against you seven times in a day, and seven times
comes back to you and says, 'I repent,' forgive him." Though Jesus never
says explicitly that unilateral forgiveness is an obligation, neither does
he ever say that it is not.[45]

In my own view, a Christian ethic of forgiveness ought to take into
account both God's restorative action and Jesus's words. In either case,
forgiveness in Christianity is restorative of relationships, as is forgiveness
in Judaism and Islam. In all three religions, forgiveness is a practice that
constructs right relationships and thus contributes to reconciliation.

Do religious justifications differ systematically from secular ones?
Most distinctively they bring into forgiveness a decisive third party:
God. Whereas secular theories of forgiveness pose the problem as one
between victims, perpetrators, and sometimes states and other collectivities, Judaism, Christianity, and Islam conceive this horizontal
process in light of the vertical action of God toward humanity. What
difference does this make for the political practice of forgiveness? To be
sure, both secular and religious accounts of forgiveness are diverse. On
balance, though, accounts involving a God who cares infinitely for victims, is willing to punish unrepentant perpetrators, and is far greater
than even the greatest evils are far more willing to advocate forgiveness
in cases where it is unilateral, involves mass atrocity, or is practiced
toward or by collectives.[46]

Political Variants

Political forgiveness, as I have defined it, is directed at a political injustice.
It need not involve the state directly. At its simplest, it involves an individual victim and an individual perpetrator of a political injustice, but it is

not always so simple. Mandela's perpetrators (apart from his jailer) were leaders of a collective that had harmed him insofar as he was also the leader of a collective. The Jesuits acted as a collective in forgiving a perpetrator who had murdered one of their own. Such complexities deserve special consideration.

A State Commends Forgiveness to Perpetrators

One sort of difficulty arises when the state advocates that victims forgive. Such activity is prone to paternalism and manipulation—the concern that Brudholm and others harbor about the South African Truth and Reconciliation Commission.

To what extent may the state encourage its citizens to forgive? Earlier I argued that there is no principled barrier to such encouragement, but there are reasons for caution when it comes to state advocacy of forgiveness. They are the same considerations that require others not to pressure victims to forgive and to respect victims' right not to forgive. First, because resentment is also a legitimate response, then states ought not to stigmatize or steer victims away from it. Second, forgiveness requires a psychological readiness that precludes others, especially the state, from pushing victims to exercise it at a given time. Third, the hope of constructive forgiveness is that victims will be transformed from objects into active subjects, a transformation that is undermined when a state pressures, manipulates, or imposes forgiveness.

Is it possible, though, for a state to advocate and encourage forgiveness without lapsing into pressuring it? South Africa, whose government advocated forgiveness most vigorously, garnering praise and scorn alike, provides the best laboratory for answering the question. Appointed by the state, seated on a dais or behind a bench, charged with conducting the proceedings, TRC commissioners exercised a formidable sort of authority vis-à-vis victims, who were ordinary citizens testifying about wrenchingly painful events. When commissioners placed words in victims' mouths, extolled forgiveness while making anger and resentment into pathologies, and confronted victims directly with the choice between embracing or refusing forgiveness, they disrespected victims' freedoms, the charges run. Such episodes occurred, as documented by Brudholm, researcher Annelies Verdoolaege, and others. In one hearing, for instance, a commission official, Mr. Dlamini, leads

Bettina Mdlalose, the mother of a son who was politically murdered, in the following way:

COMMISSIONER: But one other thing that's an objective of this Commission is that after we have ventilated about the atrocities that were committed to us, is that we should reconcile as the community of South Africa at large. The perpetrators, those who committed those atrocities to you, killed your son, according to our records haven't come forth for amnesty, or perhaps sending us to you for forgiveness. But one question I would like to ask is that, if today those perpetrators would come forth and say, "Commission, because you exist today, we would like to go and meet Mrs. Mdlalose to ask for forgiveness," would you be prepared to meet with the perpetrators? I know they haven't come forward, they have not even admitted an application for amnesty, but still we would like to ask from you, to get a view from you that if they come to you and ask for forgiveness would you be prepared to sit down with them, shake hands with them, and reconcile with them? Would you be prepared to talk to them?
[MRS. MDLALOSE:] I don't think I will allow such an opportunity.
COMMISSIONER: Thanks. Thank you for responding, because you just told us what you feel from inside. But do not feel bad...[47]

The same researchers adduce similar episodes from other hearings and quotations from victims who resented the commission's appeal for forgiveness.

Still, these efforts to unmask are not immune from criticism. Just less than 2,000 victims testified before 83 hearings of the Human Rights Violations Committee (HRVC), while the Amnesty Committee (AC) held 269 hearings of its own. In my own survey of the transcripts of the HRVC, I found that in only 4.2 percent of "victim-hearings" (instances in which a victim appeared or two or more victims appeared together) did commissioners suggest, encourage, or otherwise raise the idea of forgiveness.[48] In only a few cases did a victim forgive a perpetrator—seventeen handled by the HRCV and thirty-five appearing before the AC.

A separate analyst, Lyn Graybill, also cites examples of the refusal to forgive and resentment at being asked to do so but also cites at least as many examples (close to twenty) of victims who, on the basis of TRC hearings, came to forgive freely and spoke of it positively. Nelson Papuyana, the father of a black student and taxi driver who was murdered in 1994 by two whites who opposed national elections, described:

> I immediately knew that it was the best thing I have ever done: to face the man who murdered my son. The meeting helped me to overcome my emotional problems. Before that meeting I was convinced that I would never be able to forgive my son's murderer. In my wildest dreams I did not think that the meeting would become a situation where I would be the one trying to comfort the murderer and his wife. Mrs. Pyper was crying so much that she could not really talk. Mr. Pyper [one of the murderers] told me what had happened that night. He said that he still could not explain why he had done such a mindless thing. He repeatedly said that it had been an extremely mindless deed and that he was sorry.[49]

Graybill might have added the mothers who forgave Mbelo and the widow who forgave Eugene de Kock. The transcripts of the hearing also show the commissioners typically making concerted efforts to welcome victims, make them feel at ease, honor them for their testimony, and assure them of their freedom to testify as they wish. The commission offered psychological counseling services to victims both before and after hearings as well.

It was not just in hearings, of course, but also in the surrounding public discourse of the commission, that forgiveness was advocated. Whether this amounts to imposition or inspiration depends largely on one's view of forgiveness itself. If one views the practice of forgiveness of large-scale human rights violations to be disempowering and compromising of self-respect, then forgiveness is always going to be unethical. If forgiveness can be viewed as justice along the lines that I have argued, however, then it can be advocated, commended, and raised as a possibility, but should always be done so in a way that respects the freedom of victims to choose or reject it as well as the actual choice itself.

Collectives and Forgiveness

Two other dilemmas attending political forgiveness pertain to the dynamics of collectives. One is illustrated by a widely read story of forgiveness in politics, Simon Wiesenthal's *The Sunflower*. A Jewish inmate in a Nazi concentration camp, Wiesenthal is chosen to visit a dying Nazi SS officer, Karl, in a nearby hospital. Karl, who had been raised Catholic, explains to Wiesenthal his intense remorse for having participated in the massacre of Jews on the Russian front and asks Wiesenthal to forgive him. Wiesenthal leaves in silence. When he returns to the camp, he is unsure whether he made the right decision and debates the matter with his fellow inmates. *The Sunflower*, which tells the story, was published with accompanying commentaries by religious and moral leaders. The main issues debated were whether mass evil could be forgiven and whether a Jew such as Simon could forgive on behalf of the Jews whom Karl had killed.

It is this latter debate that is of interest here. Simon's fellow inmate Josek tells him, "[y]ou would have had no right to do this in the name of people who had not authorized you to do so. What people have done to you yourself, you can, if you like, forgive and forget. That is your own affair. But it would have been a terrible sin to burden your conscience with other people's sufferings." Simon, questioning his own decision, responds, "This dying man looked upon me as a representative, as a symbol of the other Jews whom he could no longer reach or talk to."[50]

Can one person forgive a perpetrator for what the perpetrator has done to another person? Here recall Govier's useful distinction among primary victims (those who are directly harmed), secondary victims (friends and family members), and tertiary victims (members of the same communal group—national, ethic, religious, or the like—as the victim).[51] It follows from all that I have argued that no person may forgive a perpetrator for the wrong that he has done to another person. If a person other than a primary victim were to say to the perpetrator, "since this victim coldly has refused to forgive you, I forgive you on her behalf," such an utterance would only compound disrespect for the victim's freedom to choose or to refuse forgiveness.

By the same reasoning, though, it is appropriate for a secondary or tertiary victim to forgive the harm that a political injustice has inflicted on her—a mother for the grief that the murder of her son has caused her, a community member for the harm that an injustice has done to a community. Wilson's forgiveness, as well as Bashir's forgiveness, insofar as Bashir was forgiving the killing of his brother and his uncle for the impact that it had on him, can be understood in this way. There is nothing vicarious about this repentance; these victims are forgiving what was done to them.

A more complex question, one that invokes the issue of collectives, is whether a tertiary victim—Simon Wiesenthal or the Salvadoran Jesuits—can forgive a perpetrator for the harm that the wrong against the victim has done to him, the tertiary victim, insofar as the tertiary victim is a member of the same community as the primary victim. Would Simon have been justified in saying to Karl, "I cannot forgive you on behalf of the victims whom you killed, but as a Jew I can forgive you insofar as you committed a wrong against the Jewish people"?

A leading Jewish ethicist, Elliot N. Dorff, makes the case that this sort of forgiveness can be justified. A longstanding participant in Jewish-Catholic dialogue, he asks whether a present-day Jewish leader, speaking on behalf of the Jewish community, could forgive the Catholic Church for the ways in which it contributed to the Holocaust, even though none of these contemporary parties is a direct victim or perpetrator. Dorff makes the case that the "ontological tie" of Jews to the Jewish community that exists over time and space, along with the respective ontological tie that Catholics enjoy, makes possible a "secondary" sense of regret and forgiveness. In my own version of the argument, drawing on my distinction between the individual and collective dimensions of political injustices, a representative of the Jewish community could forgive a representative of the Catholic community for the collective dimension of the wrong, that is, for what was done to Jews qua Jews. Such collective forgiveness is "logically meaningful" and ethically acceptable, Dorff argues.[52]

How widely Dorff's argument would be accepted among other Jewish ethicists is not clear. Whether any given community will regard collective forgiveness as an ethical act will depend on its members' understanding not only of its ethics of forgiveness but also of the basis of the tie between its members. The Catholic document *Memory and Reconciliation* argues that the common tie between members of the mystical body of Christ makes it possible for present-day church leaders to apologize and receive forgiveness for sins committed in the name of the church centuries ago. For the Salvadoran Jesuits, it was doubtless this tie as well as common membership in the Jesuit community that made it possible for the leader of the community to forgive the killers of its priests and their housekeeper. For other communities, the tie that binds will be understood differently, but if a community can accept that wrongs have individual and collective dimensions with respect to both perpetrator and victim and if they can allow someone who is not a primary victim to speak to the collective dimension of the wrong, then collective forgiveness is an ethical possibility.

How might collective forgiveness look in the case of Simon Wiesenthal? Here, of course, a leader is not involved. Wiesenthal had no authority to speak for the Jews as a collective vis-à-vis another collective like the Catholic Church. Had he forgiven Karl, he would have been speaking only for himself as a Jew. On the present analysis, though, without making an overall judgment about whether Wiesenthal ought to have forgiven Karl, he would have acted rightfully had he said: "I have no authority to forgive you for what you did to the Jews back on the Russian front on behalf of those Jews themselves, but as their fellow Jew I can forgive you for what you did to my people." Wiesenthal himself surmised that he might have taken this stance. Paralleling the idea of collective apology, he thus would have practiced collective forgiveness.[53]

A variant is the case not simply of a group member but rather of a group leader who forgives another collective for the wrong that it committed against the leader's own collective—one state's military invasion of another, for instance. It is rare that leaders forgive such wrongs in explicit terms—in contrast to apologies, which are far more common in global politics. Most of the examples of leaders voicing forgiveness that I have come across are ones practiced by religious leaders. In 1965 the Catholic bishops of Poland wrote to the Catholic bishops of Germany "forgiving and asking forgiveness" in regard to the Nazi invasion and occupation of Poland during World War II. It might seem strange that the Polish bishops would ask forgiveness given the rather asymmetric nature of the crimes involved. Still, the German Catholic bishops wrote back saying "we ask you to forgive…" One of the Polish bishops who initiated the letter was Archbishop Karol Wojtyla, who later, as Pope John Paul II, would apologize and ask for forgiveness on more than one hundred occasions and in regard to at least twenty-one historical incidents.[54]

I know of no explicit grants of forgiveness performed by heads of state in the name of their collective state, although I have discovered requests. In January 2000, Jewish Holocaust survivor and Nobel Peace Laureate Elie Wiesel urged the parliament of Germany to pass a resolution in the name of Germany asking the Jewish people for their forgiveness for the crimes committed by Adolf Hitler. Around the same time, German President Johannes Rau publicly asked for forgiveness from those who had been subjected to slave and forced labor during the same period. Neither Wiesel nor Rau made it clear, though, exactly whom they expected to deliver forgiveness.

Can and ought leaders forgive in the name of a collective? Some analysts doubt the possibility. Philosopher Charles Griswold, who thinks of forgiveness as forgoing resentment, does not think that collectivities like states are capable of holding resentment in a coherent fashion in the first place.[55] Political philosopher P. E. Digeser, too, casts doubt on the concept of a state changing its sentiments.[56] But what about the collective performance of forgiveness as I have construed it—as a decision no longer to count a wrong against a wrongdoer and to reconstrue him as being in good standing?

If leaders of states are to perform collective forgiveness then it must be possible for them to form enduring construals of other states in the first place. I believe they can. Such construals are not sentiments, inward states, or the expression of a group mind but are rather the official stances that leaders assume when, in the name of their own collective, they express an enduring view of another collective. During the Cold War, the U.S. and the U.S.S.R viewed each other as standing enemies. Though the degree and character of this enmity evolved, each side's head of state regularly spoke of the other as a rival. Contrary to Griswold, this rivalry might even be thought of as mutual resentment if resentment is indeed a construal of another that involves moral protest. During this same period, by contrast, the United States and Britain spoke of a "special relationship" with each other. After World War I, the victorious allies declared Germany guilty for the war in the Treaty of Versailles and continued to demand punitive reparations. States commonly declare war on other states, invite them to join economic partnerships, and in scores of other ways express enduring views of other states. Sometimes, states decide to revise these standing views. In the early 1970s, the administration of U.S. president Richard Nixon changed the official stance of the U.S. toward China and began to speak about China in a much more favorable way than earlier presidents had.

If states and other collectivities adopt such standing construals of one another, and if they sometimes alter these construals, there is no reason why they could not change these construals in the manner of forgiveness. In doing so, the leaders of one group decide to look upon the former enemy as one against whom they no longer count its wrongs. They do not merely enter an alliance or a pact or simply drop claims, but rather commit to refrain from speaking of the other state or group as being guilty of past wrongs. On this view, forgiveness between states may actually be more common than the above recounting suggests. France, Britain, and the United States may well have practiced forgiveness when, in the early 1950s, they decided to look upon the Federal Republic of Germany anew following the Second World War. Not only did they incorporate Germany into the NATO alliance and the European Coal and Steel Community (what is today the European Union) but their leaders spoke of Germany not as if it were presently responsible for its past evils but rather as a state that had committed itself to a new set of values. To be sure, the western allies neither forgot the evils of Nazi Germany nor refrained from stationing their troops in Germany, in part to guarantee the stability of the Federal Republic (as well as to defend it against the Soviet Union). But remember that forgiveness does not preclude ongoing defensive measures. What the allies forewent, rather, was the view of Germany as a mortal enemy that they held during the war as well as the view of Germany as a continually guilty nation that they had held after World War One. Through numerous speeches, memorials, and gestures of friendship, they practiced this new stance.

Willing the creation of a more just relationship, such forgiveness is not only conceptually sound but constructive of justice. But as with apologies, a leader's utterance confers only the collective dimension of forgiveness. The president of France can forgive Germany for its crimes against France but he does not supplant the right of individual French people to participate in or refuse this forgiveness of Germany or to choose whether they want to forgive individual Germans for political crimes. The ethical independence of communal and individual forgiveness also creates political risks. Just as citizens sometimes criticize their leaders for apologizing, they will also sometimes criticize leaders for forgiving the wrong collective in the wrong way at the wrong time. But we can also expect forgiveness sometimes to build a consensus for peace.

Conclusion

The potential of forgiveness to build peace arises from its being a constructive act, not merely a relinquishment, an act that performs and promotes the justice of increased right relationship. Though its occurrence in politics is rare in comparison to the other practices, there is no conceptual or moral reason why it could not become more common. Prior to the transition to democracy in Chile and the political revolution in South Africa, few predicted that forgiveness would arise in these locales or in the many other places that it has emerged in the past two decades. Sometimes, of course, forgiveness of political injustices may create peace between individuals, as it did between Lomax and Nagase, but have little impact on peace and justice on a national or international level. To build peace at this larger level, forgiveness might be practiced in two ways. First, it can be performed widely by individual victims. There is some evidence that this has occurred in South Africa and Uganda. Second, it can be practiced by heads of collectivities—states, political factions, and religious organizations—toward other collectivities. The practice of forgiveness in either of these manners is not morally appropriate at all times. Some seasons are ones when justice requires war and active opposition to unjust regimes. But other seasons are ones for forgiveness. Were these seasons to become longer and more frequent, justice would stand a better chance of growth.

Conclusion

WHAT DIFFERENCE DOES the ethic of political reconciliation make? Does it work? Has it ever worked? These are the questions posed by the action minded: the hard-bitten staffer of a U.N. peacebuilding operation, the widely traveled official of an NGO that promotes transitional justice, the experienced veteran of a faith-based relief and development organization, or even the social scientist who wants to learn whether theories beget results.

The ethic matters for five reasons. The first of these reasons shifts the question back to the one that frames the book: What does justice consist of in the wake of its massive violation? I chose this as my framing question for a deliberate reason: because justice matters for its own sake, as an end in itself, even apart from whether or how often it is enacted and with what results. To hasten to results is to ignore this intrinsic importance or else to adopt, perhaps unreflectively, an ersatz consequentialism. Two friends sit in a café hotly debating the death penalty. Neither is an employee in the criminal justice system, an activist, or a friend or relative of a victim or defendant. Their country's death penalty laws are not about to change; each of their votes matters infinitesimally. Still they argue, cajole, and rejoin, ever more heatedly. It matters to them a great deal what sort of justice their government renders, what sort of society in which they live. Conversations like this one take place continuously, ubiquitously, over innumerable issues. To the people who engage in them, justice matters. Justice matters all the more if one believes, with philosopher John Rawls, that it is the first virtue of social institutions.[1] If justice matters then its meaning and content will be of urgent interest in a setting where a great deal of justice is at stake: numerous countries around the world that are dealing with pasts of war, genocide, and dictatorship.

Second, justice motivates players in the politics of dealing with the past. The families of murdered South African human rights activists

Steven Biko and Griffiths Mxenge who protested amnesty; the mothers of the disappeared at the Plaza de Mayo in Argentina; the widow who forgave Eugene de Kock; Bishop Gerardi of Guatemala; Archbishop Tutu; Judge Richard Goldstone; President Patricio Aylwin of Chile: The actions of all of these and other figures—and of their vituperative critics as well—are unintelligible apart from convictions about justice. This is not to deny that power and pragmatism also influence outcomes—the Truth and Reconciliation Commission was shaped as much by an amnesty deal as it was by Tutu. The point is rather that convictions about justice motivate action, even in the rubble-strewn aftermath of enormities. If justice is in play, then reflection on what it consists of is all the more important.

The ethic also contains implications for action—a third reason why it matters. It is made up of practices that enact or perform the ethic's central notion of reconciliation as a concept of justice, mercy, and peace. These core concepts, both in themselves and as they take shape in the practices, serve both as standards through which a given political measure for dealing with past injustices can be evaluated and as prescriptions for what such measures ought to entail. The practices provide no fixed and determinate solution for each circumstance and leave ample room for prudential judgment. What is more, the nature and scale of the injustices to which they respond and the political possibilities in any time and place will affect greatly which of the six practices will be realized and to what degree. Still, the ethic contains concrete implications for action. For instance, it challenges the terms of a debate that has taken place all over the world between reconciliation and punishment and between forgiveness and punishment. Justified restoratively, punishment is a component of reconciliation and compatible with forgiveness. Restorative punishment, in turn, performs its reparations best—though not unqualifiedly so—in community forums, which merit further development. The ethic also shows that acknowledgment is at its ethical best when it manifests the virtue of personalism. It shows how collective apology can be both justified and compatible with individual apology as well as how forgiveness can be collective, a rarity that could become less of one. It shows why apology and reparations are complementary and incomplete without each other. It asserts that reconciliation does not negate the justice of struggles against unjust regimes and aggressor states or the justice of reforming economic structures. These and other concrete implications emanate from the ethic.

Not only does the ethic carry implications for action, but its program is distinct from other major paradigms. This is the fourth reason that the ethic matters. Reconciliation is not simply an end state where enmity becomes amity—an easily dismissed utopian ideal. Rather, it involves any incremental progress from woundedness of persons and relationships to the greater flourishing of persons and relationships in political orders. Reconciliation also does not negate such elements of justice as deserved punishment and human rights. The ethic differs from the liberal peace, the dominant paradigm of peacebuilding. Reconciliation's justice stresses rights and equality but also involves the broad restoration of right relationship with respect to the wounds that political injustices exact. It views mercy as supportive of justice, not as an exception to or departure from it. Although the liberal peace also supports several of the six practices—establishing the rule of law and human rights, truth telling, reparations, judicial punishment, and vetting—reconciliation justifies each of these as a restoration of goods that are far wider than rights alone. Reconciliation also adds two other restorative practices—apology and forgiveness. Finally, reconciliation calls for a more robust participation of victims, perpetrators, and citizens in the practices of reconciliation.

Fifth and finally, the ethic of political reconciliation reserves a place for religion in debates about dealing with the past. My claim is not just that religion has been involved in these debates. That much is clear in Germany, Ireland, Chile, Guatemala, El Salvador, South Africa, Uganda, Rwanda, Sierra Leone, Timor-Leste, Peru, and Iraq. It is rather that religious traditions are generators, hosts, and sources of the distinct concepts of justice, mercy, and peace that reside in reconciliation. By retrieving and developing these concepts and adapting them to modern constitutional democracy and international norms, an ethic emerges that offers promise for restoring damaged political orders. This ethic will not be and has not been shared unanimously by these traditions and has evolved historically within them. It finds expression in secular articulations of restorative justice. Still, the core concepts of the ethic are remarkably deep, broad, and old in religious texts and traditions. Reconciliation entered global politics at the end of a century in which war, genocide, and political oppression occurred in, well, biblical proportions. Voices within the faiths at hand, then, are asking: Could reconciliation be God's active response? If nothing else, a sense of God's purposive agency offers people of faith a basis for hope even when circumstances seem to provide none and a reason for thinking with Seamus Heaney that "healing wells" can be found "on the far side of revenge."

Another hope is that religious and secular voices can speak together about dealing with the past—at negotiating tables, at academic conferences, in public forums, in the media—more than they do at present. Constructive conversations would take place far more often, not simply because secular people are open-minded when they talk to the religious or religious people are being tolerant when they speak with the secular, but because by digging together they might discover veins of ore that, when mined, contain great potential for the troubled task of *tikkun olam*.

Notes

INTRODUCTION

1. Even as approximations, some of these numbers are disputed.
2. Andrew Mack, *Global Political Violence: Explaining the Post-Cold War Decline* (New York: International Peace Academy, 2007). According to Charles T. Call and Elizabeth M. Cousens, most studies show that somewhere between one-fifth and one-third of all settled conflicts revert back to warfare within five years. See Charles T. Call and Elizabeth M. Cousens, "Ending Wars and Building Peace: International Responses to War-Torn Societies," *International Studies Perspectives* 9 (2008): 5.
3. On the liberal peace, see Oliver P. Richmond, "The Problem of Peace: Understanding the 'Liberal Peace,'" *Conflict, Security, & Development* 6, no. 3 (2006): 291–314, and Roland Paris, *At War's End: Building Peace after Civil Conflict* (Cambridge, UK: Cambridge University Press, 2004).
4. Recovery of Historical Memory Project, *Guatemala: Never Again!* (Maryknoll, NY: Orbis Books, 1999), xxv.
5. Mark Gevisser, "The Witnesses," *New York Times Magazine*, June 22, 1997, quoted in Amy Gutmann and Dennis Thompson, "The Moral Foundations of Truth Commissions," in *Truth v. Justice: The Morality of Truth Commissions*, eds. Robert I. Rotberg and Dennis Thompson (Princeton, NJ: Princeton University Press, 2000), 26.
6. Anne Sa'adah, *Germany's Second Chance: Trust, Justice, and Democratization* (Cambridge, MA: Harvard University Press, 1998), 67.
7. Barry O'Neill, *Honor, Symbols, and War* (Ann Arbor: University of Michigan Press, 1999), 178.
8. Karen Brounéus, *Rethinking Reconciliation: Concepts, Methods, and an Empirical Study of Truth Telling and Psychological Health in Rwanda*, Report 81 (Uppsala, Sweden: Uppsala Universitet, 2008), 9.

9. See Donald W. Shriver, *An Ethic for Enemies: Forgiveness in Politics* (New York: Oxford University Press, 1995), 49–52.

10. For a more extended treatment of these claims, see Monica Duffy Toft, Daniel Philpott, and Timothy Samuel Shah, *God's Century: Resurgent Religion in Global Politics* (New York: W. W. Norton, 2011).

11. Ellen Lutz and Kathryn Sikkink, "The Justice Cascade: The Evolution and Impact of Foreign Human Rights Trials in Latin America," *Chicago Journal of International Law* 2 (2001).

12. Political scientist Samuel Huntington used the term third wave of democratization to describe this trend between 1974 and 1989. See Samuel P. Huntington, *The Third Wave: Democratization in the Late Twentieth Century* (Norman: University of Oklahoma Press, 1991). Diamond's claim of ninety democratizing countries comes in a 2008 article in which he describes the beginning of a "rollback" from democracy. See his Larry Diamond, "The Democratic Rollback: The Resurgence of the Predatory State," *Foreign Affairs* 87, no. 2 (2008): 36–48. His article was written prior to the Arab Spring, of course.

13. United Nations, *A More Secure World: Our Shared Responsibility. Report of the High-level Panel on Threats, Challenges and Change*, 34. Political scientist Monica Duffy Toft shows that between 1940 and 1989 from 75 to 100 percent of civil wars in any one decade ended in military victory while only a handful ended in negotiation. During the 1990s, in comparison, 41 percent of civil wars ended in negotiations, while only 40 percent ended in military victory. Monica Duffy Toft, *Securing the Peace: The Durable Settlement of Civil Wars* (Princeton, NJ: Princeton University Press, 2010), 6–7.

14. See Michael W. Doyle and Nicholas Sambanis, *Making War & Building Peace* (Princeton, NJ: Princeton University Press, 2006).

15. Andrew Mack, *Human Security Report 2005: War and Peace in the 21st Century* (Oxford, UK: Oxford University Press, 2005), 18.

CHAPTER 1

1. Jonathan VanAntwerpen, "Reconciliation Reconceived: Religion, Secularism, and the Language of Transition," in *The Politics of Reconciliation in Multicultural Societies*, eds. Will Kymlicka and Bashir Bashir (New York: Oxford University Press, 2008), 25–47.

2. This conception of an overlapping consensus derived without restrictions of the sort that Rawls requires has been advocated by philosopher Charles Taylor and influences the approach here. See Charles Taylor, "Modes of Secularism." In *Secularism and Its Critics*, ed. Rajeev Bhargava (Oxford, UK: Oxford University Press, 1998), 31–53.

3. Grace Clement, *Care, Autonomy, and Justice: Feminism and the Ethic of Care* (Boulder, CO: Westview Press, 1996) and Robin L. West, *Re-Imagining*

Justice: Progressive Interpretations of Formal Equality, Rights, and the Rule of Law (Surrey, UK: Ashgate Publishing, 2003).

4. Alasdair MacIntyre, *After Virtue: A Study in Moral Theory*, 2nd ed. (Notre Dame, IN: University of Notre Dame Press, 1984), 222.

5. Quoted in Michael Novak, "Human Dignity, Human Rights," *First Things: A Monthly Journal of Religion & Public Life*, no. 97 (1999): 40.

CHAPTER 2

1. See John Finnis, *Natural Law and Natural Rights* (Oxford, UK: Oxford University Press, 1980), 147–156.

2. See Robert O. Keohane and Stanley Hoffmann, "Institutional Change in Europe in the 1980's," in *The New European Community: Decisionmaking and Institutional Change*, eds. Robert O. Keohane and Stanley Hoffmann (Boulder, CO: Westview Press, 1991), 1–39.

3. Dorothy V. Jones, *Code of Peace: Ethics and Security in the World of Warlord States* (Chicago: University of Chicago Press, 1989).

4. Doyle and Sambanis, *Making War & Building Peace*, 11; *The Human Security Report: War and Peace in the 21st Century* (Oxford, UK: Human Security Centre, 2005), 23. Civil wars as a percentage of wars remained high in 2005 at 95 percent.

5. The set of standards that defines justice in a political community and, by extension, political injustices, includes human rights and the laws of war—the prohibition of aggression, noncombatant immunity, and the like. I know of no good single term for this package of standards. Throughout the book I often use the term *human rights* to refer to this package but with the knowledge that certain international norms like the U.N. Charter's prohibition of violations of political sovereignty and territorial independence (i.e., aggression) are not precisely a matter of human rights but rather of the rights of states.

6. For the view that religion is necessary for human rights, see Michael Perry, *The Idea of Human Rights: Four Inquiries* (Oxford, UK: Oxford University Press, 1998); Nicholas Wolterstorff, *Justice: Rights and Wrongs* (Princeton, NJ: Princeton University Press, 2008); Max L. Stackhouse and Stephen E. Healey, "Religion and Human Rights: A Theological Apologetic," in *Religious Human Rights in Global Perspective: Religious Perspectives*, eds. John Witte Jr. and Johan van der Vyver (The Hague, Netherlands: Kluwer Law International, 1996), 485–516. For the view that religion is strongly supportive of human rights, see Christopher D. Marshall, *Crowned with Glory and Honor: Human Rights in the Biblical Tradition* (Telford, PA: Pandora Press, 2001); David Novak, *Covenantal Rights: A Study in Jewish Political Theory* (Princeton, NJ: Princeton University Press, 2000); Pope John XXIII, "Pacem in Terris: Peace on Earth," in *Catholic*

Social Thought: The Documentary Heritage, eds. David J. O'Brien and Thomas A. Shannon (Maryknoll, NY: Orbis Books, 1992), 129–162.

7. Oliver O'Donovan, *The Desire of the Nations: Rediscovering the Roots of Political Theology* (Cambridge, UK: Cambridge University Press, 1996); Vigen Guroian, "Human Rights and Modern Western Faith: An Orthodox Christian Assessment," in *Does Human Rights Need God?*, eds. Elizabeth Bucar and Barbra Barnett (Grand Rapids, MI: William P. Eerdmans, 2005), 41–47.

8. This is the view of scholars who offer a defense of human dignity and human rights based on natural law. See, for instance, Robert P. George, "Natural Law and Human Rights: A Conversation," in *Does Human Rights Need God?*, eds. Elizabeth Bucar and Barbra Barnett (Grand Rapids, MI: William P. Eerdmans, 2005), 135–146; Finnis, *Natural Law and Natural Rights*, 198–230.

9. Jack Donnelly, *Universal Human Rights in Theory and Practice* (Ithaca, NY: Cornell University Press, 1989); James Nickel, *Making Sense of Human Rights*, 2nd ed. (Oxford, UK: Blackwell Publishing, 2007); Ronald Dworkin, *Life's Dominion: An Argument about Abortion, Euthanasia, and Individual Freedom* (New York: Knopf, 1993).

10. Richard Rorty, "Human Rights, Rationality, and Sentimentality," in *On Human Rights: The Oxford Amnesty Lectures 1993*, eds. Stephen Shute and Susan Hurley (New York: Basic Books, 1993), 111–134.

11. Desmond Tutu, *No Future Without Forgiveness* (New York: Doubleday, 1999); Jennifer J. Llewellyn, "Truth Commissions and Restorative Justice," in *Handbook of Restorative Justice*, eds. Gerry Johnstone and Daniel W. van Ness (Portland, OR: Willan Publishing, 2007), 351–371; Jennifer J. Llewellyn, "Restorative Justice in Transitions and Beyond," in *Telling the Truths: Truth Telling and Peace Building in Post-Conflict Societies*, ed. Tristan Anne Borer (Notre Dame, IN: University of Notre Dame Press, 2006), 83–113.

12. On common morality, see Alan Donagan, *The Theory of Morality* (Chicago: University of Chicago Press, 1977); Joseph Boyle, "Natural Law and International Ethics," in *Traditions of International Ethics*, eds. Terry Nardin and David R. Mapel (Cambridge, UK: Cambridge University Press, 1992), 112–135.

CHAPTER 3

1. "Ordinary men" references the title of Christopher Browning's *Ordinary Men: Reserve Police Battalion 101 and the Final Solution in Poland* (New York: Harper Perennial, 1993).

2. I fully accept the definition of *reparations* offered by the U.N. General Assembly: "[V]ictims are persons who individually or collectively suffered harm, including physical or mental injury, emotional suffering, economic loss or substantial impairment of their fundamental rights, through acts or omissions that constitute gross violations of international human rights law, or serious violations of

international humanitarian law." See United Nations General Assembly, *Basic Principles and Guidelines on the Right to a Remedy and Reparation for Victims of Gross Violations of International Human Rights Law and Serious Violations of International Humanitarian Law*, 2005.

3. Jean Améry, *At the Mind's Limits: Contemplations by a Survivor on Auschwitz and Its Realities*, trans. Sidney Rosenfeld and Stella P. Rosenfeld (Bloomington: Indiana University Press, 1980), 30.

4. Ibid., 34.

5. Antjie Krog, *Country of My Skull: Guilt, Sorrow, and the Limits of Forgiveness in the New South Africa* (New York: Random House, 1999), 176.

6. Judith Herman, *Trauma and Recovery* (New York: Basic Books, 1992), 49.

7. Ibid., 33–50, 87, 94.

8. David Becker, *Dealing with the Consequences of Organised Violence in Trauma Work* (Berlin: Berghof Research Center for Constructive Conflict Management, 2004), 6.

9. David Becker, "The Deficiency of the Concept of Posttraumatic Stress Disorder when Dealing with Victims of Human Rights Violations," in *Beyond Trauma: Cultural and Societal Dynamics*, eds. Rolf J. Kleber, Charles R. Figley, and Berthold P. R. Gersons (New York: Plenum Press, 1995), 101–102.

10. Recovery of Historical Memory Project, *Guatemala: Never Again!*, 22–23; *At the Mind's Limits: Contemplations by a Survivor on Auschwitz and Its Realities*, 27.

11. Elaine Scarry, *The Body in Pain: The Making and Unmaking of the World* (Oxford, UK: Oxford University Press, 1985), 35, 51–56.

12. Recovery of Historical Memory Project, *Guatemala: Never Again!*, 22–23.

13. Brandon Hamber and Richard A. Wilson, "Symbolic Closure Through Memory, Reparation and Revenge in Post-Conflict Societies," *Journal of Human Rights* 1, no. 1 (March, 2002): 40.

14. Alex Boraine, "Truth and Reconciliation in South Africa: The Third Way," in *Truth v. Justice: The Morality of Truth Commissions*, eds. Robert I. Rotberg and Dennis Thompson (Princeton, NJ: Princeton University Press, 2000), 150.

15. Hamber and Wilson, *Symbolic Closure Through Memory, Reparation and Revenge in Post-Conflict Societies*, 40. Their account of Argentina is drawn from the particularly rich work of Marcelo Suarez-Orozco in "The Heritage of Enduring a Dirty War: Psychological Aspects of Terror in Argentina," *The Journal of Psychohistory* 18, no. 4 (1991): 469–505.

16. Daan Bronkhorst, *Truth and Reconciliation: Obstacles and Opportunities for Human Rights* (Amsterdam: Amnesty International Dutch Section, 1995); quoted in Hamber and Wilson, *Symbolic Closure through Memory, Reparation and Revenge in Post-Conflict Societies*, 40.

17. Ibid., 41.

18. Borrowing a distinction from the philosopher Thomas Nagel, du Toit asserts a difference between factual truths—knowledge of the who, what, when, and

where of a crime—and truth as acknowledgment, public recognition of the denial of a person's dignity. André du Toit, "The Moral Foundations of the South African TRC: Truth as Acknowledgment and Justice as Recognition," in *Truth v. Justice: The Morality of Truth Commissions*, eds. Robert I. Rotberg and Dennis Thompson (Princeton, NJ: Princeton University Press, 2000), 132.

19. Ibid., 133.

20. William T. Cavanaugh, *Torture and Eucharist* (Oxford, UK: Blackwell Publishers, 1998), 48–58.

21. Hannah Arendt, *Eichmann in Jerusalem: A Report on the Banality of Evil* (New York: Penguin Books, 1994), 148–150.

22. For my understanding of this wound, I draw from the arguments of Jean Hampton. See Jeffrie G. Murphy and Jean Hampton, *Forgiveness and Mercy* (New York: Cambridge University Press, 1988), 124–138.

23. Pamela Hieronymi, "Articulating an Uncompromising Forgiveness," *Philosophy and Phenomenological Research* LXII, no. 3 (May, 2001): 546. Italics in original.

24. Timothy Longman and Théonèste Rutagengwa, "Memory, Identity, and Community in Rwanda," in *My Neighbor, My Enemy: Justice and Community in the Aftermath of Mass Atrocity*, eds. Eric Stover and Harvey M. Weinstein (Cambridge, UK: Cambridge University Press, 2004), 173.

25. Plato, *Gorgias*, trans. Robin Waterfield (Oxford, UK: Oxford University Press, 2008), 131–132.

26. Pumla Gobodo-Madikizela, *A Human Being Died That Night: A South African Story of Forgiveness* (Boston: Houghton Mifflin Company, 2003), 58.

27. Leigh Payne, *Unsettling Accounts* (Durham, NC: Duke University Press, 2008), 81. See also Tina Rosenberg, *Children of Cain: Violence and the Violent in Latin America* (New York: Penguin Books, 1992).

28. Arendt, *Eichmann in Jerusalem: A Report on the Banality of Evil*, 24.

29. Gobodo-Madikizela, *A Human Being Died That Night: A South African Story of Forgiveness*.

30. Ibid., 41–42, 50–51, 58.

31. Frederica Mathewes-Green, "The Wounded Torturer," *The Review of Faith & International Affairs* 5, no. 2 (2007): 9–12.

32. Gobodo-Madikizela, *A Human Being Died That Night: A South African Story of Forgiveness*, 46.

33. Skeptical of secondary wounds might be the accounts of conflict espoused by political scientists who doubt the role of identities, emotions, and ethnic and national loyalties in causing conflict. Such skepticism varies in its depth. Some skeptics question the view that "ancient hatreds" are behind contemporary conflict, pointing instead to the role of more recent historical processes as well as to the role of contemporary elite strategies in forming national and ethnic identities and their attendant emotions. Others argue, still more ambitiously, that ethnic and

nationalist conflict can be explained through incentives rooted in security and economics. My own view of these positions is a moderate one. I do not argue for a view based on strong ancient hatreds but only that the injustices of one period yield judgments that lead to injustices at a later time, whether that time is five, fifteen, fifty, or five hundred years in the future. I also do not argue for a monocausal explanation but suggest rather that armed conflict may arise from a combination of factors, ideational and material, cultural and structural. My own sympathies are closest to those of Roger D. Petersen, *Understanding Ethnic Violence: Fear, Hatred, and Resentment in Twentieth-Century Eastern Europe* (Cambridge, UK: Cambridge University Press, 2002); and Stuart Kaufman, *Modern Hatreds: The Symbolic Politics of Ethnic War* (Ithaca, NY: Cornell University Press, 2001).

34. Michael Ignatieff, *The Warrior's Honor: Ethnic War and the Modern Conscience* (New York, NY: Metropolitan Books/Henry Holt, 1998), 169; quoted in Hamber and Wilson, *Symbolic Closure Through Memory, Reparation and Revenge in Post-Conflict Societies*, 136.

35. Robert C. Roberts, *Emotions: An Essay in Aid of Moral Psychology* (Cambridge, UK: Cambridge University Press, 2003), 60–64, 75.

36. Petersen, *Understanding Ethnic Violence: Fear, Hatred, and Resentment in Twentieth-Century Eastern Europe*, 57, 74–75, 81–82.

37. Murphy and Hampton, *Forgiveness and Mercy*, 80–81, 88–110.

38. Roberts, *Emotions: An Essay in Aid of Moral Psychology*, 84–85.

39. For a helpful explanation of this logic, see Yinan He, *The Search for Reconciliation: Sino-Japanese and German-Polish Relations since World War II* (Cambridge, UK: Cambridge University Press, 2009), 31–34.

CHAPTER 4

1. For these terms, see Doyle and Sambanis, *Making War & Building Peace*, 18.
2. David A. Crocker, "Retribution and Reconciliation," *Philosophy and Public Policy* 20, no. 1 (2000): 6.
3. For the earliest statements of the distinction, see Martin Luther King, "Nonviolence and Racial Justice," in *A Testament of Hope: The Essential Writings and Speeches of Martin Luther King, Jr.*, ed. James M. Washington (New York: HarperCollins, 1986), 5–9; Johan Galtung, "An Editorial," *Journal of Peace Research* 1, no. 1 (1964): 1–4; Kenneth Boulding, "Toward a Theory of Peace," in *International Conflict and Behavioral Science*, ed. Roger Fisher (New York: Basic Books, 1964), 70–87.
4. For statements of this position other than those mentioned in the text here, see Reed Brody, "Justice: The First Casualty of Truth? The Global Movement to End Impunity for Human Rights Abuses Faces a Daunting Question," *The Nation* 272, no. 17: 25–30; Claire Moon, *Narrating Political Reconciliation: South Africa's Truth and Reconciliation Commission* (Lanham, MD: Lexington Books,

2008); John Borneman, *Settling Accounts: Violence, Justice and Accountability in Postsocialist Europe* (Princeton, NJ: Princeton University Press, 1997). Not all of these view reconciliation as an "oppressor's rationale" but they hold that it wrongly supplants retributive justice.

5. Quoted in Michael Ignatieff, "Articles of Faith," *Index on Censorship* 25, no. 5 (1996): 112.

6. http://www.sahistory.org.za/pages/library-resources/official%20docs/kairos-document.htm. Italics are in the original.

7. See, for instance, Mahmood Mamdani, "Reconciliation Without Justice," *South African Review of Books* 46 (1996).

8. For exemplars of all of these criticisms, see chapter 6, where I take them up in detail.

9. Payne, *Unsettling Accounts*, 1–3.

10. See, for instance, Jonathan Allen, "Balancing Justice and Social Unity: Political Theory and the Idea of a Truth and Reconciliation Commission," *University of Toronto Law Journal* 49, no. 3 (1999): 315–353; Richard Goldstone, "Foreword," in *Looking Back, Reaching Forward: Reflections on the Truth and Reconciliation Commission of South Africa*, eds. Charles Villa-Vicencio and Wilhelm Verwoerd (Cape Town, South Africa: University of Cape Town Press, 2000): viii–xiii; Kent Greenawalt, "Amnesty's Justice," in *Truth v. Justice: The Morality of Truth Commissions*, eds. Robert I. Rotberg and Dennis Thompson (Princeton, NJ: Princeton University Press, 2000), 189–210.

11. Juan E. Méndez, "National Reconciliation, Transnational Justice, and the International Criminal Court," *Ethics and International Affairs* 15, no. 1 (2001): 25–44; Naomi Roht-Arriaza, "The New Landscape of Transitional Justice," in *Transitional Justice in the Twenty-First Century*, eds. Naomi Roht-Arriaza and Javier Mariezcurrena (Cambridge, UK: Cambridge University Press, 2006), 1–16.

12. James Dobbins et al., *The Beginner's Guide to Nation-Building* (Santa Monica, CA: RAND Corporation, 2007); Stephen John Stedman, "International Implementation of Peace Agreements in Civil Wars: Findings from a Study of Sixteen Cases," in *Turbulent Peace*, eds. Chester Crocker, Fen Osler Hampson, and Pamela Aall (Washington, DC: United States Institute of Peace, 2001), 745–749.

13. Crocker, *Retribution and Reconciliation*, 5–6. See also Rajeev Bhargava, "Restoring Decency to Barbaric Societies," in *Truth v. Justice*, eds. Robert Rotberg and Dennis Thompson (Princeton, NJ: Princeton University Press, 2000), 45–67; du Toit, *The Moral Foundations of the South African TRC: Truth as Acknowledgment and Justice as Recognition*, 134–135; Trudy Govier, *Forgiveness and Revenge* (London: Routledge, 2002), 141–144.

14. John Rawls, *Justice as Fairness: A Restatement*, ed. Erin Kelly (Cambridge, MA: Harvard University Press, 2001), 3.

15. Charles Villa-Vicencio, "The Politics of Reconciliation," in *Telling the Truths: Truth Telling and Peace Building in Post-Conflict Societies*, ed. Tristan Anne Borer (Notre Dame, IN: University of Notre Dame Press, 2006), 59–82.

16. He, *The Search for Reconciliation: Sino-Japanese and German-Polish Relations since World War II*, 19–20. See also William Long and Peter Brecke, *War and Reconciliation: Reason and Emotion in Conflict Resolution* (Cambridge, MA: MIT Press, 2003). In this category also belongs certain theorists of political reconciliation, including Ernesto Verdeja, *Unchopping a Tree: Reconciliation in the Aftermath of Political Violence* (Philadelphia: Temple University Press, 2009); Colleen Murphy, *A Moral Theory of Political Reconciliation* (Cambridge, UK: Cambridge University Press, 2010); and Andrew Schaap, *Political Reconciliation* (New York: Routledge, Taylor and Francis Group, 2005).

17. Volf's views of the relationship between reconciliation and justice are most elaborated in Miroslav Volf, "Forgiveness, Reconciliation, and Justice: A Theological Contribution to a More Peaceful Social Environment," *Millennium* 29, no. 3 (2000): 861–877; and Miroslav Volf, "The Social Meaning of Reconciliation," *Interpretation* 54 (April, 2000): 158–172. In the latter piece, the author calls justice "an indispensable aspect of a more overarching agenda of reconciliation" (162) and "*a dimension of reconciliation whose ultimate goal is a community of love*" (163, italics in original). Elsewhere in his writings, though, Volf suggests a view of reconciliation (or embrace) as being justice itself—what I call the seventh view. See Miroslav Volf, *Exclusion and Embrace: A Theological Exploration of Identity, Otherness, and Reconciliation* (Nashville: Abingdon Press, 1996), 220–221.

18. For other examples of this view, see Robert Schreiter, *The Ministry of Reconciliation: Spirituality and Strategies* (Maryknoll, NY: Orbis, 1998), 123; Erin Daly and Jeremy Sarkin, *Reconciliation in Divided Societies: Finding Common Ground* (Philadelphia: University of Pennsylvania Press, 2007), 168–169, 187–189; Harold Wells, "Theology for Reconciliation: Biblical Perspectives on Forgiveness and Grace," in *The Reconciliation of Peoples: Challenge to the Churches*, eds. Gregory Baum and Harold Wells (Maryknoll, NY: Orbis Books, 1997), 1–15; Emmanuel Katongole and Chris Rice, *Reconciliation All Things: A Christian Vision for Justice, Peace, and Healing* (Downers Grove, IL: InterVarsity Press, 2008); John Paul Lederach, *Building Peace: Sustainable Reconciliation in Divided Societies* (Washington, D.C.: United States Institute of Peace, 1997); Stephen J. Pope, "The Convergence of Forgiveness and Justice: Lessons from El Salvador," *Theological Studies* 64 (2003): 812–835; and Andrew Rigby, *Justice and Reconciliation: After the Violence* (Boulder, CO: Lynne Rienner Publishers, 2001). At times, John Paul II, in his 1980 encyclical *Dives in Misericordia*, writes of reconciliation and forgiveness as encompassing justice. In other passages, though, his view seems to approximate the seventh view, in which reconciliation and forgiveness are forms of justice. See the further discussion in chapter 8.

19. Other holders of this view include Tutu, *No Future Without Forgiveness*; John W. De Gruchy, *Reconciliation: Restoring Justice* (Minneapolis: Fortress Press, 2002); Howard Zehr, *Changing Lenses* (Scottdale, PA: Herald Press, 1990); Christopher D. Marshall, *Beyond Retribution: A New Testament Vision for Justice, Crime and Punishment* (Grand Rapids, MI: Eerdmans, 2001); and Rama Mani, *Beyond Retribution: Seeking Justice in the Shadow of War* (Malden, MA: Blackwell Publishers, 2002).

20. In later chapters I will look at the meaning of reconciliation in the Jewish, Christian, and Islamic traditions. I find that most translations of the Tanakh, or Jewish Bible, contain no word for reconciliation. I argue, however, that the common concept of reconciliation from the other traditions corresponds to the Jewish meaning of justice—right relationship. The Jewish tradition, too, then, confirms that reconciliation means justice, at least, that is, as long as one is willing to accept the definition of reconciliation drawn from the other traditions as well as from a standard contemporary dictionary meaning. It turns out that the concept of reconciliation at hand also corresponds well to the first meaning of "reconcile" in the *Merriam-Webster's Dictionary,* namely "to restore to friendship or harmony." (This dictionary defines *reconciliation* as "the action of reconciling; the state of being reconciled."). As for the restorative justice tradition, writings from these sources contain the concept of reconciliation though they vary in the centrality that they give to reconciliation. It still means something quite resonant with what the restorative justice tradition means by justice.

21. I do not give extended treatment here to the issue of the responsibility of successor regimes for the crimes of previous regimes apart from a brief discussion of apologies in chapter 10. It is hardly uncommon, though, for successor regimes to act as if they have such responsibility. The Federal Republic of Germany, for instance, paid out billions of dollars in reparations and issued apologies for the crimes of the Nazi regime. Chile, under President Patricio Aylwin, similarly issued reparations and apologies for crimes committed under the Pinochet regime. Why does a government bear responsibility for what a previous government has done? Does it matter whether the new authorities are a successor administration under the same state constitution or whether they serve under a new constitution? Generally I hold a strong view of successor governments' responsibility. Broadly, this responsibility derives from the fact that victims who suffered under a previous regime were not simply harmed by individuals but by agents of the political authority whose duty it is to promote justice and the common good. The "standing victory" of this collective dimension of political injustice persists even after its perpetrators are no longer in power. Now, the present authority, which also bears a duty to justice and the common good, is required to address this legacy. Again, though, the problem bears further treatment.

22. Thomas Buergenthal, "The United Nations Truth Commission for El Salvador," in *Transitional Justice: How Emerging Democracies Reckon with*

Former Regimes, I, ed. Neil J. Kritz (Washington, D.C.: United States Institute of Peace, 1995), 321.

23. For an excellent treatment of the role of trust in reconciliation, see Murphy, *A Moral Theory of Political Reconciliation,* chapter 6.

24. For views of nationalism that see national identity as a facilitator of social action, see David Miller, *On Nationality* (Oxford, UK: Clarendon, 1995) and Yael Tamir, *Liberal Nationalism* (Princeton, NJ: Princeton University Press, 1993).

25. My understanding of social capital is drawn from Robert D. Putnam, *Bowling Alone: The Collapse and Revival of American Community* (New York: Simon and Schuster, 2000), 19.

26. This, by and large, is Howard Zehr's perspective, as he articulates it in Howard Zehr, "Restorative Justice: The Concept," *Corrections Today* 59, no. 7 (1997): 68–71. He moderates his position somewhat in a later work, *The Little Book of Restorative Justice* (Intercourse, PA: Good Books, 2002), 58–61.

27. Restorative punishment is defined by Marshall, *Beyond Retribution: A New Testament Vision for Justice, Crime and Punishment,* 131–140.

28. Gutmann and Thompson, *The Moral Foundations of Truth Commissions,* 35–38.

29. Govier, *Forgiveness and Revenge,* 141–145.

30. The phrase *incremental improvement* was suggested to me by Jason Springs.

31. Krog, *Country of My Skull: Guilt, Sorrow, and the Limits of Forgiveness in the New South Africa,* 143.

32. See Claudia Card, "Mercy," *Philosophical Review* 81, no. 2 (1972): 182–207; Alwynne Smart, "Mercy," *Philosophy* 43, no. 165 (1968): 345–59; as well as Jeffrey Murphy in Murphy and Hampton, *Forgiveness and Mercy,* 162–186.

33. St. Thomas Aquinas, *Summa Theologica,* trans. Fathers of the English Dominican Province, Vol. III: IIa-IIae, QQ. 1–148 (Notre Dame, IN: Ave Maria Press, 1948), 1311–1314. On Aquinas and mercy, see also Alasdair C. MacIntyre, *Dependent Rational Animals: Why Human Beings Need the Virtues* (Chicago, Ill.: Open Court, 1999), 124–125.

34. That two concepts overlap in their meaning may seem conceptually unsatisfactory. Should we not insist on distinctness? The argument that I am about to make about peace, however—that it contains and thus overlaps with justice—is a common one in both religious and secular writings, as is attested by the following footnote and by notes in the later chapters in the religious traditions. Just as justice and peace overlap in this fashion, so do justice and mercy.

35. For another view that associates reconciliation with a wide peace, see John Paul Lederach, *Building Peace: Sustainable Reconciliation in Divided Societies* (Washington, DC: United States Institute of Peace, 1997).

36. See Tutu, *No Future Without Forgiveness;* Jose Zalaquett, "Confronting Human Rights Violations Committed by Former Governments: Principles Applicable

and Political Constraints," in *Transitional Justice*, ed. Kritz Neil (Washington, DC: United States Institute of Peace Press, 1995); Llewellyn, *Restorative Justice in Transitions and Beyond*, 83–113.

37. John Braithwaite, a leading theorist of restorative justice, argues that the idea is present in the vast majority of cultures that have existed. See John Braithwaite, "Restorative Justice: Assessing Optimistic and Pessimistic Accounts," *Crime and Justice: A Review of Research* 25, no. 1 (1999): 6.

38. Mark Umbreit, "Restorative Justice Through Juvenile Victim-Offender Mediation," in *Restoring Juvenile Justice: Repairing the Harm of Youth Crime*, eds. G. Bazemore and L. Walgrave (Monsey, NY: Criminal Justice Press, 1999), cited in Braithwaite, *Restorative Justice: Assessing Optimistic and Pessimistic Accounts*, 2. For a description of the various restorative justice mechanisms that have been formed, see Gerry Johnstone and Daniel W. Van Ness, "The Meaning of Restorative Justice," in *The Handbook of Restorative Justice*, eds. Gerry Johnstone and Daniel W. Van Ness (Devon, UK: Willan Publishing, 2006), 8.

39. John Braithwaite, *Crime, Shame, and Reintegration* (Cambridge, UK: Cambridge University Press, 1989).

40. See Jennifer J. Llewellyn and Robert Howse, "Institutions for Restorative Justice: The South African Truth and Reconciliation Commission," *University of Toronto Law Journal* 49 (1999): 355–388.

41. See, for instance, Aristotle, *Ethics*, trans. J.A.K. Thomson (Harmondsworth, UK: Penguin Books, 1953), 173–174; Thomas Aquinas, *Summa Theologica*, 1,428–1,437.; D. D. Raphael, *Concepts of Justice* (Oxford, UK: Oxford University Press, 2001), 30–62.

42. The list includes both philosophers and statesmen who have given strong expression to liberal ideas. See Arnold Wolfers and Laurence Martin, *The Anglo-American Tradition in Foreign Affairs: Readings from Thomas More to Woodrow Wilson* (New Haven, CT: Yale University Press, 1956); Michael Joseph Smith, *Liberalism and International Reform* (Cambridge, UK: Cambridge University Press, 1992); and Michael Doyle, *Ways of War and Peace* (New York: W.W. Norton, 1997), 205–311.

43. Michael W. Doyle and Nicholas Sambanis, *Making War & Building Peace* (Princeton, NJ: Princeton University Press, 2006), 6–7.

44. See the *Supplement to an Agenda for Peace* in Boutros Boutros-Ghali, *An Agenda for Peace*, 2nd ed. (New York: United Nations Publications, 1995); and Boutros Boutros-Ghali, *An Agenda for Democratization* (New York: United Nations, 1996); "Report of the Panel on United Nations Peace Operations," (New York: 2000), also known as the "Brahimi Report," "Responsibility to Protect: Report of the International Commission on Intervention and State Sovereignty," (Ottawa, ON: International Development Research Centre, 2001), and "A More Secure World: Our Shared Responsibility: Report of the High-Level Panel on

Threats, Challenges, and Change," (New York: The United Nations, 2004), 33–34.

45. In her excellent "conceptual history of transitional justice," Arthur describes the field of transitional justice as "an international web of individuals and institutions whose internal coherence is held together by common concepts, practical aims, and distinctive claims for legitimacy" that formed in common response to practical dilemmas. "The field of transitional justice, so defined, came directly out of a set of interactions among human rights activists, lawyers and legal scholars, policymakers, journalists, donors, and comparative politics experts concerned with human rights and the dynamics of 'transitions to democracy,' beginning in the late 1980s." She also discusses debates that occurred within this web despite their broad agreement on certain values— over the desirable extent and justification for judicial punishment, for instance. See Paige Arthur, "How 'Transitions' Reshaped Human Rights: A Conceptual History of Transitional Justice," *Human Rights Quarterly* 31 (2009): 324, 353, 354, 358. For other helpful surveys and assessments of transitional justice, see Bronwyn Leebaw, "The Irreconcilable Goals of Transitional Justice," *Human Rights Quarterly* 30, no. 1 (2008): 95–118; and Ruti G. Teitel, "Transitional Justice Genealogy," *Harvard Human Rights Journal* 16 (2003): 69–94.

46. Teitel identifies Phase II of transitional justice, which encompasses much of the time period that I call here the age of peacebuilding, with a movement away from strictly legal justice to something much wider that involves a diversity of traditions and practices marshaled for the task of nation building. See ibid.

47. On the right to truth, see Verdeja, *Unchopping a Tree: Reconciliation in the Aftermath of Political Violence*, 35. The U.N. guidelines are found in United Nations General Assembly, *Basic Principles and Guidelines on the Right to a Remedy and Reparation for Victims of Gross Violations of International Human Rights Law and Serious Violations of International Humanitarian Law*.

48. See, for instance, Roht-Arriaza, *The New Landscape of Transitional Justice*, 1–16.

49. Even in *An Agenda for Peace*, Boutros-Ghali referred to multiple tasks involved in postconflict peacebuilding, as he did in his *Supplement to an Agenda for Peace*, 1995. A concern for holism grew stronger in the Brahimi Report, which discusses the importance of a strategy for peacebuilding, of viewing peacekeeping operations in terms of peacebuilding, and of incorporating a comprehensive program for national reconciliation in peace operations. In like spirit, a 2001 statement of the U.N. Security Council recognizes that "peacebuilding is aimed at preventing the outbreak, the recurrence or the continuation of armed conflict and therefore encompasses a wide range of political, development, humanitarian, and human rights programmes (*sic*.) and mechanisms. This requires short- and long-term action tailored to address the particular needs of societies sliding into conflict or emerging from it. These actions should focus on fostering sustainable development, the eradication of poverty and inequalities, transparent and accountable

governance, the promotion of democracy, respect for human rights and the rule of law, and the promotion of a culture of peace and non-violence." See "Report of the Panel on United Nations Peace Operations," (New York: 2000), (the "Brahimi Report") and "Statement by the President of the Security Council," 2001. It was then the 2004 report *A More Secure World* that proposed a U.N. Peacebuilding Commission whose mission would include coordinating the efforts of the U.N. Security Council, the Economic and Social Council, the International Monetary Fund, the World Bank, as well as representatives of principal donor countries, the target country of intervention, and regional and subregional organizations. See *A More Secure World: Our Shared Responsibility: Report of the High-Level Panel on Threats, Challenges, and Change* (New York: The United Nations, 2004). Other reports of the same period also evince a stride toward holism. See U.N. Security Council, *The Rule of Law and Transitional Justice in Conflict and Post-Conflict Societies: Report of the Secretary-General*, 2004); United Nations Development Program, "Strengthening the Rule of Law in Conflict and Post-Conflict Situations: A Global UNDP Programme for Justice and Security," 2007.

CHAPTER 5

1. Timothy Garton Ash, "True Confessions," *The New York Review of Books* 44 (July 17, 1997): 36–37.
2. Philosopher Paul Ricoeur called these thinkers "hermeneuticists of suspicion."
3. A strong connection between Nietzsche and the thought of Hans Morgenthau, perhaps the foremost figure in the realist tradition of international relations thought, can be found in Christoph Frei, *Hans J. Morgenthau: An Intellectual Biography* (Baton Rouge: Louisiana State University Press, 2001).
4. "Realism is our dominant theory," writes Michael W. Doyle in his landmark study of international relations thought, Doyle, *Ways of War and Peace*, 41.
5. Thucydides, *The Peloponnesian War*, trans. T. E. Wick (New York: Random House, 1982), 351.
6. Gary Jonathan Bass, *Stay the Hand of Vengeance: The Politics of War Crimes Tribunals* (Princeton, NJ: Princeton University Press, 2000), 8, 10, 18–20.
7. Huntington, *The Third Wave: Democratization in the Late Twentieth Century*, 211–231. Generally, though Huntington was not a straight realist and certainly not a power determinist. His long career of writing contained realist elements, liberal elements, and a rich appreciation for the role of ideas, culture, and notions of justice. This portion of *The Third Wave* is considered here only because it provides a vivid example of how power differentials can explain the approaches to justice that states arrive at in the wake of democratic transitions.
8. Jack Snyder and Leslie Vinjamuri, though their focus is on the effects, not the causes, of truth commissions and trials, nevertheless offer such an explanation at least for truth commissions. See Jack Snyder and Leslie Vinjamuri, "Trials

and Errors: Principle and Pragmatism in Strategies of International Justice," *International Security* 28, no. 3 (Winter, 2003): 31.

9. Huntington, *The Third Wave: Democratization in the Late Twentieth Century*, 231.

10. http://www.hrw.org/en/node/79211, accessed on August 17, 2010.

11. On the formation of the TRC, see Daniel Philpott, "When Faith Meets History: The Influence of Religion on Transitional Justice," in *The Religious in Response to Mass Atrocity: Interdisciplinary Perspectives*, eds. Thomas Brudholm and Thomas Cushman (Cambridge, UK: Cambridge University Press, 2009), 194–196.

12. Crocker, *Retribution and Reconciliation*, 6.

13. Among these latter liberals, see, for instance, Bhargava, *Restoring Decency to Barbaric Societies*, 60–63; Crocker, *Retribution and Reconciliation*, 6; David A. Crocker, "Truth Commissions, Transitional Justice, and Civil Society," in *Truth v. Justice: The Morality of Truth Commissions*, eds. Robert I. Rotberg and Dennis Thompson (Princeton, NJ: Princeton University Press, 2000), 108; Ash, *True Confessions*, 37–38; and Ignatieff, *Articles of Faith*, 112–113.

14. For examples, see chapter 10's section on apology.

15. Ibid., 111, 121–122.

16. See Tutu's *No Future Without Forgiveness*.

17. See Clifford Geertz, "Thick Description: Toward an Interpretive Theory of Culture," in *The Interpretation of Cultures: Selected Essays* (New York: Basic Books, 1973), 3–30.

18. Crocker, *Retribution and Reconciliation*, 6.

19. Crocker, *Truth Commissions, Transitional Justice, and Civil Society*, 108.

20. Ash, *True Confessions*, 37; Gutmann and Thompson, *The Moral Foundations of Truth Commissions*, 32.

21. John Rawls, *Political Liberalism* (New York: Columbia University Press, 1993), 19, 173–211.

22. Isaiah Berlin, "Two Concepts of Liberty," in *Liberty*, ed. Henry Hardy (Oxford, UK: Oxford University Press, 2002), 166–217.

23. Ash, *True Confessions*, 37. His quip, *"Ich bin ein Berliner"* can be found in Timothy Garton Ash, *The File* (New York: Random House, 1997), 51.

24. Michael Ignatieff, *Isaiah Berlin: A Life* (New York: Henry Holt and Company, 1998), 226.

25. Gutmann and Thompson, *The Moral Foundations of Truth Commissions*, 32–33.

26. Peter Berkowitz, *Virtue and the Making of Modern Liberalism* (Princeton, NJ: Princeton University Press, 1999).

27. Ibid., 4.

28. William A. Galston, *Liberal Purposes: Goods, Virtues, and Diversity in the Liberal State* (Cambridge, UK: Cambridge University Press, 1991), 213–237.

29. Miller, *On Nationality*; Tamir, *Liberal Nationalism*.

30. Leslie Vinjamuri, "Deterrence, Democracy, and the Pursuit of International Justice," *Ethics and International Affairs* 24, no. 2 (2010): 192.

31. Snyder and Vinjamuri, *Trials and Errors: Principle and Pragmatism in Strategies of International Justice*, 13–14.

32. See Bhargava, *Restoring Decency to Barbaric Societies*, 45–67; P. E. Digeser, *Political Forgiveness* (Ithaca, NY: Cornell University Press, 2001).

33. The Mauriac-Camus discourse is described both in Govier, *Forgiveness and Revenge*, 27–31; and Sa'adah, *Germany's Second Chance: Trust, Justice, and Democratization*, 52–56.

34. Aryeh Neier, "What Should Be Done about the Guilty?" in *Transitional Justice*, ed. Neil Kritz (Washington, DC: United States Institute of Peace Press, 1995), 182.

35. Michael Walzer, "The Moral Standing of States: A Response to Four Critics," *Philosophy and Public Affairs* 9, no. 3 (Spring 1980): 209–229.

CHAPTER 6

1. Piet Meiring, *Chronicle of the Truth Commission* (Vanderbylpark, South Africa: Carpe Diem, 1999), 30. Meiring was a member of the Truth and Reconciliation Commission from 1996 to 1998 and was involved in reparation and rehabilitation issues and in co-ordinating the TRC Faith Community Hearings.

2. Ash, *True Confessions*, 36.

3. For specific references for and further discussion of all of these cases, see Philpott, *When Faith Meets History: The Influence of Religion on Transitional Justice*, 174–212.

4. David Little, ed., *Peacemakers in Action: Profiles of Religion in Conflict Resolution* (Cambridge, UK: Cambridge University Press, 2007), 247–277.

5. Canon Andrew White, "Bringing Religious Leaders Together in Israel/Palestine," in *Peaceworks. Religious Contributions to Peacemaking: When Religion Brings Peace, Not War* 55 (January 2006): 9–11.

6. Bruce Nichols, "Religious Conciliation Between the Sandinistas and the East Coast Indians of Nicaragua," in *Religion, the Missing Dimension of Statecraft* (Oxford, UK: Oxford University Press, 1994), 64–87.

7. Andrea Bartoli, "Forgiveness and Reconciliation in the Mozambique Peace Process," in *Forgiveness and Reconciliation: Religion, Public Policy, & Conflict Transformation*, eds. Raymond G. Helmick, S. J. and Rodney L. Petersen (Philadelphia: Templeton Foundation Press, 2001), 351–372.

8. R. Scott Appleby, *The Ambivalence of the Sacred: Religion, Violence, and Reconciliation* (Lanham, MD: Rowman and Littlefield Publishers, 2000), 123–140.

9. Ibid., 121. For other general surveys of religious peacemaking efforts, see Little, *Peacemakers in Action: Profiles of Religion in Conflict Resolution*; David R. Smock, ed., "Religious Contributions to Peacemaking: When Religion Brings Peace, Not War," *Peaceworks* 55 (January 2006); Douglas Johnston, ed., *Faith-Based*

Diplomacy: Trumping Realpolitik (Oxford, UK: Oxford University Press, 2003); Douglas Johnston and Cynthia Sampson, eds., *Religion: The Missing Dimension of Statecraft* (New York: Oxford University Press, 1994).

10. Carol Rittner, John K. Roth, and Wendy Whitworth, *Genocide in Rwanda: Complicity of the Churches?* (St. Paul, MN: Paragon House, 2004).

11. The term *family of critics* is borrowed from Nicholas Wolterstorff, who discusses "a family of liberal positions" in this debate in Robert Audi and Nicholas Wolterstorff, *Religion in the Public Square: The Place of Religious Convictions in Political Debate* (Lanham, MD: Rowman and Littlefield Publishers, 1997), 74. For this formulation of the position, see Christopher J. Eberle, *Religious Conviction in Liberal Politics* (Cambridge, UK: Cambridge University Press, 2002), 12. The critics include John Rawls, Robert Audi, Charles Larmore, Gerald Gaus, Bruce Ackerman, Thomas Nagel, Amy Gutmann and Dennis Thompson, and Lawrence Solum.

12. Gutmann and Thompson, *The Moral Foundations of Truth Commissions*, 30. For similar criticisms of Tutu and the TRC, see Greenawalt, *Amnesty's Justice*, 199.

13. Eberle, *Religious Conviction in Liberal Politics*, 51–58.

14. Gutmann and Thompson, *The Moral Foundations of Truth Commissions*, 38. For a wider defense of the idea of economy of moral disagreement, see Amy Gutmann and Dennis Thompson, *Democracy and Disagreement* (Cambridge, MA: Harvard University Press, 1996).

15. Richard Rorty, "Religion as a Conversation-Stopper," in *Philosophy and Social Hope* (London: Penguin Books, 1999), 168–174.

16. Audi and Wolterstorff, *Religion in the Public Square: The Place of Religious Convictions in Political Debate*, 24–33. Rawls's position has evolved. His original statement of his view on public reason, as he calls it, is in Rawls, *Political Liberalism*, 212–254. Even here, he argues for an "inclusive" view of public reason that involves "allowing citizens, in certain situations, to present what they regard as the basis of political values rooted in their comprehensive doctrine, provided they do this in ways that strengthen the ideal of public reason itself" (247). In the second introduction of the 1996 edition of the book, he revises his position somewhat; see section 5, l–lvii. A further revised version, which he presents as his most definitive, appears in John Rawls, "The Idea of Public Reason Revisited," in *The Law of Peoples* (Cambridge, MA: Harvard University Press, 1999), 129–180.

17. Ibid., 133–134. In a series of footnotes, he discusses and addresses attendant ambiguities and contrasts his position with that of others.

18. Among these countercritics are Nicholas Wolterstorff, Jeffrey Stout, Christopher J. Eberle, Timothy P. Jackson, Philip Quinn, Michael Perry, David Hollenbach, S.J., Paul Weithman, and Stephen Carter.

19. The empirical claim that liberal democracies promote religion may come as a surprise to American readers, but in terms of the constitutional, legal, and

308 Notes

institutional separation between religion and state, the United States features
the largest degree of such separation in the world. This is clear from the rigorous work of political scientist Jonathan Fox, who has developed a quantitative
index to assess separation of religion and state that incorporates a large range
of forms of legislation and constitutional provisions that govern religion. By
his measure, the United States hosts the most separated institutions in the
world, with a score of 0. At the other end of the spectrum is Saudi Arabia,
whose measurement for 2001 was 74.62. To see the point about democracy,
consider that the United Kingdom measures 27.48, Finland 32.93, and Israel
35.34. See Jonathan Fox, *A World Survey of Religion and the State* (Cambridge,
UK: Cambridge University Press, 2008).

20. John Rawls, *The Law of Peoples* (Cambridge, MA: Harvard University Press,
1999), 126–127, 150, 176.

21. Martha Minow, "Political Liberalism: Religion and Public Reason," *Religion
and Values in Public Life* 3/4 (Summer, 1995): 4, quoted in Eberle, *Religious
Conviction in Liberal Politics*, 154.

22. Rawls, *Political Liberalism*, 4.

23. Ibid., xvi.

24. For an especially thorough listing of the reasons why religious claims can be
destructive to democratic communication, see Robert Audi, "The State, the
Church, and the Citizen," in *Religion and Contemporary Liberalism*, ed. Paul
Weithman (Notre Dame, IN: University of Notre Dame Press, 1997), 58–59.

25. See pp. xxiii–xxviii in the introduction to Rawls, *Political Liberalism*. Rawls
uses this historical narrative to frame the entire book, the major statement
of the second stage of his philosophical career. Rawls, *The Law of Peoples*,
19–23.

26. My case for this characterization can be found in Daniel Philpott, *Revolutions
in Sovereignty: How Ideas Shaped Modern International Relations* (Princeton,
NJ: Princeton University Press, 2001), 97–149. For a perspective claiming
that religion was not a direct cause of wars during this period, see William
T. Cavanaugh, *The Myth of Religious Violence: Secular Ideology and the Roots of
Modern Conflict* (Oxford, UK: Oxford University Press, 2009).

27. See Brian Tierney, *The Idea of Natural Rights: Studies on Natural Rights, Natural
Law, and Church Law, 1150–1625* (Atlanta: Scholars Press, 1997).

28. Perez Zagorin, *How the Idea of Religious Toleration Came to the West* (Princeton,
NJ: Princeton University Press, 2003), 9.

29. Rawls acknowledges and applauds this development, focusing especially on the
Catholic Church's development of religious freedom. For him, this strength-
ens liberalism's overlapping consensus. See Rawls, *The Law of Peoples*, 21–22,
164–168; and "Dignitatis Humanae," in *Vatican Council II: The Conciliar and
Post Conciliar Documents*, Austin Flannery, General Editor, New Revised ed.
(Northport, NY: Costello Publishing Company, 1975). In my view, though, it is

still not clear on what grounds religious rationales for religious freedom must be restrained or accompanied in public engagement.

30. Of Toft's forty-four religious civil wars, twenty-three are the sort where religion shapes communal identity and twenty-one are of the variety where it shapes political ends. See Monica Duffy Toft, "Getting Religion? the Puzzling Case of Islam and Civil War," *International Security* 31, no. 4 (Spring 2007): 103. Of course, it is not always the case that a conflict is purely one type or another. The Northern Ireland conflict, for instance, is propelled in part by the logic of figures such as Rev. Ian Paisley, who makes theological arguments against Roman Catholicism. The important point here, though, is that Northern Ireland unionists are not fighting to achieve a Protestant state that denies religious freedom to Roman Catholics. By contrast, conflicts in such places as Sudan and Sri Lanka are propelled in good part—though not exclusively, to be sure—by just this sort of religiously based denial of religious freedom.

31. The phrase is especially prevalent in Lecture IX, "Reply to Habermas" in the 1996 edition of *Political Liberalism*. See especially pp. 387–394.

32. Gutmann and Thompson, *Democracy and Disagreement*.

33. Jeffrey Stout, *Democracy & Tradition* (Princeton, NJ: Princeton University Press, 2004), 64.

34. Audi and Wolterstorff, *Religion in the Public Square: The Place of Religious Convictions in Political Debate*, 74–75.

35. Eberle makes the argument in far more sophisticated fashion than I do here, but this is the general structure of his objection to two broad sorts of arguments for public justification, ones that he calls populist and epistemic. The rest of the present section is strongly indebted to his work. See Eberle, *Religious Conviction in Liberal Politics*, 195–293.

36. Rawls, *Political Liberalism*, 47–66.

37. Issues of transitional justice, to be sure, involve the "basic constitutional" issues by which Rawls defines his domain. The ethic of political reconciliation proposed here deals with the establishment of human rights and the rule of law, criteria for such fundamental issues as criminal justice and the moral foundations of new regimes.

38. Eberle, *Religious Conviction in Liberal Politics*, 220–222.

39. I borrow the phrase *internal pluralism* from Appleby, *The Ambivalence of the Sacred: Religion, Violence, and Reconciliation*, 31.

40. Eberle argues that respect is furthered by a principle of "conscientious engagement" by which a religious person pursues a public justification for his political ends but is not obligated to restrain his religious justifications if this pursuit fails. See Eberle, *Religious Conviction in Liberal Politics*, 84–108.

41. It is a principle that may not be ubiquitously applicable either. The 1956 constitution of Pakistan contained a provision that no law can be repugnant to Islam. Though subject to complex interpretation, the provision obviously carries

a different criterion for judicial justification than the secular language criterion. Without raising the issue of the justice of such provisions or their compatibility with international law, I note only that judicial justification may look
different in different contexts; its secularity cannot simply be assumed.

42. A close competitor is Archbishop Juan Gerardi's leadership of the REMHI in
Guatemala. Although Gerardi did far more to bring about the REMHI than
Tutu did the TRC, his use of religious language was not as extensive.

43. Megan Shore and Scott Kline, "The Ambiguous Role of Religion in the South
African Truth and Reconciliation Commission," in *Peace & Change* 31, no. 3
(July, 2006): 309–332; Lyn S. Graybill, *Truth & Reconciliation in South Africa*
(Boulder, CO: Lynne Rienner Publishers, 2002), 16–22.

44. Indeed, the passage continues cautiously: "Neither is monolithic in its
approach; both contain strong sources of communal healing and restoration.
As such, they are sources of inspiration to most South Africans." See Truth
and Reconciliation Commission, *Truth and Reconciliation Commission of South
Africa Report*, vol. 1 (London: Macmillan Publishers Limited, 1999), 127. Note
also that the spelling *judaeo* is at it appears in the report.

45. Shore and Kline, *The Ambiguous Role of Religion in the South African Truth and
Reconciliation Commission*, 312–318.

46. My research shows commissioners using religious language in fourteen out of
1,697 "victim-hearings." For more on the definition of victim-hearing and on
my method for studying the hearings, see chapter 12.

CHAPTER 7

1. While the narrative follows roughly the same story line in both Genesis and
the Quran, there are also important differences between the two versions.
The Quranic version is shorter, less detailed, presents Joseph in a more positive light, and leaves out portions of the tale that are important to the Genesis
version.

2. Shriver, *An Ethic for Enemies: Forgiveness in Politics*, 24.

3. Genesis 41:44. Unless otherwise noted, quotations from the Jewish Bible in
this chapter are drawn from *The Jewish Study Bible: Jewish Publication Society
Tanakh Translation* (Oxford, UK: Oxford University Press, 2004).

4. Genesis 42:21.

5. Genesis 44:16. In the Quran, see Surah 12:91, 97.

6. Genesis 42:24, 43:30.

7. Genesis 45:2, 14–15.

8. Genesis 45:18; Surah 12:92; Surah 11:99.

9. Genesis 50:15–23.

10. Surah 12:94–111.

11. Genesis 48:3–4, 15; 50:19–21, 24–25.

12. Whether the Old Testament is identical to the Tanakh depends on which Christian Bible one is using. The Catholic Bible includes "apocryphal books" that are not found in the Tanakh. In the present chapter I use the term *Jewish Bible* to refer to the Tanakh, which for Jews is the Bible in its entirety. Since the Tanakh is also a portion of the Christian Bible, much of what the Tanakh says about reconciliation will contribute to the Christian interpretation of reconciliation.

13. Louis Jacobs, "The Relationship Between Religion and Ethics in Jewish Thought," in *Contemporary Jewish Ethics*, ed. Menachem Marc Kellner (New York: Sanhedrin Press, 1978), 41–57.

14. See Isaiah 2:3; Micah 4:2; Deuteronomy 8:6, 10:12, 11:22, 19:9, 26:17, 28:9, 30:16; Joshua 22:5; 1 Samuel 8:3; 1 Kings 2:3.

15. On the *imitatio dei* in Jewish ethics, see Marc Gopin, *Between Eden and Armageddon: The Future of World Religions, Violence, and Peacemaking* (Oxford, UK: Oxford University Press, 2000), 180; David S. Shapiro, "The Doctrine of the Image of God and Imitatio Dei," in *Contemporary Jewish Ethics*, ed. Menachem Marc Kellner (New York: Sanhedrin Press, 1978), 127–151; and Martin Buber, "Imitatio Dei," in *Contemporary Jewish Ethics*, ed. Menachem Marc Kellner (New York: Sanhedrin Press, 1978), 152–161.

16. Much depends on which translation is being used. In several translations of the Jewish Bible, the terms *reconciliation* and *reconcile* do not appear at all. The terms appear most often in the King James Version of the Old Testament, where *reconciliation* is used five times and *reconcile* three times. In six out of these eight instances, the Hebrew word root (transliterated) is *Kaphar*, used in the context of sacrificial atonement rituals, meaning "to cover, pursue, make an atonement, make reconciliation, cover over with pitch, pacify, propitiate."

17. John R. Donahue, S. J., "The Bible and Catholic Social Teaching: Will This Engagement Lead to Marriage?" in *Modern Catholic Social Teaching: Commentaries and Interpretations*, ed. Kenneth R. Himes (Washington, DC: Georgetown University Press, 2005), 14.

18. More literally, a hendiadys is a pairing of two terms by a conjunction to express a single notion that would normally be expressed as an adjective and a substantive. Righteousness and justice is a hendiadys that expresses what might otherwise be righteous justice. On the hendiadys righteousness and justice, see the extensive analysis of Moshe Weinfeld, *Social Justice in Ancient Israel* (Minneapolis: Fortress Press, 1995), which will receive more attention below.

19. Abraham Heschel, *The Prophets* (New York: Harper and Row, 1962), 200. G.A.F. Knight calls the two terms "Siamese twins" in G.A.F. Knight, "Is 'Righteous' Right?" *Scottish Journal of Theology* 41 (1988): 8; quoted in Marshall, *Beyond Retribution: A New Testament Vision for Justice, Crime and Punishment*, 46.

20. I am indebted to Rabbi Geoffrey Clausen for this point.

21. Ibid.

22. Elizabeth Achtemeier, "Righteousness in the OT," in *The Interpreter's Dictionary of the Bible*, ed. G. A. Buttrick, vol. 4 (Nashville: Abingdon, 1962), 80–82.

23. G. von Rad, *Old Testament Theology*, trans. D.M.G. Stalker, vol. 1 (New York: Harper and Bros., 1962), 370, 373; quoted in Marshall, *Beyond Retribution: A New Testament Vision for Justice, Crime and Punishment*, 47.

24. Moses Maimonides, *The Guide of the Perplexed*, trans. Shlomo Pines, vol. 2 (Chicago: University of Chicago Press, 1963), 631.

25. Heschel, *The Prophets*, 200.

26. Ibid.

27. See Rolf Knierim, *The Task of Old Testament Theology: Substance, Method, and Cases* (Grand Rapids, MI: William B. Eerdmans, 1995), 86–122.

28. Weinfeld, *Social Justice in Ancient Israel*, 7, 20–21, 45–47. See Genesis 18:19, Exodus 15:18, 20:2, Deuteronomy 33:4–5, Judges 5:11, 1 Samuel 12:7, Isaiah 2:1–4, 5:7, 15–16, 9:4, 11:1,4, 32:1, 51:4–5, Jeremiah 4:2, 23:5, 33:15, Amos 5:24, Micah 6:5,8, Psalms 6, 12–15; 33:5–6, 67:5, 72, 75:3, 89:3, 93, 96:10–11, 98:7–9, 99:4, 103:6–7.

29. Ibid., 9, 10–11, 13, 15, 18, 29, 35, 36, 37, 49, 51, 142, 152–156, 189, 195, 208–209. The latter quote is found on p. 11; italics in original. Eliezer Segal, "Jewish Perspectives on Restorative Justice," in *The Spiritual Roots of Restorative Justice*, ed. Michael L. Hadley (Albany: State University of New York Press, 2001), 181–197.

30. Heschel, *The Prophets*, 198.

31. Murray Polner and Naomi Goodman, eds., *The Challenge of Shalom* (Philadelphia: New Society, 1994), 2. See also Steven S. Schwarzschild, "Shalom," in *The Challenge of Shalom*, eds. Murray Polner and Naomi Goodman (Philadelphia: New Society Publishers, 1994), 16–25.

32. Perry Yoder, *Shalom: The Bible's Word for Salvation, Justice, and Peace* (Newton, KS: Faith and Life Press, 1987), 10–23.

33. On peace as God's name, see Marc Gopin, "Is There a God of Peace?" in *The Challenge of Shalom*, eds. Murray Polner and Naomi Goodman (Philadelphia: New Society Publishers, 1994), 33.

34. Ulrich Mauser, *The Gospel of Peace: A Scriptural Message for Today's World* (Louisville, KY: Westminster/John Knox, 1992), 13.

35. Gopin, *Between Eden and Armageddon: The Future of World Religions, Violence, and Peacemaking*, 77. By classical sources, Gopin seems to mean scripture as well as the Talmud.

36. Daniel Elazar, *Covenant and Polity in Biblical Israel: Volume I of the Covenant Tradition in Politics* (New Brunswick, NJ: Transaction Publishers, 1995), 71.

37. Here, I rely on the translation of the New International Version of the Bible. The *Jewish Study Bible* translates *hesed* as "goodness."

38. Mercy is linked with *sedeqah* in Jeremiah 9:23 and Psalms 36:11, 40:11, 85:11, and 143:11–12 and with *mishpat* in Isaiah 30:18, Hosea 12:7, Jeremiah 9.23, and Zechariah 7:9.

39. Louis E. Newman, "The Quality of Mercy: On the Duty to Forgive in the Judaic Tradition," *Journal of Religious Ethics* 15, no. 2 (Fall, 1987): 169. See also Weinfeld, *Social Justice in Ancient Israel*, 7; Heschel, *The Prophets*, 201.

40. The phrase *real and active* I borrow from Jon Levenson, whose analysis has influenced my own. Levenson goes further than I do, though, in distancing himself from the idea of evil as the privation of good. See Jon D. Levenson, *Creation and the Persistence of Evil* (Princeton, NJ: Princeton University Press, 1988), xxi.

41. Ibid., xvi–xxvii.

42. See, for instance, Psalms 73, 88, and 94.

43. Ibid., xxiii.

44. Susan Neiman, *Evil in Modern Thought: An Alternative History of Philosophy* (Princeton, NJ: Princeton University Press, 2002).

45. See the review of Neiman's book by Thomas Hibbs, "Seeing Evil," *The Weekly Standard*, June 9, 2003, 36.

46. Levenson, *Creation and the Persistence of Evil*, xvii.

47. Irving Greenberg, "Religion as a Force for Reconciliation and Peace: A Jewish Analysis," in *Beyond Violence: Religious Sources of Social Transformation in Judaism, Christianity, and Islam*, ed. James L. Heft (New York: Fordham University Press, 2004), 88–112. *Tikkun olam* is also a prominent concept in the Kabbalah school.

48. Levenson, *Creation and the Persistence of Evil*, xvii.

49. Isaiah 45:21. Here, the translation is from the New American Bible. See also Isaiah 46:13. The salvific significance of justice is clearer in other translations of the Bible than in that of the Jewish Publication Society. On justice and righteousness in Second Isaiah, see Weinfeld, *Social Justice in Ancient Israel*, 196.

50. Gopin, *Between Eden and Armageddon: The Future of World Religions, Violence, and Peacemaking*, 187–191.

51. See, for instance, Uriel Simon, *Seek Peace and Pursue It: Topical Issues in the Light of the Bible, the Bible in the Light of Topical Issues* (Tel Aviv, Israel: Yediot Achronot/Sifrei Hemed, 2002); Yeshayahu Leibowitz, *Judaism, Human Values, and the Jewish State* (Cambridge, MA: Harvard University Press, 1995); David Hartman, *Israelis and the Jewish Tradition* (New Haven, CT: Yale University Press, 2000); David Hartman, *A Living Covenant: The Innovative Spirit in Traditional Judaism* (New York: The Free Press, 1985).

52. Novak, *Covenantal Rights: A Study in Jewish Political Theory*, x, ix–xii.

53. Ibid., quote on 10, see also 1–35.

54. Gopin, *Between Eden and Armageddon: The Future of World Religions, Violence, and Peacemaking*, 77–78, 172–73, 177–78. *Aveilus* is often rendered *aveilut*.

55. Ibid., 169.

56. Emil L. Fackenheim, *To Mend the World* (Bloomington: Indiana University Press, 1994), quote on 225, see also 217, 225, 233, 261, 311.

57. Ibid., 249, 254, 322. John Paul II expressed these words in his pathbreaking visit to the Great Synagogue in Rome in 1986.

CHAPTER 8

1. Romans 11:29. Quotations from scripture in this chapter are taken from the New American translation of the Bible unless otherwise noted.
2. Matthew 12:18–21.
3. N. T. Wright, *Evil and the Justice of God* (Downers Grove, IL: InterVarsity Press, 2006), 64.
4. De Gruchy, *Reconciliation: Restoring Justice*, 44, 46, 51.
5. Eric Doxtader, "Reconciliation in a State of Emergency: The Middle Voice of 2 Corinthians," *Journal for the Study of Religion* 14, no. 1 (2001): 51.
6. 2 Corinthians 5:14–21.
7. Marshall, *Beyond Retribution: A New Testament Vision for Justice, Crime and Punishment*, 38.
8. Ibid., 38–39.
9. Romans 6:23.
10. Romans 5:1–2.
11. Ibid., 43; Colin Gunton, *The Actuality of Atonement* (New York: T&T Clark LTD, 1988), 96–100.
12. Marshall, *Beyond Retribution: A New Testament Vision for Justice, Crime and Punishment*, 41.
13. John C. Haughey, "Jesus as the Justice of God," in *The Faith That Does Justice*, ed. John C. Haughey (New York: Paulist Press, 1977), 283.
14. Gunton, *The Actuality of Atonement*, 165.
15. Kathryn Tanner, "Justification and Justice in a Theology of Grace," *Theology Today* 55, no. 4 (2006): 514–515.
16. Wright, *Evil and the Justice of God*, 117–118.
17. S. J. John, R. Donahue, "Biblical Perspectives on Justice," in *The Faith That Does Justice*, ed. John C. Haughey (New York: Paulist Press, 1977), 100–102.
18. Gunton, *The Actuality of Atonement*, 102–103. The argument that biblical justice can be understood as the restoration of right relationship, a definition that converges with the definition of *reconciliation*, can be found, *inter alia*, in Marshall, *Beyond Retribution: A New Testament Vision for Justice, Crime and Punishment*; De Gruchy, *Reconciliation: Restoring Justice*; Donahue, *Biblical Perspectives on Justice*, 68–112; Duncan Forrester, "Political Justice and Christian Theology," *Studies in Christian Ethics* 3, no. 1 (1990): 1–13; Tanner, *Justification and Justice in a Theology of Grace*, 510–523; Haughey, *Jesus as the Justice of God*, 264–290; Wright, *Evil and the Justice of God*; Zehr, *Changing Lenses*; Alan Torrance, "The Theological Grounds for Advocating Forgiveness and Reconciliation in the Sociopolitical Realm," in *The Politics of Past Evil* (Notre Dame, IN: University of Notre Dame Press, 2006), 50–53; Wells, *Theology for Reconciliation: Biblical Perspectives on Forgiveness and Grace*, 1–15; P. T. Forsyth, *The Justification of God* (Eugene, OR: Wipf & Stock,

1999); Volf, *Exclusion and Embrace: A Theological Exploration of Identity, Otherness, and Reconciliation*, 220–225.

19. Marshall, *Beyond Retribution: A New Testament Vision for Justice, Crime and Punishment*; Haughey, *Jesus as the Justice of God*, 264.

20. Corinthians 1:30. Emphasis added.

21. De Gruchy, *Reconciliation: Restoring Justice*, 45.

22. Colossians 1:20.

23. Emphasis added.

24. Pope John Paul II, *Dives in Misericordia, Encyclical Letter*, 1980, para. 2, 4, 6, 7, 13.

25. Tanner, *Justification and Justice in a Theology of Grace*, 513–515.

26. Marshall, *Beyond Retribution: A New Testament Vision for Justice, Crime and Punishment*, 70.

27. Donahue, *Biblical Perspectives on Justice*, 86.

28. Richard Hays, *The Moral Vision of the New Testament: Community, Cross, New Creation* (San Francisco: Harper, 1996), 163.

29. Mauser, *The Gospel of Peace: A Scriptural Message for Today's World*, 29.

30. Ephesians 2:14.

31. Ibid., 33.

32. Ephesians 2:14–18.

33. Colossians 1:15–20.

34. Gunton, *The Actuality of Atonement*, 84; Wright, *Evil and the Justice of God*, 9.

35. Matthew 18:22–35, 20:1–16.

36. John 8:3–11.

37. Hans Urs von Balthasar, *Theo-Drama: Theological Dramatic Theory. IV: The Action*, trans. Graham Harrison, vol. 4 (San Francisco: Ignatius Press, 1994), 233.

38. Quoted in De Gruchy, *Reconciliation: Restoring Justice*, 57.

39. Gunton, *The Actuality of Atonement*, 43.

40. Athanasius, ed., *On the Incarnation*, trans. Religious of C.S.M.V (Crestwood, NY: St. Vladimir's Seminary Press, 1944), 25–37.

41. Ibid., 31–64.

42. D. Bentley Hart, "A Gift Exceeding Every Debt: An Eastern Orthodox Appreciation of Anselm's Cur Deus Homo," *Pro Ecclesia* 7, no. 3 (1993): 333–349; Gunton, *The Actuality of Atonement*; Peter Schmiechen, *Saving Power: Theories of Atonement and Forms of the Church* (Grand Rapids, MI: Eerdmans, 2005), 194–221; R. W. Southern, *Saint Anselm: A Portrait in a Landscape* (Cambridge, UK: Cambridge University Press, 1990).

43. Gunton, *The Actuality of Atonement*, 87.

44. Anselm of Canterbury, *The Major Works*, eds. Brian Davies and G. R. Evans (Oxford UK: Oxford University Press, 1998), 260–366.

45. Von Balthasar makes this link with God's covenant in von Balthasar, *Theo-Drama: Theological Dramatic Theory. IV: The Action*, 255.

46. T. Smail, "Can One Man Die for the People?" in *Atonement Today*, ed.
J. Goldingay (London: SPCK, 1995), 75, quoted in Marshall, *Beyond Retribution:
A New Testament Vision for Justice, Crime and Punishment*, 60. Schmiechen
concurs that "[i]t would be fair to say that among many [Protestants, the penal
substitution theory] is an unshakable article of faith." Schmiechen, *Saving
Power: Theories of Atonement and Forms of the Church*, 109. After Calvin, prob-
ably the greatest articulator of it was nineteenth-century American theologian
Charles Hodge.

47. On Luther's doctrine, see Martin Luther, *Commentary on Galatians* (New
York: Classic Books International, 2009); Martin Luther, *Lectures on Romans*,
trans. Wilhelm Pauck, vol. 15 (Philadelphia: Westminster, 1961). In response
to Luther, John Calvin argued for a much closer relationship between justification and sanctification. Both were concurrent fruits of faith in the atoning
work of Christ. Still, though, he was characteristic of the Reformation in thinking of the two as distinct processes, even if always occurring together. See
John Calvin, "Institutes of the Christian Religion," trans. Henry Beveridge
(Grand Rapid, MI: Wm. Eerdmans Publishing Company, 1989), Book III,
37–39.

48. On this point, see Schmiechen, *Saving Power: Theories of Atonement and Forms
of the Church*, 39–40.

49. The New International Version of the Bible, for instance, uses the phrase *atoning sacrifice* instead of propitiation or expiation.

50. Romans 1:32, 6:23, 1 Corinthians 15:56.

51. Marshall, *Beyond Retribution: A New Testament Vision for Justice, Crime and
Punishment*, 59–60, 62. For Calvin's thought on this theme, see Calvin,
Institutes of the Christian Religion, Book II, 438, 439, 455, 456, 457.

52. Romans 5:8. On Calvin's thought on the general point of God's loving initiative,
see ibid., 434, 435, 437, 454.

53. Noting such an oscillation along roughly these lines are Gustaf Aulén, *Christus
Victor: An Historical Study of the Three Main Types of the Idea of Atonement*
(New York: Macmillan Publishing Company, 1969); Timothy Gorringe, *God's
Just Vengeance: Crime, Violence, and the Rhetoric of Salvation* (Cambridge, UK:
Cambridge University Press, 1996).

54. Karl Barth, *Community, State, and Church: Three Essays* (Eugene, OR: Wipf &
Stock, 2004), 168–182.

55. De Gruchy, *Reconciliation: Restoring Justice*, 67–76.

56. Orthodox theology also strongly stresses reconciliation as a real restoration of
persons and relationships. I have not found twentieth-century Orthodox theologians who apply reconciliation to the social and political realm, though, but
this does not mean that they do not exist.

57. Jürgen Moltmann, *The Crucified God: The Cross of Christ as the Foundation
and Criticism of Christian Theology* (Minneapolis: Fortress Press, 1993), 278.

Wiesel's own reference to the gallows image can be found at Elie Wiesel, *Night*, trans. Marion Wiesel (New York: Hill and Wang, 2006), 65. Wiesel seems to associate the image with his loss of religious faith in the camps.

58. Aside from theologians that I have already mentioned, see Shriver, *An Ethic for Enemies: Forgiveness in Politics*; L. Gregory Jones, *Embodying Forgiveness* (Grand Rapids, MI: Eerdmans, 1993); William Bole, Drew Christiansen and Robert T. Hennemeyer, *Forgiveness in International Politics: An Alternative Road to Peace* (Washington, DC: United States Conference of Catholic Bishops, 2004); Jon Sobrino, *The Principle of Mercy: Taking the Crucified People from the Cross* (Maryknoll, NY: Orbis, 1994).

59. See, for instance, Reinhold Niebuhr, *Christian Realism and Political Problems* (New York: Charles Scribner's Sons, 1953).

60. The Orthodox Church's support is more complex and contested. See Elizabeth Prodromou, "The Ambivalent Orthodox," in *World Religions and Democracy*, eds. Larry Diamond, Marc F. Plattner and Philip J. Costopoulos (Baltimore: Johns Hopkins University Press, 2005), 132–145.

61. William T. Cavanaugh, "The City: Beyond Secular Parodies," in *Radical Orthodoxy*, eds. John Milbank, Catherine Pickstock, and Graham Ward (London: Routledge, 1999), 182–200. For Hauerwas and Yoder, see John Howard Yoder, *The Politics of Jesus* (Grand Rapids, MI: William B. Eerdmans, 1972); Stanley Hauerwas, *Against the Nations* (Minneapolis: Winston, 1985).

62. Stanley Hauerwas, *Against the Nations* (Minneapolis: Winston, 1985), 1. I have found helpful here the critique of Timothy P. Jackson, *The Priority of Love: Christian Charity and Social Justice* (Princeton, NJ: Princeton University Press, 2003). Jackson also notes several other places where Hauerwas makes a similar statement. See p. 96, footnote 5.

CHAPTER 9

1. Karl-Josef Kuschel, *Abraham: Sign of Hope for Jews, Christians, and Muslims* (New York: Continuum, 1995).

2. Majid Khadduri, *The Islamic Conception of Justice* (Baltimore: Johns Hopkins University Press, 1984), 3–12.

3. George Hourani, *Reason and Tradition in Islamic Ethics* (Cambridge, UK: Cambridge University Press, 1985), 31.

4. A. Rashied Omar, "Between Compassion and Justice: Locating an Islamic Definition of Peace," *Peace Colloquy*, Spring 2005, 9.

5. Khadduri, *The Islamic Conception of Justice*, 6.

6. I am indebted to Asma Afsaruddin for this point.

7. Ibid., 6–7.

8. Prominent interpreter of the Quran Fazlur Rahman equates *taqwa* with "conscience" and considers it "perhaps the most important single term in the

Quran," the foundation of worship and ethics. See Fazlur Rahman, *Major Themes of the Qu'Ran* (Minneapolis: Bibliotheca Islamica, 1980), 24, 28.

9. Khadduri, *The Islamic Conception of Justice*, 7, 193.
10. Achtemeier, *Righteousness in the OT*, 80.
11. Omar, *Between Compassion and Justice: Locating an Islamic Definition of Peace*, 9 (emphasis added in quote).
12. All quotations from the Quran are derived from the translation by Abdullah Yusuf Ali.
13. Asma Afsaruddin, "The Hermeneutics of Inter-Faith Relations: Retrieving Moderation and Pluralism as Universal Principles in Qur'Anic Exegeses," *Journal of Religious Ethics* 37, no. 2 (2009): 331–339.
14. James Piscatori, *Islam in a World of Nation-States* (Cambridge, UK: Cambridge University Press, 1986), 6–7.
15. Omar, *Between Compassion and Justice: Locating an Islamic Definition of Peace*, 9.
16. Carol Schersten LaHurd, "'So That the Sinner Will Repent': Forgiveness in Islam and Christianity," *Dialog* 35, no. 4 (Fall, 1996): 288.
17. Quoted in Omar, *Between Compassion and Justice: Locating an Islamic Definition of Peace*, 9.
18. LaHurd, *'So That the Sinner Will Repent': Forgiveness in Islam and Christianity*, 288.
19. Mohammed Abu-Nimer, *Nonviolence and Peace Building in Islam* (Gainesville: University Press of Florida, 2003), 60. For an argument that peace and reconciliation are not only central to Islamic teachings but matters of the heart, not just outward action, and that these values are to be directed towards non-Muslims, see Asma Afsaruddin, "Taking Faith to Heart: Reconciliation and Peacebuilding in Islam," in *Spiritual Dimensions of Bediuzzaman Said Nursi's Risale-i Nur*, ed. Ibrahim M. Abu-Rabi` (Albany: State University of New York Press, 2008), 213–229.
20. I am indebted to Asma Afsaruddin for this point.
21. See Abdulaziz Abdulhussein Sachedina, *The Islamic Roots of Democratic Pluralism* (New York: Oxford University Press, 2001), 106.
22. LaHurd, *'So That the Sinner Will Repent': Forgiveness in Islam and Christianity*, 289.
23. Ibid., 289.
24. In this section, I rely heavily on the interpretation of Nawal H. Ammar, "Restorative Justice in Islam: Theory and Practice," in *The Spiritual Roots of Restorative Justice*, ed. Michael L. Hadley (Albany: State University of New York Press, 2001), 169–172.
25. Ibid., 172–173.
26. For my understanding of these rituals, I draw on George E. Irani and Nathan C. Funk, "Rituals of Reconciliation: Arab-Islamic Perspectives," *Arab Studies Quarterly* 20, no. 4 (1998): 53–73; and Abu-Nimer, *Nonviolence and Peace Building in Islam*, 91–127.

27. This section on *sulh* and *musalaha* draws on Irani and Funk, *Rituals of Reconciliation: Arab-Islamic Perspectives*, 53–73; and Abu-Nimer, *Nonviolence and Peace Building in Islam*, 102–108.

28. See, for instance, Jay Rothman, *Resolving Identity-Based Conflict in Nations, Organizations, and Communities* (San Francisco: Jossey-Bass Publishers, 1997). The move to incorporate such procedures as rituals of reconciliation, though, is found more prominently in proposals to move away from conflict resolution, as, for instance, in John Paul Lederach's advocacy of conflict transformation. See John Paul Lederach, *The Little Book of Conflict Transformation* (Intercourse, PA: Good Books, 2003).

29. Abu-Nimer, *Nonviolence and Peace Building in Islam*, 108.

30. Ibid., 99.

31. Afsaruddin, *The Hermeneutics of Inter-Faith Relations: Retrieving Moderation and Pluralism as Universal Principles in Qur'Anic Exegeses*, 331–354.

32. *The Times of India* reports a Gallup poll showing that 85 to 90 percent of Muslims in "Arab and Muslim states" favor democracy. See "Most Muslims for Democracy: Survey," *The Times of India*, May 29, 2007. See also Ronald Inglehart and Pippa Norris, "The True Clash of Civilizations," *Foreign Policy*, no. 135 (March/April 2003): 63–70.

33. Sohail H. Hashmi, "Islamic International Law and Public International Law: Convergence or Dissonance." Presented to a conference on "Religion and Global Politics," Harvard University, May 21, 2007.

34. *Freedom House, Freedom in the World 2006: The Annual Survey of Political Rights and Civil Liberties*.

35. Sohail Hashmi, "Islamic Ethics in International Society," in *International Society: Diverse Ethical Perspectives*, eds. David R. Mapel and Terry Nardin (Princeton, NJ: Princeton University Press, 1998), 223.

36. Khadduri, *The Islamic Conception of Justice*, 196–197.

37. Abdullah Saeed and Hassan Saeed, *Freedom of Religion, Apostasy and Islam* (Aldershot, UK: Ashgate Publishing, 2004); Abdullahi Ahmed An-Na'im, *Toward an Islamic Reformation: Civil Liberties, Human Rights, and International Law* (Syracuse, NY: Syracuse University Press, 1990); Khaled Abou El Fadl, "Conflict Resolution as a Normative Value in Islamic Law: Handling Disputes with Non-Muslims," in *Faith-Based Diplomacy: Trumping Realpolitik*, ed. Douglas Johnston (Oxford, UK: Oxford University Press, 2003), 178–209; Rahman, *Major Themes of the Qu'Ran*; Farid Esack, *Qur'an, Liberation, and Pluralism: An Islamic Perspective of Interreligious Solidarity Against Oppression* (Oxford, UK: Oneworld, 1997); AbdolKarim Soroush, *Reason, Freedom, and Democracy in Islam: Essential Writings of AbdolKarim Soroush*, trans. Mahmoud Sadri and Ahmad Sadri (New York: Oxford University Press, 2000); Abdulaziz Sachedina, *Islam and the Challenge of Human Rights* (Oxford, UK: Oxford University Press, 2009); Sachedina, *The Islamic Roots of Democratic Pluralism*.

CHAPTER 10

1. See chapter 1 for discussion and citations.
2. Daly and Sarkin, *Reconciliation in Divided Societies: Finding Common Ground*, 8.
3. Michael W. Doyle and Nicholas Sambanis, *Making War & Building Peace* (Princeton, NJ: Princeton University Press, 2006), 6–7.
4. James Dobbins et al., *America's Role in Nation-Building: From Germany to Iraq* (Santa Monica, CA: RAND Corporation, 2003), xiv–xv.
5. Roland Paris, "Bringing the Leviathan Back in: Classical Versus Contemporary Studies of the Liberal Peace," *International Studies Review* 8 (2006): 425–440.
6. For the economic dimension of these criticisms, see, for instance, Mamdani, *Reconciliation without Justice*. For the gender dimension, see Fionnuala Ní Aoláin and Eilish Rooney, "Underenforcement and Intersectionality: Gendered Aspects of Transition for Women," *The International Journal of Transitional Justice* 1, no. 3 (2007): 338–354.
7. Paul Collier, *The Bottom Billion: Why the Poorest Countries Are Failing and What Can Be Done about It* (Oxford, UK: Oxford University Press, 2007), 17–27.
8. For a criticism of the Washington Consensus, see, for instance, Joseph E. Stiglitz, *Globalization and Its Discontents* (New York: W. W. Norton, 2002).
9. Lisa J. LaPlante, "Transitional Justice and Peace Building: Diagnosing and Addressing the Socioeconomic Roots of Violence Through a Human Rights Framework," *The International Journal of Transitional Justice* 2, no. 3 (2008): 345–347.
10. Adrian Karatnycky and Peter Ackerman, *How Freedom Is Won: From Civic Resistance to Durable Democracy* (New York: Freedom House, 2005), 6–8.
11. See, for instance, Gary J. Bass, "Jus Post Bellum," *Philosophy and Public Affairs* 32, no. 4 (Fall 2004): 384–412.
12. Consider again the statistic cited in chapter 1 that 43 percent of peace agreements break down in five years. Mack, *Global Political Violence: Explaining the Post-Cold War Decline*, 5.
13. My definition draws from what is still the most authoritative work on truth commissions, Priscilla Hayner, *Unspeakable Truths: Confronting State Terror and Atrocity* (New York: Routledge, 2001), 14.
14. Kathryn Sikkink and Carrie Booth Walling, "Argentina's Contribution to Global Trends in Transitional Justice," in *Transitional Justice in the Twenty-First Century: Beyond Truth Versus Justice*, eds. Naomi Roht-Arriaza and Javier Mariezcurrena (Cambridge, UK: Cambridge University Press, 2006), 309.
15. This is the count, of course, at the time of this writing. The commissions include: Uganda (1974); United States, Commission on Wartime Relocation and Internment of Civilians (1981–1982); Bolivia (1982–1984); Argentina (1983–1984); Uruguay (1985); Zimbabwe (1985); Philippines (1986); Uganda (1986–1995); Nepal (1990–1991); Chile (1990–1991); Chad (1991–1992); Canada, Aboriginal

Peoples (1991–1996); South Africa, ANC (1992, 1993); Germany (1992–1994); El Salvador (1992–1993); United States, human radiation experiments (1994–1995); Sri Lanka (1994–1997); Haiti (1995–1996); Burundi (1995–1996); South Africa, TRC (1995–2000); Australia (1996–1997); Ecuador (1996–1997); Guatemala (1997–1999); Nigeria (1999–2000); Sierra Leone (2000–2001); Uruguay (2000); South Korea (2000–2002); Peru (2001–2003); Panama (2001); Serbia and Montenegro (2002); Ghana (2002); Timor-Leste (2002–2005); Morocco (2004–2006); Colombia (2005); United States, Greensboro (2005); South Korea (2005); Liberia (2005); Solomon Islands (2009).

16. See Louis Bickford, "Unofficial Truth Projects," *Human Rights Quarterly* 29 (2007): 994–1,035.

17. These purposes can be read in the United Nations' most important statement on transitional justice: United Nations Security Council, *The Rule of Law and Transitional Justice in Conflict and Post-Conflict Societies: Report of the Secretary-General*, 17. For the views of the transitional justice community, see Arthur, *How 'Transitions' Reshaped Human Rights: A Conceptual History of Transitional Justice*, 355–357.

18. A variant that I do not discuss is the acknowledgment of victims who are dead. Remembrance of the dead, of course, is hardly uncommon. Many societies erect memorials to their war dead, for instance. As with living victims, acknowledgment of the dead can confer recognition on those who have suffered but have been forgotten. Do the dead have an "interest" in such recognition? I believe they do. The way in which we remember (or fail to remember) the dead confers (or fails to confer) respect on what these people did or experienced when they were living. Again, this perspective is not uncommon. Think only of the efforts that the living make to clear up the reputation of dead people who have been slandered or to tell the story of dead people who they believe deserve recognition.

19. Tina Rosenberg, "A Reporter at Large: Recovering from Apartheid," *The New Yorker*, November 18, 1996, 92.

20. Cited in Hayner, *Unspeakable Truths: Confronting State Terror and Atrocity*, 144.

21. David Backer, "Comparing the Attitudes of Victims and the General Public Towards South Africa's Truth and Reconciliation Commission Process," presented at the Annual Meeting of the American Political Science Association, Philadelphia, PA, September 3, 2006, 30; David A. Backer, "The Human Face of Injustice: Victims' Responses to South Africa's Truth and Reconciliation Commission Process," PhD diss., University of Michigan, 2004.

22. Paul Jeffrey, *Recovering Memory: Guatemalan Churches and the Challenge of Peacemaking* (Uppsala, Sweden: Life & Peace Institute, 1998), 28–63; Laura Taylor, *Genocide of Indigenous People in Guatemala: Examining Social Energies of Reconciliation*, 12; Hayner, *Unspeakable Truths: Confronting State Terror and Atrocity*, 83–85; Michael Hayes and David Tombs, eds., *Truth and Memory: The*

Church and Human Rights in El Salvador and Guatemala (Leominster, UK: Gracewing, 2001), 104–107; Laura Arriaza and Naomi Roht-Arriaza, "Social Repair at the Local Level: The Case of Guatemala," *Journal of International Criminal Law* (2007): 165–166.

23. Job 34:28.

24. Jürgen Moltmann, *The Crucified God: The Cross of Christ as the Foundation and Criticism of Christian Theology* (Minneapolis: Fortress Press, 1993), 46, 53.

25. John Paul II, *Solicitudo Rei Socialis*, encyclical letter, 1987, paras. 39 and 40.

26. See, in the Quran, *Surahs* 2:177, 27:62, 51:19, 107:2–3.

27. For an application of restorative justice to truth commissions, see Llewellyn, *Restorative Justice in Transitions and Beyond*, 83–113.

28. Kimberly Theidon, "Justice in Transition: The Micropolitics of Reconciliation in Postwar Peru," *Journal of Conflict Resolution* 50, no. 3 (2006): 435.

29. Ash, *True Confessions*, 38.

30. Ignatieff, *Articles of Faith*, 111.

31. Schaap, *Political Reconciliation*, 134.

32. Audrey R. Chapman, "The Truth of Truth Commissions: Comparative Lessons from Haiti, South Africa, and Guatemala," *Human Rights Quarterly* 23 (2001): 4–9.

33. Hun Joon Kim and Kathryn Sikkink, "Explaining the Deterrence Effect of Human Rights Trials," *International Studies Quarterly* 54, no. 4 (2010): 953.

34. Kathryn Sikkink and Carrie Booth Walling, "The Impact of Human Rights Trials in Latin America," *Journal of Peace Research* 44, no. 4 (2007): 437.

35. Tove Grete Lie, Helga Malmin Binningsbø, and Scott Gates, "Post-Conflict Justice and Sustainable Peace" 2006.

36. Tricia D. Olsen, Leigh A. Payne, and Andrew G. Reiter, "The Justice Balance: When Transitional Justice Improves Human Rights and Democracy," *Human Rights Quarterly* 32, no. 4 (2010): 996.

37. Eric Brahm, "Uncovering the Truth: Examining Truth Commission Success and Impact," *International Studies Perspectives* 8 (2007): 26.

38. James Gibson, "Does Truth Lead to Reconciliation? Testing the Causal Assumptions of the South African Truth and Reconciliation Process," *American Journal of Political Science* 48, no. 2 (2004): 201–217.

39. David Backer, *Comparing the Attitudes of Victims and the General Public Towards South Africa's Truth and Reconciliation Commission Process*, 18, 28.

40. The full title is "Basic Principles and Guidelines on the Right to a Remedy and Reparations for Victims of Gross Violations of International Human Rights Law and Serious Violations of International Humanitarian Law."

41. J. D. Bindenagel, "Justice, Apology, Reconciliation and the German Foundation: 'Remembrance, Responsibility, and the Future,'" in *Taking Wrongs*

Seriously: Apologies and Reconciliation, eds. Elazar Barkan and Alexander Karn (Palo Alto, CA: Stanford University Press, 2006), 294.

42. Quoted in Ruti Teitel, *Transitional Justice* (Oxford, UK: Oxford University Press, 2000), 132.

43. Pablo de Greiff, "Justice and Reparations," in *The Handbook of Reparations*, ed. Pablo de Greiff (Oxford, UK: Oxford University Press, 2006), 455.

44. On the basis for reparations in the liberal tradition, see Randy E. Barnett, "Compensation and Rights in the Liberal Conception of Justice," in *Compensatory Justice*, ed. John W. Chapman (New York: New York University Press, 1991), 311–329.

45. Jeremy Waldron, "Superseding Historical Injustice," *Ethics* 103, no. 1 (1992): 4–28. In a later article, Waldron summarizes and elaborates on the claims of the 1992 piece. See Jeremy Waldron, "Settlement, Return, and the Supersession Thesis," *Theoretical Inquiries in Law* 5, no. 2 (2004): 237–268.

46. Ibid., 240.

47. Ibid., 238–243, 268.

48. Aviezer Tucker, "Rough Justice: Rectification in Post-Authoritarian and Post-Totalitarian Regimes," in *Retribution and Reparation in the Transition to Democracy*, ed. Jon Elster (Cambridge, UK: Cambridge University Press, 2006), 276–298; Tyler Cowen, "How Far Back Should We Go? Why Restitution Should Be Small," in *Retribution and Reparation in the Transition to Democracy*, ed. Jon Elster (Cambridge, UK: Cambridge University Press, 2006), 17–32.

49. John Hayes, "Atonement in the Book of Leviticus," *Interpretation* 52, no. 1 (1998): 11; "Tractate *Baba Qamma*" in *The Mishnah: Translated from the Hebrew with Introduction and Brief Explanatory Notes*, trans. H. Danby (Oxford, UK: Oxford University Press, 1993), 8:1; Gopin, *Between Eden and Armageddon: The Future of World Religions, Violence, and Peacemaking*, 187–188.

50. Section 1,459.

51. Bindenagel, *Justice, Apology, Reconciliation and the German Foundation: "Remembrance, Responsibility, and the Future,"* 306.

52. Brandon Hamber, "Narrowing the Micro and Macro: A Psychological Perspective on Reparations in Societies in Transition," in *The Handbook of Reparations*, ed. Pablo de Greiff (Oxford, UK: Oxford University Press, 2006), 568, 577.

53. Lisa J. Laplante and Kimberly Theidon, "Truth with Consequences: Justice and Reparations in Post-Truth Commissions in Peru," *Human Rights Quarterly* 29 (2007): 240–241.

54. Roy L. Brooks, ed., *When Sorry Isn't Enough: The Controversy over Apologies and Reparations for Human Injustice* (New York: New York University Press, 1999), 3.

55. Trudy Govier and Wilhelm Verwoerd, "The Promise and Pitfalls of Apology," *Journal of Social Philosophy* 33, no. 1 (2002): 77–79.

56. More precisely, West Germany, at least until unification in 1990. Leaders of the German Democratic Republic by and large did not apologize for Nazi crimes, preferring instead to cast themselves as liberators from this capitalist scourge. See Jeffrey Herf, *Divided Memories: The Nazi Past in the Two Germanies* (Cambridge, MA: Harvard University Press, 1997).

57. Quoted from Jennifer Lind, *Sorry States: Apologies in International Politics* (Ithaca, NY: Cornell University Press, 2008), 101.

58. Aaron Lazare, *On Apology* (Oxford, UK: Oxford University Press, 2004), 80.

59. The phrase culture of contrition, and a forceful argument for its victory, can be found in David Art, *The Politics of the Nazi Past in Germany and Austria* (Cambridge, UK: Cambridge University Press, 2006).

60. Lind, *Sorry States: Apologies in International Politics*, 26–78; He, *The Search for Reconciliation: Sino-Japanese and German-Polish Relations since World War II*, 115–288.

61. See chapter 4. These standard practices include building institutions based on the rule of law, truth telling, judicial punishment, vetting, and reparations. Apology can be found, though, in the UN's "Basic Principles and Guidelines" on reparations of 2005, in the jurisprudence of the Inter-American Court of Human Rights, and in one or two other places in international law.

62. Frederick Denny, "The Qur'Anic Vocabulary of Repentance: Orientations and Attitudes," *Journal of the American Academy of Religion Thematic Issues* (1980): 649–664.

63. On apologies in restorative justice, see Zehr, *Changing Lenses*, 202. For a rare application of apologies to politics, see Donald Shriver, *Honest Patriots: Loving a Country Enough to Remember Its Misdeeds* (Oxford, UK: Oxford University Press, 2005).

64. Collective responsibility is a large subject with a large literature and one that I do not treat extensively here. Generally, in my view, it is the internal structure of legitimate authority in a group that confers authority on members of the group to act in its name. See Larry May, *The Morality of Groups* (Notre Dame, IN: University of Notre Dame Press, 1987); and Peter French, *Collective and Corporate Responsibility* (New York: Columbia University Press, 1984).

65. Quoted in Ernesto Verdeja, "Official Apologies in the Aftermath of Political Violence," *Metaphilosophy* 41, no. 4 (2010): 576.

66. The Federal Republic of Germany, of course, *claimed* to be the legitimate government of all of Germany. At some point in time, boundaries and populations may shift so much that the same association can no longer be said to exist. It is difficult to say precisely when this occurs.

67. Govier, *Forgiveness and Revenge*, 93.

68. Victims, unlike perpetrators, do not necessarily require a single leader to accept a collective apology directed at them. Such a leader is not always easy to identify. Who speaks for the Jews, for instance? Who speaks for African Americans? If

a consensual leader is available, he could receive an apology on behalf of his people on a ceremonial occasion.

69. Melissa Nobles, *The Politics of Official Apologies* (Cambridge, UK: Cambridge University Press, 2008), 1–41.

70. Lind, *Sorry States: Apologies in International Politics*, 7, 179–198.

CHAPTER 11

1. Cited in Bass, *Stay the Hand of Vengeance: The Politics of War Crimes Tribunals*, 263, italics in original.

2. As I shall explain below, the term comes from Marshall, *Beyond Retribution: A New Testament Vision for Justice, Crime and Punishment*.

3. Vinjamuri uses her own dataset, which may not correspond exactly to the numbers in Sikkink and Walling's dataset. Vinjamuri's dataset covers only transitions from wars, whereas Sikkink and Walling's covers human rights trials everywhere. Vinjamuri reports that sixty-two trials occurred between 1945 and 2007 and that thirty-eight took place between 1990 and 2006. See Leslie Vinjamuri, "Judicial Interventions, Amnesties and Ongoing Conflict" (Paper Prepared for Annual Political Science Association, Boston, MA, 2008).

4. Andrew Reiter, Tricia D. Olsen, and Leigh A. Payne, "Behind the Justice Cascade: Sequencing Transitional Justice in New Democracies" (unpublished paper, 2007); quoted in Oskar N. T. Thoms, James Ron, and Roland Paris, *The Effects of Transitional Justice Mechanisms: A Summary of Empirical Research Findings and Implications for Analysts and Practitioners* (Ottawa, Canada: Centre for International Policy Studies, 2008), 16.

5. Herf, *Divided Memories: The Nazi Past in the Two Germanies*, 335–337. Keeping with the theme of his book, Herf also reports on trials in the German Democratic Republic (GDR/East Germany), which were far fewer and less judicially sound. Between 1945 and 1949, Soviet authorities convicted 12,500 persons of war crimes during the Nazi era, but these authorities' tendency to label Nazi war criminals widely so as to include their political opponents warrants suspicion about these figures. Subsequently, prosecutions dramatically dropped off. The GDR courts convicted only 329 Nazis between 1951 and 1964.

6. Max Rettig, "Gacaca: Truth, Justice, and Reconciliation in Post-Conflict Rwanda?" *African Studies Review* 51, no. 3 (2008): 30.

7. Mark A. Drumbl, *Atrocity, Punishment, and International Law* (Cambridge, UK: Cambridge University Press, 2007), 94.

8. Ibid., 86.

9. Louise Mallinder, *Amnesty, Human Rights, and Political Transitions* (Portland, OR: Hart Publishing, 2008).

10. Observing that the preponderance of arguments on judicial punishment is consequentialist are also Teitel, *Transitional Justice*, 28; and Leslie Vinjamuri,

"Deterrence, Democracy, and the Pursuit of International Justice," *Ethics and International Affairs* 24, no. 2 (2010): 191–211. Vinjamuri writes of "the triumph of consequences" in arguments for international judicial punishment (198).

11. Diane F. Orentlicher, "Settling Accounts: The Duty to Prosecute Human Rights Violations of a Prior Regime," *Yale Law Journal* 100, no. 8 (1991): 25–42.

12. See, for instance, the website of the ICTY: http://www.icty.org/sections/AbouttheICTY. Pierre Hazan reports that in January 2006, the website of Human Rights Watch said that "[j]ustice for yesterday's crimes supplies the legal foundation needed to deter atrocities tomorrow," in Pierre Hazan, "Measuring the Impact of Punishment and Forgiveness," *International Review of the Red Cross* 88, no. 861 (2006): 34. For others who make a deterrence argument, see Jaime Malamud-Goti, "Transitional Governments in the Breach: Why Punish State Criminals?" *Human Rights Quarterly* 12, no. 1 (1990): 12; Madeleine Albright as quoted in Bass, *Stay the Hand of Vengeance: The Politics of War Crimes Tribunals*, 290; Michael F. Scharf, "Trading Justice for Peace," in *Atrocities and International Accountability*, eds. Edel Hughes, William Schabas, and Ramesh Thakur (New York: United Nations University Press, 2007), 252; Richard Goldstone, "Justice as a Tool for Peace-Making: Truth Commissions and International Criminal Tribunals," *NYU Journal of Law and Politics* 28 (1995–1996): 490.

13. Malamud-Goti, *Transitional Governments in the Breach: Why Punish State Criminals?*, 1–16, in addition to deterrence arguments, also offers rule-of-law arguments. See also Méndez, *National Reconciliation, Transnational Justice, and the International Criminal Court*, 31–32; and the argument of Jose Zalaquett as described in Laurence Weschler, *A Miracle, a Universe: Settling Accounts with Torturers* (Chicago: University of Chicago Press, 1998), 243–244.

14. Orentlicher, *Settling Accounts: The Duty to Prosecute Human Rights Violations of a Prior Regime*, 2542.

15. Other prominent international officials cite the same effect. For a combination of peace and the rule of law as intended consequences, see Goldstone, *Justice as a Tool for Peace-Making: Truth Commissions and International Criminal Tribunals*, 485–503. Professor Cherif Bassiouni, a prominent international lawyer, legal scholar, and advocate of judicial punishment stated in 1996 that "'if peace is not intended to be a brief interlude between conflicts,' then it must be accompanied by justice." Quoted in Scharf, *Trading Justice for Peace*, 251.

16. Payam Akhavan, for instance, defended the ICC's indictment of the leader of Uganda's Lord's Resistance Army in 2005 as a potential "instrument for national reconciliation." Akhavan, "The Lord's Resistance Army Case: Uganda's Submission of the First State Referral to the International Criminal Court," *American Journal of International Law* 99, no. 2 (2005): 410–411.

17. Diane F. Orentlicher, " 'Settling Accounts' Revisited: Reconciling Global Norms with Local Agency," *The International Journal of Transitional Justice* 1 (2007): 13. She repeats the claim about reconciliation as impunity in Diane F. Orentlicher, "Swapping Amnesty for Peace and the Duty to Prosecute Human Rights Crimes," *ILSA Journal of International and Comparative Law* 3 (1996–1997): 713. More positively she calls for "balancing the demands of justice against those of reconciliation and ultimately [promoting] reconciliation within a framework of accountability," 714.

18. Drumbl, *Atrocity, Punishment, and International Law*, 169–173.

19. See, for instance, Adam Smith, *After Genocide: Bringing the Devil to Justice* (Amherst, NY: Prometheus Books, 2009). A more moderate version of the argument can be found in Helena Cobban, *Amnesty after Atrocity?: Healing Nations after Genocide and War Crimes* (Boulder, CO: Paradigm Publishers, 2006). In Uganda, the Acholi Religious Leaders Peace Initiative and the Amnesty Commission argued for amnesty in the language of reconciliation.

20. This is an epistemological claim: Liberal consequentialist arguments are of the kind that are assessable by empirical methods. See Vinjamuri, *Deterrence, Democracy, and the Pursuit of International Justice*, 193.

21. Bass, *Stay the Hand of Vengeance: The Politics of War Crimes Tribunals*, 275.

22. A handful of contemporary defenders of trials for human rights violations incorporate retributivist justifications into their arguments. See, for instance, the views of Aryeh Neier as described in Weschler, *A Miracle, a Universe: Settling Accounts with Torturers*, 244–245; Gutmann and Thompson, *The Moral Foundations of Truth Commissions*, 22–44; Drumbl, *Atrocity, Punishment, and International Law*, 150–169; Teitel, *Transitional Justice*, 50; Mark Osiel, *Mass Atrocity, Collective Memory, and the Law* (New Brunswick, NJ: Transaction Publishers, 1997), X; and Martha Minow, *Between Vengeance and Forgiveness: Facing History after Genocide and Mass Violence* (Boston: Beacon Press, 1998), 19. Others sometimes use language that is suggestive of retributivism but only vaguely. Combating "impunity" or a "culture of impunity," for instance, is a common battle cry of trials proponents. See, for instance, the preamble to the Rome Statute of the International Criminal Court. See also the respective websites of the International Criminal Tribunals for Rwanda and Yugoslavia: www.ictr.org and www.icty.org. Yet if *punity* is sought, why? Rarely do users of the term make clear the rationale. Orentlicher refers to the "harmful effects of impunity," suggesting that consequences are the problem after all. See Orentlicher, *Settling Accounts: The Duty to Prosecute Human Rights Violations of a Prior Regime*, 2,543–2,544.

23. Here I rely on the account of Jean Hampton, "The Moral Education Theory of Punishment," *Philosophy and Public Affairs* 13, no. 3 (Summer, 1984): 208–238.

24. Robert Nozick, "Retributive Punishment," in *Philosophical Explanations* (Cambridge, MA: Belknap Press/Harvard University Press, 1981), 366–368.

25. Something much like self-evidence is the argument for retributivism of Michael S. Moore, *Placing Blame: A General Theory of Criminal Law* (Oxford, UK: Oxford University Press, 1998), 117–177. That the retributive idea is a property of morality can be shown, Moore argues, through thought experiments in which people imagine situations of crime, including ones in which they are criminals. Just as they will conclude that they should suffer if they committed a crime, so they should allow that other perpetrators should suffer, too, Moore reasons. Moore's argument is sophisticated; I do not pretend to offer a full answer to it here. It does seem, though, that the evidence of ordinary people's reactions to crime ought to count as one argument against it. In addition, to be clear, I am not rejecting the moral realist idea that there are goods or obligations that are basic in the sense that they cannot be denied and require no further justification. See, for instance, Finnis, *Natural Law and Natural Rights*. I do question whether the retributivist idea is one of these naturally knowable goods.

26. Ernesto Kiza, Corene Rathberger and Holger-C. Rohne, *Victims of War—An Empirical Study on War-Victimization and Victims' Attitudes Towards Addressing Atrocities* (Hamburger Institut für Sozialforschung, 2006), cited in Drumbl, *Atrocity, Punishment, and International Law*, 42–43.

27. Immanuel Kant, *The Metaphysics of Morals*, trans. Mary Gregor (Cambridge, UK: Cambridge University Press, 1991), 142. Is this passage representative of Kant's thought? Yes, if one focuses on the *Rechtslehre*, or *The Metaphysics of Right*, rather than the rest of Kant's writings, Jeffrie Murphy argues. See Jeffrie G. Murphy, "Does Kant Have a Theory of Punishment?" *Columbia Law Review* 87, no. 3 (April 1987): 509–532.

28. John Braithwaite and Philip Pettit, *Not Just Deserts: A Republican Theory of Criminal Justice* (Oxford, UK: Oxford University Press, 1990), 158–159.

29. Hannah Arendt, "Letter to Karl Jaspers," in *Hannah Arendt Karl Jaspers: Correspondence 1926–1969*, eds. Lotte Kohler and Hans Saner, trans. Robert Kimber and Rita Kimber (New York: Harcourt Brace Jovanovich, 1992), 54.

30. Arendt, *Eichmann in Jerusalem: A Report on the Banality of Evil*, 279.

31. Among contemporary participants in debates over the trials that make up the global explosion of judicial punishment, those whose views approximate restorative punishment include Drumbl, *Atrocity, Punishment, and International Law*, 173–179; Teitel, *Transitional Justice*, 27–67; Raquel Aldana, "A Victim-Centered Reflection on Truth Commissions and Prosecutions as a Response to Mass Atrocities," *Journal of Human Rights* 5 (2006): 107–126.

32. Texts in which God destroys those whom he punishes include Deuteronomy 7:4, 9:8, 19, 25, Numbers 16:21, and Ezekiel 22:31 and 43:8. Texts in which nations are destroyed include Jeremiah 10:25, Jeremiah 50–51, Ezekiel 25, Nahum, and

Obadiah. See Marshall, *Beyond Retribution: A New Testament Vision for Justice, Crime and Punishment*, 122–170.

33. The passages expressing "slow to anger" (or a closely similar idea) are: Exodus 34:6, Numbers 14:18, Nehemiah 9:17, Psalms 86:15, 103:8, and 145:8, Joel 2:13, Jonah 4:2, and Nahum. For passages expressing God's willingness to restore, see also Jeremiah 31:20, Isaiah 54:7–8, Hosea 11:7–9, Nehemiah 9:30–32, Tobit 3:2–3, 11–12, 8:16–17, 1 Maccabees 4:24, 2 Chronicles 30:9, Wisdom 15:1, Sirach 2:11, Ekekiel 33:11, Micah 7:18, Psalms 103:3, and Exodus 34:6–7. Four passages that reveal God thinks better of punishment are: Hosea 11, Amos 5, Jeremiah 30:11, 18, and Jonah.

34. Deuteronomy 13:5, 17:7, 17:12; 19:19, 21:21, 22:21, 24:7.

35. Leviticus 17–27; Numbers 5–8; Virginia Mackey, *Punishment in the Scriptures and Traditional Judaism, Christianity, and Islam* (Claremont, CA: National Religious Leaders Consultation on Criminal Justice, 1981); G. J. Wenham, "Law and the Legal System in the Old Testament," in *Law and the Legal System in the Old Testament*, eds. B. N. Kaye and G. J. Wenham (Leicester, UK: Inter-Varsity Press, 1978), 44.; C. J. H. Wright, *An Eye for an Eye: The Place of Old Testament Ethics Today* (Downers Grove, IL: Inter-Varsity Press, 1983).

36. Rolf Knierim, "Response," in Virginia Mackey, *Punishment in the Scriptures and Traditional Judaism, Christianity, and Islam* (Claremont, CA: National Religious Leaders Consultation on Criminal Justice, 1981), 74.

37. Exodus 21: 20–25, Leviticus 24: 19–22, and Deuteronomy 19:18–21.

38. Mackey, *Punishment in the Scriptures and Traditional Judaism, Christianity, and Islam*, 3. Arguing for the *lex talionis* as restitution is also David Novak, *Jewish Social Ethics* (New York: Oxford University Press, 1992), 171–173.

39. See H. L. Strack and P. Billerbeck, *Kommentar zur Neuen Testament aus Talmud und Midrash* (Munich, Germany: C. H. Beck), vol. 1, 337–341; cited in Marshall, *Beyond Retribution: A New Testament Vision for Justice, Crime and Punishment*, 83.

40. This is not to deny that there are contemporary Jewish arguments in favor of the death penalty, but obviously, the range of capital offenses is far fewer. For an example of such an argument, constructed along the lines of an expressivist justification for punishment (which I consider a version of restorative punishment), see Novak, *Jewish Social Ethics*, 175–177.

41. R. Westbrook, "Punishments and Crimes," in *The Anchor Bible Dictionary*, ed. D. N. Freedman (New York: Doubleday, 1992), 546–556; Moshe Greenberg, "Crimes and Punishments," in *Interpreter's Dictionary of the Bible*, ed. G. A. Buttrick, vol. 1 (Edinburgh, Scotland: T&T Clark, 1962), 733–744. Elie Spitz argues that punishment, including the death penalty, has three purposes, including retribution, deterrence, and correcting the moral order of God's creation, the latter of these similar to my justification here. See Elie Spitz, "The Jewish Tradition and Capital Punishment," in *Contemporary Jewish Ethics and Morality*, eds. Elliot Dorff and Louis E. Newman (Oxford, UK: Oxford University Press, 1995), 345.

42. Matthew 5:38–42.

43. My view has been influenced by Nicholas Wolterstorff, *Justice in Love* (Grand Rapids, MI: William B. Eerdmans Publishing, 2011), 127–129.

44. R. A. Guelich, *The Sermon on the Mount* (Waco, TX: Word, 1982), 219–220; David Daube, *The New Testament and Rabbinic Judaism* (London: The Athlone Press, 1956), 257, 259–265; Hays, *The Moral Vision of the New Testament: Community, Cross, New Creation*, 325–326; Gordon Zerbe, "Paul's Ethic of Nonretaliation and Peace," in *The Love of Enemy and Nonretaliation in the New Testament*, ed. William Swartley (Louisville, KY: Westminster/John Knox, 1992), 177–222; Marshall, *Beyond Retribution: A New Testament Vision for Justice, Crime and Punishment*, 84–89.

45. As Guelich writes, "[j]ustice for justice's sake is no longer viewed as the basis of one's behaviour but the restored relationship between individuals in which the other's interests are foremost." See Guelich, *The Sermon on the Mount*, 252, quoted in Marshall, *Beyond Retribution: A New Testament Vision for Justice, Crime and Punishment*, 89.

46. Here I follow Wolterstorff, *Justice in Love*, 128.

47. *Catechism of the Catholic Church*, para. 2,266. See also the survey of statements on punishment of U.S. churches, including Catholic, Quaker, Lutheran, Presbyterian, Baptist, Episcopal, United Methodist, Unitarian, Mennonite, Mormon, Greek Orthodox, as well as the National Council of Churches and Jewish groups, in Mackey, *Punishment in the Scriptures and Traditional Judaism, Christianity, and Islam*, 59–68. For a strong statement on restorative justice, see Catholic Bishops of the United States, *Responsibility, Rehabilitation, and Restoration: A Catholic Perspective on Crime and Criminal Justice*, United States Catholic Conference.

48. R. A. Duff, *Punishment, Communication, and Community* (New York: Oxford University Press, 2001), 106–112.

49. Braithwaite and Pettit, *Not Just Deserts: A Republican Theory of Criminal Justice*, 175–176.

50. Drumbl, *Atrocity, Punishment, and International Law*, 73, 87–88. "Rwanda: CNLG to Highlight Gacaca Achievements," *Africa News*, June 2, 2009; *2008 Human Rights Report: Rwanda*, U.S. Department of State, February 25, 2009; Max Rettig, "Gacaca: Truth, Justice, and Reconciliation in Postconflict Rwanda?" *African Studies Review* 51, no. 3 (2008): 31, 43; Avocats Sans Frontières, *Monitoring of the Gacaca Courts, Judgment Phase*, Analytical Report No. 3, October 2006 to April 2007, 14–15, 17, 19, 33.

51. Bass, *Stay the Hand of Vengeance: The Politics of War Crimes Tribunals*, 296.

52. For scholars in the consensus on Tutsi killings, see Rene Lemarchand and Maurice Niwese, "Mass Murder, the Politics of Memory and Post-Genocide Reconstruction: The Cases of Rwanda and Burundi," in *After Mass Crime: Rebuilding States and Communities*, eds. Beatrice Pouligny, Simon Chesterman,

and Albrecht Schnabel (New York: United Nations University, 2007), 165–189; Alison Des Forges, *Leave None to Tell the Story: Genocide in Rwanda* (New York: Human Rights Watch, 1999); Filip Reyntjens, *The Great African War: Congo and Regional Geopolitics, 1996–2006* (Cambridge, UK: Cambridge University Press, 2009). Researchers Amaka Megwalu and Neophytos Loizides found that, to some extent, participants in the *gacaca* courts perceived justice there to be one sided. They report that 25 percent agreed with their survey statement, "justice is one-sided," while 65 percent disagree and 11 percent remained neutral. However, among those who were present in Rwanda during the genocide, 89 percent agreed that justice was a lopsided affair. Amaka Megwalu and Neophytos Loizides, "Dilemmas of Justice and Reconciliation: Rwandans and the Gacaca Courts," *African Journal of International and Comparative Law* 18 (2010): 16–17.

53. For information on the Timor-Leste CRPs, I have drawn on Patrick Burgess, "Justice and Reconciliation in East Timor: The Relationship Between the Commission for Reception, Truth, and Reconciliation and the Courts," *Criminal Law Forum* 15 (2004): 147–148, 150; Patrick Burgess, "A New Approach to Restorative Justice—East Timor's Community Reconciliation Processes," in *Transitional Justice in the Twenty-first Century: Beyond Truth Versus Justice*, eds. Naomi Roht-Arriaza and Javier Mariezcurrena (Cambridge, UK: Cambridge University Press, 2006), 180, 181, 187, 192, 194; Judicial System Monitoring Programme, "Unfulfilled Expectations: Community Views on CAVR's Community Reconciliation Process," www.jsmp.minihub.org, 9, 19, 24; Jeremy Sarkin, "Achieving Reconciliation in Divided Societies," *Yale Journal of International Affairs* (2008): 20.

54. Phil Clark, *The Gacaca Courts, Post-Genocide Justice and Reconciliation in Rwanda: Justice without Lawyers* (Cambridge, UK: Cambridge University Press, 2010), 4–7, 27–28, 342–355.

55. Timothy Longman, Phuong Pham, and Harvey M. Weinstein, "Connecting Justice to Human Experience: Attitudes Toward Accountability and Reconciliation in Rwanda," in *My Neighbor, My Enemy: Justice and Community in the Aftermath of Mass Atrocity*, eds. Eric Stover and Harvey M. Weinstein (Cambridge, UK: Cambridge University Press, 2004), 213.

56. Herbert Morris, "A Paternalistic Theory of Punishment," *American Philosophical Quarterly* 18, no. 4 (1981): 268.

57. To be clear, she was not making the case for Poncelot's execution as his participation in redemption. Préjean was and is a leading advocate of the death penalty. In addition, Poncelot was a fictional hybrid of actual persons.

58. Hampton, *The Moral Education Theory of Punishment*, 219.

59. Peter Z. Malkin and Harry Stein, *Eichmann in My Hands* (New York: Warner Books, 1990), 214–220.

60. Arendt, *Eichmann in Jerusalem: A Report on the Banality of Evil*, 95, 148–151.

61. Harry Frankfurt, "Freedom of the Will and the Concept of the Person," *Journal of Philosophy* 68, no. 1 (1971); Charles Taylor, "The Concept of a Person," in

Human Agency and Language (Cambridge, UK: Cambridge University Press, 1985), 97–114.

62. Payne, *Unsettling Accounts*, 71.

63. Ibid., 43.

64. Avocats Sans Frontières, *Monitoring of the Gacaca Courts, Judgment Phase*, Analytical Report No. 3, October 2006 to April 2007.

65. Ibid.

66. Rettig, *Gacaca: Truth, Justice, and Reconciliation in Postconflict Rwanda?*, 39.

67. Clark, *The Gacaca Courts, Post-Genocide Justice and Reconciliation in Rwanda: Justice without Lawyers*, 345–346.

68. Judicial System Monitoring Programme, "Unfulfilled Expectations: Community Views on CAVR's Community Reconciliation Process," www.jsmp.minihub.org, 12. Burgess, *A New Approach to Restorative Justice—East Timor's Community Reconciliation Processes*, 187–188. http://www.cavr-timorleste.org/en/reconciliation.htm. Ninety percent of participants, including perpetrators and victims, reported satisfaction in a midterm survey. See Burgess, *Justice and Reconciliation in East Timor: The Relationship Between the Commission for Reception, Truth, and Reconciliation and the Courts*, 152.

69. Quoted in Weschler, *A Miracle, a Universe: Settling Accounts with Torturers*, 244. See also Goldstone, *Justice as a Tool for Peace-Making: Truth Commissions and International Criminal Tribunals*, 485–503; Orentlicher, *`Settling Accounts' Revisited: Reconciling Global Norms with Local Agency*, 15.

70. Quoted in Bass, *Stay the Hand of Vengeance: The Politics of War Crimes Tribunals*, 243.

71. Phuong N. Pham et al., *Iraqi Voices: Attitudes Toward Transitional Justice and Social Reconstruction*, The International Center for Transitional Justice and the Human Rights Center at the University of California, Berkeley, 2004.

72. Burgess, *Justice and Reconciliation in East Timor: The Relationship Between the Commission for Reception, Truth, and Reconciliation and the Courts*, 152.

73. Bass, *Stay the Hand of Vengeance: The Politics of War Crimes Tribunals*, 303.

74. Ignatieff, *The Warrior's Honor: Ethnic War and the Modern Conscience*, 184. Carlos Nino also mentions the revelatory function of trials as one of their important justifications.

75. Drumbl, *Atrocity, Punishment, and International Law*, 176–178. As Drumbl says of the Milosevic trial, "the curtain fell before the closing act," 177.

76. Ibid., 80–82, 89.

77. Scharf, *Trading Justice for Peace*, 252.

78. Kim and Sikkink, p. 6.

79. Bass, *Stay the Hand of Vengeance: The Politics of War Crimes Tribunals*, 291.

80. Ibid., 290–291.

81. "[F]ailure to punish former leaders responsible for widespread human rights abuses encourages cynicism about the rule of law and distrust towards the

political system.... While [victims] struggle to put their suffering behind them, those responsible are allowed to enjoy a comfortable retirement." Scharf, *Trading Justice for Peace*, 252.

82. Judith Shklar, *Legalism: Law, Morals, and Political Trials* (Cambridge, MA: Harvard University Press, 1964).

83. Osiel, *Mass Atrocity, Collective Memory, and the Law*.

84. Kim and Sikkink, *Explaining the Deterrence Effect of Human Rights Trials*, 2–3, 24, 30.

85. Tricia Olsen, Leigh Payne, and Andrew Reiter, *Transitional Justice in Balance: Comparing Processes, Weighing Efficacy* (Washington, DC: United States Institute of Peace, 2010), 139, 143, 144–145, 148.

86. Jane Stromseth, David Wippman, and Rosa Brooks, eds., *Can Might Make Rights? Building the Rule of Law after Military Interventions* (Cambridge, UK: Cambridge University Press, 2006).

87. Megwalu and Loizides, *Dilemmas of Justice and Reconciliation: Rwandans and the Gacaca Courts*, 16–17.

88. Monica Nalepa, "Tolerating Mistakes: How Do Popular Perceptions of Procedural Fairness Affect Demand for Transitional Justice?" *Journal of Conflict Resolution*, forthcoming.

89. Longman, Pham, and Weinstein, *Connecting Justice to Human Experience: Attitudes Toward Accountability and Reconciliation in Rwanda*, 214, 216, 217, 222, 223.

90. Payam Akhavan, "Beyond Impunity: Can International Criminal Justice Prevent Future Atrocities?" *American Journal of International Law* 95, no. 1 (2001): 7–31.

91. Snyder and Vinjamuri, *Trials and Errors: Principle and Pragmatism in Strategies of International Justice*, 21–24; Hazan, *Measuring the Impact of Punishment and Forgiveness*, 19–47.

92. Megwalu and Loizides, *Dilemmas of Justice and Reconciliation: Rwandans and the Gacaca Courts*, 22, 27–28.

93. Longman, Pham, and Weinstein, *Connecting Justice to Human Experience: Attitudes Toward Accountability and Reconciliation in Rwanda*, 214.

94. Akhavan, *The Lord's Resistance Army Case: Uganda's Submission of the First State Referral to the International Criminal Court*, 403–421.

95. A. Branch, "Uganda's Civil War and the Politics of ICC Intervention," *Ethics and International Affairs* 21, no. 2 (2007): 179–198.

96. Phuong Pham et al., *Forgotten Voices: A Population-Based Survey of Attitudes about Peace and Justice in Northern Uganda*, Human Rights Center, University of California, Berkeley and The International Center for Transitional Justice, July 2005; Phuong Pham et al., *When the War Ends: A Population-Based Survey on Attitudes about Peace, Justice, and Social Reconstruction in Northern Uganda*, Human Rights Center, University of California, Berkeley and the Payson Center for International Development, Tulane University and the International Center for Transitional Justice, December 2007, 4.

97. Piers Pigou, "Degrees of Truth: Amnesty and Limitations in the Truth Recovery Project," in *The Provocatios of Amnesty*, eds. Charles Villa-Vicencio and Erik Doxtader (Cape Town: David Philip Publishers/Institute for Justice and Reconciliation, 2003), 217–236.

98. See Cobban, *Amnesty after Atrocity?: Healing Nations after Genocide and War Crimes*, 136–182.

99. Scharf, *Trading Justice for Peace*, 252–261. See also Naomi Roht-Arriaza, *Impunity and Human Rights in International Law and Practice* (Oxford, UK: Oxford University Press, 1995); Orentlicher, *Settling Accounts: The Duty to Prosecute Human Rights Violations of a Prior Regime*, 2,437–2,615. The protocol to the Geneva Convention is Article 6(5) of the Additional Protocol II to the Geneva Conventions.

100. Leslie Vinjamuri and Aaron P. Boesenecker, "Accountability and Peace Agreements: Mapping Trends from 1980–2006." Report published by the Centre for Humanitarian Dialogue. http://www.hdcentre.org/publications/accountability-and-peace-agreements-mapping-trends-1980–2006, 5, 9–11. Accessed July 25, 2011.

101. Snyder and Vinjamuri, *Trials and Errors: Principle and Pragmatism in Strategies of International Justice*, 33–36.

CHAPTER 12

1. Digeser, *Political Forgiveness*; Charles Griswold, *Forgiveness: A Philosophical Explanation* (Cambridge, UK: Cambridge University Press, 2007); Govier, *Forgiveness and Revenge*; Volf, *Forgiveness, Reconciliation, and Justice: A Theological Contribution to a More Peaceful Social Environment*, 861–877; Pope, *The Convergence of Forgiveness and Justice: Lessons from El Salvador*, 812–835; Shriver, *An Ethic for Enemies: Forgiveness in Politics*; Russell Daye, *Political Forgiveness* (Maryknoll, NY: Orbis Books, 2004); Geiko Müller-Fahrenholz, *The Art of Forgiveness: Theological Reflections on Healing and Reconciliation* (Geneva: World Council on Churches Publications, 1997).

2. Cynthia Ozick, "The Symposium," in Simon Wiesenthal, *The Sunflower: On the Possibilities and Limits of Forgiveness*, eds. Harry James Cargas and Bonny V. Fetterman, 2nd ed. (New York: Shocken Books, 1997), 216–217.

3. Jean Hatzfield, *Machete Season: The Killers in Rwanda Speak*, trans. L. Coverdale (New York, NY: Picador, 2006), 196, quoted in Thomas Brudholm, *Resentment's Virtue: Jean Améry and the Refusal to Forgive* (Philadelphia, PA: Temple University Press, 2008), 1.

4. Ibid., 3, 29, 32.

5. Ibid., 30, 65–81, 91, 98, 165.

6. Ibid., 172.

7. Thomas Brudholm, "On the Advocacy of Forgiveness After Mass Atrocities," in *The Religious in Response to Mass Atrocity: Interdisciplinary Perspectives*, eds. Thomas Brudholm and Thomas Cushman (Cambridge, UK: Cambridge University Press, 2009), 147–148.

8. Brudholm, *Resentment's Virtue: Jean Améry and the Refusal to Forgive*, 172.

9. I have relied on the account found in Bole, Christiansen and Hennemeyer, *Forgiveness in International Politics: An Alternative Road to Peace*, 63–64.

10. Eric Lomax, *The Railway Man: A POW's Searing Account of War, Brutality, and Forgiveness* (New York, NY: W. W. Norton and Company, 1995), 200.

11. Ibid., 232.

12. Ibid., 238, 241.

13. Ibid., 255.

14. Ibid., 269.

15. Ibid., 276.

16. I have drawn the information for this anecdote from Graybill, *Truth & Reconciliation in South Africa*, 16–22.

17. Pope, *The Convergence of Forgiveness and Justice: Lessons from El Salvador*, 816, 823–826.

18. See Pham and others, *Forgotten Voices: A Population-Based Survey of Attitudes about Peace and Justice in Northern Uganda*, 8, 26, 27, 42; Pham and others, *When the War Ends: A Population-Based Survey on Attitudes about Peace, Justice, and Social Reconstruction in Northern Uganda*; Pham and others, *Iraqi Voices: Attitudes Toward Transitional Justice and Social Reconstruction*, 46; Longman, Pham and Weinstein, *Connecting Justice to Human Experience: Attitudes Toward Accountability and Reconciliation in Rwanda*, 220.

19. To be sure, there are common linguistic uses of the term *forgiveness* that involve no more than a yielding up: the forgiveness of financial debt, for instance. It is true that insofar as one forgives a debtor of his financial debt, deciding no longer to hold this debt against him and, for financial purposes, to look upon him as now being in good standing, one performs crucial aspects of the notion of forgiveness that I am about to defend. But I argue that something else that is crucial for forgiveness is lacking: the reconstrual of a wrongdoer with regard to the wrong that she has committed. The concept of debt involves no necessary wrong. If Bob has borrowed money from Ellen and has not yet paid her back, he has committed no wrong (provided that he hasn't defaulted, refused, or otherwise violated the terms of repayment unjustifiably). Ellen may under some circumstances decide to release him from this debt. But this falls short of full forgiveness. Imagine that Ellen is a small time banker, has loaned money to Bob, and comes to believe that Bob is handling his money and indeed his life in such a reckless and irresponsible fashion that it is highly unlikely that he will ever meet his obligation to pay the money back to Ellen. Now, a large

corporate bank decides to take over Ellen's bank and as part of the acquisition, for some purely financial reason, it pressures Ellen's bank to release Bob from his debt. Ellen complies; Bob is now totally free—scot free, in fact—from his obligation to pay back the money. Financially Ellen's bank (and then the new merged bank) counts nothing against Bob; he is in good standing. But Ellen is now burning with resentment. She feels that Bob has deeply disrespected her and for some time continually voices this view to everyone she knows, including Bob's business associates. I argue that Ellen has not forgiven Bob, even though she has totally released him from his financial obligations. She still views him and treats him as guilty of a wrong and holds it against him. Put more simply, a victim could release an offender from his obligations yet continue to resent him. At best, the forgiveness of financial debt is a cognate version of forgiveness, at least of the concept that I am about to present.

20. Murphy and Hampton, *Forgiveness and Mercy*, 38.

21. Below, I shall argue that forgiveness is compatible with both judicial punishment and with reparations for victims. What is important here is that these are not justified according to the balance retributivist logic of "payback."

22. Robert D. Enright and Catherine T. Coyle, "Researching the Process Model of Forgiveness within Psychological Interventions," in *Dimensions of Forgiveness: Psychological Research & Theological Perspectives* (Radnor, PA: Templeton Foundation Press, 1998), 144–145. Enright and Coyle stress (p. 147) that their model is flexible and that the steps are not to be interpreted as a rigid sequence.

23. A particularly interesting case of forgiveness that involves partial reconciliation is forgiveness of the dead. Imagine that Bashir knew that his perpetrators were dead and willed and uttered his forgiveness of them. Here, forgiveness itself is partial as well, for it lacks the important element of a communication that is received by the wrongdoer. Some might say that this does not count as forgiveness at all. In my view, it is forgiveness but not full forgiveness. Forgiveness of the dead may still involve the crucial elements of a victim's will to reconstrue his view of the perpetrator, to forgo his resentment, to decide not to count the deed against the perpetrator, and to enact this decision in his words and deeds. Because shared memories of the perpetrator and his deeds remain alive, the victim's forgiveness can have an important social effect.

24. Hieronymi, *Articulating an Uncompromising Forgiveness*, 530.

25. See R. Jay Wallace, *Responsibility and the Moral Sentiments* (Cambridge, MA: Harvard University Press, 1994); Joram Graf Haber, *Forgiveness* (Lanham, MD: Rowman and Littlefield, 1991); Margaret Urban Walker, *Moral Repair: Reconstructing Moral Relations After Wrongdoing* (Cambridge, UK: Cambridge University Press, 2006); Murphy and Hampton, *Forgiveness and Mercy*; Robert C. Solomon, "Justice v. Vengeance: On Law and the Satisfaction of Emotion," in *The Passions of Law*, ed. Susan A. Bandes (New York: New York University

Press, 1999), 123–147; Bishop Joseph Butler, *Sermons* (Boston, MA: Hilliard and Brown, 1827). It is not the case that all of these theorists reject forgiveness. Most of them allow its practice though with cautions. But all of them argue for the moral value of resentment.

26. Similar is Hampton's concept of moral hatred. See Murphy and Hampton, *Forgiveness and Mercy*, 61.

27. It is fair to say that this has been the dominant view among western philosophers in the past generation. The citations are too many to list here. For a strong discussion of the relationship of resentment to forgiveness, see Griswold, *Forgiveness: A Philosophical Explanation*, 19–47.

28. http://newsreel.org/transcripts/longnight.htm. Accessed December 11, 2009.

29. Gobodo-Madikizela, *A Human being Died that Night: A South African Story of Forgiveness*, 128–129. Italics in original.

30. Robert D. Enright, Suzanna Freedman and Julio Rique, "The Psychology of Interpersonal Forgiveness," in *Exploring Forgiveness*, eds. Robert D. Enright and Joanna North (Madison, WI: The University of Wisconsin Press, 1998), 58–59.

31. Hannah Arendt, *The Human Condition* (Chicago, IL: University of Chicago Press, 1958), 241.

32. P. F. Strawson, "Freedom and Resentment," in *Freedom and Resentment and Other Essays*, ed. P. F. Strawson (Oxford, UK: Methuen, 1974), 1–28.

33. See, for instance, Griswold, *Forgiveness: A Philosophical Explanation*; Anthony Bash, *Forgiveness and Christian Ethics* (Cambridge, UK: Cambridge University Press, 2007), 63–78.

34. See, for instance, Govier, *Forgiveness and Revenge*; Jessica Wolfendale, "The Hardened Heart: The Moral Dangers of Not Forgiving," *Journal of Social Philosophy* 36, no. 3 (2005): 344.

35. Newman, *The Quality of Mercy: On the Duty to Forgive in the Judaic Tradition*, 163–167.

36. Ibid.: 159–168.

37. Abu-Nimer, *Nonviolence and Peace Building in Islam*, 67.

38. Russell Powell, "Forgiveness in Islamic Jurisprudence and its Role in Intercommunal Relations" (2009): 5.

39. Surah 39:53.

40. Ibid.: 7.

41. Torrance, *The Theological Grounds for Advocating Forgiveness and Reconciliation in the Sociopolitical Realm*, 74.

42. Jones, *Embodying Forgiveness*.

43. Miroslav Volf, *Free of Charge: Giving and Forgiving in a Culture Stripped of Grace* (Grand Rapids, MI: Zondervan, 2005), 161.

44. See Bash, *Forgiveness and Christian Ethics*, 79–100.

45. Matthew 6:15, 18: 22; Luke 17:3–4.

46. Theorists of restorative justice commonly argue in secular terms for forgiveness as a component of the justice that seeks to repair the harm of crime. The
argument of this chapter prior to this section can be read as a defense of forgiveness as restorative justice in the political realm and has been stated in mostly
secular terms. Judaism, Christianity, Islam and restorative justice, then, can
find overlapping consensus on core elements of forgiveness as a practice of
political reconciliation. These schools will differ from one another and within
themselves over issues like the priority of apology, the possibility of forgiving
perpetrators of mass atrocity, and the obligatoriness of forgiveness. As always,
the degree of consensus possible in any given locale depends on the religion
and the particular beliefs of its inhabitants.

47. Hearing of the South Africa Truth and Reconciliation Commission in Durban,
Vryheid, South Africa, April 17, 1997, found at http://www.justice.gov.za/
trc/hrvtrans/vryheid/vryheid1.htm, accessed December 7, 2009, quoted
in Brudholm, *Resentment's Virtue: Jean Améry and the Refusal to Forgive*,
32; Annelies Verdoolaege, "Managing Reconciliation at the Human Rights
Violations Hearings of the South African TRC," *Journal of Human Rights* 5,
no. 1 (2005): 67–68.

48. The idea behind a "victim-hearing" was to count the number of victims who
were exposed to the idea of forgiveness voiced by a commissioner. But in several
cases, victims did not appear alone but rather in groups, just as did perpetrators. In each hearing of the Commission, a succession of victims or clusters of
victims would appear. Each such appearance is the unit that I sought to count.
Hence the concept of a "victim-hearing," or in the case of a perpetrator or cluster
of perpetrators, a "perpetrator-hearing." By my calculations a total of 1,697 such
victim-hearings occurred over the course of 83 hearings of the Human Rights
Violations Committee. During victim-hearings, my research counts, commissioners advocated forgiveness 136 times. But many of these instances clustered
in single victim-hearings. I count that a total of 71 victim-hearings were ones in
which a commissioner advocated forgiveness. This is the 4.2 percent. Amnesty
Commission hearings were focused on perpetrators. Victims showed up in
only a minority of them. I count that in only 11 instances during 1905 "perpetrator-hearings" before the Amnesty Committee did a commissioner raise the
issue of forgiveness with a victim. As for instances of victims forgiving within
hearings, I count that 35 occurred during Amnesty Committee hearings while
17 occurred during Human Rights Violations Committee hearings.

Verdoolaege reports that her own manual counting shows that "in about
70% of the testimonies [of the Human Rights Violations Committee] the concept of reconciliation was either evoked by the commissioners themselves or
the commissioners urged the victims to express a willingness to forgive and
reconcile"—a very different result! See Ibid.: 74. What accounts for the difference? In part the fact that Verdoolaege claims to be counting for statements of

both forgiveness and of reconciliation on the part of commissioners, not just of forgiveness. Though I am not, of course, familiar with her accounting method, my own observation is that commissioners referred to the concept of reconciliation in a whole host of different manners during hearings, only some of which take the form of directly urging it upon victims.

49. Written statement by Vuyani Papuyana, amnesty hearing, Pretoria, March 26, 1998, quoted in Graybill, *Truth & Reconciliation in South Africa*, 47.

50. Wiesenthal, *The Sunflower: On the Possibilities and Limits of Forgiveness*, 65–66.

51. Govier, *Forgiveness and Revenge*, 93.

52. Elliot N. Dorff, "Individual and Communal Forgiveness," in *Autonomy and Judaism*, ed. Daniel H. Frank (Albany, NY: SUNY Press, 1992), 203–206.

53. Here I have profited from the discussion of Digeser, *Political Forgiveness*, 112–115.

54. The case of the German and Polish bishops and Pope John Paul II's many mea culpas are documented in Luigi Accattoli, *When a Pope Asks for Forgiveness* (Boston, MA: Pauline Books & Media, 1998). For the German-Polish case, see 49–50.

55. Griswold, *Forgiveness: A Philosophical Explanation*, 142.

56. Digeser, *Political Forgiveness*, 23–35.

CONCLUSION

1. John Rawls, *A Theory of Justice* (Cambridge, MA: Harvard University Press, 1971), 3.

Index